LOCAL HEROES

"Shall we ever see a side of quite such gladiatorial quality in the English county game again?" – John Arlott

Local
Heroes

John Shawcroft

SPORTS
BOOKS

Published in Great Britain by
SportsBooks Limited
PO Box 422
Cheltenham
GL50 2YN

© John Shawcroft 2006
First Published May 2006

Front cover designed by Kath Northam.

A catalogue record for this book is available from
the British Library.

ISBN 1 899807 35 7

Printed by Cromwell Press

Contents

Preface

FOR many years certain matches involving Derbyshire were not to be missed. Warwickshire, alternating at Derby over Whitsuntide and August Bank Holiday, Nottinghamshire at Ilkeston and Trent Bridge and Yorkshire at Queen's Park, Chesterfield, were the cornerstones of the county's fixture list. So it was in the natural order of things that when, at the age of ten, I was taken to my first Championship match, Derbyshire and Nottinghamshire at Ilkeston's Rutland Recreation Ground should be the choice.

Going to watch Derbyshire and Notts was something of a rite of passage for youngsters brought up in the coalfield area around Heanor and Ripley. It was a bit like wearing long trousers or having your first pint. Saturday July 27 1946 involved a bus journey to Ilkeston and a walk with my father down to the ground. My mother joined us later after doing some shopping.

The memories are sharp. Rain on Friday had cast doubt over the outing but they were able to start on time. We sat on the terraces, square to the pitch. The Nottinghamshire opening batsmen, Walter Keeton and Charlie Harris, began the innings with a partnership of 119. Harris batted all day for 106 out of 280 for six and went on to make 122 in five and three-quarter hours. It seemed more like five weeks. Contrasting hairstyles also remain in the mind: Keeton's balding head gleaming as he faced Derbyshire's red-haired fast bowler Bill Copson. And because the pit where my dad worked was closed for the holidays, we went on the second day, a Monday, joining a long queue to get in. Albert Alderman and Denis Smith made runs and Pat Vaulkhard pulled consecutive deliveries from Arthur Jepson for four and six, the six crashing into the terraces close to our seats. They had to change the ball.

It was explained to me that this duel featuring Copson, Keeton and Harris on the one hand and Smith, Alderman and Nottinghamshire's Bill Voce on the other was a continuation of epic contests which had taken place a decade earlier, when both teams competed for the Championship and Derbyshire actually won it. I was hooked. In those post-war years, when I was spending every spare moment I could find going to the cricket, nine members of the 1936 title-winning side turned out and I saw all of them. Bert Rhodes, who began his career in 1937, could be added to the collection. It did not matter that most of them were past their best. The core of that team, aided by people such as Alan Revill, Cliff Gladwin, George Dawkes and the emerging Les Jackson, nearly did it again in 1947 and 1948 before age began to weary them and the side broke up in the 1950s.

From time to time these gods became mortal. Nearly all of them had worked in the pits or been brought up in mining communities. Therefore a conversation at Derby between Copson, fielding on the edge of the boundary, and my dad on the merits of coal seams such as Tupton and Low Main as opposed to the methods required when bowling to Hutton or Compton was logical. Then there was Harry Storer, friend in his teens of an uncle who died young, asking after the family at a time when he was one of the most outspoken and successful soccer managers in the country.

In later years, I talked at length with Will Taylor, Derbyshire's long-serving secretary, and players who took part in the Championship season; Denis Smith, Alf Pope, Tommy Mitchell, Charlie Elliott and George Langdale. Jim Hutchinson and Eric Marsh did not play in the 1936 side but shed light on the beginning and the end of the era. Alan Skinner was courtesy itself in answering several written queries. There were briefer – but valuable – conversations with Storer, George Pope, the skipper Arthur Richardson, Rhodes and Copson. All have now passed on and few people are left with first-person recollections of those glory years of the mid-1930s.

Of the many titles studied in the research for this book I must acknowledge that indispensable source of reference the *Derbyshire County Cricket Yearbook*, first published in 1954 under the editorship of Frank Peach and Frank Dawn and subsequently edited by Stan Tacey and David Baggett, the present incumbent. Frank Peach made several valuable contributions to the Year Book with the advantage of first-hand knowledge of the 1936 season. The files of the *Derby Evening Telegraph*, both from the 1930s and the time when Gerald Mortimer's coverage of Derbyshire and Derby County from 1970-2002 also included numerous historical pieces, have been invaluable. Other books, newspapers and periodicals are listed in the acknowledgements.

I am grateful to the families of some of the players, Alice Carrington (widow of Elijah), Michael Copson, Neville Cresswell, Tony Pope and William Richardson (sons of Bill Copson, Jim Cresswell, Alf Pope and Arthur Richardson) and Mrs Pauline Jones, daughter of Denis Smith, for their help.

Equally valuable has been the assistance of David Baggett, John Brierley, Reg Briggs, Dennis Brookes, Peter Brookes, Ian Buxton, Brian Cox, Maxwell Craven, Mark Eklid, Ernie Fisher, Walter Goodyear, David Harvey, John Padley, Jim Sharman, Frank Shipston, Cliff Williams, Keith Williams and Peter Wynne-Thomas, and the staff of the local studies library in Irongate, Derby.

I would also like to thank the publisher, Randall Northam of SportsBooks, for his faith in the venture and for steering me back on course on occasion, my wife Gill and our son and daughter-in-law, Stephen and Tracey, for their encouragement and support, and my late parents, who started the ball rolling.

John Shawcroft

Introduction

WINNING the County Championship in 1936 remains Derbyshire's greatest triumph. Victories at Lord's in the NatWest Trophy and Benson and Hedges Cup finals of 1981 and 1993 are memories to be cherished. So, too, is the Sunday League title in 1990 but it is the Championship which is domestic cricket's most prestigious competition.

In the context of the time it was remarkable. For nearly 60 years the competition had been a closed shop, dominated by the Big Six – Yorkshire, Lancashire, Nottinghamshire, Middlesex, Surrey and Kent. Since 1877, when Gloucestershire headed the then unofficial table, only Warwickshire in 1911 had challenged their supremacy. Even their success was qualified. They did not meet either Kent or Middlesex, who finished second and third, and most of their matches were played against teams in the lower half of the table.

Small fry such as Derbyshire could count themselves fortunate to be in the competition at all, let alone harbour dreams of winning it. The club had nearly folded in 1910 and in 1920 endured a season which was staggering in its mediocrity. Eighteen matches were arranged, of which 17 were lost. The remaining fixture, against Nottinghamshire at Chesterfield, was abandoned without a ball being bowled. In 1924 they were last again, having failed to win a single game. Yet 12 years later they were champions, having served notice in 1927 and 1929 and finished sixth in 1933, third in 1934 and runners-up in 1935. Just to prove it was no flash in the pan they came third in 1937 and fifth in 1938.

Such a transformation is without parallel in county cricket. A downmarket club always on its uppers, accommodated in Spartan headquarters shared with a racecourse and with a small staff and a membership never much above two thousand produced a team which played some of the most aggressive cricket seen in that era.

It was all essentially homespun. Will Taylor, the secretary, turned the operation of a knife-edge budget, not to mention the scrutiny of players' expense claims, into an art form, with annual help from generous patrons such as the Duke of Devonshire. Sam Cadman, the epitome of a yeoman cricketer for a quarter of a century, became a highly acclaimed coach. All of the professionals were raised in the county, most of them in the coalfield area which spans eastern Derbyshire and western Nottinghamshire. A high percentage had worked in the mines, discovering a new life on the cricket field amidst the economic depression and high unemployment of the 1920s. This area also provided the nucleus of the team which brought the Championship to Trent Bridge in 1929 but the Nottinghamshire professionals were heirs to long years of success. Those from Derbyshire had to create their own tradition.

They were led into the foothills by Guy Jackson, who came from a family which owned a coal and iron company, and to the summit by Arthur Richardson, whose family had an old-established tannery business. Both were Derbyshire men and, in keeping with that era of amateur captains, they were disciplinarians. But unlike some of their kind, they were worth their place in the side, earning by deed and manner the respect of the pros.

The batsmen, Denis Smith, Albert Alderman, Stan Worthington and Leslie Townsend, with a useful middle-order formed out of the veteran Harry Storer, a talented amateur Alan Skinner, the emerging Charlie Elliott and Elijah Carrington and Richardson himself, made runs quickly enough to allow the bowlers time to dismiss the opposition twice, a priceless asset in a wet summer. And it was the bowlers who really won the day, a varied and hostile attack that as a unit was the best in the competition – the pace of Bill Copson, the sorcery of Tommy Mitchell's leg spin, Alf Pope's untiring fast-medium and Leslie Townsend's medium-paced off breaks. They were not the best fielding side in the land but they bristled with aggression, their centrepiece Harry Elliott, senior pro and one of the finest and most consistent wicketkeepers between the two world wars. They had to manage without George Pope, who was out for most of the season, while Mitchell was also injured at a crucial stage. Indeed, the players always felt their best cricket was produced in 1935, when both Popes were available.

Seven of them, Smith, Worthington, Townsend, George Pope, Harry Elliott, Mitchell and Copson, played for England during their careers but none became fully established. Perhaps this is indicative of another telling factor, for this was a team in every sense of the word, no real stars but one in which every member was capable of a match-winning or match-saving performance. It left mighty Yorkshire trailing in its wake and for a time turned the annual clashes with Nottinghamshire into conflicts which held more significance than the Roses games.

But it had been a long, hard road and its starting point can be traced to a day when Will Taylor opened an envelope and three five-pound notes fell out.

Chapter 1
The Secretary

WILL TAYLOR had been under no illusions when he took on the job of Derbyshire County Cricket Club's secretary. The air of dilapidation hanging around the bleak, windswept Racecourse Ground at Nottingham Road, Derby, was in keeping with the tribulations endured by the club since its formation in 1870.

His predecessors had not exactly covered themselves in glory. Sam Richardson, the first captain and later assistant secretary, fled in 1890 with around £1,000 belonging to Derbyshire and to Derby County Football Club. The Rams were founded as an offshoot of the cricket club and played their early matches at the ground. Richardson was born in Derby, where his father owned a men's outfitting business. He learned his trade as a tailor and appeared on course for a lifetime of success in business and sports administration before Fred Spofforth, the great Australian fast bowler, played a few games for the county and became a member of the committee. Spofforth, who married a Derbyshire girl – Richardson was a guest at the wedding – examined the books and uncovered the fraud.

As a consequence Derbyshire changed their administrative structure. Instead of an honorary secretary and an assistant, a paid secretary, W Barclay Delacombe, was appointed. He remained for 18 years before leaving amidst some acrimony, saying his farewells by burning the scorebooks and other records. Delacombe's successor RST Cochrane stayed only six months, leaving in July 1908 when he was offered a better paid job in the brewing industry in London. Sixty people applied for the vacant post, a sub-committee drawing up a short list of six candidates and on August 4 1908, during the Bank Holiday match against Hampshire, Will Taylor was appointed.

William Thomas Taylor was born in the quarry-town of Wirksworth, once a centre of lead mining and one of the earliest cricketing strongholds in the county, on April 14 1885. His father Walter was a keen cricketer and he and his four sons were mainstays of Wirksworth cricket. Will Taylor was an excellent club cricketer with Wirksworth on Saturdays and sometimes in mid-week with a touring side, the Wye Valley Wanderers, but he was not really good enough for the county game, although he played for Derbyshire at Trent Bridge in 1905 and against the West Indians in 1906. He made two further appearances, in 1910 against Kent and Surrey at Derby, and also appeared in club and ground fixtures.

In his early years as secretary he travelled frequently with the first team to away matches, sometimes acting as scorer and twelfth man. His younger brother Frank appeared in a few games for the county but the other two brothers lost their lives in the 1914-18 war.

His one regret was the restriction his administrative duties imposed on his club cricket. "I was able to play far less club cricket and was only able to practice occasionally. In those days our ground staff was small but included those two fine fast bowlers Bill Bestwick and Arnold Warren. They apparently decided they would show the new secretary what sort of cricketer he was and bowled consistently on or just outside my leg stump. Every time I was hit on the thigh, I can still see Bill grinning at the bowler's end. The trouble was I had to give the impression it didn't hurt a bit and that I couldn't care less."

At that time cricket was run by MCC and its aristocratic hierarchy, with the County Championship controlled by the Advisory County Cricket Committee. Each first-class county was represented and all its resolutions had to be submitted to the MCC committee for confirmation. In December, Will Taylor attended the annual meeting of county secretaries, who in those days arranged the fixtures. Rowland Ryder, for many years Warwickshire's secretary, left an account of those get-togethers. "Fixture making was an unhurried business, commencing in September through the agency of the penny post and culminating in a visit to Lord's in December where the silk hat and frock coat were de rigueur."

Many of the fixtures were set in stone. Nottinghamshire against Surrey and the Roses clashes endured over decades of Whitsuntides and August Bank Holidays. Derbyshire's traditional holiday opponents were Hampshire and then Essex before the 1914-18 war. When Worcestershire opted out of the Championship for a season in 1919 Derbyshire took their place against Warwickshire and, apart from a few exceptions, this continued for more than 40 years. Other set-piece fixtures were pencilled in and it was usually the last few which caused the headaches. As far as possible, extensive train journeys were limited, hence the southern or western tours of the northern sides, arranged with an eye on convenience and cost-cutting.

Such thrift became a byword for Taylor. Early in his career, Derbyshire faced a desperate financial crisis. There was a substantial loss in 1910 and it seemed likely that the club would go out of business but a saviour was found in the president, Victor Cavendish (1868-1938), the Ninth Duke of Devonshire. Nephew of the childless eighth duke, he had been at 23 the youngest member of the House of Commons as Liberal Unionist MP for West Derbyshire.

Although his Chatsworth duties changed the course of his political ambitions he took his seat in the House of Lords, acting as Conservative Whip and, in 1915-16, Civil Lord of the Admiralty. After a period in Canada as Governor-General he became a member of the Cabinet as Secretary of the Colonies in the Conservative government of 1922. The duke – who had his own problems involving half-a-million pounds death duties in addition to debts from the failure of the Seventh Duke's business ventures – made it clear in 1910 that unless sufficient financial support was forthcoming the club must close down. There was a generous response to an appeal and Taylor was able to arrange fixtures for the 1911 season. He paid tribute to the duke. "Without his inspiration, that could have been the end of Derbyshire cricket. No club could have had a finer leader, and no secretary a president who extended more kindness and consideration. He was, in my opinion, the greatest friend Derbyshire cricket ever had." It was reciprocated. For many years Taylor enjoyed game shooting with the duke on the Devonshire estates at Bolton Abbey in North Yorkshire.

For 51 years and 149 days, Will Taylor remained in office and more than 60 years after the first day at his desk he still greeted requests for a memory of a past player or some obscure point of information about the club's history with unfailing and urbane courtesy. His loyalty became the stuff of legend. Had Guy Jackson been able to lead the MCC in South Africa in 1927-28 Taylor would have been tour manager. He stayed with Derbyshire when he was invited to apply for the more lucrative and prestigious position of Lancashire's secretary in 1932. The MCC elected him an Honorary Life Member – the first and only time that a county secretary was so honoured while still in office.

When he completed 50 years as secretary the committee held a celebration for Taylor and his wife at the Midland Hotel in Derby. He was presented with a Crown Derby dinner service. On December 31 1959 he retired. Ronnie Aird, secretary of MCC, paid tribute: "He has endeared himself to a very large number of cricketers and cricket administrators and particularly to his colleagues, the other secretaries of the first-class and minor county cricket clubs. The reason is not hard to discover because a more considerate and kind-hearted man it would be difficult to find." Retirement did not end his association with the club. He was appointed to the committee and from 1962-72 was one of the hon. secretaries.

He attended home matches until April 1976, a few months before he died at his Breadsall home on August 17 in his 92nd year. It was only with reluctance that he accepted a day's cricket was too much. Instead he would telephone at the end of each day's play for a report on the match. It mattered just as much to him in 1976 as it had in former times.

Generations of players testified to the futility of seeking an increase in pay or expenses. Donald Carr, who captained Derbyshire and England, said: "I don't believe any county cricket secretary can have worked harder or more successfully against almost insurmountable difficulties. Until the formation of the supporters' club, for which he was largely responsible, Will Taylor had to think up methods of raising extra money to balance the expenditure, and he had to economise in every possible way. Sometimes the players may have thought he was a trifle keen when handing out match expenses, for he would often turn his slightly deaf ear to anyone asking for payment, but his friendship with all the players is sufficient proof of their true regard for him."

The secretary, with his trademark trilby, was a fairly heavy smoker and he kept a supply of sweets in a desk drawer. When a player entered his office, which on match days was in a small room atop of the pavilion, Taylor would say: "Do you smoke? No, well have a toffee then."

Harold Rhodes, one of the county's long line of fast bowlers, remembered practising in the nets with Keith Mohan, a batsman from Glossop, until 9pm. "We showered and then realised that the archaic shower equipment had set fire to the pavilion roof. If it hadn't been for the prompt action of the night watchman the whole pavilion could have burned down, but only a small part of the roof was affected. The following morning we were summoned to the secretary's office and walked in, assuming that we were going to get a pat on the back from Mr Taylor for saving the pavilion. Instead we got a bit of a rollicking for not, as he put it, 'letting the bugger burn' because the club was insured."

Another tale related by Rhodes concerned a 2nd XI match at Newark. Mohan discovered a couple of parrots in a cage in the hotel foyer. He was a good mimic and he spent a great deal of time teaching the birds to speak like Taylor. Next morning, as the players came downstairs, they heard a familiar voice rising to meet them. Somebody said 'bloody hell, Will Taylor's here' and there was much straightening of ties and polishing of shoes until somebody realised Mohan and his parrots had fooled everybody.

Cliff Gladwin, driving Edwin Smith and the uncapped Jim Brailsford to a game, emphasised to his passengers the importance of claiming expenses – 14s 6d train fare and sixpence for a taxi. Brailsford recalled: "Mr Taylor paid Cliff and Edwin, but said to me: 'Ah, Brailsford, you came with Clifford so you won't need anything will you?' As he walked away, Cliff called me all the names under the sun. 'He must think that my f-g car runs on f-g water.'"

Such parsimony applied only to the cricket club for this was a most generous man as a personal recollection will confirm. In August 1972, my wife Gill and I and our baby son Stephen were given a lift to Queen's Park by the club's historian Frank Peach. Taylor was in the front passenger's seat. After arriving at the ground he pressed something into our son's hand – a much-appreciated five pound note.

Three similar notes helped changed the course of Derbyshire cricket. On a weekday morning early in 1912, Taylor opened an envelope, addressed to the club's offices in St Peter's Street, Derby, which contained three crisp five-pound notes. At that time, the large, white pieces of paper were unfamiliar to many people. Fifteen pounds. A fifth of their value represented affluence to a miner, a factory employee or agricultural worker. The £15 would cover the salary of a first-team professional for three matches. It would pay the wages of a young player on the ground staff for five weeks. It was, Taylor reflected, a windfall. Later, he discovered the donor was the Hon Christopher Lowther, whose mother was of Derbyshire descent. "He commenced to take a keen interest in the club, making a number of handsome donations, attending many of our home matches, and playing in club and ground matches," said Taylor.

In autumn 1913, Lowther invited Will Taylor to London for talks about the future of the club over lunch. The consequences were far reaching.

Chapter 2
The Coach

THE lunch was at Simpson's-in-the-Strand. Will Taylor was 28, Hon Christopher Lowther 26. The two had become good friends and they discussed the cricket club's problems with all the fervour and optimism of youth.

Lowther's family connections were impressive. His father James was to be Speaker of the House of Commons for 16 years, being raised to the peerage as Viscount Ullswater after his retirement in 1921. James Lowther had married Mary Frances, daughter of Alexander James Beresford-Hope, of Bedgebury Park, Kent. The Beresfords were an ancient family – one of them fought at Agincourt – and had owned estates on both sides of the River Dove in Derbyshire and Staffordshire. Her mother had been a Cecil and Mary Frances was a niece of Robert Cecil, the Third Marquess of Salisbury, four times Foreign Secretary and three times Prime Minister.

She gave birth to Christopher, her eldest son – there would be a second son and a daughter – on January 18 1887. For Christopher Lowther, Eton and Trinity College, Cambridge, were followed by entry into the diplomatic service with spells in Morocco and Mexico. In 1910 he married Ina Pelly, daughter of a vicar, and their son John Arthur Lowther was born later that year.

It was around this time that Christopher began to develop his love for Derbyshire cricket. He was a useful player, listing shooting, cricket and tennis as his principal interests and he became a visible and popular figure among members at Derby, donating £300 to the club in 1912.

Such was the background to Lowther's invitation. "Young players were not coming forward," said Taylor. "In the autumn of 1913 he invited me to meet him in London to discuss the future of the club and how the playing strength could be improved, and incidentally entertained me to a very excellent lunch at Simpson's-in-the-Strand."

Taylor was used to taking the begging bowl around the country piles of the wealthy. But this time it was different. Far from talking about clearing debts, Lowther adopted a positive approach, with an aim of raising the standard of play. "I expressed the view that the gap between the standard of local and county cricket was such that inexperienced players coming into the side had too great a test and the only solution was an engagement on the staff for a full season of promising young cricketers and a system of intensive coaching," Taylor said. "He agreed and immediately set to work. He promised a very handsome annual subscription and obtained the services of Harry Blacklidge, a good, all-round cricketer from the Surrey club as coach and to play for the club when qualified. Blacklidge commenced his duties as coach to the newly-formed cricket nursery in 1914 and a number of young cricketers were engaged. The project showed almost immediate results."

Blacklidge was still a couple of months short of his 30th birthday when the 1914 season began. He was a left-handed batsman and left-arm medium paced bowler who played seven games for Surrey from 1908-13. Taylor described him as a delightful personality and a very fine coach. His views were echoed by the local press: "Blacklidge, the coach, has created an admirable impression. He spares no pains or time in correcting faults and giving advice. One could hardly desire to have a more capable coach or one prepared to take the requisite amount of trouble to impart his knowledge to the young players. There is no doubt that the nursery will provide much reserve strength for the county XI."

Fred Root, later of Worcestershire and England fame but then a young player on Derbyshire's staff, also recalled "happy days spent with Harry Blacklidge who had just made his presence felt at Derby."

The dressing room had a new shower bath. An extra £300 to maintain the nursery for three years until 1917 had been subscribed. Lowther donated another £200 and pledged £50 towards the nursery fund. The first nursery staff consisted of Fred Bracey, Harold Wild, Walter Reader-Blackton, Joseph Gladwin (father of Cliff), Arthur Severn and Jim Horsley. They all appeared in county cricket but Horsley was the most successful. A right-arm fast-medium bowler, he impressed Blacklidge, broke into the first team and headed the averages. It became academic when the 1914-18 war put paid to county cricket for four years.

Taylor was among the first to enlist. He found time for cricket when stationed at Lichfield in 1915, some of it played against Gilbert Jessop. "We got him out cheaply but he bowled us out with leg spinners," he said. There were matches in rest periods away from the front against units of the Royal Engineers near Neuve Chapelle and Bethune. He was invalided back to England after receiving a bad wound on the Somme in July 1916. Restored to health he returned to France only to suffer a further wound. Captain WT Taylor was about to be promoted to major when he was demobilised in 1919. Major Hon Christopher Lowther served with the Westmoreland and Cumberland Yeomanry, receiving a severe wound in France in September 1915. He was Conservative MP for North Cumberland from 1918-22, sitting in the Commons while his father was speaker. He and his wife were divorced in 1920, Lowther marrying Dorothy, daughter of Arthur Bromley-Davenport, and living in Sussex.

Harry Blacklidge was a victim of the war. A staff sergeant on the army gymnastic staff, he died of dysentery at Amara, Mesopotamia on May 23 1917.

When cricket resumed in 1919, Sam Cadman, at the age of 42, was Derbyshire's senior professional – the crucial sergeant-major role in the players' dressing room during the days of amateur captains. Cadman and Arthur Morton were, for two decades, the hewers of wood and drawers of water in Derbyshire cricket, synonymous with good, reliable professionalism.

Samuel William Cadman was born at Denton, Lancashire on January 29 1877. He soon came to live at Glossop, playing for the town club in the Central Lancashire League. An early mentor was Samuel Hill-Wood, who lived at Park Hall, near Hayfield. The family owned cotton mills at Glossop, a town which, with its adjacent moors and fells, is a gateway to the Peak District and where Melandra, the most northerly Roman fort, was situated. As SH Wood he captained the county at the turn of the century and his financial guarantees enabled first-class cricket to be played at North Road. Wood hired Derbyshire professionals to play for Glossop – the opening attack sometimes consisting of Bill Bestwick and Cadman when Derbyshire did not have a match – and dipped into his pockets to sponsor a town soccer club which reached the First Division. Most of the footballers were amateurs but the venture cost him £30,000, a fortune in those times. Sir Samuel Hill-Wood – the family name was hyphenated in 1912 and a baronetcy was conferred in 1921 – was Conservative MP for High Peak from 1910-29 and chairman of Arsenal from 1927 until his death in 1949. His four sons were to follow him to Eton and play for Derbyshire, one of them, Willie, in the Championship year.

Cadman's batting was steady and reliable, initially in the county side's middle order but later as an opener. Here he formed a useful pre-war partnership with the left-handed amateur Len Oliver, son of a Glossop tradesman. His bowling was medium paced and accurate with what was to be an interesting innovation. He was among the pioneers of in-swing or, as described in contemporary terms by two of his captains LG Wright and RRC Baggalay, "the off in-swinger or the inward swing." Cadman never achieved the classic double of a thousand runs and a hundred wickets in a season. Playing in a weak side which arranged only some 20 fixtures each summer militated against this. A better yardstick is a comparison with his county colleagues and in 1912 he headed both sets of averages.

He had joined the county staff in 1900, when he made his Championship debut. He became established in 1904 and a year later did well against the Australians at Derby, taking five for 94 in the first innings when Victor Trumper made 58 and scoring 66 in the county's second innings. Twice he exceeded a thousand runs in a season, in 1909 and 1911 and in 1910 he enjoyed his best bowling year with 67 wickets at 23 runs each. Nothing sensational, yet Cadman and Morton formed the backbone of the side for years. Cadman, twice chosen to represent the Players against the Gentlemen in 1908 and 1923 at Scarborough and The Oval, made 14,077 runs in 377 first-class matches between 1900-26, with eight centuries and an average of 21.45. He took 807 wickets at 25.25 apiece and held 277 catches.

Arthur Morton came from Mellor in the north of the county and also found his way into first-class cricket via Glossop. Morton was a steady batsman who could hit powerfully when the occasion demanded. Stockily-built, he relied on the old-fashioned virtues of length and direction when bowling his medium-paced off breaks.

Will Taylor returned to his desk early in 1919 to find that the chairman of the committee Alderman RB Chambers had managed to keep the organisation in being. The county cricket clubs obtained some financial benefits from the 1915-18 interregnum. Members continued their subscriptions – Derbyshire had 900 in 1919 – and wage bills and costs were minimal. Most of the debts were cleared, although affluence was as far away as ever.

The club set about developing its own talent and in 1920 it resuscitated the nursery, arranging a few 2nd XI matches (Derbyshire did not stage any competitive 2nd XI cricket before joining the Minor Counties in 1948) and club and ground fixtures. The scheme was worked for two years by Cadman, who supervised nets when he was not playing. Then in 1922 Fred Tate, formerly of Sussex and father of Maurice, was appointed full time coach in charge of the nursery. Posterity has been unkind to him. In his only Test – against the Australians in 1902 – he missed a vital catch and went in as England's last man with eight runs needed for victory. He made four and England lost by three runs. Tate's otherwise successful first-class career ended three years later. Using his £1,051 benefit cash he became licensee of the Burrell Arms in Haywards Heath. But cricket called and in 1921 he was appointed coach at Trent College, subsequently moving to Derby. After three years with the county Tate called it a day. He became licensee of the long-since demolished Robin Hood pub in Irongate, Derby, before retiring to Sussex where he died at the age of 75 in 1943. In the meantime, Cadman had set a record as the club's oldest centurion when he made an unbeaten 125 at Northampton in 1924 at the age of 47 years 149 days. He had a poor season in 1925, when the nursery was run for a season by Bill Bestwick, who then left with a testimonial cheque for £600 and a contract with Neath CC for the following summer in his pocket.

So, in what turned out to be one of the shrewdest appointments Derbyshire have ever made, Sam Cadman became coach in 1926. Of the professionals, every member of the 1936 team, except Harry Elliott and Harry Storer, graduated under Cadman, who was repeatedly invited to South Africa on coaching engagements.

Alf Pope said. "He was a very good coach, particularly as a bowling coach. He knew the game well and I think everybody accepted him as a good coach but he was really on his own as a bowling coach. Of course we were all young men then and probably we did not always appreciate all the techniques he was trying to impart. But he took charge of us when we joined the club and he would often coach the senior players as well.

"Sam would have them in the nets if they were out of form and he was usually able to point out any problems and remedy them. We all respected him although we were only youngsters and he would be in his fifties. He was a likeable man in many ways and a very fair-minded sort of a chap." Eric Marsh, on the pre-war ground staff, recalled two particular Cadmanisms: "play every ball on its merits" and "cricket's a funny game, a great leveller." Not original but no less true.

George Pope told a story of a leg-pulling incident in the dressing room with Cadman the victim. The coach was an expert juggler and a great kidder. Arnold Townsend's job was to make the tea and Cadman told him: "When I get these two balls going throw up the teapot and I'll juggle with that too." To everyone's amazement, when Sam gave the word, Townsend threw up the pot of tea. A thunderstruck Cadman could only remark: "Well, Arnold, I didn't think you would do it."

Some saw Cadman as a strict man and a gruff disciplinarian but he had one or two headstrong characters to deal with and he was a master of his trade. He was fortunate to some extent that his period of coach coincided with the arrival of some of the finest cricketers ever produced in Derbyshire but he was unquestionably one of the architects of the Championship success.

Chapter 3
The Moulder

GRADUALLY the nursery began to pay dividends, particularly under the influence of Cadman. Its products needed stern but sympathetic handling and they found this initially under the leadership of Guy Jackson.

He came from a family which owned a coal and iron company. This had its origins when George Stephenson, of Rocket fame, built the North Midland Railway line which provided a southern outlet for north Derbyshire coal. When the Clay Cross Tunnel was driven he saw the rich blackshale coal seams as a source of coking fuel. In 1837 he formed George Stephenson and Company, later the Clay Cross Company, to cash in, with its mines and furnaces, on the coal, iron ore and limestone. It was to develop a town, Clay Cross, five miles to the south of Stephenson's home, Tapton House at Chesterfield, which was to give its name to the company.

Among the members of the board, which included George's son Robert, was Sir William Jackson. After George's death in 1848, Robert Stephenson, Conservative MP and a renowned engineer who was a friend and rival of Brunel, succeeded his father as the largest shareholder. He sold his shares and in 1871 Sir William Jackson became sole proprietor. By 1913 it was a limited company, with the whole of the directorship members of the Jackson family. Soon it would have 4,000 employees.

The managing director, Brigadier-General Geoffrey Meinertzhagen Jackson, of Clay Cross Hall, was born in 1869, son of Thomas Hughes Jackson, of Manor House, Birkenhead. He married in 1893 Jessie Cowper Coles, daughter of the late Henry Hydman Laird, of Birkenhead. He was educated at Harrow, the county link was forged by the Clay Cross Company and the usual responsibilities associated with the wealthier classes evolved; staunch Conservative, JP, Deputy Lord Lieutenant and High Sheriff. He was associated with the Derbyshire Volunteers and Territorials for many years, commanding the local volunteer battalion from 1903 and retaining the command when it became the 6th Battalion Nottinghamshire and Derbyshire regiment in 1908. In the 1914-18 war he commanded a brigade in the 59th division and although in failing health for some months towards the end of his life he continued to deal with business matters until a few days before his death in September 1946.

GM Jackson's hobbies were listed as golf and hunting but the cricketing connections were established by two sons, Geoffrey Laird Jackson, who was born at Birkenhead in 1894, and Guy Rolfe Jackson, born at Ankerbold, near Chesterfield on June 23 1896. Will Taylor recalled Geoffrey and Guy Jackson attending Derbyshire's home matches in their school holidays, "always tremendously keen and anxious to know how Derbyshire were going on." Geoffrey was at Harrow and Oxford University and appeared four times for Derbyshire in 1912-14. He met his death at Faimpoux in Belgium in 1917.

Guy Jackson was also educated at Harrow, gaining a regular place in the school side in 1914 as a left-handed batsman. He made 59 against Eton, the second highest score, and finished second in the batting with an average of 25.08. When war broke out he joined the Derbyshire Yeomanry and served in Macedonia and Salonika. He reached the rank of Captain and was awarded the Military Cross, the French Legion d'Honneur and the Greek Military Cross for gallantry on the field of battle. He was twice mentioned in dispatches. On one occasion, advancing with his troop, he pushed a patrol through Sirlovo, the first British patrol to enter the town. It was in Salonika that, while leading his troop, he was approached by Bulgars carrying a flag of truce. They asked for an armistice and Jackson sent them to headquarters. It was the end of Bulgaria's participation in the war.

Jackson made his county debut at Bath on July 23-24 1919, when Derbyshire were all out for 37 in their second innings. He played in five games that summer, nine innings producing 183 runs with a highest score of 50. He was stumped in five of his dismissals which at least suggested aggressive intent. Further appearances followed in the next two seasons. His record for the county was modest: 417 runs in 37 innings and an average of just over 11, but he scored heavily – 1,632, average 60-plus – while captaining Clay Cross Park in the Derbyshire League in 1921, when he also played for the county 2nd XI and the club and ground.

The county had faith. George Buckston led the side for one season in 1921 and when a vote was taken to determine his successor as captain for 1922 it resulted in a unanimous decision to appoint the 25-year-old Guy Jackson.

He had much to learn, but Sam Cadman, as senior pro, was at his side and there was more old hand sagacity from Arthur Morton. There were indications that Jackson could become a very fine amateur batsman, a good fieldsman and a natural leader. There would be some early criticism of the way he handled his bowlers but that soon passed. Jackson was to emerge as a natural captain, a strict disciplinarian and, probably above all, an excellent sportsman who played the game according to the spirit rather than the letter of the laws. He was a very fair man who, after he had gained a little experience, won the confidence and respect of his players. An attractive left-hand batsman, particularly strong on the off-side, he was determined to improve and the way he applied himself to this task was an example to the team. He was a splendid fieldsman in the covers, although as skipper he usually took mid-off.

Jackson began well in 1922. He averaged only 19 but the *Derby Daily Telegraph* said: "The team has benefited from the captaincy of GR Jackson, whose acceptance of the office helped the club out of a dilemma. At first many friends of Derbyshire cricket doubted his ability but he has risen splendidly to the occasion." He exceeded a thousand runs in a season on four occasions, 1925, 1928, 1929 and 1930, with nine career hundreds. His fighting qualities as a batsman were often revealed by making the top score in a low total. And there was style. The cricket writer Henry Grierson described Jackson as almost an attractive left-handed batsman as Percy Chapman.

Notice was taken in high places. He was selected for the North against South in the 1923 Test trial at Old Trafford only to bag a pair, caught by Fender off Tate, and then run out. Tate gave him problems in such matches, dismissing him for three in a 1927 Test trial at Bristol and bowling him for 26 when he captained the MCC South African XI against CI Thornton's XI at Scarborough later that year. Jackson appeared in four Gentlemen v Players matches between 1924-27, two at The Oval and two at Folkestone. There were also tours to Germany with The Butterflies in 1924 and to Uruguay, Chile and Peru in 1926-27 with a team of amateurs captained by Pelham Warner. This included GO Allen, JC White and RT Stanyforth, who were to captain England, and Lord Dunglass, the future Sir Alec Douglas-Home, Prime Minister in 1963-64.

Captain Jackson – he continued to use his army rank in civilian life – struck up a firm friendship with Will Taylor. "Guy and myself had many interests in common, particularly cricket and shooting. His father had an estate at Dolanog in Montgomeryshire and in the early 1920s Guy invited me to join them in their annual shoot. It was always a great interest to me to visit a new shoot and I was thrilled at the thought – the trip lived up to my highest expectations. The hospitality, for which the Jackson family are so famed, was superb, the scenery simply fabulous, and the shooting really sporting. Thanks to Guy, it was my good fortune to repeat this visit for over 40 years, and every time it was a memorable experience.

"Perhaps the most outstanding feature of his captaincy was the almost uncanny success of his bowling changes. When you saw him walking to his position at mid-off, fanning his face with his cap, you knew a bowling change was imminent, and so very often it was successful. By his skill, ability and leadership, Guy gradually welded together a fine side, strong in every department of the game.

"He was absolute boss of the show and preserved complete discipline, but he was so fair and generous in his outlook to his team that he was always given 100 per cent by everyone. Some time after his retirement I saw Guy arriving at one of our matches at Derby and met him at the pavilion entrance. Derbyshire were fielding and as we walked along he said 'I never thought how much I should wish I was on the field with the boys," said Taylor.

Although Guy Jackson was not considered among the front rank of batsmen he was in July 1927, having led the North at Sheffield and The Rest at Bristol in Test trials, appointed by MCC to captain the side to tour South Africa that winter, when five Tests were scheduled. It was not a fully representative team but it included Sutcliffe, Hammond, Ernest Tyldesley, Wyatt, Stevens, Freeman and Geary, with Harry Elliott as wicketkeeper. The current England captain Percy Chapman was unavailable, and Arthur Carr and JC White, who also led the team around this time, did not go. It was an opportunity for Jackson to establish his credentials in big cricket, although it was unlikely that he would have progressed much further given Chapman's success a year later and with Jardine waiting in the wings. For example, he did not play for the Gentlemen at Lord's, where Chapman was captain in 1927.

Early in October, he was forced to withdraw from the tour. Malaria, contracted during the war and which flared up from time to time, caused his health to break down and he was taken to a London nursing home, where a long period of rest was prescribed. This was doubly unfortunate for Derbyshire. The man who replaced Jackson was Major RT Stanyforth, a wicketkeeper. He played in the Tests and this ruled out Elliott, although he did appear in the final game at Durban when Stevens led the team in Stanyforth's absence.

Amidst the disappointment Guy Jackson might have felt some relief at missing the tour. Bob Wyatt and Jackson were in the Gentlemen's team against the Players during the Folkestone Festival as the 1927 season approached its end. During the weekend, when most of the amateurs were playing golf, Jackson suggested a walk along the sea-front. They knew each other fairly well and Wyatt considered him a composed and confident figure, at his best in a crisis. But he seemed ill at ease, admitting to Wyatt that he was concerned about the forthcoming tour. "I'm not at all happy about this trip. I'm worried about all the speech-making and I'm wondering if I can possibly face it." Wyatt told him that he was attaching far too much importance to what was, after all, only a minor chore. He used Arthur Gilligan's relaxed approach to speechmaking as an example and by the time they returned to their hotel Jackson seemed in a more cheerful frame of mind. After Folkestone, Jackson went to Scarborough, where he led the MCC South African XI against Thornton's XI, Elliott keeping wicket. The news that Jackson had withdrawn from the tour came as a surprise to Wyatt.

In 1930, Guy Jackson announced that he would be stepping down after nine seasons as captain, the calls of the family business preventing him from continuing. On Monday August 25 1930, the second day of the Essex match, Derbyshire's players and officials gathered for a presentation at the County Ground. Will Taylor and the committee had known for some time but the news was officially released that day. Harry Elliott, the senior professional, presented his skipper with a silver cigarette casket on behalf of the players. Jackson reciprocated with gold cuff links, bearing on one side the club colours and on the other his initials, to Harry Storer, Garnet Lee, Leslie Townsend, Denis Smith, Stan Worthington, Harry Elliott, Archie Slater, Jim Hutchinson, Tommy Mitchell, Albert Alderman and Joe Bowden. The coach, Sam Cadman, also received a similar gift.

Then came the tributes. "For his work in leading and in inspiring the team Jackson deserves immense thanks. He took over control when the fortunes of the county were at a very low ebb, steadily raised the standard of the cricket and now retires with Derbyshire well established among the leading teams of the day," *Wisden* said. The umpire Frank Chester described him as a stern skipper but a splendid disciplinarian. "He was an unequalled judge of a cricketer and no one did more for the game in the county. When he took over the team they were rather a headstrong crowd but in a short time he nurtured the proper spirit and won the respect of all the players."

The local press was saddened to see him go, describing him as "as fine a captain as any county side could covet but he could never rely upon the comforting consistency usually associated with clubs like Yorkshire and Lancashire". It was not entirely the end, for he made 26 further appearances for the county, 1931-36, leading the side out again on several occasions.

Will Taylor said that Jackson had no legacy in a cricket sense when he took over as captain but he left a very considerable legacy to his successor, Arthur Richardson.

Guy Jackson had moulded the team into a unit which would soon be feared.

Chapter 4
The Skipper

ARTHUR Richardson, who followed Guy Jackson as captain in 1931, had been groomed for the role.

Nevertheless, Jackson's announcement that he was standing down had aroused considerable speculation about his successor. Clearly he was going to be a difficult act to follow. Although Richardson was the only serious candidate, some suggested that Jackson should retain the captaincy in name and play when he was able to do so. A deputy could be appointed to lead the side when he was unavailable. This found no takers and a few other names were bandied around, although without much conviction.

It would have to be an amateur, of course, and one of the four Hill-Wood brothers, particularly Willie, would have been suitable but none of them could spare the time. Similarly Neville Ford (Harrow and Oxford), a hard-hitting batsman who appeared in 31 matches from 1926-34, was generally lost to county cricket. Another candidate was John Dudley Harwood Gilbert, who was in the Repton XI for four years, and played in four county games in 1930. Gilbert was born at Chellaston Manor on October 8 1910. His father was one of the founders of United Dairies and a Derbyshire committee member in the early 1930s. In county cricket Gilbert, who kept goal for Derby County Reserves on occasion, was to average under ten in fleeting appearances, sometimes restricted by indifferent health, over the next few years. Another from Repton, Charles Cyril Clarke, showed promise as a 19-year-old in 1930 when he was involved with Jackson in a ninth wicket partnership of 132 against Kent at Ilkeston. Clarke's share was an unbeaten 35 but most of his cricket was played for his native Staffordshire. Although their record in county cricket was modest, Gilbert, on three occasions, and Clarke (two) were to lead the county but they were not serious contenders in 1930. Richardson had the credentials and was made for the job.

His family ran a tanning and leather business, W and J Richardson, in Eagle Street, Derby. This was established in Horsley Woodhouse in 1624, where the Richardsons had been farmers. The works, which also supplied leather to cricket ball manufacturers, transferred from Eagle Street to Sinfin in 1935. The Eagle Street site was later buried under the Eagle shopping centre.

Arthur Walker Richardson was born on March 4 1907 at Abbotts Hill House, Derby the second son of William Henry Richardson. His elder brother, Ven. John

Farquhar Richardson (1904-91) was Archdeacon of Derby from 1952-73. The house, hard by the tannery from which the family fortunes stemmed, was sold for redevelopment in 1926, the family moving to The Leylands.

By that time Richardson had completed his education at Winchester College (1920-25), where he was coached by Rockley Wilson and Harry Altham. He was in the XI in 1925, opening the innings and averaging 26, with 117 against Harrow as his top score. In that match Richardson and Edward Snell, who was to appear in a few matches for Sussex, shared a second wicket partnership of 296. Snell made 163 and Winchester completely outplayed Harrow in a drawn match. Arthur Richardson played for the Derbyshire Friars in 1925-27. He achieved little at the start but in 1927 he scored 588 runs, his highest innings being 134 not out and his average 36.75. At the age of 20 he had made his mark in public school and good quality club cricket; of equal importance he had rubbed shoulders at the Friars with the likes of Lionel (Bill) Blaxland, Rev Henry Ellison, John Chapman and George Buckston, people not without influence at the County Ground. He also did well with Derbyshire 2nd, skippered by Ellison, with Denis Smith as his opening partner and Tommy Mitchell a youthful colleague.

In May 1928 he made his first-class debut, scoring one and 17 against the West Indians at Derby. Jackson made 63 in the second innings and Archie Slater took eight for 24 but West Indians won the match by two wickets. They needed 182 in the fourth innings and collapsed from 55 without loss to 149 for eight but Learie Constantine hit out for an unbeaten 31 to get them home. Constantine claimed that Derbyshire's players had tried to put him off his game by appealing each time the ball struck his pads, regardless of whether the ball would have hit the stumps. It was a hard school.

Richardson opened with Harry Storer in the next game, against Glamorgan at Ilkeston and they put on 69 in the second innings. A week later he scored his first fifty for the county, against Somerset at Chesterfield. Rain restricted play to less than six hours, Jackson declaring immediately Richardson had reached his half-century. He was in the team which visited The Parks and then made 49 and 70 not out against Warwickshire at Derby. In July he scored 61 at Maidstone, where fielding to Woolley's 198 added to his cricketing education. Richardson was a solid and slightly ungainly batsman who scored mainly on the leg side. But he had already shown courage and determination and it was these traits, allied to a sensible application to keep within his limitations which were to turn him into a useful member of the side. The harsh, disciplined routine of Winchester and the confidence it instilled served him well on his entry into the first-class game. Eager to learn, he also became a good fieldsman at mid-off.

Richardson first captained Derbyshire in August 1928 against Sussex at Queen's Park, Chesterfield, Jackson being injured. Leslie Townsend was unbeaten with 55 in Derbyshire's total of 263 and then changed the course of the match when Sussex had reached 100 for the loss of one wicket. He took eight for 48 in 32 overs, the visitors following on under the two-day rule. Maurice Tate hit Townsend for three sixes to clear the arrears but they were only 52 ahead with two wickets remaining when the game ended in a draw. Townsend's match analysis was thirteen for 111. Richardson also led the team on two more occasions that month, at Kidderminster where Worcestershire were beaten by two wickets and against Leicestershire at the County Ground, Derbyshire winning by 242 runs. Twenty-three matches in 1928 produced 590 runs, average 20.34. The story goes that his father promised him a pound a run – if so it must have temporarily strained the family budget. A football injury prevented him from appearing in 1929 until the Whitsuntide match at Edgbaston and 60 not out against Somerset at Burton-on-Trent was his only half-century in eight games that summer. In 1930 he was restricted to four appearances, with a dismal average of 5.20, although he did reasonably well with the Friars.

The general committee met in September 1930 and Richardson accepted the club's offer to take over the captaincy. At the age of 23, he had made 35 appearances for the county and had already captained the team on three occasions. If 791 runs with an average of 19.29 and a highest score of 70 not out were relatively modest career figures at that point he had at least earned the respect of the professionals.

His career batting average remained at 19, not helped by a descent to 12.60 in the Championship year. This is misleading, for he played at least two crucial innings in 1936 and four years earlier had made his thousand runs in a season. Of his fellow captains, many fared little better in that wet summer; Lister, Chapman, Page, Sellers, Cuthbertson, Heane, Ingle and AJ Holmes averaging below 20 in the Championship, with only Dempster, Wilcox, ERT Holmes and Wyatt exceeding 35. Walter Robins and the England skipper GO Allen were in fine all-round form but Richardson was typical of the majority of county captains of that period; leadership skills honed by a public school (in 1936, eighty per cent of the county captains were public school educated) and in some cases a university background offsetting, at best, average playing ability.

Richardson said later that he inherited a going concern from Guy Jackson but this was not entirely correct. Much remained to be done before the county could rise above the middle of the table. Derbyshire had no fast bowler worthy of the name and there was a danger that the magnificent potential of Worthington would not be fully realised. A number of players were nearing the end and there were no guaranteed replacements. There was to be a period of transition before Jackson's men became Richardson's men.

Chapter 5
The Senior Pro

THERE is a lovely story in Richard Streeton's biography of Percy Fender. The veteran wicketkeeper Herbert Strudwick would bring the bowling figures into the dressing room during an interval and, if things had not gone well, the Surrey captain would ask him what he should do next. On one occasion Strudwick's answer was: 'The first thing, Mr Fender, is to take yourself off – look at these figures.' Fender roared with laughter and did not bowl again when play resumed.

Not every amateur captain in the 1920s and 1930s would have tolerated such advice, even from the most senior of professionals but Guy Jackson, particularly in the early years of his leadership, sought advice and guidance from Cadman and Morton, and Arthur Richardson forged such a partnership with his wicketkeeper and senior pro Harry Elliott. It was an alliance based on mutual respect. Elliott saw it all; from Derbyshire's lowest points to the Championship success and nobody contributed more to the club's rise.

He was born at Scarcliffe, a village in the north of the county, and worked as a miner for a time before, in 1913, becoming a groom-cum-groundsman to Sir Joseph Laycock at Wiseton Hall in north Nottinghamshire. Elliott had showed early promise as a cricketer and was in the Scarcliffe team when he was 14. In 1910-11 he kept wicket for Shirebrook, Bestwick being a colleague. At Wiseton he tended his employer's private cricket ground and tennis court, sampling the delights of country house cricket. War service in Brig-General Sir Joseph Laycock's regiment, the Royal Horse Artillery, followed in Egypt, where, during a quiet period, Elliott was given £50 to spend on cricket equipment in Alexandria to arrange games for the soldiers. After the 1914-18 conflict he returned to Wiseton.

Early in the 1920 season Sir Archibald White, a former captain of Yorkshire, came to play in a match for Sir Joseph. White noted Elliott's ability and thought he was a Yorkshireman at first. When he learned he was born in Derbyshire he recommended him to the county and he impressed in a 2nd XI match at Edgbaston during the Whitsun holiday of 1920. He replaced George Beet in the first team against Essex at Derby in June and so began one of the most successful careers in the county's history. It might never have got off the ground had Elliott told the truth about his age, for he was four years older than Derbyshire thought. It was not until a players' reunion in 1967 that he revealed the year of his birth as November 2 1891 and not 1895. "If Derbyshire had known I was already 28 in 1920 the chances are

18

that they would have said I was too old. It was often done in those days to get into county cricket. Joe Bowden had done the same thing in 1909."

When he played against South Africa at Durban in February 1928, Harry Elliott became the first Derbyshire player to win a Test cap since Joe Humphries 20 years earlier. Throughout the majority of his career he was overshadowed by Leslie Ames and George Duckworth but he kept wicket under Percy Chapman's captaincy against the West Indies at Old Trafford in 1928 and toured India with Douglas Jardine in 1933-34 when he appeared in Tests at Bombay and Madras. His four Tests represented a reward for steadily increasing competence, although his batting never developed beyond a career average of just under 14. He could be difficult to shift, however, with a stubborn and defiant dead bat and an inimitable sweep shot, mowing the ball off one knee.

The wicketkeeping record is staggering: 520 matches, including four games when he came back during an emergency at the age of 55 in 1947. He appeared in 194 consecutive matches up to 1928 when he missed two, one because of the Test match against the West Indies and the other as a result of an injury, when he was replaced by Hector Beet and Robin Buckston. The injury occurred at Blackpool when he hurt his hand tossing a ball around on the beach, Jim Hutchinson deputising in the match against Lancashire. The next game was the return against Lancashire at Burton-on-Trent, Buckston taking over. Elliott kept wicket in 518 of his 520 games. The exceptions were caused by injuries, one while batting against MCC at Lord's in 1928, Harry Storer substituting, and, after 232 consecutive appearances, another at Worcester in 1937, Albert Alderman putting on the gloves.

Between June 1920 and May 1937 Elliott missed only two matches out of a consecutive run of 436. His entire cricket in England was played for Derbyshire, with the exceptions of the 1928 Test and the 1927 MCC South African XI match. Only Derek Morgan (540) has played more matches for the club than Elliott, only Bob Taylor (1,304 for Derbyshire and 1,649 in all first-class cricket against Elliott's 1,183 and 1,206) shared in more dismissals. Elliott established a number of other county records: most dismissals in a season, 90 in 1935, most stumpings, 30 in 1931, most victims in a match, 10 at Old Trafford in 1935, a record he shares with Taylor, and six in an innings on three occasions, yielding only to Taylor, who achieved three sevens, two for Derbyshire and one for England. In 1936 Elliott allowed no byes in 25 completed innings.

He gave counsel – when asked – to a succession of amateurs, good and indifferent, who turned out for the county. For example, early in his career the Hill-Woods cemented their affinity with Derbyshire cricket. A father who had played at the turn of the century was followed by his four sons into the county side, a span of 42 years from 1894-1936 but involving only 114 matches.

The second son, Willy, subsequently Sir Wilfred, was the best of them. WW, as he was known in his playing days, was a right-hand batsman with a curious, crouching stance. He developed this to offset a habit of drawing away from the ball and although it might not have been easy on the eye it was a method which served him well. Initially he showed promise as a leg spin bowler but later turned to off breaks. He was in the Eton XI in 1919, when trouble broke out at the conclusion of the match against Harrow. As captain in 1920 Hill-Wood issued a notice that any repetition of the misconduct would lead to the fixture being taken away from Lord's. The warning had the desired effect, with no further misbehaviour. Leading a team which included his great friend Gubby Allen and Ronnie Aird, two men who would occupy leading administrative positions at Lord's, Hill-Wood dominated a match which Eton won comfortably. He earned a Blue in a powerful Cambridge side of 1922 when Hubert Ashton gave him the final place as an opener, ahead of TC Lowry. Two future England captains, Percy Chapman and Allen, were colleagues and Hill-Wood made 81, Oxford being beaten by an innings. During the winter of 1922-23 he toured Australia and New Zealand with an MCC A squad led by Archie MacLaren. His best score of 122 not out came in a rearguard action with Yorkshire's Geoffrey Wilson in an undefeated opening partnership of 282 which occupied 680 balls and lasted the whole of the final day against Victoria.

WW – at the age of 17 years 334 days – and his brother Basil, a useful right-arm fast-medium bowler, made their debuts for the county in 1919. Basil, later Sir Basil, BS Hill-Wood, was to succeed his father as the second baronet in 1949. The professionals, although addressing them as Mr, referred to WW as whisky and water and BS as brandy and soda. Dressing room humour was just as sharp in the 1920s as in other years. Charlie, the youngest of the four sons, was a left-arm fast-medium bowler who gained a Blue at Oxford in all three years from 1928-30. Denis, an opening batsman, got an Oxford Blue in 1928. He became chairman of Arsenal in 1960, his son Peter following his father and grandfather into the role. WW Hill-Wood had only one full year of county cricket, 1923, when he scored 961 runs for Derbyshire, average 34, and took 30 wickets. With Joe Bowden he shared a then-record opening partnership of 206 at Bath. A century for MCC against his old university raised his aggregate above four figures. Not yet 22, he was regarded as a possible England batsman. In the years ahead his forays into county cricket would be brief but, in Derbyshire's context, significant.

The Hill-Woods added class to an amateur content that was sometimes of dubious cricketing quality. This was to change gradually under Jackson's captaincy. He was always happy to include amateurs in the side if they were worth their place or could entertain the spectators. From the mid-1920s most of the amateurs tended to be selected on merit in addition to availability, although one or two brought in to maintain the tradition of amateur captaincy when Jackson and his successors were absent stretched credibility.

The economic climate had changed. In times past, amateurs enjoyed county cricket with its perks of first-class rail travel, top-notch hotels and lunch in committee rooms on expenses because they had private funds or occupations which allowed them time off in the summer. Now many people left the public schools and the universities facing the reality that they could not neglect a career to play cricket full-time. Instead, they were pencilled in for matches which coincided with their annual holidays, such as the schoolmasters in August. Naturally there was some resentment from professionals forced to make way. Segregation went far beyond initials before the surnames on scorecards: separate railway compartments, hotels, dressing rooms and gates leading on to the field of play were the norm. Hard pressed county secretaries such as Will Taylor could justify the inclusion of amateurs as a cost-cutting exercise.

Jim Hutchinson, unimpressed by some of the nonentities, had a different view. "We were the poorest paid county players in the country. Six pounds for a home match, eight pounds away. The amateurs used to cost Derbyshire more because their expenses were so high."

Jim Cresswell, a left-arm fast-medium bowler who was in and out of the county side for five seasons in the 1920s, provided more evidence that everything was not always sweetness and light. He came from a mining family in Marehay, near Ripley, and worked in a colliery boiler room as a stoker, getting up steam for the boilers. After leaving first-class cricket he spent 25 years with Derby Borough Police. His son Nev said: "He was popular with his colleagues but sometimes told the story of how he did not always get on with the Jacksons, Guy and his cousin Anthony." He said an early trial saw him "knock over Jackson's hob" on several occasions when he bowled to him in the nets. A balance had to be struck between impressing the hierarchy; deferential but not to the point of near-humiliation. "I remember when I used to go to the County Ground with him at Derby after his career ended. Denis Smith and Harry Storer were always very pleased to see my father. They would spend the afternoon spinning tales and they had some fascinating stories to tell," Nev added.

Some of the pros viewed the more talented amateurs as a threat. Jobs were at risk. Turning up in August wearing a 'fancy coloured cap' to bat with uninhibited freedom from contractual worries and make an effortless hundred might have been good news for the county but it meant a pro – then not paid for the season and reliant on match money for his income – losing his place in the team. When a place went to someone half as talented but with more initials before his surname then resentment was doubled.

It is unfair to tar all the amateurs with this brush. William Parrington (Rossall and Cambridge) moved to Derbyshire to sell wire ropes, mainly to collieries. He came into contact with Guy Jackson at Clay Cross and played his cricket with Belper Meadows, the Friars and sometimes as captain of Derbyshire 2nd. In 1926 he made six appearances for the county but refused further matches as he realised he was depriving a pro of his match money. Another was HGB Jordan, who made runs at Marlborough and in army cricket and played for Derbyshire when he was on leave in 1926. Captain (later Lieutenant-Colonel) Jordan bagged a pair but was still invited to go on the western tour. He declined because he felt he would be keeping a professional out of the side. Another quarter of a century would pass before Guy Willatt ended the practice of separate dressing rooms but long before then Derbyshire's amateurs were proving worthy of their places, often adding dashes of style and quality to batting which was sometimes prosaic.

In particular, Repton's masters served the county well. The public school, in south Derbyshire, has ancient ties with the club and Gilbert Curgenven, captain of the eleven for two years but never a master, was prominent. JL Crommelin-Brown was on the Repton staff for 38 years and master-in-charge of cricket from 1921-34. He batted consistently for the county during the holidays of 1922-26. Bill Blaxland, his successor in charge of cricket, became a master in 1922 and remained for 36 years. Masters or pupils John Eggar, Richard Sale, Donald Carr, Willatt and Chris Adams maintained the connection down the years. In reverse, Wilfred Carter, Garnet Lee, Harold Pope, Albert Alderman and, longest-serving of all, Eric Marsh, were professionals at the school.

It was in Guy Jackson's day that a spirit was forged between the amateurs and the professionals that led Harry Storer (St John's School, Marehay) to say of his captain (Harrow): "I like that b******, he hated losing." First with Jackson and then Richardson, Harry Elliott did as much as anyone to foster that spirit, helping to bridge the gap between amateur and professional. His ability was recognised at Loughborough in June 1933, when Arthur Richardson was ill and Jackson and Alan Skinner, who could have taken over, were unavailable. Elliott, as senior professional, deputised, in his 14th season as a player, leading out an all-professional Derbyshire team – Elliott (H) captain, Storer, Lee, Townsend, Smith, Alderman, Worthington, Elliott (CS), Pope, Mitchell and Copson.

Elliott remained proud of this honour for the rest of his life. He had been a capable lieutenant to Jackson and Richardson for more than a decade and had followed Cadman at the head of the professionals' dining table. At Edgbaston in 1930 he had tossed up when three amateurs, Jackson, the skipper, Charlie Hill-Wood and Neville Ford, failed to arrive at the ground on the Saturday morning but they were there when play started a few minutes late because of rain. And he deputised at Northampton in 1932 when Richardson was forced to withdraw after the first day.

At that time a professional captaining a county side was comparatively rare. When the outspoken Cecil Parkin suggested that Jack Hobbs should be captain of the Test side, Lord Hawke – who did so much to improve the professionals' lot – was aghast. "Pray Heaven no professional may ever captain England," he said at Yorkshire's county dinner. Pelham Warner tried to smooth it over, explaining that perhaps Hawke meant it would be a bad day when no amateur was good enough to play for his country but the damage was done. Hobbs took over in the fourth Test at Old Trafford when Arthur Carr fell ill in 1926 but the idea of a professional captain was anathema, despite the precedents of James Lillywhite, Shaw and Shrewsbury. Hammond's conversion to amateur status eased him into the Test captaincy in 1938; not until Hutton 14 years later was a pro officially appointed.

Similar feudal barriers existed among the counties. Alfred Shaw captained

Nottinghamshire in 1883 but since the Championship was formalised in 1890 professionals had led only in emergencies. Many of them would not have welcomed the job. Herbert Sutcliffe was offered the Yorkshire post but declined. However, by 1933, the custom was being breached. By then 13 of the 17 counties had used professionals as captains in matches when an amateur was not available. These included Bates (Glamorgan), Goddard, Hammond and Parker (Gloucestershire), Brown, Kennedy and Mead (Hampshire), Johnny and Ernest Tyldesley (Lancashire), Astill and King (Leicestershire), Hendren (Middlesex), John and George Gunn (Nottinghamshire), Ducat, Hobbs and Sandham (Surrey), Cornford (Sussex), Bates and WG Quaife (Warwickshire), Root (Worcestershire) and Hirst and Rhodes (Yorkshire) and now Elliott.

Some counties (Glamorgan with Turnbull, Worcestershire with Walters) got around the problem of making it worthwhile for an amateur to devote a summer to cricket by appointing their captains as paid secretaries. Leicestershire, desperate for a stopgap captain until CS Dempster, the New Zealand amateur, became available, appointed the professional Ewart Astill for one year only in 1935 and had their then best-ever season. He was the first professional captain appointed by a county for a full season in the 20th century. The committee duly stood him down in favour of Dempster and two years of poor results followed. After the war Leslie Berry and Tom Dollery broke the mould until the abolition of amateur status in time for the 1963 season changed everything.

There was a precedent in Derbyshire's history. In 1887, an amateur captain EAJ Maynard dropped out because of poor form and a paid player William Chatterton took the helm for three matches, although amateurs such as LG Wright or GG Walker were in the team. Chatterton skippered an all-professional side at Leyton in August 1887 but Essex were then second class. He was officially appointed in 1888 and 1889, when Derbyshire had lost their status among the elite.

There was no question of Elliott getting the job on a permanent basis at any time in the 1930s. He was a professional and in any event there was some prejudice against wicketkeepers as captains. In 1963 Charlie Lee was appointed, although there had been occasions of an all-pro side under Worthington and Smith in 1946.

Elliott was to captain Derbyshire on three more occasions, in 1934 against Gloucestershire at Derby and Worcestershire at Stourbridge, and in 1935 against Nottinghamshire at Ilkeston. Three of his four games in charge ended in victory, two by an innings, and the other, the Gloucestershire match, was drawn.

Chapter 6
The Veteran

ARTHUR Richardson said Guy Jackson, Harry Elliott and Harry Storer were the three rocks around which Derbyshire cricket was built. All three offered ability and brought enormous influence to the team. Only ill health prevented Jackson from captaining England, Elliott appeared in Test cricket and there was a school of thought that Storer would have done so had not soccer got in the way.

He was a man for all seasons, the best of county professionals but with a football career which was even more illustrious.

There was pedigree. His uncle William was one of Derbyshire's greatest players; his father Harry, only an average cricketer, played in seven matches in 1895 but was better known as a footballer. Harry junior was born on February 2 1898 on Merseyside, at West Derby, during his father's time as Liverpool's goalkeeper. The family roots were deep in the soil of the mining town of Ripley and his parents returned to the area when he was four. The son's pride in his heritage was evident: "Except for a freak of birth I am a Derbyshire man." When Harry senior finished playing he became licensee of the Yew Tree Hotel in Holloway, where he died of consumption in 1908 at the age of 37. Harry junior came to live with an aunt in the Peasehill area of Ripley and it was at school that he revealed his talent for football and cricket.

His cricket career began modestly. In 1918 he averaged only 14 for Butterley in the Derbyshire Alliance and there was little hint of the future opening batsman of near-Test quality. Then came a surge in 1919: 524 Alliance runs, average 34.93, and 46 wickets with his accurate medium-pace mixed up with leg breaks. Something was there but it was hidden under the rubble of 1920, when his first season in county cricket – he made his debut against Yorkshire at Sheffield – produced an average of 6.68 from 24 innings.

To their credit Derbyshire persevered with a player they considered promising but it was hard going. Storer knew it. "I found it a struggle at first with the county. It seemed easier to make a hundred in local cricket than ten runs in the first-class game."

There was a maiden century in 1921 and promise seemed about to be fulfilled in 1923. But in 1924 he averaged 6.84 in 26 innings with a highest score of 18. Disgusted with his form he left the club for Central Lancashire League cricket at Crompton, where his aim was to rebuild his game as well as earn a little money. He played three innings for the county at the end of the 1925 season, the best of which produced only 23 and came close to giving up altogether.

Storer's cricket career at this time was an adjunct to his football. After leaving school he became an apprentice fitter at Butterley Company, the famous Ripley ironworks which also owned a number of collieries. Soccer with local teams earned him a trial with Grimsby Town and the week he began training with Grimsby saw him offered a cricket trial with Derbyshire. He joined the ground staff and also finished his apprenticeship. In March 1921 Storer was transferred to Derby County and his best football was played at the Baseball Ground. He appeared mainly at wing-half, although in 1923-24 he scored 24 Second Division goals from inside-left, and won two England caps, against France in Paris in May 1924 and Ireland in Belfast in October 1927. Storer scored in a 3-1 victory in Paris but England lost 2-0 in Belfast. Derby were promoted in 1925-26 and in December 1927 he became the Rams' captain but in February 1929 was transferred to Burnley.

At 33 he seemed to have a few good years left but saw the management job at Coventry City advertised. It was a challenge and he left Burnley in April 1931 to take over at the Third Division club. A fine playing career ended: Ripley Town, Eastwood Town, Grimsby Town, Derby County, Burnley and England.

An even more memorable and colourful career in management was about to start. Coventry City owed £14,000 and the ground wasn't anything to boast about but he took them to the Second Division in 1935-1936. This was a notable achievement because there was only one promotion place from each of the Third Divisions, north and south. He remained at Highfield Road until moving to Birmingham in 1945. Promotion to the First Division was achieved when Birmingham were champions in 1948, their defence conceding only 24 goals. Then it was back to Coventry from 1948-53 before leaving on a matter of principle.

Storer was out of management for 18 months but remained in touch by adding straight-talking spice to the radio programme *Sport in the Midlands*. He succeeded Jack Barker as manager of Derby County in July 1955 after they had been relegated to the Third Division (North). The size of the task was indicated in December when non-league Boston United thrashed the Rams 6-1 in the FA Cup at the Baseball Ground. After two more years, second place in the league and a few boardroom battles Storer hauled his old club to the Third Division (North) championship and back into the Second Division. He built a side which survived in the higher sphere but, although he reduced the club's overdraft, there was never enough money to provide the class the team needed to break into the First Division. Storer stayed until he retired in May 1962, his health not good, nine months short of his 65th birthday. It was to be a duo who took him as a role model, Brian Clough and Peter Taylor, who accomplished promotion.

The tales are legendary. Storer's teams possessed skill but had their share of hard men. Taylor, assistant manager to Clough in those incredible days at the Baseball Ground and City Ground with Derby County and Nottingham Forest, had spent nine years as a player at Coventry with Storer as his boss. "Brian and I are indebted for our creed as managers to Harry Storer," he wrote. Storer was a hard man who appreciated skill but liked brave players. "He was blunt, yet also something of an orator and able to destroy almost anyone verbally, "said Taylor in his autobiography *With Clough by Taylor.* "He was ruthless and often frightening, yet always fair."

Storer had much in common with Clough. He had little time for directors and his views were candid and spared nobody. When he took over at Derby he signed a hard centre-half, Martin McDonnell, and Paddy Ryan, an experienced inside-forward or wing-half who was appointed captain. A sound defence was the watchword but Storer's teams gave the lie to any claims that he was defensively-minded. Derby scored more than a hundred goals in each of his first two seasons.

Young players learned to know their place. Ian Buxton, another footballer/cricketer, once decided the time had come to seek a pay increase. "I played for Derby when he was manager and he spent a great deal of time in the summer at the County Ground talking cricket with us. He was a very entertaining man to listen to but a hard man to work for. I was playing Second Division football at that time for about £10 a week and as I'd been doing reasonably well I thought I would go in and see the boss about a rise. I managed to get in about two words in half-an-hour and I came out of the office with the impression that I was lucky to be getting any wages at all."

Ian Hall, a colleague of Buxton with the Rams and Derbyshire, recounted a similar tale via Gerald Mortimer, of the *Derby Evening Telegraph.* A player would enter Storer's office to find that the boss's dog, Billy, normally well under control, was halfway across the room, snarling and needing careful negotiation. Storer took his time in calling him to heel and the player almost forgot what he intended to do.

Storer denied that he created hard teams at the expense of skill. "After a lifetime in this business I know that there is nothing that succeeds better than good football. I always wanted my teams to play that sort of stuff but unfortunately I was never in a position to buy really brilliant ball players. I had to get by with players of more or less moderate ability. It wasn't any free choice. Just circumstances. It was essential my players compensated with gameness and fighting spirit."

During Storer's final illness Brian Clough, newly appointed as Derby County's manager, visited him in hospital. Storer was close to signing Clough before he became a regular in the Middlesbrough side and the link was maintained during the latter's early steps into management. At the cremation in Markeaton, the service was conducted by Rev Bill Blaxland, the former Derbyshire cricketer. Storer left a request in his will that his ashes should be scattered over the pitch at the County Ground and Will Taylor was there to observe the ceremony.

In Storer's day the cricket and football seasons were distinct and dual careers were not uncommon. Albert Alderman and Charlie Elliott are cases in point. As for Storer, his cricket career never looked back after his dismal season in 1924. Dedication paid off. Will Taylor recalled how Storer came to him at the end of one season and asked if he could look through the scorebooks. He felt he was getting out too often from certain strokes and he wished to refresh his memory from the scorebook. In 1926 he scored more than a thousand runs and topped the batting averages. He exceeded a four-figure aggregate in six seasons, the best being 1652 in 1929. Then the Coventry job demanded his time and although he managed 22 of the 28 Championship matches in 1931 his appearances were restricted for the remainder of his career. From 1932 onwards he never played more than 16 matches in any one season, nine in 1936, his final year, when he was in the veteran stage of his career.

Will Taylor left nobody in doubt over his ability. "Harry Storer was a personality and in my opinion he was one of the best opening batsmen Derbyshire ever had. If it had not been for his football commitments I believe he would have played cricket for England. He was a tremendous trier and a very fine bat on difficult wickets. Harry hated the opposition and hated getting out. He was a very good cricketer who possessed an enormous amount of determination"

Chapter 7
The Opening Batsman

YOUNGSTERS aiming to make their way from club cricket through Derbyshire's nursery to the County Championship side were taught in a hard school. Sam Cadman did not mince his words and Bill Bestwick could be blunt and uncompromising. Strength of character was required, in addition to youthful promise.

Thus Denis Smith, playing for the Colts against a County XI, found himself facing Bestwick during his early days at the County Ground, a severe test for the tall 18-year-old left-handed batsman. He came through it unscathed and there was also an unbeaten, "very patient" 22 when the club and ground met the powerful Loscoe Colliery side in July 1925. Smith opened the innings with Albert Alderman and Stan Worthington was at No 3. Nobody at the Nottinghamshire and Derbyshire Border League club's ground that day could have realised the significance of that top order.

Although Smith was born in a mining village, Somercotes, on January 24 1907, he did not work in the pits. His winter job was at the nearby Codnor Park foundry. Smith's father and grandfather spent many hours bowling to him at home and at his grandparents' farm – wickets were painted on a cow shed – but his early formal cricket was played at Clay Cross Secondary School. By the time he was 16 in 1923 he was playing for Somercotes in the Derbyshire Alliance. Ironically, in view of his later reputation as an aggressive, free-scoring opening batsman, he was defensively minded during the early stages of his career. When he made his first 50 for Somercotes at Butterley, 33 came in singles. Alliance runs had currency, however, and Smith also showed promise as a right-arm medium-paced bowler. In 1926, Cadman's first year as coach, he had a week's trial at the county nets. Further trials took place in the following year and Smith made his county debut against Somerset at Taunton in June 1927. Derbyshire won but Smith, going in No 7, failed to score.

Cadman soon discovered that although Smith, who stood six feet, could hit hard he did not possess many strokes. Experience was needed and he was farmed out to the Bassetlaw League club Warsop Main Colliery, which won the championship in 1928. Colleagues were Jim Cresswell and the 19-year-old Alfred Pope, whose right-arm fast-medium deliveries brought 39 wickets at eight apiece. Smith did nothing outstanding, averaging 18.50 in a dozen innings with a highest score of 73. He scored his first century in any grade of cricket when he substituted for the regular professional for Marston's Brewery at Burton-on-Trent and he appeared in seven matches for the county in 1928. His return was modest. He was tried as Joe Bowden's opening partner against Gloucestershire at Ilkeston, when an out-of-form Storer went in at No 7 and made 167, but it took 58 against Lancashire at Burton-on-Trent in the final match to raise his average to 15.90. Cadman persevered, although there were a few misgivings in 1929. Smith failed to progress despite being given extended opportunities.

The breakthrough was achieved in 1930. There had been a few glimpses of form but it was a fighting innings against Nottinghamshire at Ilkeston which began to persuade the faithful that he might, after all, have something to offer. At lunch on Monday Derbyshire had lost half their side for 109 in reply to 349. Smith, who had come in at the fall of the fifth wicket, made 54 not out, sharing a partnership of 70 for the eighth wicket with Archie Slater. Promoted in the order he scored 85 against Worcestershire at Chesterfield, after which he was presented with his county cap, and, then, in Wilfred Payton's benefit, 83 and 105 at Trent Bridge. The maiden hundred had been a long time arriving but it helped save the match.

Ten days later Smith played an even more impressive innings at The Oval. Opening with Storer, he shared a second innings partnership of 111, going on to make 107. He finished the season only 25 short of a thousand runs and established himself as an opening batsman. Smith achieved four figure aggregates in 1931 and 1932. Although there was a hiccup in 1933, the runs continued to flow until the outbreak of the war. He was severe on the overpitched ball on middle or leg and his elegance evoked comparisons with Frank Woolley, although this was perhaps a little unfair, for he lacked the Kent man's fluency.

Selection for the Players at The Oval in 1931 (he made 16 and 24, going in at No 3 in the first innings after Hobbs and Sutcliffe had begun with 203) indicated progress and in 1935 a Test career beckoned. By now Smith had forged successful opening partnerships for his county, first with Storer and then with Albert Alderman. In the first match of the 1935 season he made 189 against Yorkshire at Chesterfield, hitting Verity into the lake.

Like so many others of the Derbyshire team he could be blunt and forthright. His opinions, straight to the point, were expressed with a rich vein of humour and cricketing lore. Personal memories remain clear. Boyhood recollections of innings cut all too short by lofted strokes are countered by his 88 out of 182 against the 1948 Australians and 97 two years later against Worcestershire at Ilkeston. In the 1970s I contacted him, seeking an interview. There was no reply for a week or two. On Easter Monday he arrived out of the blue at my home with the remark: "That wall could do with a bit of pointing." There came several hours of fascinating conversations, followed by visits to his own home and enjoyable browsing among his scrapbooks and mementoes. He regarded the 189 as a turning point in his career. He said: "I remember thinking that day, these beggars can't bowl." These beggars, by the way, included Bill Bowes and Hedley Verity.

Smith began 1935 with 667 runs from eleven innings and was chosen for the Trent Bridge Test against South Africa but had to decline after suffering a cracked rib. He was fit for the third Test at Headingley, where, going in first he saw his captain Wyatt fall to the third ball of the innings. He cut and pulled successfully, playing his legside strokes well and showed discretion in picking the right ball to drive on the off. He had made 36 out of 78 when, attempting to hook Vincent, he hit the ball on to his pads to see it bounce up for an easy catch to the wicketkeeper. In the second innings he shared an opening partnership of 128 with Arthur Mitchell in under two hours when quick runs were needed. Smith's 57 enabled him to retain his place at Old Trafford, where he scored 35 in a first wicket stand of 71 with Fred Bakewell but he was missed twice on a lively pitch and in poor light. He failed to score in the second innings and was not chosen for The Oval Test. Four innings produced 128 runs, average 32.

He was disappointed but had still made an encouraging start. Smith opened for the Players at Lord's in 1935; making 34 and 35 not out, and also at Folkestone but his best innings of the season was saved for the Rest of England against Yorkshire, the 1935 champion county, at The Oval in September. The Rest needed 262 to win in the fourth innings. Smith, opening the innings, hit 78 out of a total of 112. Nine was the next best score. *Wisden* said: "Denis Smith then stood out even more conspicuously as the one batsman capable of overcoming the difficult conditions. In an innings lasting only an hour-and-a-half, Smith scored 78 of 104 runs from the bat and was last out. While his various partners fell easy victims to Verity, Smith pulled the left-handed slows with great power and certainty. Leyland, failing to hold a catch, let the ball slip over the boundary for six and Smith hit eleven fours. Sellers also missed Smith in the long field, but, considering the collapse, the Derbyshire left-hander did wonders."

The Champion County *v* The Rest series was shelved for 12 years after this game. It began as a benefit match for William Yardley at The Oval in 1901. The weather was poor and the game not well attended but in 1903 there was a similar fixture for the benefit of the Cricketers' Fund Friendly Society and the London Playing Fields Association. The series ran until 1935, when there was a loss of £44, due to poor weather and the match ending on the third day. The Advisory County Cricket Committee decided not to renew the fixture in 1936. It resumed in 1947 and the next game was in 1955, the tradition continuing until 1960. Later came the seasonal opener, MCC v Champion County. So Denis Smith was prevented from appearing against the champion county one year and for it in the next. In 1935 it was the first time the Champion County had won since 1905, when Yorkshire beat The Rest.

The innings for The Rest brought his season's aggregate to 2175 runs, average 39.54, his 61 innings being more than any other batsman. He was one of *Wisden's* Five Cricketers of the Year for 1935.

The Test selectors were anxious to give him every opportunity and this came during the 1935-36 winter tour of Australasia. New Zealand, eager to develop their cricket, offered financial guarantees for an MCC visit, which, with fences needing to be mended after the bodyline furore, was to start with six matches in Australia.

Errol Holmes led a 14-strong party of eight amateurs and six professionals, which included Smith. Holmes was briefed on the importance of restoring good relations on the Australian leg of the tour and the team had been carefully chosen in this context. It is easy to imagine the Lord's hierarchy having a quiet word with Guy Jackson, then an MCC committee member, about Smith's credentials. While this was essentially a goodwill trip there were players with Test experience and some who would be in contention in the future, although no official Tests were played. Smith was clearly in favour, socially (when an England XI met the South Africans in the Folkestone festival he was the only pro in the side) and professionally after his not unsuccessful Test debut.

Smith made an excellent start: 83 at Perth, 52 at Adelaide and, after failing at Sydney, 109 against Queensland, where he shared an opening partnership of 204 with Wilf Barber. Smith was at the crease for 195 minutes and struck nine fours. Eddie Gilbert, the aboriginal fast bowler whose ferocious pace startled Bradman six weeks later, was in the Queensland team, conceding 111 runs without taking a wicket.

In New Zealand, Smith reached the high point of his tour with 165 in three hours against Otago at Dunedin. He hit two sixes and 20 fours, reaching his century in 115 minutes and sharing an opening stand of 239 with Jim Parks. Three of the four unofficial Tests against New Zealand produced scores of 26, 48, 16 and 40 not out – 130 runs, average 43.33. The final innings proved frustrating. MCC trailed by 139 on the first innings and lost Parks and Barber in reaching 63 in their second attempt. Smith and Joe Hardstaff took the score to 142 for two by close of play and with the arrears cleared an interesting third and final day was in prospect. Continuous rain overnight and in the morning put paid to it all and to Smith's opportunity of going on to make a big score in a representative match. In addition an elbow injury proved a handicap.

It was not quite good enough: 711 tour runs, average 47.40, second in the averages to Joe Hardstaff but no big scores when it really mattered, such as the representative games in New Zealand or against an Australian XI at Sydney. *Wisden* said: "Smith would have been a greater force as a batsman but for a tendency early in his innings to 'feel' at deliveries outside the off-stump." Errol Holmes found him "a merry, enthusiastic personality and full of fun. He possessed a Derbyshire accent so pronounced that some of us had difficulty in following him even at the end of the tour. When he was fit he played forceful cricket and fully lived up to expectations." Only once did Smith lose his cool, when he felt national honour had been violated. That occurred when a match was postponed because of the death of King George V. Smith heard a member of the opposing side decrying the king's death because it robbed him of an opportunity of making a hundred against MCC. Smith, in high indignation, told his skipper that he had had "half-a-mind to stick one on" the offending player but it was all sorted out over a couple of beers in the end.

India came in 1936 and there was an Ashes tour following. Hardstaff made the trip to Australia in 1936-37 but there was no place for Smith after an unsuccessful time on the wet pitches. His season was rescued only by a return to form in August. Herbert Sutcliffe, too, was discarded. He was in his 42nd year and averaged only 33 in 1936 but some felt he still should have gone in place of Arthur Fagg. Smith thought highly of him as an unselfish opening batsman. In the 1935 Scarborough Festival they shared a second wicket partnership of 84 for HDG Leveson-Gower's XI against the MCC West Indies Team. Their association was cemented when they opened for Leveson-Gower's XI against the MCC Australian Team and the Indians at Scarborough in 1936. Smith said: "He is wonderful. I reckon that if Herbert was my regular partner I'd average another 15 runs an innings." In the first match Smith faced the bowling of his county colleague Bill Copson, who was in the MCC team. The duel was inconclusive. Copson dismissed Sutcliffe for three in the first innings (he made 102 in the second) and Kenneth Farnes twice accounted for Smith (22 and four). Sutcliffe and Smith shared a second innings opening partnership of 88 against the Indians. Other openers came to the fore. Smith returned to his best in 1937 but he never played for England again. The feeling persists that he was a little harshly treated.

Smith became the first Derbyshire batsman to reach 20,000 runs in his career, his 20,516 remaining a county record until Kim Barnett exceeded it. In 1946 he shared a fourth wicket partnership of 328 with Pat Vaulkhard at Trent Bridge. During that season he took over the county's wicketkeeping duties as opposed to his regular position at first slip. He had first kept in the Bradford League during the war and made 28 appearances in the post, most of them prior to the arrival of George Dawkes. Smith was also a useful right-arm medium bowler whose best performance was five for 37 at Trent Bridge, including the wicket of Hardstaff, bowled for 99 with a ball intended to give him his hundred. There was the 88 against the 1948 Australians, during which he hooked Keith Miller to the boundary and dealt with the inevitable bouncer which followed with considerable aplomb. Three years earlier he had made 109 for the North of England against the Australian Services at Blackpool before falling to Miller, although this was not a first-class match.

He was appointed coach in 1952, succeeding Harry Elliott, and could be hard to please. Young players, chastened by his brusque comments, were sometimes afraid of him but they held him with high regard and respect. "They said I was too harsh with them but they were men, not boys. They did not want mollycoddling. They learned to fight back at me in the nets and this taught them how to fight back in the middle. Nobody could hold their hands out there, could they?"

A word of encouragement from Smith was worth a volume of fulsome praise from others. The pipe, his faded England blazer and his tall, gritty figure was a familiar sight at the County Ground. In the nets he could turn his hand to anything – leg-spin, off-spin, in-swing, out-swing – and occasionally he would pick up the bat to demonstrate a particular shot.

There was a day when a young amateur fast bowler was given a trial. He had pace but sprayed the ball all over the place. At the end of the session he roared away from the ground at high speed in a noisy sports car. "Don't worry," said Denis. "If he drives like he bowls he'll not hit anything." When a former playing colleague turned up in a new suit, of which he was obviously proud, he was told by Denis: "By that's cleaned up well."

Ernie Fisher, a bowler who had a long career in the Nottinghamshire and Derbyshire Border League and the Derbyshire County League, played for the club and ground and the 2nd XI when Smith was coach. "He was a character. He would have us bowling flat out for an hour or so to build up our fitness and, puffing away at his pipe, tell us in no uncertain terms what we were doing wrong." When it came to paying out expenses Smith was from the Will Taylor school of parsimony. "Fisher," he'd say, 'what are your expenses?' I would reply, 'five shillings bus fare'. There would then be a great show of slowly counting out the five shillings, with mutterings of "I don't know, thart getting more money than I am."

Bob Taylor had a similarly blunt introduction to Derbyshire. He was due to play for Derbyshire 2nd against Lancashire 2nd at St Helen's and arrangements had been made for Smith to pick him up in Leek. "I was to look out for a black Morris Minor – registration number 695 DTO – they were impressionable years and I can still recall that number plate – and this meant that I had to get a bus from Hanley, one of the Five Towns of the Potteries, at around 7.30am. I waited for a long time but no black Morris arrived. I had arrived ridiculously early but after about an hour and still no sign of Mr Smith I was ready to return home.

"I decided to give it another five minutes before catching the bus back to Hanley, convinced that Derbyshire had found someone else to keep wicket and did not want me. Then suddenly, around the corner came this black car. Denis Smith leaned out and said 'Where the bloody hell have you been?' Such was my introduction to Derbyshire cricket." Taylor also recalled being bawled out as a second team player by Smith for not wearing a jacket when watching cricket on a hot day.

Curiously Smith was not the highest-scoring Derbyshire-born batsmen of his era. The Nottinghamshire and England opener Walter Keeton made more than 24,000 runs in first-class cricket, exceeding Smith's 21,843. He was born at Minerva Street, Shirebrook, which is part of Derbyshire although close to the border. The postal address gave an impression it was in Nottinghamshire, although this is incorrect. Keeton always said he was born in Nottinghamshire, possibly because he preferred a career at Trent Bridge.

Once, when Will Taylor mischievously issued a challenge, Nottinghamshire's secretary claimed the county boundary passed through the house and the bedroom in which Keeton was born was in the Nottinghamshire half.

Chapter 8
The Perfect Foil

HARRY Storer was a role model for Denis Smith's burgeoning career as an opening batsman. His peak seasons coincided with Smith's breakthrough and years later due tribute was paid. Smith recalled how Storer would shield him from the most difficult of bowlers with a laconic 'I'll take him for a bit' if the younger batsman was struggling.

However, it was not Storer who became Smith's most successful partner but Albert Alderman. His career ran parallel to that of Smith's but took longer to develop. Somewhat unusually in the 1930s team, the majority of which came from the coalfield communities, Albert Edward Alderman was born in Derby, at Allenton, then a hamlet in the parish of Alvaston, on October 30 1907. At school he learned the rudiments of cricket and football and he developed in both sports after starting work in the offices at Rolls-Royce. A century for Rolls-Royce 2nd when he was 17 earned promotion to the first eleven and he headed the batting averages for two seasons.

Fair-haired, Alderman became a solid and dependable right-hand batsman. Sam Cadman, who had been a patient batsman himself, was duly impressed and the youngster appeared in several trial and club and ground matches. In March 1927 Alderman signed as a professional with Derbyshire at £4 a week and joined Derby County the same month. He first appeared for the Rams on New Year's Day 1929 and had two spells at the Baseball Ground, mainly at inside-right, from 1929-31 and 1932-34. He played for Burnley in 1931-32 and was again at Turf Moor in 1934-35. He then ended his soccer career to concentrate on cricket.

Alderman made his debut for Derbyshire in August 1928 against Leicestershire at Derby, making 26 in his only innings that year. The following year produced an extended trial: 276 runs, average 25.09 in 13 matches and his first half-century, 53 not out at Dover when he shared a 103-run partnership for the ninth wicket with Elliott. Seventeen games in 1930 resulted in 386 runs, average 18.38 and he found difficulty in establishing himself. Figures do not tell the whole story. In May 1930 Derbyshire dismissed Sussex for 121 at Derby. Then Derbyshire made heavy weather of it against Maurice Tate and Albert Wensley, despite 60 from Worthington. Alderman spent three hours making 52, helping his side to a lead of 70, enough, in fact, to secure victory by an innings. Dour he might have been but he could be a thorough nuisance to the opposition.

The Perfect Foil

That summer found Smith realising his potential and it was Alderman's turn in 1931. The third match of the season was at The Oval, when he went in at the fall of Derbyshire's first wicket after Surrey had been dismissed for 184. Alderman made 113 not out in a total of 307 and he was again undefeated with 50 in a fairly meaningless second innings. Now a regular, his aggregate was 965 (29.24) and although there was a dismal 1932 he became a valued member of the team, scoring more than a thousand runs in every season from 1934-39. He began to cement a position as an opener, sometimes with Storer but by the mid-1930s regularly with Smith, and the pair shared eleven century opening partnerships, which established a county record (since equalled by Lee and Hamer and surpassed by Barnett and Bowler).

Alderman was also an outstanding fieldsman, especially in the deep. He earned fame for a spectacular one-handed catch at The Oval, when Tom Barling, batting at the pavilion end, swept Bill Copson high to fine leg in 1936. Barling had just sent up the hundred by hooking Copson round to leg for four. In the same over he repeated the stroke. As Alderman sprinted 30 yards around the boundary the ball appeared to swerve in the air and instead of going to the fieldsman's left it passed over his right. Alderman jumped and seemed to make a round-about face movement in the air, thrusting his right hand over the boundary line and grabbing the ball back within the field of play. The boundary was marked not by a white line but by planks set up edgeways. Two years later there was another remarkable one-handed catch, high above his head when running at full tilt to dismiss George Heane in front of the pavilion at Trent Bridge.

In *To the Wicket*, Dudley Carew wrote: "Smith and Alderman respectively represented a dashing adventurousness and a sober orthodoxy. Smith was left-handed, with something of Woolley's willowy tallness and a trace, too, of his ease of stroke. He was that rare type of No 1 batsman – (Charlie) Barnett and Bowley were others – who can set a game alight in the first over, and he had the left-hander's natural shot through the covers to perfection. He would get himself out, or just get out, unexpectedly, and a lack of consistency could, perhaps, be laid to his charge, but when he got going there were fewer batsmen in the country more exhilarating.

"Alderman, fair and stolid, was his antithesis. He had an unlimited supply of patience and was proof against temptation. He had the strength to hit, and occasionally he would wallop the ball uncommonly hard just to show, as it were, that he could do it, but normally his game traced its lineage to Scotton and was dedicated. In the outfield he was a different man. At the wicket he gave an impression of ponderousness, but in the field he was wonderfully fast and light on his feet."

Alderman also kept wicket in 13 games in 1937, 1939 and 1947, holding 16 catches and his career total of 202 catches in 318 matches for the county indicates his value as a deep fieldsman.

Chapter 9
The Runmaker

IN one match, at least, Stan Worthington was compared not unfavourably with Wally Hammond, England's greatest batsman of the 1930s. Worthington, of course, was no Hammond but he became Derbyshire's equivalent, enjoying his most memorable season, batting mainly at No 3 during the Championship year.

Thomas Stanley Worthington, was born at Bolsover, a mining community also famed for its 17th century castle, in the north-east of the county, on August 21 1905. He showed considerable promise as a fast right-arm bowler at Netherthorpe Grammar School, where he performed a couple of hat-tricks. After leaving school he became an apprentice electrician at Bolsover Colliery and soon worked his way into the pit team's first XI which played in the Bassetlaw League. Here he was noticed by Fred Tate and he went to Derby for a trial in 1923. Burly and powerfully built, Stan Worthington was destined to become one of the great names of Derbyshire cricket. He was, in his early days, principally a medium-fast bowler who was able to move the ball in, with an ability to keep going for long spells on the hottest of days, producing the occasional ball which would beat the best batsmen.

He joined the staff in 1924 and made his debut in August at Trent Bridge, when he bowled George Gunn for 23 and also dismissed Willis Walker and Ben Flint in taking three for 66 in the first innings. After three matches in 1925 Worthington became a regular in 1926, with 56 wickets and 656 runs. He started the season 10th in the batting order but improved to such a degree that he was promoted to seventh. He ended the summer with a fine performance in the match against Kent at Derby, which started on his 21st birthday. Worthington took five for 74, including the wickets of Hardinge, Woolley and Seymour, and made 84. Earlier he scored 60 at Bramall Lane when Yorkshire were made to follow on.

In the late 1920s he was establishing a reputation as a fast-medium bowler, often taking the new ball in the post-Bestwick years, and a hard-hitting lower order batsman. He got through a prodigious amount of work, although he never took one hundred wickets during a season. It was not until 1935 that his bowling began to tail off. Worthington exceeded a thousand runs in 1928 and 1929 and from 1932, under Richardson's influence, his batting gradually superseded his bowling.

The selectors regarded him as a bowling all-rounder when he was chosen for The Rest against England at Lord's in the 1928 Test trial. Two years later he made 29 in The Rest's total of 138 against an England attack comprising Larwood, Tate, Geary,

Robins and Woolley. Worthington also made two appearances for the Players against the Gentlemen, both of them at Folkestone. In 1928, going in eighth, he top scored with 77, surpassing this with 129 (a six and 20 fours) in 1932, but he never appeared in the prestigious Lord's fixture.

Greater glory awaited Worthington. He was in the 1929-30 MCC team to Ceylon, Australia and New Zealand, captained by Harold Gilligan. The tour began with five games in Australia, where the 24-year-old Worthington did well with 66 against Queensland at Brisbane. In the New South Wales game at Sydney he bowled Bradman, although The Don had made 157 by this time. In 13 first-class games he made 370 runs (24.66), with 125 against Auckland as his best performance, and took 30 wickets at 26.86. Worthington appeared in four matches against New Zealand which came to be regarded as Tests, although his record was modest – 0, 32 and 0 and seven wickets at 26.57.

He also proved popular. There is a record of the tour, *The Book of the Two Maurices* by MJ Turnbull and MJC Allom, Cambridge Blues and amateurs. Of Worthington, they said that he was 'just his name'. "When one sees him bowling and fielding tirelessly one thinks of 'On, Stanley, on!' And for the rest, as stockily built as is a Worthington bottle, well poised on his feet, he is just like a glass of English ale, the steadiest friend in the world, a cure for ailments, a consolation in failure, someone to rejoice with in success. Worthington is a generous beer: one that is out to give all that it has got; always there at your elbow, never frothing about and pushing itself forward like champagne. Stan we hardly knew on the boat, but now we recognise him as a good man on the piano and by no means a bad mimic."

Playing alongside cricketers such as Duleepsinhji and Woolley caused Worthington to think deeply about the game and he began to pay more attention to stroke play than in the past. It was to be a lengthy process but the seeds of his development from an all-rounder into a batsman of Test quality were sown on that tour and nurtured by Sam Cadman.

It took several years to make the transition but by 1936 he had become a specialist batsman and was in the form of his life. When an injured Maurice Leyland withdrew from the England team for the second Test against India at Old Trafford, Worthington replaced him. He took one for 15 in India's total of 203 and then, joining Hammond, was on five at the close, when England's score was 173 for two, Hammond 118 not out. On Monday the pair took their third wicket partnership to 127. Hammond, 167, dominated the early batting but Worthington drove with power and decision. The runs came in 75 minutes and Worthington also shared a fifth wicket stand of 86 with Nottinghamshire's Joe Hardstaff. He had batted almost two-and-a-half hours when he was brilliantly caught by CK Nayudu off his brother CS, one-handed and high up at cover for 87.

He retained his place for the third and final Test at The Oval and it was in this match that Worthington made history for Derbyshire. Going in at 156 for three shortly after lunch on Saturday – the first day – he shared in a fourth wicket partnership of 266 with Hammond, who made 217. A crowd of 17,000 saw Worthington make 128, the first Derbyshire batsman to score a century in a Test match. He hit 19 fours, mainly in front of the wicket, and at times outscored Hammond, driving and pulling to good effect and square cutting perfectly. He had a bit of luck, edging through the slips on more than one occasion and he was missed at the wicket off Amar Singh when 104. It was a magnificent innings which ended when he played on having a go at Nissar that evening. His place on the boat for the 1936-37 tour of Australia now looked secure but he had his critics. He was acknowledged as a strong batsman with many strokes but it was felt his bat was not straight enough to satisfy the purists. His square cut was effective but there was an element of danger in the manner in which he dealt with some deliveries outside the off stump.

Nevertheless he was in the MCC party, led by GO Allen, which lost the series 3-2 in Australia after taking a two-match lead. Injuries and illness dogged the tour and the team never found a settled opening pair. Worthington made 89 against a Combined XI at Perth and was selected for the first Test at Brisbane, opening the innings with Charlie Barnett.

Neville Cardus described the start of the series: "The beginning was catastrophic; McCormick's first ball, which he bowled like a hurricane, pitched short, and rose high at Worthington's left shoulder. Worthington hooked impulsively, foozled his stroke, skied it, and Oldfield, after starting late, ran forward in a panic, and held the catch. Poor Worthington stood dazed a moment, then departed head down." Stumped for eight in the second innings, he was dropped for the second Test. But he was back for the third at Melbourne where England were caught on a gluepot. Australia declared at 200 for nine to send England in on a pitch from which the ball often reared up almost straight and at other times kept low. Worthington was caught at silly point from the third ball and it was small consolation to him that his side could manage only 76 for nine declared. He opened again with Barnett in quest of an unlikely 689 to win. His fielding had been top class during a Bradman-dominated Australian second innings and now he got his head down and battled, only to fall to a Ward leg spinner for 16.

There was a 50 at Launceston but he missed the fourth Test and did little in the games running up to the fifth Test at Melbourne. The problem relating to the opening pair was still unresolved – Fagg had to return home early with rheumatic fever – and Verity had gone in first with Barnett at Adelaide. So Worthington returned to the team for the final game, with the Ashes at stake. Australia made 604 and England began their task at 12.30 on the third day.

After Barnett was out, Worthington and Hardstaff added 63 with steady but positive batting. Soon after lunch Worthington, 44, hooked Fleetwood-Smith, a fine shot, but caught his heel against the wicket and knocked a bail off before completing his stroke. Later Cardus wrote of a conversation with Bradman. It turned to Worthington's wretched luck in the series and his dismissal at Melbourne when he seemed on course for a century. "Yes", said Bradman. "He was playing well, and it was a shame." Then, after a pause – "Still, you know, a batsman shouldn't tread on his wicket." He made only six when England followed on, caught by Bradman off a skier at mid-wicket and his Test career fizzled out, the future in the hands of young batsmen such as Hutton, Edrich, Compton, Gimblett and Washbrook. In three Tests against Australia, Worthington scored only 74 runs in six innings; on the tour, which included New Zealand, 571, average 23.79. His bowling was expensive and of little consequence.

There was a final flurry. To mark its 150th anniversary, MCC arranged two matches at Lord's in May 1937, North against South and MCC Australian XI against the Rest of England. Worthington did not play in the first but opened the MCC innings with Barnett in the second. He batted throughout a total of 376, making 156 not out in five-and-a-quarter hours. Aggregates of 1734 (41.28) in 1936 and 1774 (41.25) in 1937 placed him close to the front rank but the days at top level were over. He toured India with Lord Tennyson's 1937-38 team but averaged only 33, although he played some attractive innings. When Tennyson became fatigued after making a hundred against Sind at Karachi, Worthington took over the captaincy before he was struck above the left eye while fielding at short leg. He was also involved in a practical joke which was played on His Lordship. In his biography of Tennyson, *Regency Buck*, Alan Edwards says the team saw relatively little of the skipper, who was frequently entertained by Indian princes and high-ranking representatives of the Crown. In Bombay, where he lodged with the governor, Lord Brabourne, after whom the new stadium was named, the players asked their captain to join them in a drink. "He celebrated with his usual uninhibited enthusiasm and then fell asleep. Gover, Wellard and Worthington loaded him into the Governor's barge and asked the captain to take him on a tour of the vast Bombay harbour. He woke up at four o'clock, feeling the early morning chill. The trio expected to receive a reprimand but the Governor, with a distinct twinkle in his eye, instead complimented them on their efforts." The players thoroughly enjoyed the tour and Worthington finished in style, driving and pulling his way to 68 in the fifth unofficial Test at Bombay.

So there was to be no prolonged Test career for Stan Worthington – just nine matches which produced 321 runs, average 29.18 and eight wickets at 39.50. He was somewhat unfortunate in being tried too high in the order in Australia, forced by circumstances to open when he was better suited to numbers four or five.

But there are many county cricketers who would settle for nine Tests and a century to boot.

Chapter 10
The All-rounder

IN a side of only average batting ability the value of a player who could achieve the double of a thousand runs and a hundred wickets in a season speaks for itself. Leslie Townsend performed the feat on three occasions and he remained an all-rounder of high quality in the Championship year.

Leslie Fletcher Townsend was born at Long Eaton on June 8 1903, where his father was in the lace trade, the town's major industry. His mother was a member of the Fletcher family which founded a successful lace business in the Midlands. His father was a good batsman in club cricket with Long Eaton and Leslie played his first senior match when he was nine and the town team found themselves a man short. Living only seven miles from Trent Bridge, Townsend saw much of his early cricket on this ground and his first serious forays into the game were with Lenton United during the war years. His medium-paced off breaks impressed in a match for Derby Road Wesleyans against Long Eaton Conservatives in 1919 and Billy Locker, a former Derbyshire player, recommended him to the county. He was invited to attend the county nets in May 1920 for a week's trial. "The first man I met was Sam Cadman, but I couldn't tell half he said in his Glossop accent. He took me up to the office in the old pavilion for my first meeting with Mr Taylor."

The first bowler he faced was Bill Bestwick's son, Bob. Townsend recalled that he was a much better bowler than his record showed. "The trouble was his father, who would not leave him alone." Townsend never forgot his first meeting with Bill Bestwick. "What a frightening spectacle. I was always scared of him, but not of his bowling. In fact I thought he was a nice, friendly one for a fast bowler. He never bounced them around your ears, but make no mistake, he was a fine bowler, but he did bowl a nice lot of half volleys."

The club engaged Townsend for two months in 1920 and gave him a place on the staff in 1921. He justified this with an unbeaten hundred for the 2nd XI at Edgbaston. There was sound advice from Cadman and Bestwick and Morton taught him how to spin the ball. In 1922 he made his first-class debut at Northampton. A right-hand batsman, Townsend was often to lose his wicket through impatience in his early days but he became a reliable player with plenty of powerful strokes, his off-driving being particularly good. He developed a nice, easy action to deliver his off breaks and he was a good fieldsman.

After a few appearances in 1923 he broke through in 1924 with 556

Championship runs, average 15.88, and 26 wickets at 27.8. He was awarded his county cap shortly before his 21st birthday after a good, all-round performance against Worcestershire at Derby. Townsend was to number dismissals of George Gunn, Jack Hobbs, Walter Hammond, Bill Ponsford and Don Bradman among the outstanding memories of his career but his maiden hundred, against Kent at Ilkeston in 1930, was a long time coming. Long Eaton's captain WA Wallis was determined to be there and present Townsend with a new bat. Will Taylor was asked to let him know when Townsend approached three figures but there were to be several fruitless journeys before the target was achieved. Townsend was also a fine billiards player and excelled at ice skating.

He was chosen for the North against the South in the 1927 Test trial at Bramall Lane and was in the Players' teams at Lord's in 1929 and 1933 and in the Scarborough match in 1934. A double in 1928 was followed by another in 1932 (1,373 runs and 113 wickets for the county – the first man to perform the feat solely in Derbyshire matches) and a remarkable performance in 1933. In that season Townsend made 2268 runs, average 44.47, with six centuries and took 100 wickets at 18.71. His county aggregate of 1966 established a new club record.

In 1929, when he was 26, the England selectors felt he was worth a closer look. MCC organised two tours in which Tests were played that winter, to New Zealand and the West Indies. Neither side was fully representative. Townsend was in the party for the West Indies, led by Freddie Calthorpe, the captain of Warwickshire. He played in one Test, the third at Georgetown, making 3 and 21 and taking two for 48 and two for 25. In eight first-class matches he scored 278 runs, average 25.27, his best innings being 97 against Barbados at Bridgetown, when he shared a seventh wicket partnership of 323 with Patsy Hendren, who made 211 not out. Townsend's bowling proved expensive, ten wickets at 40.60 each. But he learned a great deal from Wilfred Rhodes, Hendren and George Gunn, registering astonishment at Gunn's ability to deal with high pace delivered by bowlers half his age.

Off spin, whether medium paced or slow, was held in low regard when teams were chosen for overseas tours in those days and there was no place for Townsend in the bodyline series, although he came close to selection for the first Test against the West Indies at Lord's in 1933 when he was in superb all-round form. He was named as twelfth man and certainly the local newspapers felt he was unfortunate not to gain a place in the team ahead of Maurice Turnbull. He went on the MCC tour of India and Ceylon in 1933-34, captained by Jardine, and did well with 566 runs, 31.44, and heading the bowling averages with 43 wickets at 14.13. He played in all three Tests, averaging 18 but taking only two wickets in 43 overs for 132, although he bowled well to a leg-side field. Townsend suffered from food problems on this tour and he was also struck a painful blow when Mahommad Nissar bowled something approaching bodyline at Calcutta.

Harry Elliott also toured, getting into the party when Ames withdrew. He kept wicket in two Tests, catching six and stumping three and making 37 not out in the first at Bombay. In this match two spectators ran on to the playing area when Amarnath completed his century, intending to garland the batsman. Nayudu, his partner, had just completed a run and he set off down the pitch to hurry them off. The ball was still in play and when it was returned to Elliott he swept off the bails as an acknowledgement of good fielding. Elliott then realised Nayudu was out of his crease but Jardine, acting out of sportsmanship, instructed him not to appeal. It gives a rounder portrait of a Jardine so often vilified for the bodyline tactics.

Later Townsend expressed his regret about going to India, although he got on well enough with Jardine. "It injured my health, it upset my cricket. It was the food, and the accommodation at times, and I got very, very tired. I wasn't well for quite a few years, not up to the war," he told Nigel Smith (*Wisden Cricket Monthly* July 1992).

So in four Test matches against the West Indies and India, Leslie Townsend can be said to have failed, only 97 runs (16.16) and six wickets at 34. His dedication and general demeanour was noted at Lord's, however, and his reputation as a lifelong teetotaller and non-smoker did him no harm. When the New Zealand cricket authorities wrote to MCC asking for them to suggest a reliable player to coach and help develop their cricket, Lord Hawke recommended Townsend. He spent two winters in Auckland and would have gone for a third but Derbyshire felt he was suffering from a surfeit of the game and, concerned about his health, asked him not to go again in 1936-37.

Townsend might not have made the grade at the highest level but he was a tower of strength in the county game. His predecessors as all-rounders, Sam Cadman and Arthur Morton, spent most of their careers trying to retrieve lost causes. As time passed, Townsend became a match-winner in good sides.

"Les was a fine player," said Charlie Elliott. "He often played simply as a batsman because there was a bit of everything in our attack. What you have to remember is that we played on uncovered wickets and, if it had rained, we turned to Les for off spin. He might not have bowled for a week or longer but he dropped straight into the right line and length. Once he had opened up their batting order, he could go through the rest because the new man would have no peace to play himself in. He was very highly rated as a player and a man."

Townsend also shed interesting light on travel in the 1920s and 1930s. A rail journey from his home in Long Eaton to Chesterfield, for example, meant a 9.30am train arriving at 11am, with a scramble to cross town and reach the ground in time. The 7.50pm return involved a connection at Ilkeston Junction and arrival in Long Eaton at 10.10pm. Not surprisingly he bought a Velocette Two Stroke motor-cycle in 1926 and a car four years later.

Chapter 11
The Middle Order

FOUR batsmen, then, each capable of making a thousand runs in 1936 but what of the middle order which followed Smith, Alderman, Worthington and Townsend? It was a question which confronted Richardson from time to time in those golden seasons because two players who would have solved the problem, an amateur Alan Skinner and Harry Storer, were available for only half a season.

Storer in 1935 had usually opened with Smith, Alderman dropping to number three, before his departure to Highfield Road and he tended to be regarded as an opener in his final season when Smith's loss of form was another factor. A full summer of Storer might have changed things but he was then 38, out of full time practice and past his best. It was difficult to envisage him at number five after so many seasons of going in first.

Skinner was another matter. He enjoyed a good deal of success from 1931-38 as a forcing right-hand bat, a fine stroke-player who cut both square and late although he watched the ball carefully. He could be the most attractive batsman in the side, happy to open or go in lower down. He was also a good fielder anywhere, although he usually stood in the slips. Skinner became a key member of the team, captaining the side on 28 occasions. Frank Peach recalled one idiosyncrasy. "He wore two caps, one for fielding and the other for batting, one being a Quidnunc and the other a Crusader cap." He tended to be available for the county only in July and August.

Alan Frank Skinner was born at Brighton on April 22 1913 but the family moved to Derbyshire just after the war when his father was appointed assistant clerk to the county council. Skinner was educated at The Leys School in Cambridge and was in the XI from 1928 to 1931, being captain in his last year. He opened Derbyshire 2nd's innings against Warwickshire 2nd at Edgbaston in 1931 and scored 117, making his first-class debut at Trent Bridge in August 1931 and playing in six matches in the following year. Skinner did well at Cambridge University, where he obtained degrees in law at Trinity, but an injury incurred while playing for Derbyshire at The Oval in June put him out of the reckoning for a Blue in 1934. On coming down from Cambridge he was articled to his father, now clerk to Derbyshire County Council.

There was also competition from two young professionals, Charlie Elliott and Elijah Carrington, for a middle order place.

Charles Standish Elliott was yet another product of the coalfields and the Bassetlaw League. He was born at Bolsover on April 24 1912, a nephew of Harry

Elliott, and raised in Scarcliffe. In many respects the Elliotts were more like brothers since they were brought up by the same relative. When Charlie left school at 14 he worked on the pit top at Glapwell Colliery before getting a better mining job at Bolsover. His early cricket was played at school and for Scarcliffe in the Portland League, a rung below the Derbyshire League. He earned a place in the Bolsover Colliery side which competed in the Bassetlaw League. He did well in 1929 here, making a league hundred and averaging more than 30 and Derbyshire invited him for a trial. Brought down by his uncle, the young Elliott had already spent time helping in the nets at the County Ground and he was one of 20 hopefuls who attended trials.

From these Derbyshire would hope to find half-a-dozen or so players who could turn out for the seconds and it was Elliott who impressed. He was offered a job on the groundstaff, found digs in the town and settled down to the life of a young professional cricketer. Soccer also called and he was taken by Harry Storer to Coventry. Elliott was a rugged defender at right-back between 1931-32 and 1947-48, serving six months as caretaker manager in 1954-55 and balancing his dual careers in the manner possible in that era.

Charlie Elliott made his county debut against Warwickshire at Derby in 1932. It was an unspectacular first summer but although he averaged only 13 in 19 first-class matches he gained richly in experience, trying to fill a gap left by Storer, who made only nine appearances. In truth, Elliott's performances during the 1930s were modest; infrequent for the next three seasons, not on the staff in 1935 but back in 1936. His appearances increased to double figures in 1936 and 1937 but four half-centuries in 62 games scarcely set the world on fire. Nevertheless he was capped after the match against India in 1936 before falling victim to financial cutbacks a year later. "In those days, when you got your cap, you automatically went on to a fee of £4 per week all year round, plus so much per match when you played. Well, the powers-that-be – and it was WT Taylor then – said, 'We think that as you're playing football as well, you can forego the £4 a week in the football season.' So I said, 'Well, in that case, that's it,' and I stopped playing for Derbyshire." The club released Elliott after the 1937 season and he became professional with Stourbridge. His best years as a solid opening batsman and superb, close-to-the-wicket fieldsman, were to occur after the 1939-45 war.

Elijah Carrington made his debut as a 20-year-old right-hand batsman against Hampshire at Portsmouth in June 1934. There was a vacancy in the middle order left by Garnet Lee's retirement and the injury to Skinner, and Carrington took advantage. He averaged 20 in eleven matches in 1934, with 80 against Worcestershire at Queen's Park as his highest score.

Again, this is a story of a man who had to contend with the most basic of upbringings before graduating from the pits into county cricket. Carrington was born at Blackwell on March 25 1914, and worked there as a miner. He played for the Blackwell Colliery team on the ground where John Chapman and Arnold Warren shared a world record partnership of 283 for the ninth wicket against Warwickshire in 1910, later appearing in the Bassetlaw League with Glapwell Colliery and Teversal Welfare. Carrington, also a good local footballer, was an attractive, attacking batsman, although he never quite made the grade with Derbyshire: 50 first-class matches from 1934-37, average 20.13.

His widow, Alice, said he enjoyed his career and was "good friends with all of the Derbyshire team." They met when she was in service at Blackwell and their early married life took them to Ayr and Bath, where Carrington was professional after his days with the county ended. He returned to the mines and eventually bought property which included a fish and chip business in Hilcote, a village only a short distance from Blackwell. Former colleagues such as Cliff Gladwin, would call from time to time. The shop closed when the couple grew too old to run it but their home remained on the premises, a framed picture of the Derbyshire side sharing pride of place with family photographs. Disappointment at Carrington's failure to establish a first-class career of substance paled into insignificance when set against the tragic death of the eldest of his two sons, in the Norfolk Broads at the age of 26.

Now only hints of Hilcote's mining legacy remain: B Winning Colliery site given over to development, a new community centre planned to succeed the miners' welfare, the Co-op branch, opened in 1914, long gone but the building still used for retailing. Along with the Carringtons' fish and chip shop, The Hilcote Arms pub has closed but there are modern new houses and bungalows and a post office with friendly staff. At 88, Alice Carrington remained active and clear of mind, happy that somebody should wish to talk about her husband's cricket after so many years.

Another young player trying to establish a place in 1936 was Leslie Townsend's younger brother Arnold. The third of four cricketing brothers, Arnold Frederick Townsend was born at Long Eaton on March 29 1912. He showed promise as a youngster with both bat and ball and as a 17-year-old in 1929 he took all ten for 20 runs playing for Long Eaton Bible Class against Shardlow 2nd XI. Townsend made his debut against Leicestershire at Chesterfield in the final game of the 1934 season and this was followed by six matches in 1935 when he averaged 15.42, with a highest innings of 47.

His best seasons were to be a decade hence and middle order speculation as the 1936 season approached centred on Skinner and the promise of Carrington, with runs to be expected down the order from Richardson and Harry Elliott.

Chapter 12
The Brothers

DERBYSHIRE'S hopes of winning the Championship in 1936 suffered a grievous blow at the end of May when George Pope developed cartilage trouble which put him out for the rest of the season. This meant that in 24 of its 28 matches the team was below full strength.

Pope, who was developing into an all-rounder of great potential, had followed his brother Alf into the side and the pair had played a large part in Derbyshire's rise in 1935.

Alfred Vardy Pope was born in the coal mining village of Tibshelf, not far from Clay Cross, on August 15 1909. His father Fred, later at Edgbaston for many years, became groundsman at Chesterfield Cricket Club and in 1913 the family moved to the town. Alf started work as a coalminer at 14 but he left the industry after the General Strike of 1926.

He began his cricket career in the Derbyshire League when he was 15 and he grew into a 6ft 4ins powerfully built man with a varied repertoire of deliveries at a sharp right-arm fast-medium pace. Pope was also a good fieldsman and a hard-hitting late-order batsman and he soon graduated into the Bassetlaw League. Warsop Main won the Championship in 1928 under the stand-in captaincy of Pope's uncle Fred Vardy, another miner. Alf Pope's son Tony – whose local league career as a slow left-arm bowler also included 500 matches for the MCC and eight for 51 for the Friars against Repton Pilgrims in 2005 when he was aged 71 – said Vardy had the potential to play first-class cricket. "He was a slow left-arm bowler and my dad said he was good enough to be given a try in county cricket.

But he married young, had a family and could not afford it or spare the time. In those days there were only a few 2nd XI and club and ground games and it was sometimes a case of going straight from club cricket into the county side."

Warsop's success was something of a family celebration, the 19-year-old Pope topping the bowling averages and Vardy, the leading wicket-taker, finishing second. The colliery manager and official captain, Rex Ringham, used his influence to bring in talented youngsters such as Pope, Denis Smith and Jim Cresswell and they learned much from the likes of German Whysall, brother of the more famous WW (Dodge), who, although in the veteran stage, was still the leading batsman. Warsop fielded four present or future Test players on occasions in 1928, Dodge Whysall, Walter Keeton, Sam Staples and Smith. Pope remained one of the leading bowlers in the competition for the next four seasons but by then he was beginning to establish himself in county cricket.

He joined Derbyshire's groundstaff in 1928, performing the typical nursery youngster's duties of helping to tidy the ground, working on the square, putting out and collecting seats on match days and bowling to members in the nets. His cricket was the traditional mix of club and ground and the 2nd XI, with Saturday matches for Warsop Main. There was a year's contract which guaranteed pay for half the county matches, after which pay for the remainder of the season was only £4 groundstaff wages unless you made the first team. For a regular the pay was £8 for a home match, £10 for an away Wednesday fixture and £11 for an away weekend game. Professionals had to pay their own hotel bills, unless they stayed at the home of an opposing player. Travel was mainly by rail, although sometimes cars would be shared on the roads.

Alf Pope made his first-class debut against Middlesex at Burton-on-Trent in 1930 but his opportunities were restricted to a total of four matches during his first two seasons. These were to rise to 13 in 1932 and he became a regular in 1933, remaining so until the outbreak of the war. His stock balls were a late in-ducker and the leg-cutter and he was a good enough bowler to dismiss Herbert Sutcliffe on eight occasions and Walter Hammond on seven. Such ability earned him a taste of big cricket. In the North v South trial match of 1937 at Lord's, Alf Pope opened North's bowling with Bill Voce, dismissing Hammond, with his "in-ducker" and James Langridge for 59 in the first innings but meeting no success in the second. Nevertheless he had been in good company, with Hutton and Hammond making centuries and Farnes and Verity being the pick of the bowlers.

If Alf Pope became the epitome of a reliable county cricketer, his younger brother not only played in a Test but had the potential for a brilliant future at the highest level.

George Henry Pope was born at Tibshelf, on January 27 1911, sixteen months after Alf. As a youngster he showed promise as a footballer but his father advised against a soccer career and he escaped the mines when he was taken into the family business of sports ground contractors. He made a study of grasses and specialised in the production of bowling greens and cricket squares. George played for Chesterfield and in 1932 was professional with Kelburne at Paisley in Scotland, where he enjoyed an outstanding season. A fine, all-round sportsman, Pope considered taking up golf as a profession – he was assistant pro at Chesterfield – but chose cricket, following his brother to the County Ground. He made his debut against Worcestershire in 1933 at Queen's Park, Chesterfield, earning his cap in 1935, when he broke through as a key all-rounder.

Tall, at 6ft 3ins, an inch shorter than his brother, George, bald-headed and magnificently built, was a hard-hitting middle order batsman and a fine, close fieldsman. He could move the ball sharply at a fast-medium pace slightly below that of Alf. His bowling was in the finest of Derbyshire traditions, quick enough to be nasty, devastating on helpful pitches and begrudging of every run conceded off a mean length. He soon became one of the leading cricketers of his type in the country, although the war – he was 28 when it broke out – curtailed his career when he seemed on the threshold of the Test team.

His record is good enough: the double in 1938 and 1948, a tour of India with Lord Tennyson's side in 1937-38, a Test trial and selection for the England party at Trent Bridge in 1938, although he was not in the final eleven against Australia, the Players at Lord's in 1939, chosen for the aborted MCC tour to India in 1939-40, three Victory 'Tests' in 1945 and, at last, a full Test cap against South Africa at Lord's in 1947. He was also close to selection for the first Ashes Test of 1948 when he was called to Trent Bridge on the eve of the match but did not play. Career figures of 677 wickets at 19.92 and a batting average of 28 are testimony to Pope's ability, yet, as *Wisden* stated, he "somehow came to seem the embodiment of the county's professionals: hard, rough-hewn, under-appreciated."

The facts were that George Pope was one of most combative, aggressive and talented cricketers of his day. Michael Parkinson, who faced him on a grassy Bramall Lane pitch during Pope's awesome post-war league days with Sheffield United, described him as not so much playing cricket as conducting master classes. "The point about facing George Pope was that it was the ultimate examination for any young cricketer," he wrote in *The Daily Telegraph* in 1993. "He had a relaxed action and a high delivery and total command of line and length. He bowled outswing and inswing, snapped the ball back from outside off stump and had a lethal leg-cutter." Parkinson said Pope left the legacy of a generation of cricketers prepared to testify that he was the best bowler they faced. "He was a master of his craft and not many of us will go to our graves with that as our epitaph."

Pope was taught to bowl the leg-cutter at Cadman's behest by the great Sydney Barnes in return for a few nets at the County Ground when Barnes, still playing for Staffordshire, kept the Palm Court at Allestree. It took two years to perfect it. There is an interesting continuity here for it was at Derby in May 1903 that Barnes discovered his ability to bowl what Neville Cardus was to describe as the 'Barnes Ball'. This was the leg break, swinging into the batsman and then cutting away and rising at pace, which was to prove so devastating against Australia and South Africa a decade later. It was all too much for Derbyshire as Barnes returned a match analysis of 52-26-59-14, Lancashire winning in two days. Pope passed the knowledge down to Alec Bedser, who first bowled the leg-cutter in the second Test at Sydney in 1946 but also took a couple of years to master it. The leg-cutter, pitching leg stump and missing off, became the most lethal weapon in Bedser's armoury. Keith Miller, who played against Pope in the Victory Tests of 1945, was another beneficiary.

Opinions about Pope's potential as a Test match all-rounder were mixed in the 1930s. Dudley Carew described the brothers as "so much alike in their caps that it was almost impossible to tell them apart – George was rather the sparser of the two when it came to hair". They carried their physical resemblance into their style of play. "AV looked a shade the faster in his bowling, but that was the only difference between them, and as batsmen they knew how to mingle defence with the kind of shot that clears the ropes. Both gave the impression of being natural hitters who had schooled themselves into a sensible restraint without overdoing it. They were adaptable and could regulate their game by the state of the circumstances; they were, however, undoubtedly happiest when the earlier batsmen had made enough runs to release them of the responsibility of keeping their wickets up. They were county cricketers of the best type, and although Worthington went to Australia with GO Allen's team, it is no insult to him to write that he was essentially of their class."

County cricketers of the best type; an opinion echoed by Terence Prittie, who wrote two charming books of cricket recollections from the era before and just after the 1939-45 war, *Mainly Middlesex* and *Lancashire Hot-Pot*. "The Pope brothers, both fast-medium bowlers and hard-hitting batsmen, were county players pure and simple. But for the outbreak of war, the younger, GH would have toured India with an MCC side. I do not think this would have led him further. Though only 29 years old, I think he had gone as far as he was ever likely to go. This may be personal prejudice on my part, but I have always suspected fast bowlers with definitely clumsy actions."

Similar views from two writers who saw a lot of county cricket in the 1930s. But these are only opinions, admittedly based on sound judgement. So what do the facts tell us? The yardstick has to be George Pope's record at top level. His single Test match, against South Africa at Lord's in 1947, was unsuccessful. This was the summer of Edrich and Compton. They shared a third wicket partnership of 370 and Doug Wright's leg-spin accounted for ten Springbok batsmen in the match. Pope, going in at 541 for six, was reduced to eight not out before the declaration and took only one wicket, the No 11 Ian Smith, for 85 runs in the game. His bowling was steady, accurate and economic but no more. Too much should not be read into Pope's failure at Lord's. Alec Bedser fared even worse, conceding 96 runs without taking a wicket in the match. It must be remembered that Pope was now 36 years of age, still an all-round force in county cricket but past his best at the highest level. It was his first Championship season since 1939 – he had a league engagement with Colne in 1946 – and hindsight suggests there should be no surprise that he was found wanting at Lord's.

More pertinent are his pre-war performances. In 1937-38 Lord Tennyson's team which toured India played five unofficial Tests against a strong home side. The party which left Victoria Station for the journey overland to Marseilles and boarded the Viceroy of India to Bombay included Bill Edrich, Joe Hardstaff and Norman Yardley, who were to make their mark in Test cricket and James Langridge, Stan Worthington, Arthur Wellard, Jim Parks, Peter Smith and Alf Gover who failed to establish regular places. Pope also comes into this category but he was a key member of the party. While Tennyson's team was by no means the finished article it was a powerful unit and offered an opportunity for promising young cricketers. The fact that it won the 'Test' series 3-2 is testimony.

Pope had an outstanding tour. He scored 441 runs, average 24.50 and took 58 wickets at 15.93 each to head the bowling averages. He was the leading wicket-taker and took five in an innings six times. More to the point Pope achieved three of these five-fors in the four 'Tests' in which he appeared, at Calcutta, Madras and Bombay. His 20 wickets in these matches were taken at a cost of 16.15 each and among his victims were Merchant, Amarnath, Mushtaq Ali and Mankad, the leading Indian batsmen of the time. It gives the lie to any suggestions that he could bowl only in English conditions, such as a Queen's Park greentop.

This placed him on the threshold of the full England side and he did his chances no harm in the 1938 Test trial at Lord's. He hit an undefeated 47 and took the wickets of Wyatt and Compton for 57 runs in 27 overs for The Rest. "Pope used his height to advantage and was chosen among the thirteen players for the First Test," said *Wisden* but he was excluded from the starting eleven and did not appear in any other representative match that season. There was an interesting end-of-summer festival match when the Pope brothers opened the bowling for Sir Pelham Warner's XI against England Past and Present, Alf having a field day.

George Pope was not picked for the 1938-39 tour to South Africa or the 1939 series against West Indies. He was in the Players' team at Lord's and was chosen for the MCC party which was to tour India in 1939-40, under AJ Holmes. It was very much an England second team squad, probably not as strong as Tennyson's two years earlier. Three official Tests were scheduled and, given his performances with Tennyson, it seems likely that Pope would have played in all three. It is conceivable that he might have earned a regular place against South Africa in the planned visit to England in 1940.

Mere speculation but it disposes of the 'county cricketer only' label, as did his three Victory Tests against the Australians in 1945: 15 wickets at 21, with five for 58 at Bramall Lane. It was a pity he missed first-class cricket in 1946 for he might have appeared in the Tests against the Indians and toured Australia and New Zealand in 1946-47. He did not play for the county after 1948, finishing because of his wife's illness, and concentrated, instead, on a league career with Heywood and then Sheffield United. He made another visit to India with a Commonwealth team in 1949-50, where he played in an unofficial Test. So he was restricted to one Test, eight unofficial games, a Test trial and the Players in which he took 40 wickets at 21 but had little success with the bat. The evidence is clear. George Pope could more than hold his own in the best company. He can be regarded as above-average as a county all-rounder and would have been very much in contention for a place in the England team of the years lost to the war. Immediately afterwards he was bracketed with Keith Miller as the finest all-rounder in the world. An element of regret, then, for what might have been, succinctly put by Will Taylor: "George Pope was an all-rounder of abundant possibilities whose natural talent should have produced better results than it did."

In later years he became an umpire and an entertaining after-dinner speaker who was much in demand, sometimes with the theme: "It was more fun in my day. We'd have played for nothing." Gerald Mortimer, who shared one such evening with him as a fellow-speaker, recalled: "Among those who knew their Derbyshire history, there were a few wry smiles. George Pope was the fiercest of competitors, in county and league cricket, and disputes with Derbyshire were not unknown. He was very much his own man."

A third Pope, Harold, joined Derbyshire's staff in 1938 and the three brothers played for the county against the West Indians a year later, the only time they all appeared together in first-class cricket. Harold, a leg-break bowler who began his career at Chesterfield, was to play in only ten games for Derbyshire with limited success. He never fully overcame the effects of a head injury received in a plane crash during the war, when he served as a navigator with the RAF. In 1946 the opportunity was there to become Tommy Mitchell's successor but Pope failed to measure up and this led to Bert Rhodes switching from medium-pace to leg breaks and googlies. Instead, Harold played league cricket and was secretary of the Bassetlaw League for almost 20 years, later becoming its president.

George and Alf Pope played their cricket hard, although Alf's was slightly less obviously combative. Perhaps one story sums up not only George's attitude to the game but the toughening of Derbyshire's approach. In the 1930s Yorkshire were the dominant team, captained by the autocratic Brian Sellers, a disciplinarian who did not mince his words. The cricket was stern but also good humoured. Pope told the story about batting against Hedley Verity with Sellers fielding close in at silly mid-on. The batsman decided to remove the threat and went down the pitch to Verity, hammering the ball through midwicket and just missing Sellers. The Yorkshire captain became angry and said accusingly: "I think you deliberately tried to hit me then." Pope replied: "Just stay where you are Mr Sellers and you'll be in no doubt about the next one."

He had not finished with Sellers. In 1948 Yorkshire were dismissed for 44 on a Saturday morning at Chesterfield. Sellers was top scorer with eight and Pope returned figures of 14.1-9-12-6. He made 73 in Derbyshire's 277 and had taken two wickets as Yorkshire ended the first day – watched by 14,000 people – on 15 for three. Nothing could be done because of rain on Monday and there was an impasse on the time play could begin on the short, final day. This was due to finish at 4pm, extra time having been allocated to the first two days to allow Derbyshire time to make the journey to Worthing for their next match. Sellers, wily as ever, managed to get the start delayed to 2.15pm and Yorkshire, 37 for six, escaped with a draw. Pope's match analysis was 31-20-25-10.

Performances such as this indicate Pope's ability as a match-winning all-rounder at county level. Whether his destructive powers could have bridged the gap to the Test arena remain a subject for fascinating speculation. Pope never had a doubt.

David Harvey, a member of the Association of Cricket Statisticians and Historians, recalled sitting next to him at a cricket dinner. "He spent the entire evening explaining why he should have played more than once for England," he said.

Chapter 13
The Magician

COAL miners were a hard-headed lot who, despite the attractions, did not always snatch at the first opportunity to play county cricket. The rewards had to justify it.

Consequently, when Guy Jackson took a county side to meet Creswell Colliery during the 1926 strike, he found a young leg spin bowler driving a hard bargain when offered a place on the groundstaff. Jackson had been impressed by Tommy Mitchell's ability to turn the ball and invited him to the County Ground. Mitchell refused the initial offer of £3 a week, arguing that he could earn more as a miner. He accepted when it was raised to £4. The extra pound ranks as one of the best investments ever made by the county.

Thomas Bignall Mitchell was born near Chesterfield, at Creswell – a village developed in the 1890s by the sinking of its colliery – on September 4 1902 and like most of his peers went down the pit. As a boy he possessed a good singing voice and when he was nine he was selected by his school to perform a solo before King George V and Queen Mary at Welbeck Abbey. An audience of 11,000 heard Tommy sing 'Oh, for the Wings of a Dove' and his father wanted him to become a professional singer. But coalfield economics and a love of cricket – paradoxically, he once said if he had played for nothing he would still have enjoyed every minute of it – prevailed. Will Taylor said his discovery was unusual and intriguing. "With time on his hands during the General Strike of 1926, Mitchell, a miner, practised bowling near the pit-head of the Creswell Colliery at which he normally worked. An old cricketer who saw him turning the ball prodigiously from leg at once recommended him to the local cricket club. They invited Mitchell to play for them." There was also a story that he had been seen performing amazing feats of spin with billiard balls during the strike. Herbert Slater, brother of Archie (their mother was a Bestwick, aunt of Bill), witnessed this and encouraged him to play in an inter-departmental competition. His success here led to some matches with Creswell Colliery 2nd XI and then the colliery first team. Mitchell said later that he was bowling leg breaks long before the billiard ball incident.

Creswell Colliery were members of the Bassetlaw League and Mitchell was one of the long line of future county cricketers who played in the competition. He was a mercurial character, who wore spectacles and he became a highly skilful leg break bowler who later added the googly to his repertoire and also bowled some off spin. He was no batsman, although he sometimes hit out to good purpose, but he became a fine fieldsman in the covers and to his own bowling. His sorcery with the ball in an era of quality leg spin was paramount. One writer commented: "The ball had only to see those twinkling spectacles to start spinning madly on its own." Neville Cardus wrote: "Mitchell reduced first-class players to helpless mediocrity with a few snaps of his fingers."

Statistics tell part of the tale. More than a hundred wickets in ten consecutive seasons, 1929 to 1938, with 168 (and 171 in all first-class matches) in 1935 a club record, a season in which he took all ten in an innings against Leicestershire. A total of 328 first-class matches produced 1483 wickets at 20.59, ten in a match on 30 occasions and five in an innings on 118. At Chesterfield he dismissed Sutcliffe and Duleepsinhji each twice in a day.

His sense of humour made him a popular character in the dressing room and with the spectators but there could be blunt speaking amidst the jokes and this sometimes got him into trouble. His career with Derbyshire might never have started, for Sam Cadman caught him drinking in a pub. "Earlier I'd been told there was to be no pub crawling, but he knew I liked a pint," said Mitchell, who was reprieved with a warning. Rough edges needed smoothing and this occurred in club and ground and 2nd XI matches under Henry Ellison's captaincy and with Cadman casting a stern eye in his role as umpire. His marriage to Doris in 1927 – they were to have a son and a daughter – was a steadying influence and seven for 38 for the seconds in the 1928 Whitsun match at Edgbaston led to his first-class debut against Essex at Chesterfield in June. He took the wickets of Jack O'Connor and Jack Russell for 68 in the first innings but conceded 63 runs without success in the second. It was a high-scoring match which ended in a draw, notable for Worthington's maiden century, four sixes and 12 fours in 133, coming in at number eight. Mitchell appeared in 13 matches in 1928, capturing only 19 wickets at 44 but Cadman had seen something and the committee took heed. Guy Jackson also played his part, urging the committee to persevere, just as he had a few years earlier when there were doubts about Townsend.

The reward was 111 at 19 in 1929. The selectors took note of some fine early-season performances and he was chosen for The Rest, captained by Percy Fender, in the Test trial against England at Lord's in June. He was up against it – Hobbs, Sutcliffe, Hammond, Ernest Tyldesley and Leyland – but he dismissed Leyland and Sutcliffe at a cost of 115 in 33 overs although his ten overs were punished in the second innings. Mitchell was impressed with Fender, "because he would do anything to get wickets, and he encouraged the bowler to make the batsman play."

By 1931 Mitchell was numbered with Ian Peebles, Walter Robins and Freddie Brown among the young leg spinners who might cause Bradman problems. Peebles had got The Don out at Old Trafford in 1930 and the later bodyline tactics tend now to mask a school of contemporary thought that he was vulnerable to leg spin. Mitchell had troubled him at Chesterfield in May 1930 but it was Worthington who had him caught at the wicket by Elliott for 44. Tich Freeman was the daddy of all such bowlers in the Championship but he was in his mid-forties and had been costly in Australia. Peebles did well in South Africa in 1930-31 and, with Robins and Brown, played in the 1931 Tests against New Zealand. But Mitchell was never far away and the 1931 Gentlemen v Players match at Lord's was something of a leg spin fest, with Brown, Marriott, Robins and Mitchell impressing.

In 1932 there was only one Test against India, in which Brown and Robins appeared, so the selectors, Pelham Warner, Percy Perrin and Tommy Higson, gave themselves every opportunity to make their choices for the 1932-33 tour of Australia and New Zealand by arranging two Test trials, North v South at Old Trafford and England v The Rest at Cardiff. In addition, there was Gentlemen v Players. Mitchell was selected for both trials but Robins and Brown, leg spinning all-rounders, were selected for Douglas Jardine's tour party, with Verity providing the left-arm spin. Robins then withdrew for business reasons and Mitchell replaced him. Such was the irony for Derbyshire, a club with seam bowling traditions, providing a leg spin bowler for a series dominated by pace.

It was an honour, but there was also the matter of the travel, £400 and a post-tour bonus which turned out to be £75. In the mid-1930s a county cricketer received on average £300 per annum, while a coal face worker got £149. The lure remained obvious.

Mitchell suffered as the SS Orontes passed through the Bay of Biscay but a few days later he was spinning viciously off the timber deck as the nets went up during the passage across the Arabian Sea. He had the company of fellow-miners Larwood and Voce and was proving to be a popular life-and-soul-of-the-party. Team-mates hid his wallet and false teeth when he fell asleep, taking pity on him only after he had searched for them for several hours. Ever the joker, Mitchell was to get even with a local fisherman in Tasmania who was boasting about the fish he had caught by going down to the harbour and buying a load of fresh fish which he dumped on the man's Launceston doorstep. He enjoyed his cricket there, too, taking 11 for 144 against Tasmania.

In Australia, Mitchell appeared in eight first-class games, taking 25 wickets at 19.68, plus some purple patches in up-country games. He confronted Don Bradman in the return game against New South Wales at Sydney shortly after the third Test, dismissing him for one after bowling Jack Fingleton round his legs on the first day. RES Wyatt, Jardine's vice-captain, led MCC and in that innings Mitchell took three for 32. Years later, he recalled the incident, saying that he had seldom bowled the googly before that tour, concentrating on leg breaks and the occasional off spin. Like many of his kind he had two googlies, one he allowed the batsman to read, the other less obvious.

He was fascinating on the subject of The Don as I discovered when I contacted him specifically to ask him to speak about his experiences when bowling to Bradman. After a typical 'will there be a few bob in it for me?' he said that Bradman was unquestionably the outstanding batsman of the era. "I always felt, whether I was playing for Derbyshire or England, that he could murder my bowling and yet I was confident I could take his wicket. I bowled the googly in the nets to Herbert Sutcliffe and Walter Hammond before trying it out in the matches. When I bowled Bradman at Sydney it was the second ball I bowled to him and it was a googly which he failed to spot. He came forward to me and then back and tried to cut it and was bowled leg stump." Some reports describe the delivery as a top spinner. In the second innings Mitchell bowled only five overs and Bradman made 71 not out. But he had won £20 in a bet that he would take Bradman's wicket.

A fortnight later, with England leading 2-1, Mitchell was included in the team for the fourth Test at Brisbane, replacing Voce who had influenza. "Bradman used to play shots that no other batsman seemed able to play so that bowlers would have no idea how to bowl to him or what to bowl," Mitchell said. "He was a wonderful batsman but because he played so many shots you sometimes felt you had a chance of getting him out. Jardine brought me into the Test team to try and get Bradman out." He added that the batsmen he found most difficulty bowling to were Hammond and Patsy Hendren, particularly Hammond who made 2,158 runs, including six hundreds, against Derbyshire and averaged 63. Soon after the match against Queensland finished Jardine took Mitchell to the middle and had him practice bowling on the worn pitch. In the first innings he bowled the Australian captain Bill Woodfull, who was beaten coming down the pitch, commentator Alan Fairfax saying: "Mitchell has bowled Woodfull, the unbowlable." He took two for 49 in 16 overs and in the second innings had Woodfull caught by Hammond, taking one for eleven in five overs.

Mitchell had a high opinion of Jardine. He told Guy Williams (*Wisden Cricket Monthly* July 1986): "I was at fine-leg at Brisbane, having some fun with some spectators, and they sent me down a bottle of Burton beer. Jardine, fielding at short-leg to Larwood, was watching all this through his legs. When I went to mid-off next over Jardine said: 'You are getting too familiar with those buggers. You're stopping here.' He was a ruthless captain but we were behind him to a man. Before one Test, he considered dropping himself because his average wasn't good enough. But he was outvoted by the selection committee. He was so thorough: when I was twelfth man, he'd say 'Take a few autograph books into the Australian dressing room and see what they're talking about.'"

Mitchell also caught Bradman in the second innings for 24 off Larwood. He had wandered a few yards from his original position at cover when Bradman clipped the ball straight to him. There were only two fielders on the off-side, Wyatt at third man and Mitchell at cover. Bradman was cutting Larwood past point and Mitchell had moved squarer to cut off the stroke. "Well caught, Tommy," said Jardine, "but I'll move you when necessary." England won the match and took the series 4-1. Mitchell went on to New Zealand, playing in the second Test at Auckland, taking one for 49. In this match Hammond made the then-record Test score of 336 not out, having borrowed Mitchell's brand new Gunn & Moore bat.

Mitchell did not play in the Tests against the West Indies in 1933 or tour India with Jardine, who had been impressed with his bowling and fielding in Australia, in 1933-34. He was dropped for two county matches in 1933 after swearing at one of Derbyshire's amateurs Tommy Higson, the son of the Test selector, who was slow to move to where Mitchell wanted him in the field. "The game was at Leyton and an Essex committeeman heard the swearing and reported me to Derbyshire. I refused to apologise and was then dropped," he told Guy Williams.

William Richardson, son of Derbyshire's captain Arthur, said his father sometimes found Mitchell a problem. "Father was a disciplinarian and wouldn't stand any nonsense from anybody but he had to give Tommy some rope because he was a match winner."

Honours were even when Mitchell took on Will Taylor, a story related to Alan Hill (*The Cricketer,* September 1992). The secretary's customary greeting to the professionals was 'Good morning troops'. One day Tommy responded: "If it wasn't for us bloody troops, you wouldn't have a job." Next morning Taylor amended his greeting: "Good morning, troops – and Mr Mitchell." On another occasion, at Taunton, Mitchell was at third man when he borrowed a telescope from a young boy and entertained the crowd by holding it to his eye. Derbyshire's skipper, Robin Buckston, an old Etonian, was not amused and told Mitchell he would send him home if he did not behave. Tommy replied: "You'll be a good player short, Mr Buckston."

It was impossible to keep him down for long and in 1934 he took wickets at Lord's for the Players and for England in the Test trial against The Rest, although his bowling was punished because of his inability to maintain a length. He was back in the England team for the Ashes series, having little success at Trent Bridge (the Australian leg spinners Clarrie Grimmett and Bill O'Reilly did), but he again caused Bradman a few problems at Chesterfield, only for Townsend to take his wicket, caught by Harry Elliott for 71. He was recalled for the fourth Test at Headingley but Bradman left nobody in any doubt about who was in charge here. He made 304, adding 388 for the fourth wicket with Ponsford. Mitchell conceded 117 runs in 23 overs without taking a wicket. He finished the series with one wicket at a cost of 225 runs yet things might have been different.

Of the first Test, Cardus wrote: "Mitchell's spin was beaten by the Trent Bridge wicket; he is dependent considerably on his spin; his bowling bites rather than cogitates or connives." And at Leeds: "Mitchell occasionally sent an excellent spinner, but frequently he omitted to hit the ground." Yet he might have had Bradman stumped in the fifties by Ames and he nearly bowled Ponsford when he was also in the fifties. Mitchell, himself, said he strained too hard at Test level. Herbert Sutcliffe, dismissed by Mitchell twice in a day at Chesterfield, said in 1934: "Mitchell is one of the finest bowlers in the country – let there be no mistake about that. If he could have struck the form he showed against Yorkshire, the Ashes might have remained in England."

He continued to speak his mind and the classic confrontation with the establishment came at Lord's when England met South Africa in 1935.

Pelham Warner said the choice of the England team involved the longest selection committee meeting of his experience, from eleven in the morning until seven in the evening. The point at issue was whether Robins or Mitchell should play. The selectors wanted an all-rounder, Robins. Bob Wyatt, the England captain, was emphatic in supporting Mitchell. The leather-jackets, the larvae of the daddy-long-legs, had been at the Lord's pitches and Wyatt, who had been impressed by his bowling in a county match at Edgbaston, felt Mitchell could win the match. "We pointed out that Mitchell, good bowler as he was, had been a complete failure against the Australians in the previous summer, and that in no sense could he be compared with Robins either as batsman or fielder. No argument, no comparison of previous performances, could convince him, and in the end, physically and mentally exhausted, we gave way," wrote Warner.

The outcome was disastrous. South Africa won by 157 runs, the first time they had won a Test in England, and Mitchell's three wickets in the match cost 164 runs; 20-3-71-1 and 33-5-93-2. In contrast the leg breaks and googlies of Xenophon Balaskas accounted for nine England wickets in the game at a personal cost of 103.

Warner added: "In his management of the bowling Wyatt leaned far too heavily on Mitchell and did not make enough use of Hammond in either innings. On the loose surface of the wicket more use of Hammond should have produced good results but Wyatt seemed obsessed with Mitchell. Wyatt, at silly point, stopped several hard hits, but his fielding there meant that Mitchell, a leg-break bowler, had a gap in his field, and this meant runs." But Wyatt told a different tale about the meeting of the selectors. He challenged the unanimity of the opposition to him and the length of the meeting. "I had particularly outspoken support from Perrin," he said. He believed that, with the match lost, Warner tried to lay the blame entirely on his captain by not accepting any corporate responsibility of selection.

Frustration had spilled over on the field. Mitchell said Wyatt wanted him to bowl at the leg stump from the pavilion end. "I refused," said Mitchell. "He was telling me how to bowl and I didn't like it. So I turned to him and said, 'You couldn't captain a box of bloody lead soldiers.'" Mitchell had just bowled Siedle, who tried to hook a googly and missed. One of the umpires, Tiger Smith, said Wyatt moved from gully to mid-on to coach Mitchell. "Tommy got so fed up with Wyatt telling him what to send down that he told him to go on himself – with a few colourful adjectives thrown in – and he was taken off." He never played for England again, although he was honest enough to acknowledge his form, eight wickets in five Tests at 62.25 each, had not been good enough. At Lord's he was somewhat unjustly maligned for, although there were too many four-balls, he bowled some good spells, in particular before lunch on the first day, suffered from a missed stumping, and twice dismissed Jack Siedle, also accounting for Jock Cameron, two of the Springboks' heaviest scorers.

Contemporary cricket writers sought explanations. Raymond Robertson-Glasgow described him as one of the great bowlers, "an artist of spin and deception, a master of flight and variety," but with a temperament that was torrid. "Yet mostly he argues with intangible enemies, with leg breaks that have spun just too much, catches that have defied instructions, puffs of wind that have interfered with his own private theories of ballistics. There is something of the Donald Duck about him. No cricketer so conveys to the spectators the perplexities and frustration of man at the mercy of malignant fate. He has much in common with that golfer who missed short puts because of the uproar of butterflies in the adjoining meadows. He is the comedian of tragedy." Robertson-Glasgow added that he took valuable wickets "but, most of all, he has taken pomposity and convention by their noses and tweaked them sharply."

Alan Gibson wrote that Mitchell may have tried too hard in Test cricket, particularly at Lord's, and did not do himself justice. Dudley Carew felt that only some particular private quirk, some personal humour, prevented him from achieving even greater fame than he did. He found Mitchell the greatest fun as a person. "There was no stock, routine up-and-down stuff when Mitchell was on, and, even when he was being hit, he somehow contrived to be at the centre of the picture rather than the disconsolate spectator of the batsmen's prowess."

Charlie Elliott put it in perspective. "Tommy was an easy-going sort of bloke who liked his pint, a game of snooker and a gamble. It was probably this that limited his success in Test cricket." Elliott added that he was a magnificent bowler who won match after match for Derbyshire. "He had tremendous strength in his forearms and was able to turn the ball prodigiously in all conditions." The sense of fun was not lost on opponents. Nottinghamshire's Frank Shipston told a story of Mitchell going out to face Larwood and Dodge Whysall saying: "You'll not be staying long, will you Tommy?"

Guy Willatt wrote: "Even in his latter years and a different age, he referred respectfully and affectionately to Mr Jackson and Mr Jardine (his county and England captains), describing them as 'real gentlemen' with no concessions to modern familiarities; but for those captains for whom he had no respect he, on his own admission, bowled but refused to spin the ball!" In short, amateur captains were respected by the professionals, providing they were fair to them.

Life, then, was usually fun for Tommy Mitchell. There is a splendid tale of an engagement with Blackpool after the 1933 county season. He enjoyed himself so much that an anxious Mrs Mitchell asked Derbyshire officials when the cricket was due to finish. She was told by Will Taylor "My dear, it finished some time ago". The other side of his character was an inconsistency that was sometimes reflected in his bowling. Jim Hutchinson said: "Tommy Mitchell was Guy Jackson's biggest headache. He was a wonderful bowler but so moody. Like Bill Bestwick, his biggest enemy was himself. He could be difficult to handle, very moody. You could never tell when he was going to sulk. He couldn't help it. He was born like that."

After 1935 there would be no more Test matches and no further appearances for the Players against the Gentlemen but he continued to take wickets in county cricket. England looked to others for leg spin in the remaining pre-war Tests but they fared little better than Mitchell.

Chapter 14
The Fast Bowler

NO county won the Championship between the wars without pace or, at least, a bowler on the sharp side of fast-medium. Middlesex had Durston, Yorkshire Waddington and then Bowes, Lancashire Macdonald and later Pollard and Nottinghamshire Larwood and Voce. At The Oval Fender was usually trying to make bricks without straw and Kent, for all Freeman's prodigious efforts, found the lack of pace a handicap after Wright (AC) had finished.

The absence of a fast bowler was a major concern for Richardson when he took over the captaincy of Derbyshire. It was something that would need to be addressed if the county was to progress much further. Since Bestwick had retired in 1925 the gap had never been satisfactorily filled and it remained the missing piece in the jigsaw. Wilfred Shardlow was tried but he dropped out after 1928 and the persevering Worthington was left to shoulder most of the burden.

The coalfields solved the problem. There had been colliers who had bowled fast for the county before; Mycroft from the ironstone mines, Bestwick, and Warren who was raised in a mining area. Alf Pope would develop, although not as the spearhead, and he was unproven in May 1932. But it was the emergence of Bill Copson which really gave rise to the legend 'Whistle down a pit in Derbyshire and up comes a fast bowler'.

William Henry Copson was born at Stonebroom on April 27 1908, although during his lifetime the year was given as 1909. It was a basic upbringing and he did not play formal cricket as a boy because the school he attended had no facilities for the game. Stonebroom developed as a mining village as a result of the sinking of Morton Colliery in 1865. The Stonebroom Blocks, five rows of houses in the lower part of the village, were built for the miners. There were no water toilets, such facilities consisting of a wooden form over an outdoor ash pit which was emptied weekly. Tin baths hung on nails outside the homes and water was heated by the fire. It seems staggering that families existed in such deprivation and yet a strong community spirit was forged which remained at the time the Blocks were demolished in the 1950s. The Clay Cross Company also established Stonebroom British School for the children of their employees at Morton Colliery. Boyhood cricket in such areas took place on the local recreation ground or waste land or in the ginnels between the houses. "You learned how to bowl straight in the ginnels because if you didn't the ball hit the walls on either side," said one ex-miner.

The family – it knew tragedy when one of Bill's brothers died in a fire – moved from Stonebroom to live in Morton. Inevitably Copson had found his way into the pit at the age of 14 and he was working underground at Morton Colliery at the time of the General Strike in 1926. Whiling away the days, he joined his colleagues in some games of cricket at the local recreation ground, one in which the miners played the police who were guarding the pit head machinery. Not far away, in Whitwell, the five-year-old Leslie Jackson watched with growing fascination the impromptu games which the men and boys staged during that long, hot summer.

It was in such games that the 18-year-old Copson discovered that he was a natural bowler by simply running up and delivering the ball as fast as he could. He found he could pitch it on a length and wreck the stumps. Initial mutterings from the batsmen about "beginner's luck" soon gave way to the realisation that here was someone special. Bill was given a place in the Morton Colliery second team for the rest of the season. A year later he was in the first team and after four years with Morton joined Clay Cross in the Derbyshire League. All ten Staveley wickets for five runs indicated that this was a bowler who was out of the ordinary. Later the Bassetlaw League connection was forged with Warsop.

Fred Marsh, the Morton secretary, recommended him to Derbyshire in 1931 after his performance against Staveley and there was support from the local vicar. Copson was 23 and had a reputation in the league. It was time for Cadman and Richardson, to take a proper look. They were impressed.

Copson was ginger-haired, slightly-built, but with long arms and strong shoulders toughened by his years in the mine. He took an easy, relatively short, run up to the wicket and hesitated briefly before releasing the ball. Right-arm fast, he was able to obtain a great deal of pace out of even the most lifeless of pitches and could swing the ball either way with a disconcerting break back. Alf Pope said that Copson generated deceptive pace and lift through having unusually long arms. There was one major problem. That magnificent potential was handicapped by illness and injury. Life was not easy and Copson's health was affected by this. There were few luxuries in the homes of miners, the men often out of work or on short time, their women striving to make ends meet and dreading the onset of childhood illnesses such as diphtheria, scarlet fever and whooping cough.

Dudley Carew wrote of Copson's debut: "He seemed a very frail, thin boy at the time, and his hair seemed redder than it appeared on further acquaintance. Even in those days he managed to come very quickly off the pitch, and he showed, for one so apparently lacking in stamina, a remarkable hostility. Personally I never liked Copson's action; there was a pause at the moment of delivery, and I sometimes wondered whether umpires ever allowed themselves a shade of doubt as to the absolute fairness of his delivery. Copson, personally, was a charmingly shy youth who survived his sudden ascent to fame and a world which at the first must have seemed strange to him with innate manners and good sense."

Action aside – and nobody else seems to have complained – another telling opinion was provided by Terence Prittie: "As a fast bowler Copson was on the fringe of representative cricket for several seasons. Possibly his physique alone stood between him and the highest honours. He was always good, always hostile, but he never had the dynamism of a Larwood, or of a Macdonald, even of a Farnes or Allen."

This sits comfortably with the opinions of contemporary spectators, many of whom were miners and as such could converse easily with Copson. A personal memory is of my father, who saw him many times and reflected: "Some people hoped he might be a successor to Harold Larwood and you could see why. But you could never imagine him bowling with the pace and stamina Larwood showed on his visits to Australia." It was an unfair comparison. Copson was a different animal, effective in short bursts. It was to Richardson's credit that he was quick to realise the fact.

One of the best assessments of the young Copson was related by the Derby cricket writer John Twells. "Sam Cadman, that great moulder and maker of bowlers, said to my father one day: "Look at that lad in the net. I've found a gorilla-armed 'un." Then morosely: "Trouble is, he's had more dinner times nor dinners." Arthur Richardson recalled: "I had a painful introduction to Bill when, after I had been injured, I went to the County Ground for a net. It soon became obvious that Bill was very quick but, as I pointed out rather testily to Sam Cadman, the coach, I had no wish to have another four bones broken."

Under the guidance of Cadman Copson made progress. He was outbowled by Alf Pope when Derbyshire 2nd came close to defeating their Warwickshire counterparts at Edgbaston in August 1931. Skinner made his 117 out of a total of 377and Warwickshire were dismissed for 145, the slow left-arm bowler Tommy Armstrong taking five for 26 and Pope four for 33. Copson failed to take a wicket, delivering 17 overs and conceding 37 runs. In the second innings the home side clung on for a draw, 220 for nine, Armstrong four for 65, Copson three for 37, his victims including Aubrey Hill and James Ord, future county stalwarts.

The 16-year-old Cyril Washbrook, who was brought up in Shropshire, made one and 41 for Warwickshire but was soon to move to his native Lancashire. Rain washed out play when the teams met again at Edgbaston on Whit Monday 1932. The pitch was badly affected and wickets tumbled on the Tuesday: Warwickshire 2nd 96, Pope four for 28, Copson four for 30, and 50 for six, Pope three for five, Copson one for eight; Derbyshire 2nd, captained by JDH Gilbert, 61. Although curtailed, it was a significant match in which Copson and Pope served notice of things to come.

In June, Derbyshire undertook a southern tour: Surrey at The Oval, Hampshire at Southampton and Kent at Tonbridge. Copson was included in the party.

On Wednesday June 8 1932, Bill Copson followed his captain Arthur Richardson, Tommy Higson, Harry Elliott and the rest of the team – Lee, Alderman, Smith, Townsend, Worthington, Charlie Elliott and Mitchell – to join the umpires Bill Reeves and Tiger Smith in the middle at The Oval. Surrey's openers were Jack Hobbs and Andy Sandham. Older heads among his colleagues advised Copson that anything remotely offline would be punished. Worthington bowled the opening over, from which Hobbs took four runs. Then it was Copson's turn – and his first ball in first-class cricket secured a wicket – Sandham, beautifully caught by Charlie Elliott at second slip. It was a remarkable beginning. Not only had Derbyshire separated one of the most redoubtable opening pairs in county cricket but their debutant fast bowler had made an immediate impression. Sandham, out without scoring, returned to the pavilion to warn his side that the ginger-haired b***** was a bit quick. And, with luck, Charlie Elliott might have caught Hobbs off Copson with only 14 scored.

Surrey soon repaired the damage. Hobbs and Tom Barling added 110 for the second wicket before Hobbs left for 67 and Barling (82) and Tom Shepherd carried the score to 195 for two wickets. The shock from Sandham's early loss had been absorbed and the foundations had been laid for a big score. Copson then returned to dismiss Jardine (lbw), Shepherd, bowled for 49, and Fender, also bowled, in quick succession, restoring Derbyshire's advantage. It did not last for long. Whitfield's unbeaten 47 helped Surrey to a total of 315, Copson finishing with four for 43 in 25 overs in which he maintained a good length at slightly above medium pace, according to *Wisden*.

Denis Smith made 52 but Derbyshire trailed by 147 on the first innings and fine batting by Jardine enabled him to declare and leave the visitors an unlikely 355 for victory. In Surrey's second attempt Copson took two wickets for 46. Although Richardson and Townsend batted soundly Surrey were comfortable winners, by 199 runs.

Copson bought his first pair of cricket boots for this match. His feet were pinched and blistered and his colleagues cut slices off the new boots to enable him to keep going. The boots finished in shreds.

At Southampton Derbyshire batted consistently to reach 318. Hampshire were dismissed for 234, Copson taking five for 45 in 27 overs, and after Smith completed a century, Richardson declared at lunch on the third day, setting Hampshire a target of 304 at 76 an hour. Phil Mead and John Arnold each scored hundreds and the home side got home with six wickets and 35 minutes to spare. Copson's solitary wicket cost him 54 runs from 13 overs.

Next it was Kent, with Frank Woolley, Les Ames and Bill Ashdown. Nought for 53, following on from the punishment his bowling suffered at Southampton, gave Copson plenty of food for thought. In Kent's second innings he came back with five for 40 in 24 overs. At this point he had taken 17 wickets at 16 apiece and Richardson awarded him his county cap after only three matches, not one of them in Derbyshire.

He ended his first season with 46 wickets at 27.58 from 18 matches, increasing his total to 90 in 1933 and 91 at 18.10 in 1934. A series of injuries limited his number of appearances to 18 in 1935, when he took 71 wickets at 16.53 and at the end of June, Derbyshire sent him to Skegness to regain his health. Two examinations by specialists in the summer and another in January 1936 disposed of fears that his health was seriously affected.

A fully fit Copson was crucial to Derbyshire. The 1936 Championship success was a team effort in every sense of the word but if individuals have to be singled out then Copson and Mitchell – so aptly described by AA Thomson as 'brimstone and treacle' – were indispensable. Had either of them been out for a long period then it is unlikely the title would have been won.

Chapter 15
The Slow Left-armer

DERBYSHIRE'S bowling attack in the mid-1930s was varied, balanced and aggressive: Copson, Alf and George Pope, Mitchell and Leslie Townsend forming a quintet which few counties have matched or surpassed in Championship history. A slow left-arm bowler of quality would have completed the set. It is difficult to imagine how he could have been accommodated – George Pope higher in the order at number five and Richardson at six, perhaps. However, for a time it appeared possible that Tommy Armstrong might establish a permanent place.

Until Mitchell came along there was little tradition for spin in the county. Fred Bracey produced some notable performances with his left-arm slows but his career was cut short by a 1914-18 war injury to the fingers of his bowling hand so Armstrong found few precedents. Thomas Riley 'Tosser' Armstrong had a curious career. He was born at Clay Cross on October 13 1909 and did well outside the first-class game, with Clay Cross, Ollerton in the Bassetlaw League – where he won the bowling prize in 1937 with 89 wickets – and Smethwick in the Birmingham and District League.

Armstrong worked as a clerk in the Clay Cross Colliery Company offices, later moving to Ollerton Colliery, and was on the county staff for a time. Despite some fine performances for the second team, he could only get into the side when somebody was injured, Mitchell was absent or conditions, such as the rain affected pitches at Buxton, simply demanded his inclusion on a horses for courses basis. His performances were usually respectable and in modern times he would, no doubt, have sought pastures new, although later he put his job first. He made his debut in 1929 against Worcestershire at Stourbridge, appearing twice in 1930 and in six matches in 1931. Early in the 1932 season it appeared that the 22-year-old Armstrong might be quite a discovery. He bowled well at Old Trafford and played his part in something rare in Derbyshire cricket – a match won by spin. This was the Whitsuntide fixture at Derby in which Charlie Elliott made his debut. It was a low scoring affair. Derbyshire made 108 but Mitchell (seven for 48) and Armstrong (three for 22) bowled Warwickshire out for 111. Fine batting by Lee, supported by Smith and Worthington, enabled Richardson to declare and set the visitors 212 for victory. They were helpless against Armstrong (five for 27), with Mitchell, Worthington and Townsend getting among the rest and Derbyshire got home by 123 runs. Seldom have Derbyshire possessed spin of this quality to exploit turning pitches.

In that season Armstrong took 18 wickets at 22 from ten matches. His best season proved to be 1933; 13 matches, 36 wickets at 26.83 with seven for 57 against Somerset at Frome and seven for 87 against Northamptonshire at Chesterfield. A breakthrough seemed close but after a relatively unsuccessful 1934 – 18 wickets at nearly 39 each from 12 matches – he was not retained. Although no longer on the staff, he appeared in half-a-dozen matches from 1935-39, dramatically so against Somerset in the crucial game at Wells in 1936. In 1937 he achieved the best figures of his career; seven for 36 against Gloucestershire at Buxton, and in 1946 headed the county's bowling averages with 28 at 17.60. During a 21-year span from 1929-50 Armstrong appeared in 58 matches for the county, taking 133 wickets at 24.35.

Roy Genders, who played a few games for Derbyshire in 1946, was a colleague at Smethwick. He described Armstrong as "that very excellent Derbyshire left-arm bowler who would no doubt have reached the England team if he had not thought more of his job than he did of cricket. But then he had to take a back seat in the Derbyshire side of the 1930s, a side which with Bill Copson, George and Alf Pope, Tommy Mitchell, Leslie Townsend, Stanley Worthington and later Clifford Gladwin was perhaps the strongest bowling side ever to play at one time for a county. Of his time in the Birmingham and District League, Genders added: "With his constructive criticism and quiet help whenever his opinion was invited, Tommy Armstrong proved himself an ideal clubman."

Armstrong had some good days at Buxton and it is revealing to note a couple of examples when Derbyshire decided it was worth weakening the batting to accommodate him in a five-man attack. He played against Worcestershire at Queen's Park in July 1933 in a team which read: Skinner (captain), Storer, Townsend, Smith, Worthington, George and Alf Pope, Elliott, Mitchell, Armstrong and Copson. This was George Pope's debut but he did not bowl. Six years later Armstrong was part of a similar attack except that Rhodes replaced Mitchell, with George Pope at number five.

Another slow bowler on the 1936 staff flickered even more briefly. Samuel Walter Hunt, who was born at Doe Lea, Chesterfield on January 9 1909, had played soccer for Lincoln City and Mansfield Town and was currently with Torquay United. A centre-forward who could also play as an inside-forward, Hunt was Mansfield's second highest scorer in 1934-35 with 15 goals. After leaving the Stags he scored eight goals in 28 appearances for Torquay in 1935-36. During the summer he moved to Rochdale. Hunt was a middle order right-hand batsman and right-arm leg-break bowler who remained on Derbyshire's staff for just one season.

More spin of sorts was provided towards the end of the season by an amateur, George Langdale, a 20-year-old student at Nottingham University. Langdale, who was born at Thornaby-on-Tees in Yorkshire on March 11 1916, played some local cricket with marked success as a left-hand batsman and right-arm off-break bowler.

Chapter 16
The Groundsmen

GENERATIONS of Derbyshire fast bowlers regarded Queen's Park as their killing ground as visiting batsmen suffered nightmares about facing Bill Copson, the Popes, Les Jackson, Cliff Gladwin, Harold Rhodes or Mike Hendrick on Chesterfield green tops.

The small playing area, situated in a public park in a lovely tree-lined setting and overlooked by the famed crooked spire of the parish church of St Mary's and All Saints, also earned itself a reputation as a fast scoring ground. Brown and Tunnicliffe began the Yorkshire innings with a partnership of 554 in 1898. Six years later Derbyshire defeated Essex by nine wickets after facing a first innings total of 597. The pitch was hard, the outfield like glass after a heatwave which lasted for several days. But Percy Perrin, who made an unbeaten 343 for Essex, recalled a Bestwick delivery early on the first day which pitched outside his off stump and passed behind him. Jim Hutchinson said it was a good wicket but there was usually something in it for the bowlers first thing.

Walter Goodyear tended the ground for Derbyshire's six matches at Chesterfield in the Championship year. "The Queen's Park pitch gained a reputation for being fast and bouncy after the war following work which was carried out on the square but in 1936 it was more even," he said.

Goodyear was born at Hasland, near Chesterfield in February 1917, the son of a railwayman, and joined the Queen's Park staff in March 1931, when he was 14, working first under Tinker Simpson and then Fred Pope, who eventually went to Birmingham. He was in charge of the ground from 1932-38. "We were never asked to carry out any special preparations to the pitches which would have suited Derbyshire's bowlers in those years," he said. "Mr Richardson was a gentleman who just let you get on with the preparation work in your own way. He always had the respect of the professionals and so did Guy Jackson, although they were both disciplinarians. I can remember Captain Jackson going into the pavilion with a walking stick. The professionals' white shirts were hanging in the dressing room and he lifted them up with his stick to inspect them, saying 'Are these the cleanest you can find?'

Hutchinson appreciated the beauty of Queen's Park. "Chesterfield was my favourite ground although I suppose Lord's ran it close. It was a lovely ground and I enjoyed playing in such a beautiful setting. The crowd was always good to me, even if I hadn't done very well." Some players might have thought he was in the minority as far as the spectators from the mining communities who poured into the ground when they had finished an early shift were concerned. Norman Yardley and Jim Kilburn, with first-hand knowledge from years of annual Yorkshire fixtures in the park, described them as: "a crowd with a reputation for unambiguous expression of opinion."

Arthur Richardson told a tale to illustrate this. It concerned a miner who had allegedly played against Larwood and Voce before their England heyday. Richardson asked him if they were fast. "Oh ar," replied the miner. "Bad wickets and bumpers?" Richardson said. "Oh ar. Up rahn yer chest and showders." Richardson then asked how the miner played such bowling. "Well, way just fronted 'em. Turned and chested 'em. W'arnt nowt much when yo' fronted 'em."

These tales fail to do justice to the vast store of knowledge inherent in the Queen's Park faithful, although they illustrate generations of spectators who did not suffer fools gladly and were sparing in their praise, even when it was one of their own from the nearby mining country. "When you got praise at Chesterfield you knew you had earned it," said Hutchinson.

He had good cause to remember the bleak panorama of the County Ground at Derby from his playing days. In the 1920s there was little hot water and inadequate covering for the square. The long-serving groundsman Albert Widdowson faced an uphill struggle due to lack of investment. He had been at Lower Broughton, Manchester before coming to Derby in September 1889. Later he said that when he first saw the state of the ground he nearly caught the next train back to Manchester. Derby County used part of it before moving to the Baseball Ground and an FA Cup final replay and an international match were played there. From 1878-1939, race meetings took place and Derby Racecourse was famed for its straight mile and a grandstand with a copper-domed viewing cupola and stables.

Widdowson had found the ground sadly neglected. He discovered a missing cricket net rotting beneath piles of cut grass and it took years to bring things up to standard. Steve Bloomer, the great Derby County and England player, made an apt comment. "We had no high falutin' gadgets but we did have plenty of fresh air and cold water."

The cricket ground was a bare and remote place, thoroughly miserable in cold and wet weather, although its open nature was pleasant on warm and sunny days. It changed little until major alterations were made in 1955. The old pavilion had charm, despite being on the small side, with a balcony and some six rows of seating either side of the central steps leading to the playing area.

The nets were behind the pavilion. Wickets were pitched from north to south (today they face east-west); with the bowling taking place from the Pavilion end (north) and the Nottingham Road end. A couple of stands close to the pavilion eventually offered a decent view from the third man area but the remaining accommodation consisted of wooden forms. The racecourse grandstand was too far away for any practical use as far as the cricket was concerned until the pitch was moved during the post-war changes.

Widdowson remained groundsman until he retired in September 1930, a span of 41 years. He was succeeded by Harry Williams, who was born at Pershore in Worcestershire and had been groundsman at Queen's Park. Williams remained at Derby until October 1935 when he moved to Old Trafford. His successor was Harry Fletcher, who had been groundsman to the Burton Gentlemen CC on The Meadows where Bass and Allsop also had grounds. Fletcher was in charge at the County Ground in the Championship year but he only had a short time at Derby for he became ill during the 1937 season and died in October at the age of 55. Alfred Pope looked after the ground until January 1938, when Walter Goodyear was appointed.

It was a busy life. The county side, the 2nd XI, the Friars, half-a-dozen Saturday club sides and in the winter Derbyshire Amateurs FC and Derby Hockey Club demanded his attention on the vast expanses of Nottingham Road. Then there was the players' kit to sort out and the dressing room to keep tidy, his wife helping him with the cleaning. A friendly and fair man and one of the game's true characters, Walter Goodyear became known as a craftsman and a 'players' groundsman.

He remained at Derby until he retired in February 1982, the 50-year span interrupted only by service with the Nottinghamshire and Derbyshire regiment, the Sherwood Foresters during the 1939-45 war. After his retirement, he continued to help out at Belper Meadows' and Quarndon's club grounds for many years afterwards. He holds a unique record. In 1936, the Championship year, he was at Chesterfield and in 1981 he prepared the County Ground pitches which were used in the quarter-final and semi-final of the NatWest Trophy, which Derbyshire won.

From 1925, Ilkeston's Rutland Recreation Ground replaced Derby and Chesterfield as the venue for Derbyshire's home match against their neighbours, Nottinghamshire. Close to the border, in the county's third-largest town, it was near to the main centres of interest. The Duke of Rutland presented the recreation area to the people of the town, offering it to the borough council to mark the visit of King George V and Queen Mary in 1914.

The local authority enlarged the ground and laid it out for county cricket. Situated in picturesque surroundings, it had a spacious pavilion and a terrace with 3,000 seats. The first match, against Nottinghamshire in July 1925, attracted around 7,000 people. From 1925-80 only Chesterfield (1937 and 1966) and Derby (1959, 1978 and 1979) staged the fixture other than Ilkeston. The last such game at Ilkeston was played in 1994 but despite sponsorship from Erewash Borough Council, Derbyshire lost money and the Rutland venue went the way of other outgrounds. It hosted 46 Nottinghamshire visits, with a few more 1939-45 wartime friendlies.

Burton-on-Trent Cricket Club's Town Ground in Staffordshire staged 13 fixtures from 1914-37. Derbyshire then switched to the Ind Coope (later Allied Breweries) venue for 38 games from 1938-80, with a couple of matches at Bass-Worthington in

1975-76. Another club ground, The Park at Buxton, suffered from above-average rainfall which often left damp or drying pitches. It is the only ground on which Championship cricket has been played at more than a thousand feet above sea level and one where snow ruled out play for the day on June 2 1975. Summer days brought charm, with the woods in full growth helping create a setting of beauty. The 1878 Australians played there and Derbyshire used it for 48 first-class matches, many of them against nearby Lancashire, from 1923-86.

In 1936 six matches were played at Chesterfield, five at Derby (including one against the tourists, India), two at Ilkeston and one each at Buxton and Burton-on-Trent.

Chapter 17
The Prodigal

NO doubt Bill Bestwick raised a glass in salutation to his old county in 1936. He was now a first-class umpire and under the laws of those days was not allowed to stand in Derbyshire matches. Instead, he spent the summer travelling up and down the country, from Trent Bridge and Edgbaston to a sequence around August Bank Holiday in which he stood at The Oval, Hove, Canterbury, Hastings and Lord's. South coast air and local ales added to the pleasure.

Bestwick was 61 and his playing days were far behind him but he had been a figure of some influence as far as the Championship-winning side was concerned. Although sciatica meant he made his last appearance for Derbyshire in 1925 his wickets were crucial to the future of the club in the early 1920s and he helped nuture young talent on the ground staff.

He was born at Heanor on February 24 1875, one of 14 children of a collier. At the age of eleven he was working at Coppice Colliery, close to his home. He developed into a man of magnificent physique, broad of shoulder, big of heart and with great strength, possessing immense stamina and consistency. Heavily-built, he could keep going for long spells because he relied on a comparatively short run, the power of his arm and body giving his deliveries pace and lift off the pitch. Bestwick enjoyed success as a fast-medium bowler in local cricket and, after trials with Warwickshire and Leicestershire, he was snapped up by his native county and made his debut in 1898.

An early mentor was SH Wood, who captained the county in his formative seasons. In 1906, his success was overshadowed by crisis in his personal life. The death of his wife left him with a seven-year-old son Robert and they moved into Bill's parents' home. Things continued to go downhill. A few months later Bestwick was accused of the unlawful and felonious killing and slaying of William Brown at Heanor on Saturday January 25 1907. Brown died from wounds received in a knife fight in which Bestwick was wounded. They had been drinking and an argument developed. An inquest jury found the cricketer acted in self-defence. No further evidence was offered and he was cleared. Then in August 1909 he failed to turn up for a match against Northamptonshire at Derby. The club, fed up with his erratic behaviour and his drinking, had had enough. He was suspended and, at the end of the season, sacked.

When cricket resumed in 1919 after the war, Derbyshire found themselves down to the bare bones. Jack Chapman captained the team in most of the games but only Morton, Cadman, Oliver and Horsley remained as established players. Two others, Archie Slater, an all-rounder and Joe Bowden, a solid opening batsman, found league cricket more lucrative. Consequently, to its eternal credit, the club offered an olive branch which led to the return of the prodigal son, Bill Bestwick. He was now 44 and had been out of first-class cricket for nearly 10 years. His burly frame was giving way to corpulence and much of his former pace had gone. For all that he remained a fine bowler, his stamina unimpaired. After his sacking, he played for Shirebrook – where Ray Wilson, a member of the England soccer team which won the 1966 World Cup was born – in Derbyshire league cricket and found work as a miner in South Wales, where he met and married his second wife, Dora Allen of Neath. He was pro with Llanelli and Neath and took part in some matches for the second-class Glamorgan in 1914. During the war he worked in Derbyshire's pits and took a prodigious number of wickets for Heanor. This persuaded the county club that he still had something to offer. Peace made, he signed up for a season's county cricket.

Joint ninth out of 15 counties – they headed the table briefly in mid-June with three wins out of five matches – in 1919's limited programme of two-day Championship games was respectable enough, with Bestwick taking 90 wickets at 18.62 each. In July there was a 36-run victory over the Australian Imperial Forces at Derby. The AIF – Derbyshire were the only county side to defeat them – was a powerful team, drawn from cricketers who served in the European theatre of the war. The captain HL Collins led the 1926 Australian team to England and the AIF also included Jack Gregory, who formed with Ted McDonald one of the fastest bowling attacks in Test match history on the 1921 tour. Len Oliver captained Derbyshire, who struggled to totals of 181 and 112 against Gregory's pace. The tourists had little answer to the bowling of Horsley and Morton. They were dismissed for 125 in the first innings, Horsley taking six for 55, including a hat-trick, and Morton four for 66. In the second innings, needing 169 to win, they were all out for 132, Horsley six for 62, Morton three for 54. The pair bowled unchanged for all but eleven deliveries in the second innings. "I had hurt my ankle so I was prevented from having a go at the last man but Arthur and I virtually bowled them out twice on a good batting wicket," said Horsley. Derbyshire were without Bestwick, who was selected for the Players against the Gentlemen at Lord's. This was honour indeed, reward for his splendid form and an indication that, in spite of all his ups and downs, he was welcome at headquarters.

Bestwick and Horsley each opted for the leagues in 1920. Bestwick's engagement was with Neath and he also played for Glamorgan in their last season as a second-class county. Horsley went to Burnley. At that time Derbyshire were not alone in finding it difficult to hang on to their professionals. Cash and the relatively poor rewards the counties could offer were at the root of the problem. League cricket was of high quality and fiercely competitive but represented less work for more pay. Lord Hawke accused Lancashire League clubs of poaching county pros and Lord

Harris warned that league cricket had become a real competitor to county cricket. Kent countered the threat by saying they would only grant benefits to professionals pledging themselves to the county for at least seven years, playing in the leagues only with prior consent. The Advisory County Cricket Committee then decided that no player could be selected for representative and overseas tours unless he was prepared to put his county first. The crisis eased after the early 1920s and few players forsook the county game until their best days were behind them, although approaches continued.

Bestwick, who played just once for Derbyshire in 1920, appeared set to finish his career in Wales with a residential qualification when Glamorgan achieved their goal of first-class cricket in 1921. The county agreed terms with four professionals but Derbyshire, anxious to re-sign him after the disasters of 1920, made a better offer, with a promise of some coaching. By now the county had accepted him for what he was – a magnificent bowler whose behaviour, because of his drinking, was sometimes erratic. Fellow seam bowler Raymond Robertson-Glasgow held him in high regard. "He belonged to the now less fashionable school of faster bowlers, who, having been put on, are left on; or, rather, left alone; not interfered with... The art of nursing had not yet come to relieve and insult the toilers under the sun. Bestwick, tall enough and tremendous of shoulder and arm, didn't need a nurse. A batsman who could fight, an umpire with two out of his five senses, a quart or so of beer at mid-day and sunset, earthy laughter and cursing – these were his game." And later in Bestwick's umpiring days, Robertson-Glasgow found him "full of rough comfort and homely counsel for the young imitator."

Derbyshire's 1921 western tour consisted of consecutive matches at Bath, Bristol and Cardiff in June. At Bristol, Will Taylor and the youthful Wally Hammond had to field as substitutes when Joe Bowden was injured and Bestwick the worse for wear after a night out. Nearly 80 years later, Jim Hutchinson, a colleague for five years, would gaze at a photograph of the county side, point to Bestwick and give a shake of his head and a good natured chuckle. "Bill was his own worst enemy. It was such a pity. He was an outstanding bowler who was capable of getting out any side on his day. Guy Jackson was a very good captain but he had a pretty rough time with him. Jackson was a former army man who introduced some military discipline into the side but it didn't work with Bill. Yet he could be a very generous man. He was a great help to anybody coming into the side for their first match and he was kind to the youngsters.

"Out of drink he was lovely but when he had had a few he could be awkward and difficult to handle. It was best to keep out of his way at times like these. I don't know why but he seemed to go mad celebrating whenever we got anywhere near Wales."

At Cardiff on Saturday June 18 1921, Glamorgan made 168, Derbyshire collapsing to 83 all out. Will Taylor recalled the second day's play. "On the Sunday evening Bill was again hors-de-combat (he had spent the evening drinking heavily with some of his friends from Neath) and this was reported to our skipper

(George Buckston) who decided to try him out first in Glamorgan's second innings. He commenced with that lovely run and beautiful action and in his first over bowled their opening batsman Whittington. He then continued throughout the innings and accomplished the memorable performance of taking all ten wickets before lunch (seven clean bowled and three in his last over in four balls) in 19 overs at a cost of 40 runs."

Bestwick's generous nature was revealed as an offshoot of this performance. The committee decided that collections should be made for him at the next two home games at Derby and Chesterfield. "In those days, the players were paid match fees with a small retaining sum in the winter and Arthur Morton had been seriously injured in a motor-cycle accident early in June," said Taylor. "When I handed the proceeds of the collection to Bill, he counted out half and handing it to me said 'give this to 'owd Arthur, he needs it more than me.' This was a typical gesture on the part of this great-hearted cricketer, who, in spite of his peccadilloes, was, I consider, the outstanding personality in Derbyshire cricket during the whole time I have been associated with the club. The side were short of bowling and frequently I saw him commence and continue without a break for two hours up to the luncheon interval and then start again for at least another half-hour."

Figures confirm this. In 19 Championship matches in 1921 he delivered 935.3 overs and took 147 wickets at 16.72 each. *Wisden* said: "Naturally, he had not the speed of his younger days but he kept up something more than medium pace and retained his old accuracy." Form and commitment, then, from Bestwick appeared almost beyond reproach – but only almost. In 1922 Guy Jackson took his team to Worcester for the final match of the season and there came a drink-related incident which entered the game's folklore. Bestwick did not arrive, but turned up later to barrack his colleagues. Guy Southern, a young amateur who had made 43, Derbyshire's highest score against the AIF three years earlier, was hastily summoned and went in at No 10 due to his late arrival.

The game was drawn but what really livened up proceedings was beautifully described by *The Times* correspondent Dudley Carew in his book *To the Wicket*. He refrained from naming Bestwick, contenting himself by describing him as a bowler on whom the club depended. "As tea-time approached the players became aware of a disturbance somewhere in the crowd. A voice, thick and belligerent, was asking who were playing and what county was in the field. Derbyshire, he was told. 'Derbyshire,' exclaimed the voice, disgustedly in a dialect which defies print. 'Derbyshire. If I'd known it was that ****** county I'd never 'ave wasted a ruddy sixpence getting in.' It was the bowler, richly confused in whereabouts and circumstance, but certain and confident in opinion."

Bestwick was the county's leading wicket-taker in 1923 and 1924 but played only seven matches the following year when he spent most of the summer in charge of the youngsters in the nursery. Two teenage batsmen, Denis Smith and Albert Alderman, found his bowling a handful in trials. So did Leicestershire at Burton-on-Trent, where seven for 20 and ten in the match make him the oldest player, at 50 years 130 days, to accomplish the feats for the county.

A month later he appeared in his final match. Replying to Derbyshire's 134, Warwickshire were 68 for one at the close of Saturday's play, Bestwick's figures being 11-2-34-0. He took 1,457 wickets during his first-class career at 21 each, impressive in a struggling team, significantly so in 1921 when his haul of 147 was crucial to the future of the club when its status as a first-class county hung in the balance. Later he became an umpire, standing in three Tests.

It was at Whitsuntide in 1936 that Denis Compton made his first-class debut for Middlesex against Sussex at Lord's. On Whit Monday, in front of a 15,000 crowd, he went in at No. 11 to join Gubby Allen, with Middlesex needing 24 runs for a first innings lead. They had added 36 when Jim Parks appealed for lbw against Compton and Bill Bestwick's finger went up at once. Allen was unimpressed. "Bill," he said. "you're a so and so cheat... Young Compton wasn't out and well you know it." Bestwick was unperturbed. "I know he wasn't, sir," he answered, "but you had your first innings lead, and I was dying to spend a penny so I gave him out."

Bestwick died at Nottingham General Hospital on May 2 1938, aged 63, a victim of cancer. The vicar and rural dean of Heanor, Rev DG Smith, conducted the service in St Lawrence's Church, assisted by Rev Henry Ellison. The mourners included Guy Jackson, Will Taylor, his old fast bowling partner Arnold Warren and the wicketkeeper Joe Humphries; the floral tributes some from friends and relatives in Neath and South Wales.

Chapter 18
1920

A RUN of eight consecutive victories propelled Middlesex to the top of the Championship table in 1920. They stayed there; gaining a thrilling victory over Surrey at Lord's to set the seal on their captain Pelham Warner's final season.

Wisden waxed lyrical. "Never has the competition excited such widespread interest and never has the actual finish been more dramatic." Lancashire were runners-up, Surrey third, with Yorkshire and Kent fourth and fifth. Sussex were sixth and Nottinghamshire, weak in bowling, seventh. It was no coincidence. The Championship was the playground of the Big Six. During the first 42 seasons of the official Championship from 1890-1935 Yorkshire won 18 titles. Lancashire and Surrey each won seven, Kent four, Middlesex three and Nottinghamshire two. The exception was Warwickshire in 1911. The Big Six are still the only counties to have a credit margin of victories over defeats in the list of Championship results since 1864. Essex joined them for a time in 1996-97 but soon slipped back into the red. Warwickshire are the only other county within striking distance but it would take a number of successful years for them to erase the deficit. Four or five of the Big Six invariably filled the leading positions; in 1893, 1925 and 1926 they took the first six places in the table.

Their collective confidence was such that whatever means of deciding the Championship was cobbled together, one or the other of them would come out on top. Matches among themselves attracted huge crowds, with standards of play not far below the Ashes Test matches and the best of Gentlemen v Players. They were the most sought after as opponents when the secretaries compiled their own fixture lists at the annual meeting at Lord's. Derbyshire usually managed to arrange home and away matches against Lancashire, Yorkshire and Nottinghamshire but fixtures with the southern trio were less frequent.

From time to time they sought official segregation. Lancashire suggested two divisions in 1911, with a top section of 11 teams. The remaining five would form a second division with the leading minor counties. One side would be relegated and one promoted each season. Nothing was achieved. A year later, Yorkshire and Lancashire sought to limit the competition to 11 clubs. Derbyshire, Essex, Northamptonshire, Somerset and Worcestershire, the counties with the smallest crowd appeal, would go. Then, independently of each other, Warner and Fender came out in favour of two divisions in 1923. There was a similar suggestion from the Lancashire chairman Tommy Higson a year later and some newspapers offered support. Again it led nowhere. Nobody wanted to play in a second division. Cash-strapped counties feared spectators would drift away from lower category matches. Not until 2000 would two divisions come into being.

It was a wonder anybody bothered. Effectively two divisions, verging on three, already existed – the predatory Big Six, a handful of mid-table sides and the perennial minnows at the bottom of the food chain. Natural financial selection was close to achieving a split in the Championship. Derbyshire faced extinction in autumn 1910. Gloucestershire and Northamptonshire might not have been able to compete in a 1915 season lost to the war. Worcestershire, near to winding up in 1913, did not take part in 1919 because of financial circumstances, although they did arrange a few first-class fixtures. Their return in 1920 was disastrous. In 18 matches they won once, against Gloucestershire. Only three professionals were regulars and of 29 players who turned out, 23 were amateurs. The gap, evident since the competition was expanded in 1895, had reached worrying proportions.

Wisden's editor, Sydney Pardon, pulled no punches. "A disappointing feature of our otherwise brilliant season (1920) was the extreme disparity between the strongest and the weakest counties... I should be the last to throw cold water on county cricket, but there is no getting away from the fact that since the scope of the Championship was so widely extended a lot of our so-called first-class cricket has been quite second-rate." Pardon pointed out that the leading teams were often engaged in soft matches which under equal conditions of weather they could scarcely help winning. "Things will be worse than ever in the coming season, Glamorgan having secured sufficient fixtures to rank as first-class." There was more about the weakness and excess of county cricket placing England's Test match prospects at a serious disadvantage, although he acknowledged the Championship had to be kept open to new aspirants.

Derbyshire had long been among the small fry which aroused so much scorn from *Wisden* and elements of the national press. From 1895-1919 they won 60 and lost 215 of 386 Championship matches. No side won fewer or lost more. Their infrequent victories were, in the main, gained over their fellow-strugglers. Of the Big Six, Yorkshire were defeated in 1895 and 1905, Lancashire in 1895 and 1911, Surrey in 1903 and 1904 and Nottinghamshire in 1903, 1908, 1913 and 1914. They had not met Middlesex and no win had been recorded against Kent for close on 40 years. In five seasons, but not since 1907, they finished last. In 1919 five counties were below them, indicating that a gradual improvement which had started before the war was being maintained.

They started 1920 with eight professionals but only Sam Cadman and Arthur Morton were of genuine quality, although George Beet seemed established as a wicketkeeper and a useful batsman. Jack Chapman and Len Oliver were named joint captains but Chapman, never entirely happy with leadership, handed over to Oliver. His form with the bat was woeful and he probably felt he had enough on his plate trying to score runs. Oliver led the side in each of the 12 matches in which he played, even when Chapman was in the team. Chapman was skipper in only three, when Oliver was absent. Two other amateurs, FG Peach and GF Bell, stepped in for the two games when neither Oliver or Chapman was available.

The campaign began with a visit to Bramall Lane, where Yorkshire proved far too powerful, winning by an innings and 223 runs. Lancashire were the next opponents, the margin of defeat at Chesterfield being an innings and 160 runs. Derbyshire were unfortunate in that the pitch had turned difficult when they batted. Totals of 41 and 62 reflected the conditions and their own shortcomings. An eight-wicket reverse at the hands of Warwickshire at Derby followed and Derbyshire were left to reflect on three consecutive defeats in matches which failed to reach the third day.

There was now a three-week gap before the next fixture against Essex at Derby. Early in June Derbyshire crossed the Irish Sea to meet Ulster, officially the Northern Cricket Union of Ireland team, at Belfast. The match, not first-class, was a low scoring affair on a pitch which helped the bowlers, Morton taking 13 wickets and Derbyshire gaining a heartening win by 114 runs. Changes were made for the Essex match, Harry Elliott making his debut. The match was lost by six wickets but he made a good start with an unbeaten 25 in the second innings. Beet was to make only three more appearances in 1920 and those as a batsman. A competent enough wicketkeeper, Beet was unfortunate in the quality of his rivals, first the ensconced Joe Humphries and now Elliott.

Although they had lost their first four games Derbyshire retained hope. Northamptonshire, their next opponents at Queen's Park, had lost seven out of eight but had beaten Leicestershire on their opponents' ground. Consequently there was everything to play for as Derbyshire approached a game that was eminently winnable. Again they made changes, in fact Derbyshire were to alter their side for every match in 1920. The most interesting found Arnold Warren returning at the age of 45 for one of two games he played that summer. Warren had not played first-class cricket since 1913 but he had been taking plenty of wickets for Langwith Miners' Welfare in the Bassetlaw League. He struck an early blow and finished with four for 45 in Northamptonshire's first innings of 196, Morton dismissing five batsmen for 61.

The pitch, already helping the bowlers, was further affected by rain on Sunday. Only Harold Wild and Elliott reached double figures in Derbyshire's 71. Northamptonshire, with a lead of 125, fared little better. They managed only 89 in their second innings. Warren, four for 46 and Morton, six for 35 and taking his match analysis to eleven for 96, bowled unchanged. This left Derbyshire 215 for victory but it was never on. Oliver made 46 and Elliott 22 but Northamptonshire won comfortably by 114 runs, well within two days.

It was a major setback but some fighting spirit remained. For a time Derbyshire gave as good as they got against Lancashire at Old Trafford. Oliver (73) and Cadman (47) added 120 for the second wicket, the captain batting especially well. Morton was left high and dry with 30 in a total of 225. On the second day Ernest Tyldesley's

169 not out was the cornerstone of Lancashire's 528 for six. Rain fell in the night, James Tyldesley performed a hat-trick and Derbyshire, on a damaged pitch, were routed for 75. Six matches, six defeats. The next fixture, against Nottinghamshire at Chesterfield had been given to Joe Humphries for his benefit. He replaced Elliott as wicketkeeper on the teamsheet, Bill Bestwick also returning. But rain prevented any play.

Bestwick remained for a visit to Leicester and for the first time that summer Derbyshire found themselves in the driving seat. Bestwick and Morton wrecked the Leicestershire first innings and Derbyshire led by 61. Morton fought hard but they could manage only 118 in their second innings, setting the home team a target of 180. Struggling sides and ill-fortune go hand in hand and Derbyshire found plenty of that. Rain on Friday morning eased the pitch; Leicestershire got the runs for the loss of only four wickets.

Confidence and morale were now in freefall. Yorkshire inflicted further humiliation at Derby and then the club found itself in hot water at Lord's following defeat by Sussex at Hove. On the second day, Thursday, Derbyshire made a reasonable start in their quest for 300 to win the match, Oliver getting 43. They soon fell away and with eight wickets down the captains agreed to finish the game in two days to save expenses. Just on seven o'clock Sussex won by 134 runs but MCC reprimanded the captains for their unorthodox procedure.

By now Oliver must have been at his wit's end. The free day at least meant a comfortable journey home for the next match against Somerset at Derby but he ran into more controversy. The captains found a plumb, hard pitch which was not consistent with the prevailing weather – an interesting point of view when compared to modern standards. Albert Widdowson was ordered to cut a new strip, to the instant benefit of the home side. Elliott made 42 not out in a total of 149 and Morton, 36.4-20-37-8, reduced Somerset to 98 all out, a lead of 51. The second day found Derbyshire with a genuine chance of victory. Whether it was the conditions, exploited by Ernest Robson and Jack White, or the lack of confidence born of repeated failure or a combination of both, the result was disastrous. Five wickets were down for 35, the last one fell at 67 and Somerset needed only 119. Morton again bowled well but the visitors, who fielded nine amateurs, got home by five wickets early on the final morning. Salt was rubbed into the wounds a week later at Northampton. Oliver won the toss and tried fielding first. Cadman took six for 34 and eight for 70 – a match analysis of 45.3-9-104-14 – and top scored in the second innings with 22. The margin of defeat, 80 runs, scarcely did justice to Northamptonshire's superiority.

Eleven defeats. People had lost direction and morale was on the floor. Rumblings began to appear in the press about relegating Derbyshire to minor status. The nightmare continued as Warwickshire won at Edgbaston. Here an amateur, Frederick Peach, resisted Howell's pace with 61 not out in the second innings but at the age of 37 and with a brewery company career he was hardly a long term prospect.

Peach was missing for the fixture against Sussex at Queen's Park, Chesterfield. Four changes were made, one involving the return of Warren but he withdrew because of a knee injury. His replacement was to make cricket history. James Metcalf Hutchinson was born at New Tupton, Chesterfield on November 29 1896. When he died on November 7 2000 he was 22 days short of his 104th birthday. Eighty years and 62 days had passed since his county debut. He remained lucid until the end, a treasure house of information about those distant days, related from the comfort of his armchair at his home in Thurnscoe, between Barnsley and Rotherham. The longest-lived first-class cricketer of them all was a credit to the game but a greater achievement was his career in the mining industry.

He was the second in a family of seven children, his father being under-manager at Oscroft Colliery in North Derbyshire. Jim Hutchinson was down the pit at 14, studied mining at Sheffield University and was on the threshold of a promising career in the industry when cricket began to attract his attention. As a teenager, he demonstrated he could hit hard and showed glimpses of the fielding skills which made him one of the best cover-points in the game. In 1920 he played for Bulcroft Main Colliery, near Doncaster, and took part in a charity match at Hull after somebody had dropped out. He made 55 not out, an innings watched by Joe Humphries. Archie Slater also knew something of Hutchinson's ability and the two of them recommended him to Derbyshire. When Warren withdrew, a telegram arrived at Hutchinson's home asking him if he was available on the Saturday at Queen's Park.

"I hadn't even seen a county match, but I turned up early with my kit crammed into a small bag. After waiting for a time I nearly left the ground before somebody came up and introduced themselves. The head coach Sam Cadman gave me a poor reception. I don't think he liked me, simply because he didn't introduce me to Derbyshire. That was the trouble. Joe Humphries had recommended me to the club and Cadman was annoyed because he hadn't dealt with me. Cadman was a good all-rounder but I hadn't much time for him. Now Arthur Morton was a different person altogether."

Sussex won by an innings but Hutchinson made a creditable start; bowled in the first innings by Arthur Gilligan for five, his 22 in the second was Derbyshire's highest individual score of the match bar Cadman's 25.

Business commitments ruled Oliver and Chapman out for the next game, Leicestershire at Derby, Peach leading the team. This was the final home game and a third wicket partnership between Peach and Morton produced 89 runs. Morton's bowling had been consistent throughout the summer but his pre-war batting form had eluded him. Now he came good, carrying his bat for 105 out of 204 – the first hundred made for the county in 1920. By the third day the match seemed destined for a draw, the long sequence of sickening defeats ended at last. The visitors, aware that the pitch would prove difficult, declared with a first innings lead of 67. Astill and King played havoc, five wickets falling for 10 runs. Morton and Cadman, who opened the batting in the first innings and then the bowling, added 28 before Morton left for 16. Cadman was still there at the finish, with 19 out of 53, Leicestershire taking the final wicket a quarter of an hour before stumps would have been drawn. It was a close call but, in the end, another innings defeat.

There was another flicker at Southend, where an old Reptonian Geoffrey Bell must have harboured hopes of skippering the team to its first win. Essex, fielding eight amateurs, made 225 and Derbyshire got within five runs of this. A fourth innings target of 202 looked attainable when Wild and Wilfred Carter began with 41 for the first wicket but Louden then carried all before him and the remaining nine went down for 56. Sixteen matches, 15 defeats, one abandoned.

The end of the season could not come quickly enough. Four changes, including the return of Oliver and Chapman, were made for a visit to Trent Bridge. Again Morton and Cadman toiled away as Whysall made 142 and Nottinghamshire put the game beyond Derbyshire's reach with 382. Richmond's leg spin then caused problems and half the side was out for 72 on the second morning. There then followed the most pleasant period of cricket in Derbyshire's 1920 campaign. Oliver and a veteran amateur CJ Corbett took control. They had added 108 in 75 minutes for the sixth wicket when Corbett was bowled for 61. Elliott batted well and at 253 for six, Oliver's share was 128. He had been steady and cautious until the follow-on was averted but then began to score freely. He took 16 off one over from John Gunn and reached 170 before falling to a splendid slip catch by George Gunn off Arthur Carr's bowling. Oliver batted for three hours 40 minutes, hitting two sixes and 18 fours. Derbyshire's total of 302 was their highest of the season. It was not enough, Nottinghamshire winning on the Saturday by 173 runs, but they had been made to fight far harder than they expected.

So to the final match, Weston-super-Mare, scheduled for the first three days of September. Nobody in the wider world of cricket cared overmuch. The drama at Lord's, where Middlesex won the Championship, was the main talking point. Only two days were needed on a rain-affected pitch, Somerset winning by 10 wickets. Sixteen amateurs, seven of them in Derbyshire's side, took part and all 20 Derbyshire wickets fell to amateur bowlers. Major Llewellyn Eardley-Simpson, a club official for 47 years, recalled the game. "In the Somerset innings, with a wicket likely to suit Arthur Morton, John Daniell made up his mind that drastic action was required – and he provided it with a vengeance. He was eventually disposed of when he had made 102, out of which he actually scored the first 50 out of 53 in less than half-an-hour." Somerset required a mere 29 to win, Daniell and PR Johnson getting them off 71 balls delivered by Morton and Cadman.

Thus the two all-rounders finished the season in their accustomed manner, toiling away in a lost cause towards an ending which came as a profound relief to everybody.

Played 18, won none and drawn none, one match abandoned without a ball being bowled and 17 defeats.

Chapter 19
Sifting through the Wreckage

WILL TAYLOR needed no array of statistics to emphasise the crisis. They remain, however, fascinatingly awful.

Of the 17 defeats in 1920, six were by an innings and one by 10 wickets. The narrowest margins were five wickets (Somerset at Derby) and by 80 runs at Northampton. In 34 completed innings Derbyshire were dismissed for fewer than a hundred 16 times. The lowest total was 41; the highest 302 and 200 was exceeded on only four occasions. A first innings lead was obtained twice, at Leicester and against Somerset at Derby. Seven matches finished in two days, something of a mixed blessing. It saved on expenses and eased the rigours of long-distance rail journeys against the clock after matches ended late on the final day. A few towels were sometimes thrown in by the weaker counties when the cause was hopeless, either during the second evening or early on the third morning.

Oliver headed the batting averages, 546 runs, average 22.75, followed by Cadman 527, 15.96 and Elliott 299, 15.73. A degree of respectability was achieved with the ball. Morton took 89 wickets at 20.31 and, in all first-class cricket, 95 at 19.96, in which he passed 500 runs. Cadman's 58 wickets for the county cost 20.87.

By far the most damning set of figures relates to the sheer number of people who turned out. Thirty-nine players appeared in 17 completed matches. Cadman and Morton were ever-presents. Chapman and Elliott each played in 14 games, Oliver and Storer 12. Eleven played once and eight twice so 19 players appeared in no more than two matches. For nine cricketers 1920 was the only season in which they took the field in a first-class fixture. Eighteen amateurs, many with few pretensions to first-class ability, were selected. Joe Humphries was chosen for his aborted benefit and WM Limb was in the team which won in Belfast: 41 players for 18 scheduled first-class matches and one other. Changes ranging from two to five were made for every game.

Eardley-Simpson – prominent in Derby's legal, social, political and sporting life and a noted historian – said the selection committee had about as many meetings as there were matches. "On more than one occasion it was not too easy to find a full eleven. As the end of the season approached it became a question of whether it was worth while trying to keep the county flag flying."

Will Taylor said: "A panic policy was pursued by our selection committee which was far too large and no fewer than 39 players represented the club that season. If a young player coming in failed, he was immediately dropped and another youngster tried with the same result. The side was dispirited and completely lacking in fight." Yet he could look back on those dismal days with a touch of gallows humour. Derbyshire's record was the worst experienced by any county since the competition started. "I've always had mixed feelings about the Nottinghamshire match being abandoned. It was a change not to lose but it did deprive us of an unbeatable record, that of losing every match, for I've no doubt we should have lost."

Jim Hutchinson said: "It was a very poor side and we had a terrible time. Losing so often meant confidence and team spirit was very low. There was hardly any money and sometimes Mr Taylor found it a struggle to pay us."

A new face was needed and it came from an unexpected source. George Moreton Buckston was born, fittingly in the light of Derbyshire's parlous state, at Hope, a Peakland beauty spot with its valley and associations with Castleton and Kinderscout. He was educated at Eton, playing his cricket as a wicketkeeper and lower-order batsman. In 1900 he scored 45 and four at Lord's in a splendid match which Harrow won by one wicket. Buckston got a Blue at Cambridge in 1903, a late choice for the team which was beaten by Oxford. Two years later he was in the Derbyshire side alongside Bestwick, Cadman and Morton. He averaged 20 in 1906 with a highest score of 96 but fared poorly the following season and had played no further Championship cricket. Captain GM Buckston emerged from the 1914-18 war with malaria and little or no intention of playing first-class cricket again. Instead, he turned out in club cricket and captained the amateurs, the Gentlemen, against the Players in a Derbyshire trial at the County Ground in 1919, when the pros were led by Joe Humphries. It was obvious that morale, pride and self-respect needed injecting into the side. Nevertheless, at the age of 40 in 1921, he was an unlikely knight on a white charger.

"I remember him telling me at the end of the 1920 season that unless there was a radical alteration in the general set-up he believed the club would cease, but if the committee so desired, he was prepared to undertake the captaincy for one year only, in an effort to pull things together. He was appointed to lead the side and only those intimately connected with the organisation of the club can possibly realise the great services he rendered to Derbyshire cricket," said Taylor. Similar views were expressed by Eardley-Simpson, who saw the bold experiment as "the last effort to stave off the approaching collapse."

For the 1921 season, Buckston still had Cadman, Oliver and Morton. Promising youngsters such as Storer, Hutchinson, Carter and Elliott had started their first-class careers. An old Reptonian, Gilbert Curgenven, who had been a hard-hitting middle-order batsman before the war, was available. Joe Bowden was attracted back from the leagues and Bill Bestwick returned.

The most interesting of the early-season fixtures pitted Derbyshire against Worcestershire, a confrontation which would have been fascinating amidst the miseries of 1920 had it occurred, for Worcestershire's record was only slightly better.

Sifting through the Wreckage

Derbyshire had lost their opening match at Edgbaston, where Bestwick took nine for 65 in Warwickshire's second innings, but at New Road, the first day was marginally in their favour. Morton and Bestwick took the bowling honours as Worcestershire were dismissed for 214. By close of play Derbyshire had lost two wickets for 81. Buckston, who opened, was going well and on Thursday the position was consolidated. The captain reached 71 before he was fourth out after two hours at the crease, Cadman made 91 and Curgenven 43 in a total of 332. But Worcestershire cleared the arrears of 118 with only one wicket down and it was anybody's game going into the final day.

It became a battle of the veterans. Dick Pearson, for years the backbone of his county's cricket, made 87 but Bestwick caused a breakdown and the innings closed at 213. Bestwick took seven for 67, returning a match analysis of 75-24-144-11. Just 96 to win. Even this modest target might have been beyond the 1920 side but Len Oliver, who had endured more than most in those disasters, left nothing to chance. His sound 47 calmed the nerves and victory was achieved with eight wickets to spare.

Thus ended a run of 18 consecutive defeats. Not since the AIF was beaten in July 1919 had a first-class match been won: it was the first win over a county since June 14 1919 when Northamptonshire lost at Derby. Confidence and self-esteem restored, Derbyshire promptly defeated Nottinghamshire by 23 runs at Chesterfield, Morton taking thirteen for 128. At Cardiff, where Bestwick took all ten in an innings, Glamorgan were beaten but it was a close call. Derbyshire, needing 192 to win, lost eight wickets for 116 before Carter and Elliott added 77 to record a two wicket victory. Glamorgan were defeated in the return at Chesterfield – Bestwick took 23 wickets against his former colleagues that summer – and there was a victory over Leicestershire. Five matches were won and Derbyshire rose to 12th place in the Championship table.

Buckston had achieved his aim of righting the sinking ship. Eardley-Simpson wrote: "He did more as a bat than we had a right to expect, while as captain he would have been well worth his place had he never scored a run. Long before the season was over, he had pulled the side together and was in a fair way to produce a team instead of a number of disorganised players." The local press said he proved himself above all things an optimist – just what was needed when he was chosen for the post – and a most popular captain.

He was, however, past 40 and the strain had told. It was time to go. "Having accomplished his mission, Buckston refused to be dissuaded from his decision to retire," wrote Will Taylor. "Instead, he was elected chairman of the committee." In an era when MCC was dominated by peers, baronets, military officers of high rank, Conservative politicians and an Old Boy network based on a public school background Buckston's Etonian credentials did homespun Derbyshire no harm at all.

But the club was to strike riches from a far more basic source.

Chapter 20
The Seedbeds

THE riches in the cricketing sense were located amidst the county's most precious natural asset, its coalfields.

These occurred in three main areas, near Axe Edge in the north-west, the south around Swadlincote and Newhall; but mainly in the east, merging with those of western Nottinghamshire. Landowning families; the Devonshires, Sitwells, Cokes, Drury-Lowes, Mundys and Morewoods, and newly-formed companies such as Butterley, Clay Cross and Barber Walker were quick to exploit them. By 1922, when Guy Jackson became captain, the influence of the coal mines was becoming a feature of Derbyshire's dressing room, the flat East Midlands' vowels of the professionals blending with the broad localised accents of the miners. Jackson was a future joint managing director of the mine-owning Clay Cross Company. His second cousin Anthony, a right-hand fast-medium bowler and a useful batsman, became a mining engineer. An amateur lost to the mines was Harry Watson Smith, a wicketkeeper and useful batsman who might have made a good county captain but who became an engineer, mining consultant and managing director of Hardwick Collieries. Jim Hutchinson's principal career was to be mining, although he was also paid for playing first-class cricket for a decade. Harry Elliott, now established among the country's leading wicketkeepers, had worked in the mines. Bill Bestwick divided his time between the pit, the pub and the cricket pitch.

It was their heritage. For all the rugged grandeur of the Peak District and the beauty of the Dales, the cradles of Derbyshire cricket lay within the industrial belt, the lead mines of Wirksworth, the lace and rail heritage of Derby, the pit hills, winding houses, smoke-misted sheds and fussy shunting engines of the coalfields. Chesterfield and the North East Derbyshire area spilling over into Nottinghamshire became a forcing ground for sporting talent. Further south, for 20 miles the boundary between the counties is formed by the River Erewash, an unprepossessing stream far removed from the lovely scenery of the Wye or the Derwent. The Erewash Valley is flanked by hill towns such as Ripley, Heanor and Ilkeston on its western slopes and by Eastwood and Kimberley to the east in Nottinghamshire. From the mines, ironworks and the hosiery mills came the cricketers and footballers and a fierce soccer and cricketing rivalry which found its zenith at Trent Bridge, the City Ground, Ilkeston Rutland Recreation Ground and at the Baseball Ground and Pride Park.

Almost every town and most of the villages in North East Derbyshire and parts of West Nottinghamshire had its own pit. DH Lawrence mourned lost opportunity. "These mining villages might have been like the lovely hill towns of Italy, shapely and fascinating. And what happened... " The pits may have appeared to Lawrence as "in a sense an accident in the landscape" but they provided a living, albeit creating a lifestyle which was hard and basic. From Lawrence, through the novels of Walter Brierley to Owen Watson's *Rhymes of a Marlpool Miner* (which relate to pits near Heanor), the collier's lot was engraved in poetry and prose.

The mining terms, snap tin (lunch), face (the coal wall where the coal is dug), gate (an underground road), motty (a check, tally or token), loose-all (time to go home), overman, onsetter and deputy, and the coal seams, deep soft and hard, piper, low main, blackshale, silkstone, top hard, Tupton, Mickley, Kilburn and Norton, would be as familiar in the professionals' dressing room conversation as debates on in-swing or pad play. There was much to talk about. More than a million colliers worked in 3,000 mines throughout the country. Lads went down the pit at 14, learning to dig coal with pick and shovel, handle pit ponies, pumping and how to set explosives. The homes of the miners – some purpose-built in model villages such as New Bolsover – were in rows of small terrace houses, the living room fireplace, with its black-leaded firegrate, heating an oven on one side and a copper on the other: the fire, fed by giant, shiny lumps of coal from the loads cocked up outside every entry and backed up with rough stuff, burning for months on end until the glow from the firegrate was extinguished for the pre-Christmas chimney sweep. Mining towns and villages became self-sufficient. Miners' welfares sprung up, with facilities for social evenings and sport. Co-op branches offered everything from basic food to items of hardware and paid a dividend on purchases vital to the household economy. Gardens and allotments provided fresh vegetables and opportunities to grow giant leeks and onions for the annual show. Homing pigeons, whippets and breeding game fowls (and sometimes cock fighting) occupied the pitmens' leisure hours. Comradeship and neighbourliness was balm for all the bruises and shattered bones suffered in the clammy heat or intense cold, the coal dust, damp, and the backbreaking slog at the face. And there was also lingering death from dust in the lungs or of the kind described by Lawrence in *Odour of Chrysanthemums*, where a wife waits with increasing irritation for her man to come home from the pit only to learn, at length, the terrible truth.

It was a time of unrest in the coalfields. There was a strike in 1921, when a slump found two-and-a-half million unemployed. The Government, under Prime Minister Stanley Baldwin, subsidised the mine owners to maintain wages but this could last only until April 1926. Unemployment continued to rise and the mine owners proposed pay cuts as a way of moving the industry forward. It cut little ice with their employees, who rejected new terms of hours and pay. Matters came to a head when the Trades Union Congress pledged support for the miners. On May 4 1926 a General Strike was called in an attempt to force the Government to accede to the miners' demands. A leading role was taken by the Derby MP Jimmy Thomas, who was secretary of the National Union of Railwaymen. The strike lasted only eight days and failed to gain any concessions. The miners, feeling they had been sacrificed in the interests of industrial peace, refused to compromise. They continued their strike. Food and coal were in short supply. Ends were made to meet. Coal was picked from the slag heaps. Queues formed at the soup kitchens. It was bearable in the summer but, as autumn bit, the drift back to work began. First back would get the best jobs, said the owners, but there would be short shrift for the militants and union men.

The Jacksons and the Clay Cross Company had their problems, along with a dozen similar coal and iron firms. The Clay Cross Company had carried out a paternal role, a form of welfare state which helped the workforce. There was assistance to schools, chapels, institutes and sport and a coal allowance for miners. It built a cricket ground, Sharley Park. But Guy's father GM Jackson met a hostile reception in Morton in 1921 when he outlined the owners' proposals to the miners. James Randle, a member of Derbyshire County Council and a miners' leader, asked a number of questions. He was ordered to leave and the meeting broke up in disorder. Shouts of abuse rang in Jackson's ears as he drove away. He was one of the owners trying to reopen their collieries in the summer of 1926. In June a number of men resumed work at the Staveley Company's Markham No 2 colliery on new terms. There were some hostile demonstrations by the strikers. Jackson and RCA Palmer Morewood, the owner of the Swanwick Collieries, followed Staveley's example. Miners employed by Butterley Company had raised enough coal to keep the pumps going and soon went back.

Most of the striking miners only sought the wherewithal to look after their families rather than bring down the government. It was likely the strike in the Midlands would have ended long before it did but for the activities of AJ Cook, secretary of the Miners' Federation of Great Britain. His militant leadership and powers of oratory kept the men out for months before defeat was accepted. By November it was over. The dawn chorus of pit boots echoing on Derbyshire streets resumed. Later, after loose-all, there would be the walk home, in many cases to a house owned by the colliery company. Then a strip-wash or a warm and comforting soak in the tin bath before a blazing coal fire. Porridge for breakfast, the contents of the brown earthenware stewpot for dinner. Two or three pints in the pub to follow and bread and cheese for supper.

The 1926 strike left bitterness in the coalfields. One outcome was an increase in the working day. It had been limited to seven hours in 1920. Cook's slogan had called for "not a penny off pay, not a minute on the day." After the failure of the General Strike the hours increased to eight. They were reduced to seven and a half under the Coal Mines Act of 1930. But the industry continued to struggle. In Derbyshire, pits closed and in November 1927 the Grassmoor Colliery Company alone dismissed around 500 men. Miners on a three-day week with stoppages found problems feeding their wives and children. Some lived in conditions which were described as a disgrace to civilisation. In fact, the depression – the slump of the 1920s and 1930s – caused

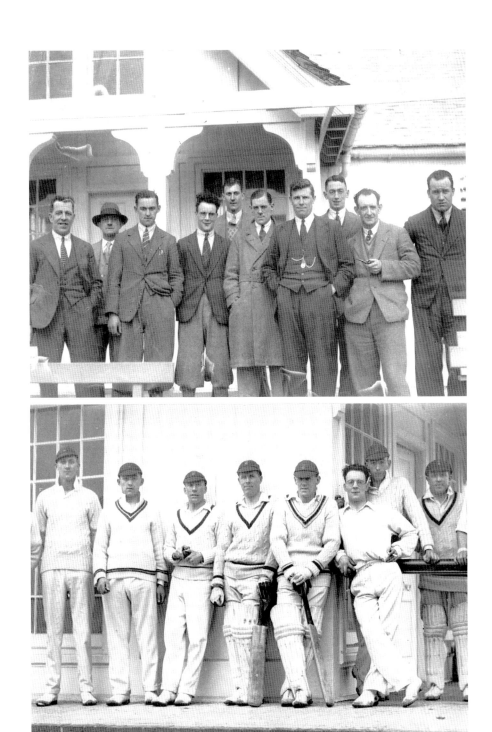

Two views of the 1931 team gathering before the start of the season and ready for action. (courtesy Derby Evening Telegraph)

Derbyshire take the field for the match with Gloucestershire at Burton-on-Trent on Saturday July 20 1935. (Top) deep in conversation are Arthur Richardson and Harry Elliott. It worked: Gloucestershire 160-2 at lunch crumbled to 234 all out. (courtesy Derby Evening Telegraph)

(Top) Bill Copson (left) goes to practice with Albert Alderman and Denis Smith.
(courtesy Michael Copson) (Bottom): meeting before the start of the 1930 season. (left
to right) Stan Worthington, back from the MCC tour of New Zealand, Tommy Mitchell,
Archie Slater and Garnet Lee. (courtesy Derby Evening Telegraph)

(Top) Will Taylor, Derbyshire secretary for 51 years. (Raymonds Photographic Agency)
(Bottom): 1938, and Derbyshire now led by Robin Buckston (extreme right) take the
field against Worcestershire at the County Ground. Derbyshire won by six wickets.
(courtesy Derby Evening Telegraph)

The 1936 team: (back row) Harry Elliott, Leslie Townsend, Bill Copson, Harry Parker (scorer), Alf Pope, Denis Smith, Charlie Elliott. (front row) Harry Storer, Stan Worthington, Arthur Richardson (capt), Tommy Mitchell, Albert Alderman

Former players gather for the opening of the new ground at Derby in 1955. (back row) Buckston, C Elliott (third row) H Elliott, G Pope, Lee, Horsley, Hutchinson, Storer, Burnham. (second row) Smith, Worthington, Copson, Skinner, Will Taylor, Watson-Smith. (front row) Sale, Richardson, Jackson, Gothard, Eggar, Vaulkhard (courtesy Derby Evening Telegraph)

(Top) May 1939 and the County Ground's new concrete stand. The bar afforded shelter from the cold winds (courtesy Derby Evening Telegraph)
(Bottom) The eve of war and after six consecutive seasons finishing in the top six Derbyshire fell to ninth in 1939. (back row) Tommy Mitchell, Albert Alderman, Sam Peters (hon, scorer), Bill Copson, Denis Smith, Stan Worthington, George Pope. (front row) Alf Pope, Harry Elliott, Robin Buckston (capt), Leslie Townsend, Bert Rhodes

The last link with the golden decade. Denis Smith as coach casts an eye over Harold Rhodes.

more misery in the coalfields than the 1921 and 1926 strikes. In Derbyshire's mining towns and villages there were few choices of employment. A town such as Ripley, for example, found its youngsters leaving school and heading for the pit, the quarry, the factory or the ironworks. Jobs with the Co-operative Society or in Butterley Company's offices were cherished. It was the most severe and protracted economic downturn experienced by the British economy since the mid-19th century. The miners remained victims of a decade of recession from 1925-35.

In the autumn of 1931 the dreaded Means Test was introduced. This was aimed at those receiving unemployment insurance beyond the statutory six months period. Claimants had to undergo a household means test carried out by the local Public Assistance Committee. Any form of income and savings were taken into account. Its debilitating effect was captured in Walter Brierley's novel *Means-Test Man*, published in 1935. Brierley came from Waingroves, a small mining village near Ripley. His father was an engine-winder at nearby Denby Hall Colliery and the family was prosperous working class. Brierley left school at 13. His mother wanted him to work at the Co-op but he followed the rest of the village boys into the pit 'not yet quietened by the persistent drag of the cramped and half-blind world of the mine ... to turn most of them into prematurely old and worn-out men.' Studies were to take him out of the mines but first he endured four years on the dole, an experience which led to his famous novel.

It describes a week in the life of an unemployed Derbyshire miner awaiting the visit of the means test man. The public assistance committee allows 25 shillings and three pence a week, six shillings of which went on rent and rates and two shillings in sick clubs. The rest provided food, clothes, coal, light and the hundred and one things which were needed in a home. On the Saturday the miner wants to take his young son to a village cricket match. His wife was aware of the cricket team but it had little significance. "But her husband going to watch the cricket club play a match was a different thing, it had significance, had to be considered." She wanted to know how much of the 25 shillings it would soak up.

"How much is it to go in?" she asked at once.

"Oh, they charge us a penny if we show our dole card. It's fourpence bi reights." He was dropping into dialect in his bitterness. "Us an' kids a penny."

There follows the shame of displaying his yellow card at the entrance, the letters WU, "wholly unemployed" in the bottom right-hand corner.

The village team is captained by the colliery manager's son, just out of college and clad in striped cap and gaudy blazer. Earlier he had complained to the committee about an unemployed miner who turned up to play in a pair of grey flannel trousers instead of whites. A spectator took exception to this. "Tellin secretary an' one a tew on 'um w'ose on t' committee nobody owt ta be picked w'o didna come togged up reight... Some a them wants a lick a' t' dole. 'E'd non come in striped get-up, then, 'e'd 'appen 'a'e a empty belly ta plee on."

Things gradually improved and GM Jackson played his part as president of many sporting, philanthropic and social organisations. He was chairman of Derbyshire Miners' Welfare Committee and the Derbyshire Coal Owners' Association. Jackson was involved in helping create the Derbyshire Miners' Welfare Holiday Centre at Skegness. The Derbyshire Miners' Association fought long and hard for improved conditions and in 1925 it bought nine acres of land at Winthorpe in Skegness, where it built a convalescent home. The 'con home' overlooked the sea and had direct access to the beach. It opened in 1928, accommodating 120 men and 30 women. Miners obtained time off for an annual holiday with money to spend. A holiday savings scheme started in 1936, enabling Derbyshire pits to close for a week in the summer with a guaranteed payment to each miner. The miners contributed savings from their pay, with the colliery owners also making a contribution. On May 20 1939 the Derbyshire Miners' Holiday Centre was officially opened at Skegness, with a capacity for 900 visitors each week. Cheap railway fares and special trains enabled the miners and their families to enjoy a week's holiday at a cost well within the family budget. The principal driving force behind the building of the camp was Harry Hicken, who had left school at the age of 12 to work underground at Pilsley Colliery. Hicken became a member of the national executive of the Miners' Federation of Great Britain, the forerunner of the National Union of Mineworkers. When Billy Butlin opened the first seaside holiday camp at Skegness in 1936, Harry Hicken wanted nothing less for the county's hard-working colliers and so the idea of a miners' holiday camp was born.

County cricket seemed a world away to the miners, with their strong allegiances to their families and the local community. A shilling admittance to the ground was a considerable outlay. Membership of a county club represented half the adult weekly wage of those who were employed and was not an option unless you belonged to the higher and middle classes. It was far cheaper and more convenient to watch the local team. Nevertheless the pilgrimage to a day's first-class cricket was made, although the journey was sometimes undertaken on foot to economise on train or bus fare.

The cricket field represented an escape from the hardship of the coal face, both for players and spectators. A summer playing for the county or in the leagues, with a possibility of a winter tour, was an ideal. Bestwick and Hutchinson never experienced international cricket but they obtained reasonable financial terms in both worlds, returning to the mines in the close season. At worst, Saturday afternoons playing soccer or cricket provided a few hours in the fresh air after the depths of the coal seams. The miners' cricketing ability was initially reflected in the local competitions.

Leagues evolved, the Alliance, Derby and District and the Derbyshire League. The latter's member clubs, mainly from the Chesterfield area, are revealing: colliery sides from Blackwell, Bolsover, Glapwell, Oxcroft, Morton, Tibshelf and Whitwell; works teams representing Butterley, Grassmoor, Pilsley and Staveley, Chesterfield itself and Clay Cross Park. On August 12 1903 the Bassetlaw and District League was founded at the Lion Hotel, Worksop. The first match was played on April 30 1904 between Whitwell and Retford and the competition – although it took its name from a parliamentary division of Nottinghamshire – actually brought together clubs from Derbyshire, Nottinghamshire, South Yorkshire and Lincolnshire, handily linked by the railways. It grew apace in the 1920s and produced a number of strong sides. During the 21 inter-war summers the championship was won every year bar one by a colliery club – Dinnington seven times, Whitwell four, Langwith two and Mansfield, Manton, Kiveton Park, Warsop Main, Bolsover and Glapwell once each, with Glapwell sharing the honours with Ollerton in 1939. The exception was Gainsborough Britannia in 1935 and then only by a narrow margin of one point. Leslie Townsend recalled several tough matches at Dinnington when he played for Derbyshire Club and Ground. "We never beat them, in fact they beat us once," he said.

Roy Genders was a league cricketer of vast experience. "Mostly colliery sides compose the Bassetlaw League and it is from these clubs that so many of the famous Derbyshire and Nottinghamshire players originate. In fact they never really leave the clubs until extreme old age compels it for the collieries find their cricketers work during the non-cricketing season and when their first-class careers are over. The young player who achieves certain success in league cricket is given every encouragement to take up the first-class game for he knows full well that he has his colliery work to fall back on if he does not make the grade, while he has a definite job to return to in the winter."

The league produced an impressive list of Test cricketers. The 1932-33 MCC party in Australia included three players who had played their early cricket in the competition, Harold Larwood, Bill Voce and Tommy Mitchell. Four years later the league was represented by Voce, Stan Worthington, Bill Copson, Kenneth Farnes, who played for Worksop while a master at the college, and Walter Robins, who occasionally turned out for Worksop. Mike Hendrick, Geoff Miller and Derek Randall maintained the tradition 40 years on.

Larwood was every inch a product of the coalfield area. He was born in the village of Nuncargate, where houses were built for the miners working at Annesley Colliery, in 1904. Larwood was soon playing for Nuncargate and at 17, after three years as a pit-boy at Annesley, he moved to the nearby Langton Colliery night shift, cleaning away dirt with a pick and shovel with a three feet clearance to work in at the coal face, laying bare the seams for the daytime workers. "Down the mine I dreamed of cricket; I bowled imaginary balls in the dark; I sent the stumps spinning and heard them rattling in the tunnels."

Joe Hardstaff senior lived at Annesley and he arranged a trial for the young fast bowler at Trent Bridge in 1923. Nottinghamshire broke him in gently, one county game in 1924, 2nd XI cricket and farming him out on Saturdays for Bassetlaw League matches with Mansfield. Two years later Larwood was helping England regain the Ashes at The Oval; the epic duels with Bradman just over the horizon. His county captain – and his first Test match skipper – Arthur Carr was illuminating on the stamina-building properties of beer in those days. "You cannot be a great fast bowler on a bottle of ginger pop or a nice glass of cold water. Your fast bowler is in much the same case as your harvester and your navvy; he uses up an immense amount of physical strength on hard out-of-doors exercise and he must have something to give him a kick. Beer is best. A pint too much may make him slightly tiddly for a little while, but only for a little while. He very quickly perspires it out of his system. When I have particularly wanted to get Larwood's tail up in order to get a quick wicket or two for Notts I have seen to it that he has not wanted for a glass of beer."

The former Warwickshire and England wicketkeeper Tiger Smith said many of the fast bowlers of his era, such as Warren and Bestwick, would have a couple of pints before play so that they could sweat freely. That way they didn't sap any energy. "But they certainly weren't boozers – they were hard, fit men doing a strong man's job."

Fast bowlers hunt best in pairs and the name of Bill Voce will forever be linked with that of Larwood. He was born three miles away from his colleague, at Annesley Woodhouse in 1909 and was working down the pit at 14. It was while playing for Annesley Colliery 2nd XI that he was recommended to Nottinghamshire by Fred Barratt and he was engaged on the ground staff in 1926, graduating to the first team through 2nd XI and the Bassetlaw League. Voce began as an orthodox slow left-arm bowler but changed to his quicker style in 1928 with marked success.

League cricket was centred on collieries and works teams, such as the Bassetlaw League and the Notts and Derbyshire Collieries League. Then, on the evening of Thursday September 25 1919, a meeting was held at the Lord Clyde Inn in Kimberley. About 40 representatives of clubs served by the tramway route which linked Ripley with Nottingham attended. It led to the formation of the Nottinghamshire and Derbyshire Border League, somewhat lower in status than the Bassetlaw League but a strong competition nonetheless. Its knock-out trophy, the Lady Readett-Bayley Cup, attracted big crowds to its August Bank Holiday Monday final. Colliery teams dominated the inter-war period, although not quite to the same extent as the Bassetlaw League. A pioneer club was the splendidly-named Derbyshire and Nottinghamshire Electric Power Company, albeit a relatively unsuccessful one.

Such leagues were a forcing ground for talented young players and by 1922, when Fred Tate was placed in charge, Derbyshire's cricket nursery was fully equipped to sift through the dozens of hopefuls eager to swap the pits for summer days at Queen's Park or the County Ground at Derby. Competition was keen. Youngsters turned up for trials and at the Easter nets; a few were taken into the nursery for a season with the hope of ascending to the staff. They played in 2nd XI friendlies against Warwickshire over the Bank Holidays and there were club and ground fixtures against public schools such as Repton, Trent College and Denstone and colliery sides. Here the nursery seedlings were put on their mettle. The public schools were usually strong and there were any number of players in the colliery teams anxious to prove themselves. Perhaps a good performance would lead to an opportunity with the county, with a chance of a match or two for the club and ground during the annual holidays.

The Seedbeds

The youngsters usually played under the leadership of Rev Henry Ellison, a tower of strength in the development programme and, as honorary secretary from 1930, in the club's administration. HRN Ellison was born at Blyth in Nottinghamshire and educated at Rugby. He was a good club cricketer with Free Foresters and Incogniti and played for Lincolnshire and later Wiltshire but he made only one appearance in first-class cricket, for Nottinghamshire against the Philadelphians in 1897. Ellison's father played against the Grace brothers; his grandson Richard, of Kent and England, appeared in eleven Tests from 1984-86. Sadly the grandfather did not live to see Richard's success and neither did Richard's father, Peter. Henry Ellison died at Elstead in Surrey nearly eleven years before Richard was born. Peter Ellison died when his son was only eight.

It was as Rector of Aston-on-Trent, a village six miles south-east of Derby, that Henry Ellison developed links with Derbyshire cricket. He captained the second team until he was 60 in 1928 and represented the county at meetings of the Advisory County Cricket Committee at Lord's. Eardley-Simpson wrote of him: "A great leader himself, he has the flair for spotting a good player almost at sight, and his advice has been even more important than his leadership on the field." Ellison also turned out for the Derbyshire Friars. Formed in 1878, it became one of the leading amateur wandering clubs in the Midlands. The Friars' fixture list included matches against schools such as Repton, Shrewsbury, Derby and Trent College and the army and similar amateur clubs. For years its home matches took place on the County Ground; today they are at Belper Meadows.

Thus the influential links were forged, the personnel put in place for the reshaping of Derbyshire cricket. Will Taylor, who also captained the second team and the club and ground on occasions, ran the club with the help of a typist; the Duke of Devonshire and a few others dipped into their pockets to help it keep afloat. Guy Jackson was emerging as one of the best young captains in England, Morton, Cadman and Bestwick seemed destined to go on for ever and Tate and Ellison looked after the youngsters. Stuart McMillan, manager of Derby County when they won the FA Cup in 1946, Richard Pratt and Colin Leech flourished for a time in the second team and made fleeting appearances in the Championship but failed to make the grade. Wilfred Carter and Leslie Townsend made more of a mark, Townsend particularly so.

Chapter 21
The Harvest

IN the 1922 season, Guy Jackson's first as captain, Derbyshire won six matches – all over counties below them – and finished in eleventh place. Morton took a hundred wickets and Bestwick's contribution was 92 at 17. It was on Whit Monday at Derby in the match against Warwickshire that the celebrated occurrence of Bestwick and his son Bob bowling for six overs to William Quaife and his son Bernard took place. WG Quaife made 3,188 runs against Derbyshire, more than any other batsman, 107 of them in this innings, which was ended by Bob Bestwick.

The new skipper's tentative steps into captaincy found firmer ground in 1923. His team was strengthened by the return of Jim Horsley after three seasons of league cricket and the availability of WW Hill-Wood. Four matches, Warwickshire at Edgbaston, Leicestershire at Ashby-de-la-Zouch and Northamptonshire and Glamorgan at Chesterfield – were won and tenth place achieved. But the last six games passed without a victory and the trend continued into 1924. By the end of the season Derbyshire were back where they had been four years earlier, in bottom place, without a single win in 24 fixtures, 13 of which were lost. It was a wet summer and the cricket sometimes matched the weather. The 1925 campaign started with three defeats and it was not until June 5 that a win was recorded when Worcestershire were beaten by 212 runs at Stourbridge. During the period, July 27 1923 to June 5 1925, Derbyshire had gone 36 matches without a win, 35 of them in the Championship. There had to be change. Bill Bestwick was 50, Sam Cadman 48 and Arthur Morton 42. It was beginning to show and in the field Derbyshire sometimes looked heavy-footed. Opposing batsmen took note. They could not take chances against Hutchinson in the covers but they knew there were runs elsewhere. Soon all three had gone, Bestwick to Neath, Cadman to take charge of the nursery and Morton to don an umpire's coat. Jim Horsley also left and the search began for replacements.

Cadman found a nursery brimming with promise but seasoned pros were needed. Garnet Lee, a hard hitting batsman and leg spin bowler who had been released by Nottinghamshire, joined the club at the age of 38 in 1925 to add experience and quality. Archie Slater, a batsman and medium-paced off-break bowler, returned in 1927. Slater was a fine all-rounder and but for the lure of league cricket and the loss of four seasons to the war, might have reached Test match standard. At 36 his best years were gone but he made an immediate impact. For all their ability, Lee and Slater represented the relative short term. To progress Derbyshire needed young talent to flourish under Jackson's leadership, alongside the more experienced Elliott, Hutchinson, Lee, Slater, Bowden and the developing Harry Storer.

Leslie Townsend and Stan Worthington, had emerged, however, and through this period of transition Derbyshire's form was respectable. They finished the 1925 season with five victories – Worcestershire (twice), Essex, Somerset and Glamorgan – and three counties below them in the Championship. In 1926 ten matches passed without a win, including Cadman's final appearance when he turned out against Kent at Chatham. On June 29, Derbyshire were last in the table after an innings defeat at Bath at the start of their three-match western tour. The next fixture, against Gloucestershire at Bristol, ended the drought. Then Somerset were beaten at Derby, a weakened Yorkshire made to follow on at Sheffield and the double achieved over Worcestershire. An innings success over Northamptonshire at Chesterfield ensured respectability with five victories and eleventh place in the table.

Storer, Bowden and Lee each exceeded a thousand Championship runs. Worthington took 56 wickets in 746 overs, followed by Morton (49 in his final season), Storer (41), Lee (40) and Townsend (38). Critics noted Worthington's improvement as a batsman during the last six weeks of the season and Storer's all-round ability. "The nursery, which is in the hands of Cadman, has been largely responsible for the all-round improvement this year, and as there is some promising young talent, Derbyshire's prospects next season should be even better," said *The Cricketer*.

Hopes were high in 1927 but results exceeded all expectations. Notice was served in the opening game of the season at Chatham. Kent were set 391 to win in four-and-a-half hours and Woolley led the chase with 187. Worthington, Slater and Townsend each took three wickets and Derbyshire were home by 64 runs – their first win over Kent since 1881. Lancashire were then given a fright at Ilkeston. Needing 106 to win in an hour, they were reduced by Townsend to 68 for seven in 19 overs when the game ended. Kent avenged their defeat by winning at Derby at the end of May when the home side had the worst of the pitch but high summer brought riches aplenty. Ten matches passed without a defeat, albeit four affected by rain, and four were won. The biggest disappointment was at the end of June when Derbyshire, third in the table, threw down the gauntlet at Old Trafford. Only 25 minutes play was possible, during which Derbyshire reached 28 without loss.

Defeat at Leicester ended the sequence but three consecutive victories carried Derbyshire into third place, behind Nottinghamshire and Lancashire with Yorkshire fourth by the first week of August. Warwickshire had been beaten in a thrilling finish at Derby and a prodigious all-round performance by Garnet Lee, 100 not out, five for 65 and seven for 78 for a match analysis of 77-27-143-12, set up a comfortable victory at Northampton. Crucially, however, Derbyshire failed to win any of their last five Championship matches, although there were two honourable draws against Yorkshire and one at Trent Bridge.

Nevertheless the Championship could still be won as the season entered its closing stage. With two games remaining, Nottinghamshire headed the table, followed by Lancashire and Derbyshire, who each had one game left. If Nottinghamshire won their final two games the title was theirs, even if Lancashire gained a victory. Nottinghamshire and Lancashire could tie for top position but if they each lost their fixtures then Derbyshire could be champions. So Nottinghamshire's penultimate game at Ilkeston – Derbyshire's last of the season – was vital. Nottinghamshire were without Larwood and Carr but managed to dismiss the home side for 141 on the Saturday. When bad light stopped play Nottinghamshire were 78 for three and on Monday they placed themselves in an impregnable position. A century by Wilfred Payton laid the foundations of a total of 353. Derbyshire, 212 in arrears, had made 107 for four by the close. Storer took his score to 106 on Tuesday, adding 84 for the sixth wicket with Worthington. By lunch they were 253 for nine and Sam Staples took the final wicket in the second over after the break to return figures of five for 83. Needing only 47, Nottinghamshire lost George Gunn to the first ball of the innings, bowled by Shardlow, but they knocked off the runs with ease.

Lancashire could only draw at Leicester so Nottinghamshire travelled to Swansea needing only to avoid defeat to take the title. Chickens were counted and a civic reception booked to greet the homecoming champions. It was hastily cancelled, Glamorgan gaining their only victory of the season, leaving Lancashire as champions, Nottinghamshire runners-up and Yorkshire third. Kent were fourth. Derbyshire finished fifth with eight victories and three defeats from 24 scheduled games. Surrey came sixth, Middlesex, the odd one out of the Big Six, having to be content with ninth.

Only 15 players appeared in the competition for Derbyshire in 1927. Three made fleeting appearances so the team was virtually picked from twelve men – Storer, Bowden, Slater, GR Jackson, Lee, Hutchinson, Worthington, Townsend, Elliott and Shardlow, with the final place going to Anthony Jackson or another amateur, EF Loney. Nobody reached a thousand Championship runs or took one hundred wickets. Slater, 941 and Lee 72, were the leaders, and there was no genuine fast bowler, Shardlow, aiming to fill Bestwick's shoes, was not helped by the soft pitches in a wet summer. However, the side possessed five genuine all-rounders in Lee, Townsend, Slater, Worthington and Storer and, with the veterans gone, it was much sharper in the field. Hutchinson was outstanding at cover, fielding so brilliantly that Jackson, normally excellent in that position, posted himself regularly at mid-on. *Wisden* described them as almost without superiors in the field, citing Guy Jackson, Hutchinson, Storer, a fine slip and Elliott as examples. *The Cricketer* described it as "a young side, with a fine fielding record, inspired by a keen and popular captain." Although Jackson and Townsend were given recognition in Test trials, it was the 22-year-old Worthington who attracted the most attention from the magazine. "Worthington is a cricketer of future possibilities. Blessed with a rare physique he is one of the best natural hitters in the country and his fast-medium deliveries will be more effective in a dry season, as he comes quickly off the pitch."

Nevertheless some thought it all a flash in the pan and 1928 brought knowing nods. Six wins and six losses left Derbyshire tenth. Individually, there was no falling-off. Jackson was said to have eight professionals, of whom six could bowl. Their table manners must have been improving, too, for 1928 marks a point when Derbyshire were becoming socially acceptable again. Sussex were added to the fixture list and visits to Lord's for a match against MCC and to Oxford, where Neville Ford and two of the Hill-Woods were Blues, were milestones. Worthington made 101 against MCC and returned to Lord's ten days later when he appeared for The Rest against England in a Test trial. A year later Derbyshire met Middlesex for their first-ever Championship match at Lord's. Middlesex usually arranged fewer games than some of the other counties and Leicestershire and, to an extent, Warwickshire, had also been out in the cold. GR Jackson, Storer, Lee, Slater, NM Ford, Worthington, Hutchinson, Townsend, CK Hill-Wood, Elliott and Mitchell formed the team which made history, nearly 59 years after the formation of the club.

Chapter 22
Best of Enemies

TOMMY MITCHELL'S sorcery added a cutting edge to a Derbyshire bowling attack that had been accurate, steady and persevering but lacked bite.

Benefits were reaped in 1929. Lancashire won the opening game, Mitchell taking five for 34 in their first innings but being outbowled by Richard Tyldesley who captured twelve wickets in the match. After rain deprived them of a probable victory at Leicester, Derbyshire gained handsome wins at Portsmouth and Edgbaston. Mitchell's haul in the two games was 21 and the county found itself among the front-runners in the Championship table, in third place behind Lancashire and Nottinghamshire.

It was merely the hors-d'oeuvre. There was frustration at Ilkeston when Northamptonshire, set 305, had lost half their side for 117 at tea on the last day. Rain caused a delay and Derbyshire claimed the extra half-hour but the visitors, 174 for eight, escaped with a draw. Derbyshire then embarked on a surge unprecedented in their history. Storer made 119 and 100 and Worthington took a career-best eight for 29 as Sussex were beaten at Derby. Derbyshire, with three wins in six games, now headed the Championship from Kent and Middlesex. It delighted their followers, who did not now require a degree in mathematics to work out the positions in 1929. Every county played 28 three-day matches, which eliminated the need for percentages.

Hampshire were seen off in two days and with an innings to spare at Chesterfield and eleven wickets in the match by Mitchell set up another innings victory, this time over Somerset at Burton-on-Trent. It was their third consecutive victory and the fifth in a sequence of six matches. Derbyshire now had 50 points from eight matches, two ahead of Lancashire, with Middlesex, 37 from six, in third place.

There was a break from the Championship programme when the South Africans visited Derby for a rain-ruined fixture. The county resumed the campaign with a 116-run win over Worcestershire at Stourbridge. It carried the run to four consecutive Championship victories and six in seven, enabling them to regain the first place they had lost during the South African game. The sequence was maintained in less demanding circumstances when Oxford University were defeated by seven wickets and for three heady weeks until the middle of June Derbyshire were in pole position apart from one Saturday when Lancashire led by a single point.

Consequently Kent's arrival in Chesterfield on Saturday June 22 1929 aroused massive interest. Derbyshire began well, 96 for two at lunch, but Freeman took over in the afternoon and they were all out for 202. Kent then began to establish an impregnable position as Hardinge and Woolley took the score to 170 with only one wicket down by the close. The second wicket partnership reached 255 on Monday, both batsmen making centuries, and Kent, 442 all out, piled up a lead of 240. Mitchell's four wickets cost him 159 runs, Townsend taking three for 107. By the close of the second day Derbyshire had lost seven wickets for 123 and went down to an innings defeat early on the third morning. Freeman set Mitchell's figures in perspective with 14 wickets for 180 in the match – but then he did not have to bowl to Frank Woolley.

The upstarts had been put firmly in their place by one of the Big Six. It was a reverse but Derbyshire had recovered well by the following Saturday. Harry Storer and Joe Bowden created a record with an opening partnership of 322 against Essex at Derby. Storer hit 29 fours in his 209, made in four hours, and he slapped his pads with his bat in annoyance when he was bowled. Uncle William's career-best was 216 and the nephew had aimed for a new family record. Bowden went on to make 120, Derbyshire declared at 418-4 and forced Essex to follow-on but the match was drawn. Worcestershire were beaten at Ilkeston and there was a win at Bath to revive hopes. On July 20, Gloucestershire led the table with 100 points from 17 matches. Kent had 93 from 17 and Derbyshire and Nottinghamshire 87 from 15.

It was an open race, but Derbyshire failed to win any of their next seven games and fell away, finishing seventh with 10 wins and 133 points in 28 games. It was still cause for celebration. Storer headed the batting averages with 1,532 runs (36.47) and in all first-class matches for the club 1,652, only 64 behind LG Wright's then record aggregate of 1,716. Lee, Worthington and Jackson also topped the thousand in all games. Slater had a fine, all-round summer with 876 Championship runs and 81 wickets and Worthington was not far from the double with 1,031 runs and 89 wickets in all county games. Townsend, who in all first-class cricket in 1928 had completed the double, sent down 1056 overs in the Championship and captured 91 wickets at 20.52, reaching 100 in all games. Elliott's 71 victims were five short of Humphries' 1906 county wicketkeeping record.

Storer had honed his game to a high level. Determination and combativeness allied to a thoroughly good style of play – he was a particularly fine cutter – had, by 1929, raised him almost into the front rank of professional opening batsmen. The local derby clashes with Nottinghamshire generally brought out the best in him. For decades these had been one-sided but in the 1920s the gap was narrowing. The fixtures developed a pattern, mainly in July and August, coinciding with colliery or factory holidays. It was Nottinghamshire who took up the baton as it fell from Derbyshire's grasp in 1929. They had not won the Championship since 1907 although consistency had been their hallmark throughout the decade: runners-up in 1922, 1923 and 1927 and third in 1928.

Derbyshire, spent as contenders, entered the equation. The rivalry was becoming intense, fanned by that between the soccer clubs, Nottingham Forest and Derby County. Between the end of the 1914-18 war and 1969 there were only four seasons when the Rams and Forest were in the same division, the old second. The Clough-Taylor era awakened allegiances that had slumbered in the Erewash Valley and along the A52, roused briefly only by a handful of league meetings and wartime games. There had also been the FA Cup fourth round ties in 1936, won by Derby, and in 1928, when Forest were the victors in a replay after a draw on a Baseball Ground quagmire. Here a personal interest should be declared. Among the 60,000 people who saw the 1928 matches was my father. He had known Harry Storer from his schooldays, although Storer had been a closer friend of an elder brother who was killed in the war. Consequently a great deal of satisfaction was obtained by Derbyshire's followers, my father included, when the county visited Trent Bridge in August 1929.

Echoes of the cup defeat and disappointment over the failure of the Championship challenge were assuaged to some degree as Derbyshire dealt the Nottinghamshire attack a fearful hiding. Storer (176 in five hours 40 minutes, hitting 20 fours) helped his team to 457-8 declared. Nottinghamshire averted the follow on with four wickets in hand, crawling to 353 all out in 182.5 overs.

Nottinghamshire went into their final fixture of 1929 at Ilkeston in almost the same situation as the Glamorgan match of two years earlier. If they avoided defeat they would win the Championship. They began on Saturday with extreme caution. Rain caused only 95 minutes play to be possible and the visitors were 40 for the loss of George Gunn at the close. Around 9,000 spectators packed the ground on Monday and watched Nottinghamshire struggle to 175 in 113.4 overs. When Derbyshire batted, Lee made 45 out of 49 in three-quarters of an hour before Voce uprooted his off stump but they held the advantage at 114 for one when play ended for the day, only 61 behind. The headlines proclaimed: 'Notts Falter in Crisis. Wickets fall steadily at Ilkeston. Derbyshire rapidly catching up'. In short, Derbyshire could not win the title but they could prevent their neighbours from doing so. Everything changed on Tuesday. Rain fell until three o'clock at Ilkeston – and news filtered through that Yorkshire were unlikely to beat Sussex at Hove in their final match. Thus Nottinghamshire were sure of the Championship. In the event Yorkshire lost and Nottinghamshire finished the season with 158 points, winning 14 of their 28 matches and losing two. Lancashire and Yorkshire each had 148, while Gloucestershire, with more wins, 15, than anybody else, and Sussex 145.

Derbyshire could claim that had had the better of their two matches against the champions in 1929. But in 70 first-class matches they had defeated their neighbours on only five occasions and only once, in 1921, since the war had ended.

Chapter 23
A New Era

ARTHUR Richardson's first move after his appointment as county captain at the end of the 1930 season was to take stock. To some extent, Guy Jackson's last year at the helm was a minor disappointment. It began full of hope that the achievements of the previous year could be repeated. Instead there was a decline, seven wins, eight losses in 28 games and ninth place in the table, two places lower than 1929. Nevertheless, some of the highlights indicated the progress made under Jackson's leadership. Sussex were routed by an innings at Derby which put the club in good heart for the Australians' arrival at Chesterfield.

At that point of the tour Don Bradman, on his first visit, had scored 626 runs, average 125, of the thousand he was to make in May so even this early in the season the Derbyshire bowlers had no illusions about what awaited them. His first impression was with the ball, dismissing Storer for 65 as Derbyshire reached 215, Worthington top-scoring with 79.

Bradman began batting at 127-1 in decidedly unpleasant conditions. The light was poor, there was drizzle about and almost immediately he was struck on the left thigh by a ball from Worthington which restricted his movements for a while. Ponsford made 131 before Bradman was caught by Elliott off Worthington for 44.

After the Australian fixture there was a surprise when Derbyshire suffered an eight-run defeat by Northamptonshire, the eventual wooden spoonists, at Derby. This was followed by a tremendous victory over Kent, fifth in 1930, at Ilkeston. Next came a landmark win over Middlesex at Burton-on-Trent, Derbyshire's first over the Londoners. Hendren and Hearne were absent at the Test trial, as was Worthington, and Middlesex had a dreadful summer but it still represented two consecutive victories over Big Six counties. But Derbyshire's final ten games passed without a victory

Storer, who headed the averages for the fourth time in the past five years, Townsend and Jackson exceeded a thousand Championship runs and Smith was only 25 short. Bowden's age and loss of form – he retired at the end of the season – had opened the way for Smith. Early in the season, Lee had been promoted from his usual first wicket down to open with Storer, Bowden dropping to No 3. It was not a success, Lee's desire to get after the bowling costing him his wicket on several occasions. Bowden lost his place to Smith, who took over the opener's spot in July, Lee reverting to first wicket down.

Richardson found that the cost of running the club in 1930 was heading for £8,000 and this did not include the nursery. Membership had risen by 200 to 2,300, the highest between the wars. Subscriptions brought in £3,323 and some 70,000 paying spectators produced gate receipts of £3326. Worries were eased by a £,1285 share of Test match receipts, enabling a profit of £378 to be returned. The accounts had shown results on the right side only in 1921 and 1930 since the war, both in the years of an Australian visit. The nursery fund was kept separate from the club's general accounts but year after year, despite donations from people such as Major Christopher Lowther, it struggled to meet the £500 needed to keep going.

Richardson spoke warmly of Guy Jackson. In a 1971 interview with Gerald Mortimer in the *Derby Evening Telegraph*, he said: "I do not think Derbyshire cricket would have existed had it not been for him. He took over a wreck. By the time I became captain Derbyshire were a good side and we had young players coming on. GR, Harry Storer and Harry Elliott – those were the three rocks around which Derbyshire cricket was built."

Nevertheless, in its review of the 1930 season the *Derby Daily Telegraph* sounded a warning. "One thing, however, is certain. If the club is ever to rise to the top of the Championship table new batsmen and new bowlers must be found." Members and the cricket writers were beginning to lose patience with what was perceived as underachievement. For the 1931 season, Richardson had the support of Cadman as coach and a first-class senior professional and wicketkeeper in Elliott, his skills undiminished at 40. The batting was unreliable. Too much depended on Storer, theoretically with years of good cricket left but his career soon to be curtailed due to soccer managerial commitments.

Townsend, at 27, was one of the country's leading all-rounders, already an England player and with his best years ahead. Smith had emerged as a left-handed batsman but Hutchinson's form was in decline and although Lee remained capable of making a thousand runs, age – he was 43 – was against him. Alderman, despite an extended run in 1930, was having difficulty in establishing himself. The bowling was balanced but lacked pace. Mitchell's leg-breaks were the cutting edge, with Townsend in support. Slater and Worthington had used the new ball in 1930 and would do so again in 1931. Slater still had days when he could destroy a side – at Chesterfield in 1930 he had taken three wickets in four balls in returning seven for 31 and seven for 17 against Somerset – but he had turned 40.

The biggest enigma was Worthington. His career seemed to be in regression at that time, with concern that at 25 he might fall between two stools. Fifty-eight wickets in 1930 cost 29 apiece; the player who had twice exceeded a thousand runs in a season failed to score a hundred for his county in 1929, 1930 and 1931, his average hovering around twenty. Only in the field did he escape criticism, with an ability to hold more than 20 close-to-the-wicket catches each summer and deliver some 700 overs.

Wet pitches dulled his stroke play, the local press saying he spoiled his batting by over-concentration on defence and on on-side strokes. "A batsman of his build and natural driving power should aim at splintering the pavilion rails." Hindsight points to a period of transition; contemporary opinion was expressed out of frustration.

Richardson faced a challenge. Not only had he to follow a respected and popular captain but there was the matter of replacing Jackson's thousand runs per season to be considered. Storer, Lee and Townsend could each virtually guarantee such a figure in 1931; Smith, too, probably and, possibly Worthington. Hutchinson and Alderman, at extreme poles in their careers, had much to prove. The bowling attack – Slater, Worthington, Mitchell and Townsend with Lee and Storer in support was adequate. Slater and Elliott would also provide useful runs. It was an experienced dressing room and it could be an outspoken one, too, but there would be no challenge to the skipper's authority. Derbyshire's captains possessed the power to bring to an end the career of a professional. All of the pros realised that it was in their best interests to play in the style the captain wanted. Charlie Elliott recalled that a professional who disputed the decision of an umpire on the field was immediately told by his captain that he would never play for Derbyshire again if he repeated such behaviour. In practice, Richardson – the players referred to him as Mr or sometimes Skipper – seldom had cause to use his full authority, his enthusiasm and warm personality earning support from his team. The captain then turned his attention to the practice facilities. He took Townsend and the groundsman Harry Williams to his family's Eagle Street works and asked Townsend if he could fix up an indoor net inside a large empty warehouse. Thus Derbyshire became one of the few counties to have the equivalent of an indoor school. It was used until the remaining part of the works moved to Sinfin.

So, in 1931, the new era began with a match against Leicestershire at the County Ground. It was a tedious, drawn match, Leicestershire toiling to 216 in 141.4 overs and Derbyshire responding with 224 in 127.4, typical of the slow scoring which occurred in some of the matches in that era. Although the tempo of the game generally was quicker, with the rate of overs per hour considerably higher than in modern times, run rates could be tardy. It is to Richardson's credit that Derbyshire began to score at a faster pace, always allowing that the batting became much more powerful than in Jackson's day.

In 1931 Derbyshire did not register a victory until their eighth game, when Sussex were beaten by an innings at Chesterfield under Gilbert's captaincy. After the home side had made 343 Mitchell wove his spells. He took six for 11 in Sussex's first innings of 67 and six for 19 in their second attempt, which produced 88. Match figures of 20.4-7-30-12 included the dismissal of Duleepsinhji for six and eight on the second day, stumped and then caught by Elliott. Richardson was back in charge for the second win of the summer, by eight wickets over Hampshire, also at Queen's Park, where Smith made a century. It was part of a seven-week run of a dozen undefeated matches, ending at Hove early in July.

Seven of the 28 fixtures were won – Sussex, Worcestershire and Glamorgan, with doubles over Hampshire and Northamptonshire – and seventh place attained in the Championship table. For the only time between the wars no matches against Yorkshire were arranged. There was a close tussle at Blackpool, where Slater and Worthington bowled their side to a first innings lead of 107. Richard Tyldesley destroyed Derbyshire's second innings and Lancashire needed 173 to win. Three wickets fell for 31 before Charlie Hallows and Ernest Tyldesley added 53 for the fourth wicket. At 69 Elliott believed Hallows had been bowled when the bails were dislodged. He appealed but Dolphin at the bowler's end was unsighted and the square leg umpire Buswell could not say definitely what had happened. Hallows claimed the ball rebounded from the wicketkeeper's pads and neither umpire would give him out. He went on to make 74 and Lancashire got home by three wickets.

Storer, lost to soccer after August Bank Holiday, Lee and Smith each scored more than a thousand Championship runs and Alderman did well. Lee made three hundreds, Smith two and Alderman and Storer one apiece. But Townsend, average 21, Worthington (19) and Hutchinson (16) fell far below expectations. Richardson missed only one game but never got beyond 49 and averaged 13. Slater took 106 wickets at 16 each, Mitchell 105 at 21, Townsend 72 at 15 and Worthington 57 at 24. Elliott had a magnificent year, sharing in the dismissal of 75 batsmen, 45 caught and 30 stumped.

As for Richardson he earned praise from the *Derby Daily Telegraph*. "The young captain made no mistakes, he did a number of clever things and he came through the ordeal of his first season's captaincy with flying colours." Already he was warming to the task of assessing the diverse personalities in the squad and getting the best performances out of them. Certainly a few mutterings about an amateur figurehead, with Elliott making the on-field decisions, proved unfounded.

It was Slater's last season. Although he had just enjoyed his best-ever year with the ball he saw his future with Colne in the league. Another to go was Hutchinson, who was not retained after 1931. Two lean seasons did for him and his future lay in the mines, mainly in South Yorkshire. During the winters he had returned to the pits and they now became his full-time occupation. He was involved in opening a new colliery at Markham Main and later became safety manager at Hickleton Main. Hutchinson skippered the colliery team in the Yorkshire Council. Hutchinson and Slater had played significant roles in Derbyshire's revival but their day was over. Storer would continue for several years but his priority now was soccer duties at Highfield Road, increasingly reducing the time and energy he could devote to cricket.

Now hopes rested on promising youngsters such as Tommy Armstrong, Charlie Elliott and Alfred Pope.

Chapter 24
Whistling down a Mine Shaft

ONCE again Derbyshire entered a period of change. The loss of Slater's bowling left a gap, particularly on hard pitches. It seemed unlikely that he would be adequately replaced in 1932 and possibly in the following year. Cricket writers speculated that Townsend might fill the role, opening the attack with his medium-pace off-breaks. But it was Alf Pope who shared the new ball with Worthington when the 1932 season began at Old Trafford.

The dilemma over the opening attack was soon trivialised by the weather. The match at Old Trafford was lost but Warwickshire were beaten at Derby and there was a comfortable victory at Northampton, where Mitchell took thirteen for 98 in the game. Here, Arthur Richardson became ill, Harry Elliott taking over the captaincy for the second and third days. Heavy rain then swamped the county over the weekend. On Sunday May 22 1932 the town centre was awash with the worst floods Derby had known since 1842. After 36 hours of torrential rain the Markeaton Brook gave up the ghost. It became too full for the culvert that took it under the streets and the water welled up, rapidly turning the centre into a Venetian scene. "Torrents tear up roads and wreck homes and shops" said the *Derby Evening Telegraph* headlines. On Sunday evening the swollen Derwent overflowed and the County Ground became a victim of the floods.

The rain played havoc with the cricket. The Yorkshire fixture at Chesterfield, for which Jackson was named as Richardson's deputy, was abandoned without a ball being bowled. Gilbert was skipper against Kent at Ilkeston but play was possible only on the middle day, Thursday. The Sussex match, due to begin at Derby, was transferred to Chesterfield but more rain caused its abandonment without a ball being bowled. Of nine scheduled days from three consecutive home matches, play had been possible on only one day. It was a serious blow to hard-pressed finances.

When the season got under way again Nottinghamshire won by an innings at Trent Bridge, where Jackson took over the captaincy from Gilbert. Richardson returned for the eighth fixture of the season, which Hampshire won by two wickets at Chesterfield. Worthington and Townsend had opened the bowling but the new ball problem was to be solved by the emergence of Bill Copson at The Oval, Southampton and Tonbridge, although despite his success all three matches were lost – five consecutive defeats.

At least, the skipper had found his fast bowler and was also on the way to solving another problem – his own lack of form with the bat. Despite some dogged performances his career average at the start of the 1932 season was around 17. More runs were needed from the captain of a team in which runs were often at a premium. He dealt with the difficulty by leading from the front. An answer had to be found to the question posed by Storer's late starts and early finishes to the cricket season. It was Richardson who provided the solution by opening the innings himself. Initially the returns were modest; a few 30s and 40s but enough to justify the experiment. Storer did well at Queen's Park, where the Leicestershire match was drawn to halt the run of defeats, and then made 170 against Middlesex at Derby. Here he shared a fourth-wicket partnership of 209 with Smith (107 not out) after Derbyshire, following on, looked to be heading for defeat. It was in this match that Copson came up against two more batsmen of high quality after bowling to Hobbs, Mead and Woolley. At Derby, Jack Hearne and Patsy Hendren each made centuries, Copson returning a respectable three for 66 in the total of 404.

Seven weeks, encompassing ten scheduled matches, had passed since Derbyshire had won. A draw with Middlesex was no disgrace, for anything positive against a member of the elite was a rarity. Kent, Middlesex and Surrey were beaten in 1930 but Lancashire and Yorkshire remained impregnable as far as Derbyshire were concerned and, so, too, were Nottinghamshire.

Against this background, Nottinghamshire made the journey across the Erewash for the annual match at Ilkeston. At the time of their arrival at the Rutland Recreation ground, on Saturday June 25 1932, they were well within striking distance of the leaders, Kent and Yorkshire. It was the summer in which Larwood and Voce, shrewdly handled by Carr, unleashed their fury on county batsmen. Larwood took 141 Championship wickets and Voce 106. Film exists of the matches with Derbyshire and Hampshire at Trent Bridge which show the pair operating to orthodox fields, sometimes with a couple of short-legs and a few batsmen backing away from Larwood's shorter deliveries. As the season drew to a close they gave an airing to what became bodyline the following winter.

The planning came to a head in the famous get-together in the grill-room of the Piccadilly Hotel, when the England captain Douglas Jardine, Carr, Larwood and Voce exchanged views. This was during the Surrey v Nottinghamshire match at The Oval during the August Bank Holiday of 1932. Jardine had been made aware of Bradman's discomfort against Larwood when the pitch turned spiteful in the final Test of the 1930 series.

The idea grew. Frank Foster was consulted about his 1911-12 series field-settings for sharp left-arm in-swing and it was clearly in Jardine's mind when he captained Surrey at Queen's Park, Chesterfield a month before the grill-room meeting. William Richardson said Jardine discussed it with his father. "Jardine was a Wykehamist, like my father and when Surrey played at Queen's Park he stayed with him. They talked about the tactics. If bodyline was not exactly hatched in the sitting room of my father's home it was certainly discussed."

Crucially the Notts' expresses missed the Ilkeston match which gave Derbyshire their first victory over their neighbours in 11 years. Voce was playing in the Test match against India at Lord's and Larwood was injured. Nottinghamshire's followers were left to rue several chances which went down in the slips and might have changed the complexion of the game which ended in a seven wicket victory for the home side, restoring local bragging rights. Fifteen matches followed the Ilkeston fixture and only two – against Lancashire at Buxton and Yorkshire at Headingley – were lost. Four were won; Essex and Northamptonshire each by an innings at Chesterfield, India at Ilkeston and Leicestershire at Ashby-de-Zouch.

Richardson finished the season with 1,258 runs, average 29.95, and opened the batting in 39 of his 44 innings. He had broken the barrier of a thousand runs in a season and although it was to be the only season in which he completed a four figure aggregate, it erased any lingering doubts about his quality. Smith, Worthington and Townsend also reached the target and Lee was not far away. Storer made only nine Championship appearances but scored 538 runs (average 41.38). The downside was that Alderman and Charlie Elliott had little to show from extended trials.

It was the bowling which gave the most cause for optimism. Mitchell finished with 121 wickets for the county at 21.17, 111 in the Championship and was selected for the 1932-33 tour. Townsend completed the double by taking 104 wickets in the Championship. Worthington also produced some sterling all-round performances: 26 Championship matches, 1232 runs and, in 686 overs, 53 wickets at 28.73. As the younger bowlers developed and offered Richardson more options, so the reliance on Worthington would decrease. Suffice it to say that in 1932 the all-round contributions of Townsend and Worthington were essential to the balance of the side. And what of these younger prospects? Copson made 17 Championship appearances, taking 46 wickets from 554.5 overs at 26.76 each. Alf Pope had fewer opportunities but returned similar figures; 12 matches, 25 wickets at 24.40. The jury was still out on both of them but the signs were good.

Six victories in 28 Championship matches, eight defeats, tenth place in the final table and a continuing cash crisis aggravated by the weather and the nation's economic crisis. But that significant victory at Ilkeston served notice of things to come.

Chapter 25
Into the Big Six

TOMMY MITCHELL returned to Derbyshire's dressing room in 1933 to find colleagues anxious to hear a first-hand account of the bodyline series.

The county's other involvement was political. The furore got as far as the Dominions Office, where Derby's MP JH (Jimmy) Thomas was Secretary of State. In February 1933 an MCC deputation met Thomas, who had little interest in cricket, to discuss the bodyline crisis. Although it was played down publicly – official interference was denied – there is little doubt that the Government was concerned about the possible effects on trade and Empire relations. A few months later Thomas attended a farewell lunch at Claridge's for Sir Julien Cahn's private cricket team which was leaving for Canada. "No politics ever introduced in the British Empire caused me so much trouble as this damn bodyline bowling," he said.

Although bodyline was a talking-point for a time in Derby it was quickly placed into the background. The county greeted the 1933 season with much optimism. There was a change once again in the method of deciding the County Championship with a reversion back to percentages.

Each county had to play a minimum of 24 matches to qualify, although more could be arranged, hence the need for percentages. Fifteen points were awarded for a win, five for first innings lead in a drawn game and three for first innings lost. In a match where no result was reached on the first innings each side received four points. The county obtaining the greatest number of points on a percentage basis would be champions.

The system was to be used from 1933 to 1937 inclusive. Derbyshire arranged home and away matches with 14 counties, Glamorgan and Surrey not being met. Of the home games six were played at Chesterfield, four at Derby, three at Ilkeston and one at Buxton, with the match against the West Indians at Derby.

There was some grumbling among members over the lack of quality teams allocated to Derby. Yorkshire at Chesterfield, Nottinghamshire at Ilkeston and Lancashire at Buxton reflected proximity to county borders but the main tourists were seldom seen in Derby. The Australians paid four consecutive visits to Chesterfield from 1926-38 and the 1935 South Africans went to Ilkeston. The County Ground had to make do with West Indians and New Zealanders and, in 1936, the Indians, all of whom were taking tentative steps into Test cricket. The Warwickshire match alternating over the Bank Holidays was usually the principal attraction at Derby. The reasons were purely financial, gate receipts being higher elsewhere. Derby retained its quota between the wars only because most of the membership lived in its area.

The 1933 fixtures could not have thrown up a tougher start. For the opening match at Hull, Yorkshire, the reigning champions, fielded ten players who had appeared in Test cricket, and won by six wickets in a match which yielded only 260 runs.

It was a bad start but defeat by Yorkshire in a dogfight on their home ground was no cause for alarm. Three consecutive victories over Somerset at Ilkeston, Kent at Derby and Leicestershire at Chesterfield were gained despite the absence of Richardson, who was ill. Clarke deputised in two of these games and Jackson in the Kent match. Richardson was back at Portsmouth in which Derbyshire escaped with a draw after a dramatic batting collapse in their first innings. From 41 for the loss of one wicket they subsided to 47 all out, nine wickets going down for six runs.

There was a fourth victory by June 2 with Essex routed by eight wickets at Derby. They made two respectable totals: 283 and 306, but Derbyshire piled up 455 in their first innings, Richardson declaring with seven wickets down. Storer hit 20 fours in his 232 in five hours, thus becoming the first Derbyshire batsman to make two double centuries. He had to cope with some leg-theory sent down by Stan Nicholls, who opened England's bowling against West Indies at The Oval that year. The fast bowler posted five men in a packed leg-side field but it made little difference to Storer. He maintained his form with 94 and 70 at Edgbaston but an improving Warwickshire side won by eight wickets and despite a battling performance at Worcester, Derbyshire had to be content with the worst end of a draw.

Eight matches, four wins, two defeats and a couple of draws. It was satisfactory and they were not too far away from the leaders. For a week or two Lancashire matched the pace but on May 23 Yorkshire forged ahead, butchering their rivals in the Old Trafford match at Whitsuntide. As Derbyshire made the short trip to Loughborough for their match against lowly Leicestershire, which began on Saturday June 10 1933, they could reflect that Yorkshire already had what seemed an unassailable lead. They had won seven of their eight matches and taken maximum first innings points from the other one. Nobody could cope with this and in the event nobody did. Sussex chased them but after June 27 the positions never altered; Yorkshire first and Sussex second. Essex and Kent had a rare tussle for third place, Kent's form in August proving decisive and Lancashire ended fifth.

It was at Loughborough where, in Richardson's absence, Harry Elliott captained an all-professional Derbyshire team. The only amateur present was Leicestershire's captain, E W Dawson, and Elliott, a former coal miner and veteran professional cricketer, accompanied his opposite number, an old Etonian, Light Blue and a batsman who had played Test cricket and for the Gentlemen, to toss for innings. Elliott and Dawson had been in Stanyforth's MCC party in South Africa in 1927-28 and made their debuts for England in the same match, the fifth Test at Durban. Elliott returned home on the Union Castle but Dawson stayed behind, having become engaged to be married while on the tour. Then in 1929-30 Dawson was a colleague of Worthington's on the 1929-30 visit to Australia and New Zealand so he was known to the Derbyshire team outside of the occasions they had met in Championship matches.

At Loughborough Town Ground – which had relatively short boundaries – Dawson won the toss and elected to bat on an excellent pitch. Leicestershire reached 346 and Elliott had to undertake the duty of nightwatchman as Lee went before the close.

He shared a record third wicket partnership of 222 with Townsend before being bowled by Berry for 94. It was a crushing disappointment for the wicketkeeper. This proved to be the highest score of his career and he fell victim to an occasional bowler who took only ten first-class wickets during a career of 609 first-class matches. By the close Townsend was unbeaten with 183, taking his score to 233 on Tuesday. He was at the crease for five hours 20 minutes and hit two sixes and 27 fours. It allowed Harry Elliott to declare at 508-7. Mitchell, six for 36, and Townsend, three for 22, then took advantage of a wearing pitch and Derbyshire were home by an innings and 77 runs. It was a victory which lifted them to third place in the Championship table. For Harry Elliott the match was a triumph. He caught two batsmen and stumped two in the second innings, did not concede a single bye, indeed Derbyshire did not give away any extras at all in the match, and he earned praise for his captaincy. "The wicketkeeper handled the bowling and batting with remarkable skill, without allowing his responsibilities to interfere with his own play," said the *Derby Evening Telegraph*.

Richardson's absence from the next match against the West Indians at Derby led to a record relating to the captaincy. Alan Skinner, who took over from Harry Elliott, was aged 20 years 53 days on the morning of the match, the youngest skipper in the county's history. Kim Barnett is the youngest ever to be appointed as Derbyshire's captain; 22 years 315 days old on his first day in 1983. Among the amateurs who deputised between the wars Willie Hill-Wood and JDH Gilbert were only 20 but older than Skinner, and Clarke 22. Skinner quickly proved that he was not merely just a convenient amateur making up the numbers. He made 68 against the tourists – George Headley amassed a double century – and finished the season with 788 runs, average 28.14, from 16 matches. Skinner embarked on a lengthy spell as stand-in for Richardson until Guy Jackson became available early in August. Richardson was back at the end of the season but led the team out on only nine occasions in 1933. Skinner was captain in 12 matches, Jackson four, Clarke two and Elliott and Blaxland one each.

A new opening partnership also had to be discovered as a result of Richardson's absence and Storer's soccer duties. About a dozen combinations were tried, Storer, Skinner, Alderman and Lee featuring, among others. It was unsettling and it was, to some extent, reflected in the results. A great deal of positive cricket was played and it usually brought a finish, wins and losses being evenly split. Nottinghamshire gained a crushing win at Trent Bridge; then remarkable bowling by Townsend (14 for 90) brought Derbyshire victory over Gloucestershire at Queen's Park. This was followed by three consecutive defeats, although they went down fighting in the return against Nottinghamshire at Ilkeston. Needing 313 to win Derbyshire lost seven wickets for 102 but Worthington and Harry Elliott added 117. Worthington struck four sixes in making 108 in 70 minutes, reaching his hundred in an hour, then the fastest century made for the county.

The summer of spectacular cricket continued to delight members. Worthington's undefeated 200 helped Derbyshire to declare at 513-7 against Worcestershire at Chesterfield. Townsend made 172 not out in 448-8 declared against Warwickshire at Derby, the home side winning by 317 runs after Jackson decided against enforcing the follow on. Yorkshire were given a fright at Queen's Park, where Derbyshire won on the first innings, and history was made at Lord's, where Middlesex went down by 141 runs – the first time Derbyshire had won a county match at headquarters. Richardson was now back and made 61 in the second innings but it was the bowling of Copson, Mitchell and Townsend which proved decisive.

The eleventh win of the season – a new club record – was gained emphatically at Northampton. On a perfect pitch Derbyshire scored at 77 an hour to declare at 538-3. Lee scored 128, while Townsend had 142, his sixth hundred of the season, establishing a club record which endured for almost half-a-century. Smith, 129 not out, and Worthington, 70 not out, added 112 in 50 minutes as the slaughter continued and Derbyshire won by an innings and 184 runs.

In their final game of this exhilarating season Derbyshire enjoyed the better of a drawn game at Blackpool. Richardson, 65 not out, and Copson, 43, shared a last wicket partnership of 80, the fast bowler hitting a six and seven fours in making a career-best. Mitchell took eight for 38 to give his side a lead of 106 and Alderman's unbeaten 83 led to a declaration but Lancashire were never in danger of defeat. Mitchell remained by the seaside to deputise for an injured professional in Blackpool's last match and appear in a play-off which secured the Ribblesdale League title. There was some grumbling that Blackpool had "bought" the title by employing Mitchell. His 16 wickets at fewer than four each in the two games were a major factor.

Twenty-eight matches, eleven wins, eleven losses, six draws with three wins on first innings. It was a year of positive cricket in a dry summer and it earned sixth place. A memorable summer, too, for Townsend. He shattered Wright's record with 1,954 runs in the Championship, averaging 44.40. In all matches for the county Townsend made 1,966 runs (42.73) and in all first-class games 2,268 runs (44.47). He headed his club's Championship bowling averages with 87 wickets at 16.91, took 90 wickets for Derbyshire and completed his hundred with the help of end-of-season festival matches. His 100th was the last taken in the 1933 season. Townsend was in the Rest of England side which met the Champion County at The Oval and in Yorkshire's second innings the chief interest centred on Freeman and Townsend. Freeman took three wickets but finished on 298 for the season; Townsend's four included the last two which enabled him to complete his remarkable 2,000 runs-100 wickets double. His figures would have been even more impressive but for a road accident in July.

Townsend was a passenger in a car which overturned. He escaped with a shoulder injury but he was unable to bowl for half-a-dozen games, although he played as a batsman. He also appeared for the Players at Lord's and was one of *Wisden's* Five Cricketers of the Year.

Storer, 1,109 runs, average 44.36 in 15 Championship matches, and Worthington, 1,221, 29.78, two centuries and 50 wickets also did well. Lee reached his thousand in his final innings, at the age of 46 the oldest Derbyshire player to do so, Alderman got into the 900s but Smith had a poor season, averaging only 20. Harry Elliott, 694 runs and 89 wicketkeeping victims, had his best season and Alf Pope, 697 Championship runs and 23 wickets, made a big advance.

Townsend led the bowlers but it was Mitchell who took the most wickets, despite missing three games. He delivered 1,124 Championship overs to take 136 wickets at 18.88 and in all first-class cricket his total was 142 at 19.30. "His skill in spinning the ball combined with deceptive variation of flight and pace enabled him to achieve some remarkable performances," said *Wisden*. The almanack was also full of praise for Copson, who took 90 wickets at 21.34 each in 26 matches. "Nothing was more gratifying than the advance of Copson, the fast right-hand bowler in his second season with the county. The promise he revealed on his debut in 1932 was well fulfilled, for he obtained forty-four more wickets and at considerably less cost. His pace off the pitch provided an effective contrast to that of the slower bowlers."

But it was Townsend and Worthington who were the backbone of the side, *Wisden* saying that once again the county owed them a tremendous debt. Stan Worthington often took the new ball and maintained his reputation as a reliable stock bowler with an occasional 'magic' ball which would defeat the best of batsmen. Old Supporter (*Derbyshire Year Book* 2000) recalled watching them at their best. "It was a joy to see them batting together, whether hurrying the score along or in a defensive situation. When in form Worthington was masterful against fast bowling and Townsend similarly against spin. Stan played well all around the wicket but was strongest on the leg side with pulls and finely timed glides. Les rarely missed a chance to step out and drive the slow bowlers. He had great power in that stroke, either straight or bisecting the off-side and a useful late cut bringing runs behind the wickets. Les Townsend was described by Herbert Sutcliffe as a spot bowler, one who could consistently pitch the ball on a chosen spot, containing batsmen on good wickets and taking wickets on helpful ones." If Townsend was the more destructive bowler, Worthington was reliable and after becoming a change bowler he would often come on to break a stand that had defied the opening bowlers. "Whereas Les was sound in the field Stan was brilliant, either at short leg or deeper on that side, his sturdy frame being no bar to agility. His face rarely showed his feelings on the field whereas Les could hardly suppress his emotions; grim if he had failed but pure delight at his own or his side's success."

Derbyshire, said *Wisden*, impressed everyone as a strong and promising team which thoroughly deserved the reward of finishing sixth.

Chapter 26
Among the High Peaks

TALES from the east added spice to the conversation as Derbyshire's cricketers prepared for the 1934 season. Three of them had now toured under Jardine; Mitchell in Australia and New Zealand and Harry Elliott and Leslie Townsend with the MCC party which visited India and Ceylon in 1933-34. Townsend suffered something of a breakdown in health as a result of his experiences in India but the stories remained exotic to sons of the mining communities. Travel had been arduous, sometimes the food and the accommodation indifferent, the whole experience tiring.

Set against this was the rich hospitality from assorted Maharajahs, Nawabs and wealthy English expatriates. *The History of Indian Cricket* by E W Docker says that when MCC played against Patiala a banquet was held at the Maharajah of Patiala's palace. It went on until three or four in the morning and the players were awakened to take part in a deer hunt at 7am. Eleven of them then had to take part in a full day's cricket. Townsend was not in the side but Elliott kept wicket. At least he could put his feet up when MCC batted for the whole of the first day. Jardine, typically, showed no sign of a hangover in making the top score. Another party was followed by a panther hunt. To nobody's surprise the three-day match ended in a dull draw. From the point of view of the cricket Derbyshire's players had cause for satisfaction. Townsend played in three Tests, Elliott in two. Reputations were enhanced.

A familiar face was missing from the pre-season gathering. Garnet Lee was not re-engaged after 1933 as the gradual changes continued. Jackson, Bowden, Hutchinson, Slater and Lee had gone over the past three years to be replaced by Richardson, Smith, Alderman, the Popes and Skinner. The average age was thus reduced without any loss of quality. Looking back on 1933 the *Derby Evening Telegraph* said: "The past season has, without doubt, provided a fine illustration of the value of the nursery which Mr WT Taylor has been so keen to cultivate." Without it, added the paper, Derbyshire might have had only an average season.

Where did it leave them in 1934? The County Championship remained the prerogative of the Roses counties. Yorkshire had won seven and Lancashire four of the last 12 Championships. But in 1933 there was some evidence that the collective powers of the Big Six were on the wane. Yorkshire, the champions, Kent, who were third and Lancashire (fifth) were the only representatives. Sussex (runners-up), Essex (fourth) and Derbyshire (sixth) replaced the others. Getting into the top half-dozen was one thing, winning the Championship was quite another matter. Between the wars all of the six remained strong but whereas Yorkshire were all-powerful the others went through periods of quiescence before emerging again sooner or later.

What of the pretenders? Under Bev Lyon's dynamic captaincy and with Hammond to make the runs and Charlie Parker and Tom Goddard taking wickets by the sackful Gloucestershire were runners-up in 1930 and 1931. Under almost any other points system used to decide the competition they would have been champions in 1930. As it was, 15 wins and four defeats against Lancashire's ten victories and no losses through the 28 matches was not good enough under that year's method. In both seasons they made a magnificent effort and played some attractive cricket but they never quite got there.

It was Sussex who mounted the most sustained challenge. With Maurice Tate the spearhead, they had been a useful side for years but in 1932 they rose from fourth to second under the captaincy of Duleepsinhji. He was succeeded by RSG Scott in 1933 and they were runners-up again, achieving a double over Yorkshire. They faced 1934 under yet another new captain. Scott had to give up to run the family business after the death of his father and Alan Melville, past Oxford and future South African skipper, was appointed. In 1933, John Langridge and Ted Bowley shared an opening stand of 490 against Middlesex at Hove but Bowley retired at the season's end and this left a gap. Sussex remained as the likeliest challengers. John and James Langridge, Jim and Harry Parks, Melville and Tom Cook were established runmakers. Tate was still a fine bowler, with Jim Cornford an accomplished new ball partner. James Langridge, Jim Parks and Wensley provided variety. Sussex had an attractive, powerful, confident and popular team, with their nursery at Hove flourishing. Improvement had been shown by Essex and Warwickshire but the odds were on Yorkshire, Lancashire and Sussex. Derbyshire were among some half-a-dozen teams on the fringes.

They faced immediate trials. Four matches were scheduled in May – Lancashire at Ilkeston, Sussex at Hove, Warwickshire at Derby, Northamptonshire at Northampton and Yorkshire at Chesterfield.

Lancashire were held up by rain but there was enough time for them to declare at 337-3 and dismiss Derbyshire for 115 by the end of the second day. Following on, the home team crawled to 88 for the loss of Richardson, Townsend, who opened with him, just managing to post an unbeaten fifty. It was a salutary lesson and Derbyshire were relieved to escape with a draw. The team – Richardson, Storer, Townsend, Smith, Alderman, Worthington, Elliott (CS), Pope (A), Elliott (H), Mitchell and Copson, with Harry Storer replacing Armstrong – made the journey to Hove for the following weekend's game against Sussex. This aroused considerable interest beyond the two counties; significant because it pitted two of the pretenders against each other at an early stage.

Sussex scraped home by two wickets despite a late charge by Derbyshire and it was a disappointed side which travelled back for the fixture against Warwickshire at Derby. That ended in a win and spirits were lifted even higher with an innings victory at Northampton which owed much to Worthington's 147 and Mitchell's bowling. Then came the fourth of the fixtures which appeared to have been especially created to test Derbyshire's mettle to the full. Yorkshire had crushed Lancashire by an innings in the Roses match at Bramall Lane but initially they found Derbyshire a real handful at Queen's Park. On Saturday 21 wickets fell; Yorkshire 99 and 41 for one, Derbyshire 102. Mitchell baffled everybody, dismissing Sutcliffe twice in the day, caught by Harry Elliott for 15 and 23. That was the extent of Derbyshire's mastery. Mitchell took his match analysis to 11 for 122 but Derbyshire, needing 269 to win, were all out for 166.

As May gave way to June, Derbyshire's season already appeared set in stone; too good for the lowly clubs, a match for the mid-table and top six pretenders but out of their depth against the leaders. They went to Trent Bridge without Copson, injured against Sussex, Mitchell (playing in the Test trial) and Storer. Leslie Townsend arrived late after being released from the trial squad. Copson's absence was crucial. Larwood bowled only a few overs in 1933 due to the broken bones in his left foot, a legacy of the bodyline series, but was now close to full speed. Voce remained, hostile as ever, and Harold Butler, a young fast bowler, had shown early promise in Larwood's absence. All three were in the team and without Copson, Derbyshire had nobody approaching such pace, although as it turned out that did not matter over much as Voce reverted to slow left-arm in Derbyshire's second innings, proving adept at it with seven for 53.

The visitors batted first, crawling to 263 in 126 overs and stretching the innings to Monday morning. The wearing pitch was exploited by the spin of Armstrong (five for 72) and Townsend (four for 59) and Nottinghamshire were all out for 203. The visitors crumbled to 135 all out, leaving Nottinghamshire to make 196. This was when Townsend and Armstrong took over. Townsend returned figures of 31-7-47-7 and Armstrong took three for 76. Spin had prevailed over speed and Derbyshire had won a Championship match at Trent Bridge for the first time.

They were soon brought back to earth with defeats at The Oval, where Alan Skinner suffered an elbow injury after being struck by a ball from Gover which probably cost him a Blue, and at Portsmouth, when Guy Southern stood in as captain. It was a lean spell, seven consecutive matches and only a solitary win at Leicester to show for it. Twelve matches had produced only 76 points out of a possible 180. Then the return with Sussex at Buxton was left unfinished after rain washed out play on Thursday.

At this point of the season Derbyshire scarcely had the look of Championship contenders or even a place in the first six. Their percentage of points from 13 games was far below Sussex, storming away at the top with Lancashire snapping away at their heels. Yorkshire, deprived by Test calls in an Australian year, spluttered uncharacteristically, indeed Sussex routed them by an innings at Sheffield just before the Buxton fixture.

The tide turned for Derbyshire with a comfortable victory over Somerset at

Chesterfield in the first few days of July. Storer made a hundred here and then showed his quality at Tunbridge Wells. By now Copson was in full flight and again demonstrated his ability to remove top batsmen before they had a sight of the ball. Woolley was taken at the wicket before he had scored, one of Copson's five victims in a total of 114. Freeman possessed too many tricks on such a pitch and Derbyshire were shot out for 92, of which Storer made 38. Kent, 31 for two at the close of a day on which 22 wickets fell, could make only 120, Mitchell finishing off the tail. With the Nevill Ground clearly taking spin, Kent pinned all their faith on Freeman and Lewis as Derbyshire faced a target of 143, the highest total of the match. Storer got his head down, battling through 62 overs for an unbeaten 54. It was one of the finest innings of his career and it saw his side home by four wickets. This match ended inside two days, as did the next game at Stourbridge, where an all-professional team led by Harry Elliott defeated Worcestershire by an innings. Mitchell was unplayable, eight for 22 in six overs in a first innings of 48 and five for 66 when Worcestershire batted again. Derbyshire's top scorer at Stourbridge with an unbeaten 70, was Elijah Carrington, who filled a vacancy in the middle order left by Lee's retirement and the injury to Skinner.

Derbyshire now lay fifth in the table, behind the leaders Sussex, Lancashire, Nottinghamshire and Yorkshire. They gained their fourth consecutive Championship victory by defeating Middlesex at Derby, where Mitchell took 13 wickets. Crucially he now missed three consecutive matches due to the Leeds Test and Players v Gentlemen at Lord's and Derbyshire failed to win any of them. He returned to take ten Hampshire wickets at Derby in a match won comfortably by Derbyshire, Worthington scoring 154. It lifted Derbyshire into fourth place, behind Sussex, Lancashire and Yorkshire and with matches imminent against the Roses' counties it left them an opportunity to gain ground.

Proof that Derbyshire were genuine challengers was demonstrated at Bramall Lane on August 1, 2 and 3 1934. Yorkshire were at full strength but Derbyshire batted first reaching 345 and then forcing Yorkshire (187) to follow on thanks to Mitchell, five for 81, and Townsend three for 71.

Enforcing the follow-on was one of the high points of Arthur Richardson's career. Guy Jackson had enjoyed a similar experience eight years earlier but then Yorkshire were missing key players. In Richardson's case it was something of a gesture for there was time for only 31 overs to be bowled and Sutcliffe and Mitchell eased their way to 97 without being separated.

Storer marked his annual farewell after the August Bank Holiday match with 69 at Edgbaston, sharing an opening stand of 112 with Alderman but rain washed out the final day. Then Len Hopwood's left-arm slow medium proved too much at Old Trafford, where Lancashire won easily. After the following weekend's round of matches, Lancashire replaced Sussex at the top of the table on Tuesday August 14 1934 although they had to thank a sporting declaration by Nigel Haig which enabled them to beat Middlesex. Sussex had led since May 22.

Derbyshire bounced back after their defeat at Old Trafford with an innings win over Somerset at Weston-super-Mare. Smith and Alderman began with a century partnership, Townsend made 106 not out and took six for 66 and five for 64. But an 84 run defeat at Lord's spoiled their chances of the Championship. This proved to be Derbyshire's last visit to headquarters until 1939. Their 28-match programme, home and away against 14 teams excluded two counties in the pre-war years. Consequently no fixtures with Glamorgan were arranged after 1931. Middlesex joined the Welsh county in isolation from 1935-38, Hampshire replacing them in 1939.

Fourth position remained there for the taking, however, as Lancashire, Sussex and Yorkshire battled for top spot with Derbyshire some way behind. Nottinghamshire, with Carr out of the team because of illness, had faded and at Ilkeston they suffered a signal defeat. Alf Pope (40) was the top scorer in Derbyshire's first innings of 220 and he followed this with a spell of four wickets for three runs. Nottinghamshire were all out for 130, Pope completing figures of 25-13-21-6 and with Worthington making 93 Derbyshire extended their lead to 302. Copson wrecked the second innings with five for 40 and Nottinghamshire went down by 201 runs. It was the first time Derbyshire had recorded two wins in a season against their neighbours.

While Derbyshire enjoyed the euphoria, a match took place at Eastbourne which decided the Championship. In June, the Lancashire v Sussex encounter at Old Trafford ended in a draw, with Lancashire winning on the first innings. Sussex were to finish the season having won only one of their last 12 matches after July 17. Lancashire travelled south in the knowledge that avoiding defeat was a priority and after gaining a first innings lead of 53 they made the game safe with a big score at the second attempt. Lancashire duly took the title and brought Yorkshire's run of three consecutive Championships to an end.

Derbyshire ended with a 42-run victory over Leicestershire at Chesterfield, which ensured third place. Their 12 victories constituted a new club record. It was the first time they had finished above Yorkshire since the Championship was formally organised in 1890. They achieved this despite the handicaps of losing Copson and Mitchell for seven matches and Richardson and Storer for 13. It led to some chopping and changing in the captaincy, with mainly Skinner but also Elliott, Jackson and Southern filling in. Derbyshire never seemed to make up their minds about the openers, with some eight combinations involving several players.

There was a lack of stability about the batting as a whole which a full season of Storer would probably have eradicated. Smith gave some brilliant exhibitions of fast scoring. *Wisden* said his spirited play had an uplifting effect upon his colleagues. Alderman, if inclined to be slow, became a more prolific scorer on the off-side and at the same time one of the most dependable men in the team. He proved himself an ideal opening partner for Storer, *Wisden* continued. Townsend, suffering the after-effects of India, enjoyed nothing like the success of 1933 with the bat, averaging only 27.35, which was still ahead of Worthington's 26.93. The Almanack found special praise for Alan Skinner. It said he acted very efficiently as deputy for Richardson and turned out to be the most improved, and probably the most attractive batsman in the eleven.

Mitchell took 159 wickets in all first-class matches. Copson did well and many competent judges predicted he had a brilliant future. "Many of the best batsmen found his late swerve and pace off the pitch difficult to counter," *Wisden* said. Harry Elliott's 78 victims established a new record and he enjoyed a well-deserved testimonial at the end of the season.

Of the ground staff, George Pope began to establish himself in first-class cricket and Arnold Townsend, Leslie's younger brother by nearly nine years, made his debut in the final match of the season against Leicestershire. Tommy Armstrong was not retained after 1934 but was still to be called on irregularly for many years to come. Sam Weaver, the Newcastle United and England footballer who pioneered the long throw-in, was also axed after a year on the nursery staff but a young slow left-arm bowler, Bedford from Grassmoor, was engaged. Neither played for the first team, although Weaver had a couple of games with Somerset in 1939.

By not retaining these young players Derbyshire made a gesture towards cutting costs for they suffered a financial loss of £1,217 in the 1934 accounts. Subscriptions remained disappointingly below £3,000 at £2979 while the gate receipts, boosted by £931 from the Australian match provided £3,552. Membership stood at 2,150, half that of Lancashire and Surrey and one-third of Yorkshire's but on a par with some of the smaller clubs. Even with a share of Test profits it was still not enough to make ends meet and the financial difficulties always have to be borne in mind when considering Derbyshire's successes of the mid-1930s.

The separate nursery fund was also struggling. It had an income of £468, compared with £492 in 1920, but a £200 legacy from the late Alderman Eastwood helped. Fund raising events were another boost and one such took place at Derby's Assembly Rooms on Tuesday January 8 1935. Rev Henry Ellison, Major Llewellyn Eardley-Simpson, Will Taylor, Arthur Richardson and his fiancée Kathleen Taylor – a niece of TL Taylor, who played as an amateur for Yorkshire and was later president of the club – Alan Skinner, Harry Elliott and Denis Smith attended.

A day earlier, Hon Christopher Lowther, who had worked so diligently and generously to help establish the nursery, had died in a London nursing home, eleven days before his 48th birthday. He never fully recovered from his war wounds. Tribute was paid by the *Derby Evening Telegraph*. "By the death of the Hon. Christopher Lowther, Derbyshire County Cricket Club loses an old and valued friend. His family associations with Derbyshire were somewhat remote – his mother was a Beresford – but his interest in the game and his personal friendship with some of the leading county supporters were sufficient reasons for his active interest in the cricket. A donation of £200 and a handsome annual subscription were followed by a promise of £50 a year towards the nursery fund and he can claim to have taken an important part in the formation of the nursery."

Christopher Lowther's son Lieut John Arthur Lowther was private secretary to the Duke of Kent and lost his life with him in an air crash in August 1942. Ullswater was eventually succeeded as second viscount by his great grandson.

At least Lowther lived to see Derbyshire's rise from sixth to third in the Championship. They were entitled to feel they were now a genuine member of the new Big Six.

Chapter 27
Heading for the Top

ARTHUR RICHARDSON'S wedding took place in February 1935 at Christ Church in Lancaster Gate, London. Guy Jackson, Alan Skinner and Neville Ford were among the guests and the couple received a Davenport tea service from the club and Crown Derby from the family firm. The couple made their home at the Old Vicarage in Quarndon.

The newly-wed skipper received congratulations when the pros assembled for the 1935 season but there were more pressing matters to discuss. Legislation in the wake of bodyline outlawed direct attack and there was an experiment involving the law covering leg before wicket. Under the existing lbw law a batsman could be given out only to a ball pitched in a straight line between wicket and wicket. This enabled him liberal use of the pads to anything pitched only a fraction wide. Pad play was developed to a virtual art form, a second line of defence, and there was a need to redress the balance between bat and ball. MCC took action and in 1935 gave a trial to a rule which held that a batsman could given out if the ball pitched outside the off-stump, providing the point of contact was on a line between wicket and wicket.

It helped bowlers, many batsmen getting out to balls they would have padded off or left alone. They now had to play forward to a good length ball pitching just outside off stump and a great deal of pad play had been eliminated. *Wisden* welcomed it and in the end the players adapted to it. The law was fully adopted in 1937 after two seasons of trial. Of 1,560 lbw decisions in 1935, 483 were under the new rule, signalled by the umpire raising his right hand, palm outwards, after giving the decision. Derbyshire's batsmen coped, the leading players each falling lbw(n) on a couple of occasions apiece, although Worthington avoided the fate. Of the bowlers Alf Pope was the main beneficiary and George Pope and Tommy Mitchell, who could turn it in any direction albeit not always with full control, also enjoyed a share of the spoils.

Denis Smith lost no time in allaying fears. Yorkshire – and Yorkshire at full strength had been considered by many good judges to be the best county side in 1934 – were still smarting over their failure to win the previous season's Championship. That Lancashire, of all counties, should take the title hardly sweetened the pill. There was a determination that 1935 would set matters to right and restore the status quo. First, some the pretenders had to be put in their place and they lost no time in establishing their authority over one of these at Chesterfield.

Heading for the Top

It was Derbyshire's opening match of the season and Smith watched from the non-striker's end as Yorkshire's Bowes had Alderman and Worthington back in the pavilion with only ten runs scored. Leslie Townsend helped him to add 105 but the real fireworks started when Elijah Carrington arrived at the crease. These were products of mining villages only a few miles apart and with their Bassetlaw League associations thrashed an attack including Bowes, Smailes and Verity in a fourth-wicket partnership of 202 in two hours. Carrington made 74 and Smith 189. He drove and pulled superbly, skilful timing and accurate placing bringing him a six and 25 fours. It was a faultless display. This was the innings Smith regarded as a turning point in his career giving rise to his comment: "I remember thinking that day, these beggars can't bowl." Queen's Park was among his favourite grounds. He made seven hundreds at Chesterfield, all before the war, but only one at Derby during the same period. After all this mayhem there was something of a collapse, Derbyshire subsiding from 317 for three to 382 all out in 91.2 overs but it was still a considerable total. Herbert Sutcliffe and Arthur Mitchell continued the White Rose fightback against an attack missing Copson and were still there at the close of play with 67 on the board.

Yorkshire's initial target on Monday was 233, which would ensure avoiding the follow-on but with seven wickets down for 174 it seemed unlikely. Teams captained by Sellers, however, did not roll over and Arthur Wood, Hedley Verity and Frank Smailes not only prevented this ignominy but carried the score to 328, a deficit of only 54. Derbyshire, 158 for three at the close, consolidated their position. Alderman, 63 overnight, was missed three times in an unusually aggressive display in making 100. Richardson's declaration set Yorkshire 266 in three-and-a-quarter hours and Sutcliffe and Mitchell gave them a flying start with 89 in three-quarters of an hour. A mixture of rain and snow intervened and the visitors finished the match on 102 for four, Derbyshire taking five points and Yorkshire three.

It was a good start and it was followed by some of the most remarkable cricket in Derbyshire's history. The rain followed them to The Oval and play could not start until three o'clock. Copson started a collapse on the wet pitch, Mitchell and Townsend took advantage and Surrey were all out for 60 in 85 minutes. Townsend and George Pope added 113 for the fifth wicket, helping to give Derbyshire a lead of 193. Surrey, despite a fine innings by Fender, broke down against Mitchell (eight for 78) and were all out for 210. Derbyshire duly completed a nine-wicket victory inside two days and followed this with a ten wicket win over Leicestershire at Derby, again in two days. Copson took nine wickets in the match but enjoyed his unbeaten 22 just as much. His magnificent form continued at Brentwood, where he took five for 29 as Essex were routed for 116, Mitchell taking the other five wickets. Derbyshire fared little better and led by only 34, Essex finishing on 85 for three. On the second day they left Derbyshire a target of 186 on a doubtful pitch. Smith and Worthington put on 102 for the second wicket, but after tea Eastman caused problems and five wickets fell quickly, among them Smith's for 82 in 90 minutes. Richardson and Alf Pope stayed, however, and got Derbyshire home by four wickets, their third consecutive victory, each in two days. They now headed the Championship table, with Middlesex in second place.

After a defeat by the South Africans at Ilkeston, Derbyshire consolidated their position at the top with a superb display against a weakened Hampshire at Queen's Park. Copson was absent but an attack consisting of Worthington, the two Popes, Mitchell and Townsend dismissed the visitors for 140. By the close of play Derbyshire had made 301 for two. Smith was unbeaten with 203 and Townsend 47 and on Monday they carried their partnership for the third wicket to 235, then a club record. Townsend made 52 and Smith 225. At one point he threatened George Davidson's individual record of 274. *Wisden* described his innings as magnificent. "After starting rather shakily on Saturday, Smith adopted forcing methods with marked success. Exceptionally quick on his feet and driving with power and certainty he reached three figures out of 166 and, missed when 156, altogether defied Hampshire for four hours." He hit four sixes and 31 fours. Derbyshire declared with nine wickets down on a now rain-damaged pitch and a lead of 238. Hampshire had little answer to the varied bowling and were all out for 134.

Four consecutive two-day victories and even at this early stage a gap was appearing at the top of the table although Yorkshire had now joined Middlesex in the chase. Derbyshire's run look set to continue at New Road when after some good batting by Carrington and Richardson and fine bowling from Mitchell they led by 36 on the first innings after being put in on a sweating pitch. When Derbyshire went in again, a treacherous wicket after rain made Richard Howorth almost unplayable and they were shot out for 54. Worcestershire were left to get 91 and rain threatened to frustrate them. A storm broke over the ground as the winning hit was made, their nine-wicket success a check to Derbyshire's progress.

Worse was to follow over a damp Whitsuntide, when Jackson captained the team in Richardson's absence. Only three hours play was possible at Edgbaston on the Saturday but it was enough for Warwickshire to dismiss their opponents for 119. Of these Smith, who drove and hit to leg splendidly for two and a half hours, made 61 and Carrington 21. There was heavy rain on Monday and wickets toppled like ninepins. Warwickshire emerged with a six-wicket victory. That was not all. Smith, 667 runs in his first eleven innings, had been selected for the England party at Trent Bridge from which the team to meet the South Africans in the first Test would be chosen. It was at Edgbaston that he discovered an injured rib suffered in the Hampshire match was cracked, compelling his withdrawal from the England squad and also from Derbyshire's next two games. The defeats at Worcester and Edgbaston were costly. Yorkshire now led the table, Warwickshire having risen to second, with Kent third, Middlesex fourth and Derbyshire trailing in fifth place. An unlikely success story of 1935 was that of Leicestershire. Under the captaincy of Ewart Astill they rose to sixth place in a remarkable reversal of fortune. The bowling of Smith and Geary had much to do with this and the pair were in fine form when Derbyshire went to Aylestone Road.

Their captain for this match was Gilbert Hodgkinson, a 22-year-old amateur who did well in club cricket and made 44 on his debut against the South Africans. Hodgkinson was a prisoner of war in the 1939-45 conflict and his death was recorded in the 1941 edition of *Wisden*. Happily it was incorrect but he had suffered a severe head wound in France and this took its toll in later years. Hodgkinson, who ran a high quality greengrocery business in Derby, was appointed captain in 1946, although business commitments restricted him to about half the scheduled matches.

Hodgkinson was dismissed for a pair at Leicester but few noticed as Tommy Mitchell produced an outstanding individual performance, taking all ten wickets. Derbyshire made 140 after being put in but Mitchell reduced the home side to 68 for six by the close of Saturday's play. On Monday he took the remaining four wickets, Derbyshire having a lead of 17. Mitchell's analysis was 19.1-4-64-10, all ten in an innings, five bowled, one lbw(n), three caught by Worthington and one stumped. "Flighting the ball with considerable skill and varying his spin, Mitchell tempted the batsmen to hit, but his ten wickets cost only 64 runs," said *Wisden*. Derbyshire left Leicestershire to get 245 but rain ruled out a positive result.

Arthur Richardson returned against Somerset at Derby and promptly demonstrated his positive approach to the game. On Wednesday, Derbyshire made 152 for four but miserable weather resulted in a blank Thursday and the match seemed destined to a draw. Few people bothered to turn up on Friday but Alf Pope struck three consecutive sixes off Frank Lee, enabling a declaration at 237-8. Somerset lost nine wickets for 82 but Lee and Arthur Hazell added seven which was just enough to save the follow on by two runs. That seemed to have put an end to any meaningful cricket, particularly when, to general astonishment Harry Elliott and Mitchell came out to open the innings. Elliott pushed a ball from Reggie Ingle, the Somerset captain, for a single, and everybody then made for the pavilion. "That was a quick one," a spectator said to Mitchell. "I was playing for my average," Tommy replied.

Richardson had declared, setting Somerset to score 150 in 90 minutes. Ingle took up the challenge, sending in the hitters Arthur Wellard and Bill Andrews to open. Copson, operating from the Nottingham Road end, removed Andrews's off stump with his first ball and soon had Wellard caught behind. Somerset never recovered on the rain affected pitch. They were all out for 35, Copson five for 15, Townsend three for one, and Old Supporter was delighted. "The little crowd gathered round to applaud in their team and I can still remember some of the facial expressions; Elliott and Copson dour and determined, Storer very well pleased and Townsend a picture of pure delight."

Derbyshire were now back at the top of the table, ahead of Kent and Yorkshire. It was a remarkable performance but it was quickly overshadowed by the next two games. First came a short journey to Old Trafford and a match against the champions. Lancashire had been inconsistent, suffering from injuries, declining form and the vagaries of the weather. They were more than satisfied by Derbyshire's dismissal for

227 from 113 for one on Wednesday, the returned Smith top scoring with 63. Four Red Rose batsmen were back in the pavilion for 51 by the close and the whole side out for 168 on Thursday. Storer and Smith began Derbyshire's second innings with a stand of 138 and the lead had been stretched to 241 by close of play.

On Friday, Richardson's declaration left Lancashire 320 to make in four hours and a half. Copson struck an early blow but with Frank Watson and Jack Iddon going well the hundred was passed with only one wicket down. By tea Lancashire were 153 for three and after the break Iddon and Oldfield added 54 in 30 minutes before Elliott stumped Oldfield off Mitchell. Then came the key moment. At 213 Iddon was caught behind for 131 (14 fours) "three yards wide off a fast ball from Copson – another marvellous piece of agility and anticipation by Elliott", wrote Neville Cardus in the *Manchester Guardian*. Pollard and Phillipson added 47 in 35 minutes before the former was run out (260 for six) and Booth, who had just pulled Mitchell into the ladies' pavilion for six, was stumped to give Elliott his sixth victim in the innings and his tenth in the match. Parkinson was caught off Mitchell by Worthington at silly mid-off: 276 for eight: 44 needed in an hour. Peter Eckersley, Lancashire's captain, and Phillipson added 36 before the skipper was caught by Alf Pope on the boundary having a dip at Mitchell. He had scored 30 in 20 minutes and Lancashire were 312 for nine, eight runs short of victory. In the next over Alf Pope bowled Duckworth with the score unchanged and Derbyshire had won a most exciting match by seven runs, with five minutes remaining. Mitchell took four for 116 from 29 overs in the second innings but the starring role was Elliott's, caught eight, stumped two, ten victims in the match, and six in the second innings, when he held four catches and made two stumpings.

This was Derbyshire's first victory over Lancashire – their oldest rivals – since 1911 and they could scarcely have been in better fettle for the clash with Nottinghamshire at Ilkeston as June gave way to July. Mitchell was playing in the Lord's Test and Richardson was missing with an injury to his right hand received at Manchester. So it was another rare occasion when an all-professional team was fielded: Harry Elliott (captain), Storer, Smith, Alderman, Worthington, Leslie Townsend, Carrington, Arnold Townsend, the Popes and Copson. Nottinghamshire, the post-bodyline upheavals behind them, had just crushed Sussex by an innings and were hovering on the edge of the challengers.

The mid-1930s were the high noon of the Derbyshire-Nottinghamshire clashes. Both clubs were strong and the spectators could identify with the players. Of the 22 men engaged in this game, Derbyshire fielded an all-county raised side. Of their opponents only Willis Walker (Gosforth) was an outsider. The majority were born within a 20-mile radius and some very close to the border. The atmosphere was akin to a match between neighbouring villages, though on a much higher plane. The setting at Ilkeston ideally placed geographically, the local derby aspect reflected by a Saturday attendance of 8,000 packing the terracing and elsewhere. There was, too, the ever-present Bassetlaw League influence, with most of the players having appeared in the competition. The crucial Derbyshire v Nottinghamshire matches of those days aroused an intensity of feeling not far removed from the epic Roses games and in some seasons were of greater significance.

Nottinghamshire performed indifferently on Saturday on what was a batsman's pitch. They collapsed from 75 for one to 107 for six before GV Gunn (George Vernon was the son of George who retired in 1932) and Heane added 71. Gunn hit well to leg and cut gracefully in making 78 but the total was a disappointing 205, the Pope brothers and Leslie Townsend each taking three wickets. There was an interesting point about Derbyshire's field placing in this match. First and second slip at the start usually consisted of Denis Smith and the bowler, in this case Worthington or Copson, with Alderman at third slip. When Alf Pope replaced Worthington, Alderman went out to the boundary.

Voce dismissed Smith and Alderman but Storer stayed 80 minutes for 56. By the close Derbyshire were 122 for four, with Worthington going well and the game evenly balanced. On Monday Worthington completed his first century of the season and went on to make 126 in three hours, an innings which included 17 fours. Nobody else could do much against Voce (five for 87) and Derbyshire were all out for 253, a lead of 48. Nottinghamshire set about the task of recovery, Charlie Harris making 92 and Joe Hardstaff 42, both being run out. They were all out on the final morning for 233, leaving Derbyshire to make 186 on a wearing pitch.

They lost Storer, bowled by Larwood, without a run on the board but Smith (47) and Alderman took the score to 70 and then Worthington helped Alderman add 83. Alderman gave a splendid display, hitting eleven fours in an unbeaten 76 and showing great skill on the worn pitch. Derbyshire got the runs in just over two hours, winning by seven wickets and retaining their position at the top of the Championship table. They had won seven of their 11 games. Yorkshire, unbeaten with seven wins out of 13, were second. Kent also had seven wins in 13 but, like Derbyshire, had lost twice. In fourth place was Middlesex, five wins and three defeats in 11.

Surrey, Lancashire and Nottinghamshire of the Big Six had been defeated by Derbyshire and Yorkshire given a fright. Furthermore, Yorkshire were being weakened by the demands of the selectors, Leyland and Verity each appearing in four Tests, Mitchell, Sutcliffe and Barber in two and Bowes in one. In addition Barber, Leyland and Bowes were in the Players' side at Lord's, although this match coincided with the county's innings win over hapless Northamptonshire. It meant that if Derbyshire could maintain form then the Championship was there for the taking.

All was not well. Bill Copson might have joined Denis Smith in the South African Tests if he had played anything like a full season. Instead, he was being dogged by injury and an apparent lack of stamina. Derbyshire sent him to Skegness at the end of June in an attempt to restore his health. At one time it was feared that he was suffering from a serious ailment and the club had him examined by specialists. Their reports dispelled the doubts. It was found that he was suffering from a strained sacro-iliac joint in the lower part of his back. Copson had two examinations by specialists in 1935 and was to have another in January 1936 before he received a clean bill of health. He played in 18 of the 28 Championship matches in 1935 and in some of those was not 100 per cent fit.

Copson, Mitchell, with a groin injury suffered at Lord's, and Richardson were missing for the Surrey match at Queen's Park, where Willie Hill-Wood returned 10 years after his last appearance to captain the team. Errol Holmes made a double century after Surrey lost three wickets for 12, a four-man attack of the Popes, Worthington and Townsend, plus ten expensive overs from Hill-Wood, conceding 430 runs. Worthington (107) ensured respectability, Holmes set a target of 351 but a three-figure opening stand by Storer and Smith removed the possibility of defeat.

The draw cost Derbyshire the lead in the Championship. Yorkshire, in the midst of a run of six consecutive victories, moved to the top on July 5. Derbyshire slipped further behind although the next match against Lancashire at Buxton was drawn in their favour. The recalled Armstrong took five for 13 in Lancashire's first innings of 86 all out after Derbyshire made 237. Alan Skinner did not enforce the follow-on and his declaration set Lancashire 343 at a run a minute but they crawled to 176 for four in 145 overs, of which Townsend and Armstrong were responsible for 101. The absence of Copson and Mitchell might have been felt less at Buxton than other grounds. Leslie Townsend said they never had much success there "because the ball would not go through for Bill and Tommy made it turn too much."

The run without a victory was extended to four games by defeats at Bristol and at Trent Bridge, where Nottinghamshire, set 291, reached the target with three wickets to spare, GV Gunn making 113 not out. Here, for the second time in a week, a Derbyshire captain, on this occasion Richardson, decided against the follow-on. The lead was 166 but Eardley-Simpson felt the decision was correct. "I was in the dressing room when the decision was made and I never had the slightest reason to doubt that it was the correct one. What lost the match was slow batting and an hour's rain on the last morning; we had to declare – in the hope of forcing a win – before we were really safe, Notts put up a great display and won a fine victory against odds." The Championship dream appeared to be over. Yorkshire had opened up a huge gap, ahead of Middlesex and Warwickshire. Derbyshire were fourth and Nottinghamshire fifth. It was then that Derbyshire, seemingly out of the reckoning, launched a sustained assault.

It began with an innings victory over Kent at Chesterfield, followed by one of ten wickets against Gloucestershire at Burton-on-Trent. There was a hiccup when Sussex won by seven wickets at Derby as Storer bid the 1935 season farewell but Northamptonshire were crushed by 10 wickets at Chesterfield and the Sussex defeat avenged by a win at Hove. Just to put the icing on the cake Yorkshire went down to a shock defeat against Essex at Huddersfield, being humbled for 31 in their first innings.

It all added spice to the August Bank Holiday programme, in which Yorkshire won the Roses match at Bradford and Derbyshire defeated Warwickshire before large crowds at Derby. With Middlesex beaten at Hove, the Championship was turning into a two-horse race, Yorkshire now having a percentage of 67.57, Derbyshire 62.85 and Middlesex 58.14.

Derbyshire travelled to Northampton and the prospect of easy pickings. They received a massive shock. Fine bowling by Nobby Clark and Reg Partridge sent back the first five batsmen for 11 and although Carrington, with 35 not out, rallied the side Derbyshire were all out for 85. Mitchell took seven for 73 but Northamptonshire gained a first innings lead of 101. Batting a second time Derbyshire lost Alderman and Worthington for 39 but Smith (44) helped Townsend take the score to 122. Townsend gave a fine display, making 102 (16 fours) out of 167 before he was fourth out at 206. Carrington, missed twice, drove and cut well for 71 and the total reached 362, leaving Northamptonshire to make 262. Copson took two wickets before a run had been scored on Thursday evening and finished with five for 44 as Derbyshire got home by 100 runs. It was their 13th victory of the season – a new club record. Then they won a bowlers' match against Essex at Chesterfield by 21 runs to establish another club record of five consecutive victories.

Seven wins marred only by the defeat by Sussex in the last eight games had put Derbyshire firmly back into the race for the County Championship. Yorkshire's percentage was 70.27 from 24 matches, Derbyshire's 66.08 from 23. Such was the position when Derbyshire travelled to Scarborough for what was at that stage the most crucial match in their history. Victory would put them marginally ahead in the race.

Bill Bowes was absent from the Yorkshire team but all of their other Test stars were playing. Derbyshire, missing Storer, were otherwise at full strength: Richardson (captain), Smith, Worthington, Alderman, Skinner, Townsend, George and Alf Pope, Elliott, Mitchell and Copson. Derbyshire began well. Yorkshire lost half their side on Wednesday for 131 before Arthur Wood and Brian Sellers, both missed, added 72 before Wood was bowled by Copson for 39. Mitchell had Frank Smailes stumped at 244 and by the close Yorkshire were 266 for seven, Sellers 69 not out. They had shaded the day but neither side had established mastery. That was to change on Thursday. Sellers went on to 73 as Yorkshire were dismissed for 304 and Derbyshire began their innings against a new-ball attack including a bowler who was a relative unknown.

Thomas Alec Jacques (always known as Sandy) was a 30-year-old right-arm fast bowler, a farmer by occupation. He made an impressive debut as an amateur in 1927 and after only six matches he took four for 53 in a Test trial at Lord's. His ability to maintain pace and length for long periods impressed observers and he turned professional, amid high expectations the following year. It soon became clear that his legs could not stand the strain of cricket six days a week; he even tried wearing five pairs of socks to reduce the pain. Jacques played only 28 times from 1927-36 and the match at Scarborough, in which he came in for Bowes, was his only appearance in 1935. He was to devote himself to league cricket and his farm near Selby.

Richardson and Smith began steadily with 20 for the first partnership before Jacques had the left-hander caught at the wicket. Then, trying to pull a no-ball from the same bowler, Worthington, on three, received a severe blow in the face which fractured his jaw and he took no further part in the match, or, indeed, the remainder of the season. In a spell of nine overs Jacques, forcing life out of the pitch, had a spell of three for nine, finishing with four for 35 as Derbyshire were dismissed for 133. Only Richardson (31) showed any sort of form and Sellers had no hesitation in enforcing the follow on with a lead of 171. Going in again Derbyshire lost two wickets for nine and six were down for 102. Skinner played a stern, watchful innings of 43 not out in two-and-a-quarter hours and George Pope (33) joined him in a fifth wicket stand of 42 but the side was dismissed for 174, Frank Smailes and Cyril Turner each taking four wickets. Jacques delivered 13 overs without success but the damage was done. Yorkshire were home by 10 wickets in two days and the race was over.

Skinner said: "Yorkshire produced an almost unknown fast bowler in Sandy Jacques who proceeded to subject us to probably the most hostile attack I ever had the misfortune to suffer. That Stan Worthington had his jaw broken and lost several teeth did not improve our morale, but the fact was that on such a lively wicket we allowed Yorkshire to make too many runs; so they won the match and won the Championship." Alf Pope recalled Arthur Mitchell coming into the Derbyshire dressing room before play began to tell them that Jacques was playing and would liven things up for them.

Hopes virtually dashed, Derbyshire prepared for the run in of four more games before the season ended. Leslie Townsend hit 180 against Worcestershire at Derby but the bowlers were on the receiving end at Dover, where Kent made 560. Bill Ashdown struck 47 boundaries in making 305 not out but Derbyshire escaped with a draw.

Alf Pope maintained that he had Ashdown caught by Harry Elliott when he had scored 19. The ball lifted, found the shoulder of the bat and Elliott dived in front of first slip and held the catch. This was an era when most batsmen walked if they knew they had been caught. If a batsman knew he was out but was given not out by the umpire, it was not usual to leave as this would be construed as being offensive to the umpire. In Ashdown's case, everybody expected the batsman to walk and when he did not move an appeal was made but the umpire said 'not out'. Later in his innings the fielders suggested to Ashdown that it was time he got out. The batsman said he had been trying to do so since he reached his hundred.

Pope could take solace from his ten wickets in the match at Bournemouth, which was won by Derbyshire. The season ended with a victory at Taunton.

Sixteen victories in 28 matches and runners-up. For the second consecutive year Derbyshire set a new benchmark with by far the finest season in their history. "Had they made 'safety-first' their policy, they might have ousted Yorkshire," said *Wisden*. "As it was Derbyshire, acknowledged as exponents of attractive cricket, continued to hold victory as the highest prize, and if at times this urge caused their downfall the county gained tremendously in popularity and respect among both supporters and rivals."

There was nothing better than the progress made by the Popes, Alfred with 87 first-class wickets and George with 63 and 729 runs. Carrington played some resolute innings, Worthington, called upon to bowl fewer overs with the advent of the Pope brothers, could devote more time and care to his batting and it was only a pity that Storer and Skinner could not play more often. This was echoed by the *Derby Evening Telegraph* correspondent, who felt that Skinner would solve Derbyshire's middle-order batting deficiencies if he could appear regularly. "His batting is always a delight to watch and while he is noted for his quick scoring he is also capable of holding up his end when he knows that the consumption of time is almost as valuable to the side as runs." It added that the Pope brothers had been the biggest find in years.

With 160 Championship wickets in 25 games Mitchell exceeded Bestwick's seasonal record and in all matches he took 168 for Derbyshire at 19.54, in all first-class cricket 171 at 20.16. Harry Elliott in his testimonial year – a North against South match was played for him at Chesterfield – caught 69 batsmen and stumped 21, his total of 90 exceeding by one his 1933 record. In the field Worthington, in the slip cordon or at short leg, held the most catches, getting into the twenties, and Alderman, the Popes, Smith, Mitchell and Copson also reached double figures. Denis Smith, one of *Wisden's* Five Cricketers of the Year, made 1,767 runs in all games for the county (42.07) and 2,175 in all first-class matches.

The *Derby Evening Telegraph* paid what was becoming an annual tribute to the nursery: "There is no doubt that the Pope brothers and Carrington have benefited from the experience gained on this staff and there are a number of other youngsters under the care of Mr Sam Cadman who are showing signs of developing into useful players."

Rev Henry Ellison also made some interesting points about the 1935 season as he looked forward to the following year. He began by paying tribute to Will Taylor, who had received a testimonial as recognition of his 26 years service as secretary. The club donated £100 and there was another of £50 from the nursery account. Derbyshire's annual report said: "It is impossible to overrate what he has done for Derbyshire cricket, and your committee have every confidence in asking members and supporters throughout the county for a liberal response to the appeal which has been made by the president."

Ellison added: "The advance of the county may be traced to a great extent to his hard work and tact. There was a time when the Derbyshire professionals had an unenviable reputation both on the field and in the dressing room, but today one hears at Lord's how popular they are and a nicer lot of fellows never stepped upon the sward. The gradual improvement in the club's position in the Championship table dates from the inauguration of the nursery; by this means youngsters of promise could be under constant supervision, coached, and when ready brought into the side as friends, instead of outsiders who were not infrequently made to realise their position."

Ellison paid tribute to Harry Elliott and Smith and described Skinner as a fine, steely attacking player. He said that Alderman "had learned to give the bat a chance and that offence is the best defence. One can't help feeling that he has the new lbw rule to thank. His fielding has been magnificent."

Of the Pope brothers, 'wonderful young triers from the Vatican' Ellison wrote: "AV does something with the ball which nobody can explain, not even the bowler, but when it does happen batsmen have to seek a seat in the shade. His action is not so good as GH, who unwinds himself well, keeps his arm well up, and is on his day quite fast." He added: "As Worthington is called upon to do less with the ball his batting should go ahead. There are plenty of runs left there and when he is getting them well no one is better worth watching. When Carrington has learnt to give the ball a little less air he should be fifty per cent better. He is a fine fielder. One more class opening bat like Sutcliffe and a slow left-arm bowler like Verity or Parker would have given Derbyshire their first Championship."

Although the South African game at Ilkeston was a financial disappointment – it yielded only £220 compared with £931 from the Australian visit to Chesterfield in 1934 – there was an increase in receipts, gates going up by nearly £1,000 to £4,549 and subscriptions bringing in £2,944, slightly down on 1934. The cost of running the side now was £8,521 and the loss on the season was cut to only £155.

It had been a stunning rise from obscurity and near oblivion. Major Llewellyn Eardley-Simpson's book, *The Rise of Derbyshire Cricket 1919-1935*, described the confidence gained by the team and the consequent change of approach. "We have now a set of really good players, but so we had in the past, and yet there is something different. It is the psychology of thing that counts; in the old days when a match started players and spectators were wondering "What shall we lose by?". Next came the question "Is there a chance of winning?" And now it is more likely "Will it be another win in two days?"

The club was, indeed, entitled to rejoice that after so many lean years it had achieved success. "Eleven years ago, Derbyshire – for the second time in five seasons – was at the bottom of the table without a single victory; in the last three years we have been three times in the Big Six... The side is young, keen and successful; there are few players who should not do even better with more experience and I know they mean to keep Derbyshire in its proud position among the leading counties," Eardley-Simpson wrote. He made no rash promises about going one better and winning the County Championship, content enough to say they would keep on trying. On all fronts, then, Derbyshire had cause for celebration in 1935.

Chapter 28
A New Season

POETICALLY, cricket's pre-season ritual involves mowing and rolling the square, the smell of freshly cut grass and linseed oil and net sessions taking place on fine spring days. The reality can be different. Two days after the coldest Easter Sunday since 1919, Derbyshire's professionals reported for duty on Tuesday April 14 1936 in chilly weather.

In the fashion of new seasons, they arrived in dribs and drabs. Leslie Townsend, Denis Smith and Albert Alderman were en route from New Zealand, Smith with the MCC team and his colleagues from coaching engagements. Harry Storer and Charlie Elliott were still with Coventry City. Another absentee footballer was Wally Hunt, who joined the ground staff in the spring. On that bitterly cold day Cadman, George Pope, Arnold Townsend and Carrington laid matting on a concrete pitch. Youngsters from public schools were to spend a fortnight practising, among them 16-year-old David Skinner, brother of Alan. The much-maligned ground at Derby at least earned praise from the local newspaper: "The County Ground at Nottingham Road today presents a picture that must delight the heart of every lover of our summer game. The turf has received attention throughout the winter, and it is now to be seen in all its verdant grandeur."

Will Taylor said that in the first few days there had been no indoor practice. Priority was given to physical training. "All the players are fit and looking forward to the start of the season. In view of our performances last season we have something to live up to but I think we shall succeed."

Tommy Mitchell was back, although it had been touch and go. Offers from Royston and Colne in the Lancashire League had been considered. He was 33, had taken more than a thousand first-class wickets and was unlikely to play Test cricket again after his experiences at Lord's in 1935. Mitchell opted to stay with the county. He also had problems with a damaged leg muscle and thought he might have to miss a few matches in 1936. In the event he was able to carry on and suffered no ill effects from this.

The most pleasant surprise was Bill Copson. Derbyshire had given a lot of consideration to his health and the fast bowler had spent the winter training with Chesterfield at Saltergate. The outcome was a stone gained in weight and greater strength. Ellison wrote: "Copson has been wisely hardening himself on the Chesterfield football ground during the winter and should come into form straight away. England has need of a man with his pace off the pitch." Marriage to Emily Titterton in 1935 added stability to his life. The couple made their home in Hepthorne Lane, North Wingfield, Bill later having a house built in Clay Cross in 1937 or 1938. During the close seasons he worked at the Clay Cross Company. "The Jacksons were his sponsors or mentors," said his son, Michael. "During the winter they employed him at the works and generally looked after him." The high regard of the Jacksons was reciprocated. At Guy's funeral in a packed Morton parish church in 1966, Bill Copson was one of the bearers.

There was sad news. Arthur Morton had died aged 52, in December 1935 after a long illness. During the summer he had been forced to relinquish umpiring engagements due to ill health but he had been retained on the first-class list for 1936. Another former player, Ernest 'Nudger' Needham, died in March at the age of 63.

Latent talent was now coming into full flower as the sons of the mining communities who had developed through the nursery reached full potential. This was a team which had been together for several years, most of them either at the peak of their careers or close to it. Harry Elliott, at the age of 44 when the season began, was in the veteran stage but there were no signs of receding powers. Harry Storer (38) was past his best but of the other over-thirties Tommy Mitchell (33), Leslie Townsend (32) and Stan Worthington (30) were close to their finest seasons.

The remainder achieved a near-perfect balance of age and experience: Arthur Richardson and Denis Smith were 29, Albert Alderman and Bill Copson 28, Alf Pope and Tommy Armstrong 26, George Pope 25, Charlie Elliott and Arnold Townsend 24, Alan Skinner 23 and Elijah Carrington 22. Places in the field were automatic. The slip cordon could be formed by any of Copson, Mitchell, the Popes, Smith, Skinner and Worthington, with the latter also fielding at short-leg. The vital positions in the covers were filled by Carrington and Storer, with Richardson taking mid-off. The outfielders were Alderman, Townsend and Charlie Elliott.

The players were becoming familiar to a wider audience. An occasional newpaper photograph, or perhaps a cartoon was the most exposure a county cricketer could expect in the 1930s, when there was no television and radio commentary was in its infancy. The tobacco firms were taking notice of Derbyshire's success and some players were featured in the cigarette cards which were becoming increasingly popular. Players' Cricketers 1930 included Mitchell and the 1934 set Townsend and Mitchell. By the time the 1938 set was issued Copson, Smith and Worthington had graduated and they were also included in Churchman's Cricketers of 1936.

There was experience and capability at top level. The club president, the Duke of Devonshire, was aged 68. George Buckston (55), captain in 1921, was the chairman and the two honorary posts of treasurer and secretary were filled by Major Llewellyn Eardley-Simpson (56) and Rev Henry Ellison (67). And there was Will Taylor, the secretary, now aged 51, linked in *Wisden* to a familiar address, 18 St James's Chambers, Derby.

The Championship fixtures for 1936 consisted of home and away matches against

14 counties, Glamorgan and Middlesex being excluded. These covered five home grounds and included a cricket week at Chesterfield in July when Warwickshire and Hampshire would be the visitors. The Bank Holiday matches reverted to the pre-1914-18 war arrangements with Essex the opponents for the next two seasons. Practice for members would start on May 1. Admission at the home grounds would be a shilling, and sixpence for pensioners. The *Derby Evening Telegraph* headlined its preview 'Derbyshire's cricket reputation never so high', while pointing out that there was a need for a sound batsman at No 3. There were several players who could score quickly but somebody was needed to take the edge off the attack. The paper felt that the attack should be better than ever, although it lacked a quality slow left-arm bowler.

The bowlers received a workout against the Derby and District League, when the side was captained by Mac Walker in the absence of Richardson, unavailable for the opening three games. Walker, a 40-year-old army officer who was adjutant of the 5th (TA) Battalion Sherwood Foresters, led out a side consisting of Worthington, the Pope brothers, Carrington, Harry Elliott, Mitchell, Copson, Bedford, Rhodes and David Skinner. Derby and District League were restricted to 36 for eight on a rain-affected day. Walker also skippered a club and ground team at Chesterfield a few days later.

The 1936 season started with a nine-day tour; Hampshire at Southampton, the university at Oxford and Kent at Gravesend. It was announced that, with Richardson out and Alan Skinner unavailable until later on, the matches would be played under three captains – Willie Hill-Wood at Southampton. John Gilbert at Oxford and Mac Walker for the Kent game. The committee selected a team for all three: Smith (recovered from pre-season lumbago), Alderman, Leslie Townsend, Worthington, Carrington, George Pope, Alf Pope, Elliott, Mitchell, Copson and the captain. Charlie Elliott travelled as twelfth man.

From the modern perspective the wonder is that Harry Elliott was not placed in charge but even after four successful matches as captain, Elliott was still regarded as a last resort, given the job only when there was no suitable amateur available. The Derbyshire professionals were, by now, a hard-headed lot. Denis Smith, George and Alf Pope and Harry Storer were men of forthright opinion which they were not slow to express. Tommy Mitchell clashed with a number of people in authority. Nevertheless they had to toe the line. Contemporary thinking remained heavily in favour of an amateur skipper who wielded considerable power. It was the way of things. Hill-Wood had scored his thousand runs in 1923, disappeared for a decade and returned as captain for a couple of matches in 1935. He played a fair amount of club cricket in the intervening years and made 56 for the Viceroy's XI in India three years earlier in a first-class match. Gilbert and Walker were prominent in 2nd XI and club cricket.

On Wednesday May 6 1936, Hill-Wood lost the toss at Southampton's County Ground and led out the team, Bill Copson delivering the first ball of what was to be an outstanding season. The pitch was soft after rain and Mitchell, four for 93, found some turn. Phil Mead (62) was the sheet anchor as Hampshire were dismissed for 256, Derbyshire losing Smith and Townsend in making 40 by close of play.

Hampshire took control on the second day. They had a first innings lead of 52 and it would have been more but for an aggressive display by Carrington. He was missed off successive balls and was lucky again when a huge drive struck a fieldsman's hands and went for six. His 72 included two sixes and nine fours and although Harry Elliott made an unbeaten 35 Derbyshire were all out for 204. Then Dick Moore, in his first match as Hampshire's captain, and Cecil Paris made hundreds, the declaration on the final day leaving Derbyshire to make 387 in 240 minutes. It was a tall order and Derbyshire concentrated on saving the game and the three points for a loss on the first innings. Smith and Alderman opened with 64, Worthington made 44, Townsend 67 and the score reached 148 with only two batsmen out. The middle order crumbled, however, and eight wickets were down for 235, Hill-Wood getting an invaluable 38 in what was to be his final innings for the county. Hampshire claimed the extra half-hour, Elliott spent 55 minutes over a single, Mitchell laid about him and the end came with Derbyshire, 255 for eight, playing out time.

On to The Parks and an admirable start. Gilbert won the toss; Alderman failed but Smith (77) and Worthington added 139 for the second wicket in 90 minutes. Townsend then joined Worthington in a partnership of 136, the score being 306 when the third wicket fell. Worthington made 174 in three hours, hitting two sixes and 25 fours. He batted faultlessly in making his hundred, hit out at everything afterwards and was missed four times. George Pope drove vigorously in an unbeaten 62 and Derbyshire had raced to 456 all out when bad light ended play at 5.15pm. Sixty-five fours were struck during the day's play. On Monday, Oxford University were forced to follow on, 303 behind, after being dismissed for 153. Copson took four for 14 and although Mitchell was punished only the Dark Blues' captain, Norman Mitchell-Innes, with an undefeated 67, resisted for long. Copson's pace was simply too much for the undergraduates and in bowling Michael Barton middle stump before he had scored, he sent a bail flying 35 yards. Barton (70) batted well in Oxford's second innings but they could make only 173 and Derbyshire won by an innings and 130 runs in two days.

It was an encouraging outing, marred only by a knee injury to George Pope, which caused him to miss the next match against Kent at the Bat and Ball ground in Gravesend. Walker took over the reins from Gilbert and Charlie Elliott replaced Pope. Nearly everything went wrong. Freeman, at 47, fell away dramatically in the latter part of the summer, the muscles in his right arm no longer able to bear the strain, and he was not re-engaged at the end of the season. There was as yet little evidence of this and Derbyshire had no answer to him after rain delayed the start and affected the pitch.

The visitors had made 37 without loss at lunch but afterwards Freeman gave yet another reminder of his skill with seven for 29. The young Doug Wright provided a demonstration of what was to come as Derbyshire foundered against the leg-spin and were all out by 3.30pm for 119. Alderman made 47 but the last six wickets went down for 30. Free hitting by Frank Woolley and a fine display by Leslie Todd gave

Kent the upper hand but there was no prolonged stand against Copson and Mitchell and by the close of play they had been dismissed for 179.

On the second day Derbyshire again collapsed against spin. Three wickets were down for 27 and although Alderman and Carrington tried to pull the game round by clearing the arrears Wright (five for 31) accounted for both of them and then destroyed the tail. A humiliating ten-wicket defeat before lunch on the second day when many of the crowd had only just arrived left no room for excuses. It was Kent's third consecutive victory, a 100 per cent return of 45 points. Derbyshire had three from a possible 30 and all the hopes and predictions were already looking highly optimistic. To rub salt into the wound they were asked to fill in with an exhibition match but refused on the grounds that they wanted to get back home on the same day.

There is evidence that Mac Walker failed to win many friends as skipper. Tony Pope said his father Alf used to speak of 'an army officer' who took over in 1936 when Arthur Richardson could not play. "The professionals knew nothing about him when he turned up and said he was going to captain the side. It soon became obvious that he was not good enough to play at their standard. My dad was batting and when the captain called for a risky single he sent him back. He marched down the pitch and said to my dad: 'When I say run, you bloody well run.' The pros were not impressed."

Two years earlier, a Royal Navy commander John Dunlop Southern (known as Guy because his birthday was November 5) had stood in at Portsmouth when Arthur Richardson and Alan Skinner were injured. Southern was no more than a good club player and this was his fifth and final match for the county, the penultimate one having been in 1922, although one or two of the younger players were aware of him from his captaincy of the club and ground and 2nd XI in the 1930s, when the Pope brothers were forcing their way to the front. "My dad also mentioned this," said Tony. "It was all very feudal. Again it was a case of an officer arriving and taking over as captain of a side which hardly knew him. You can imagine the feelings of seasoned pros being told what to bowl and where to field by somebody some of them had never seen before."

But there was one occasion when Alf Pope rebelled. After an all-professional Derbyshire team had beaten Worcestershire at Stourbridge in July 1934, three amateurs made themselves available for the visit of the Australians to Chesterfield. Guy Jackson, who was captain, Alan Skinner and Neville Ford replaced Carrington and the two Popes. Alf Pope had given way to Ford earlier for the Warwickshire match at Whitsuntide and he was not pleased. "He made a bit of an issue about it because it meant he would lose his match fee and eventually he received his money," said Tony. To be fair to Ford, his 37 was the second-highest score in the first innings. The Australians won by nine wickets, Bradman making 71, caught by Harry Elliott off Leslie Townsend, and six not out.

They even had their moments with Guy Jackson. He was travelling first class, as was usual, on one long rail journey, with the professionals segregated lower down. "Four of them, including my father and Stan Worthington, were together in a carriage," said Tony. "Worthington had done well in the previous match and had bought a lot of newspapers which praised him in glowing terms. When Guy Jackson came down the train this was pointed out to him and somebody started to read the reports out aloud. "Right," said Jackson. "Pope, you're playing in the next match. Smith, you're playing," and so on until he pointed to Stan. "But Worthington you are not playing. Your head's too swollen." Such stories illustrate the respect the team had for Richardson. The other stand-in captains were acceptable – they had grown up under Jackson, some of them were playing in 1923 when Hill-Wood topped the batting averages and the youthful Gilbert seems to have caused them no problems – but others were different.

Somewhat chastened, the team returned from Gravesend and reported to Derby for the first home game of the season, against Surrey. They found a change at the County Ground. The pavilion balcony had been extended so that it covered a greater part of the terracing. This offered better shelter for members and included a section reserved for the professionals. Rev Henry Ellison said there would now be no excuse for them not sitting in the light before batting. "No man can do himself justice if he walks straight out of a rabbit warren into sunlight," he wrote. The work was made possible by a legacy of £500 from the late Alderman GA Eastwood, of Chesterfield, who had been a member of the committee. It was formally opened by his niece on Saturday May 16, the opening day of the Surrey match.

Arthur Richardson was present at the ceremony and skippered the side for the first time that season, the fourth captain in as many matches. George Pope, who had received treatment at the Derbyshire Royal Infirmary for his strained knee, replaced Charlie Elliott, although he played only as a batsman, the injury preventing him from bowling.

Even at this early stage of the season fast bowlers Bill Copson and Surrey's Alf Gover were in competition for a place in the England team. Bill Bowes and Gubby Allen, captain for the three Tests against the Indians and the man who was to lead in Australia, opened the MCC attack against the tourists at the time of the Surrey match but Gover and Copson remained among the front runners. Gover lost no time in making his mark when play began at Derby, removing Smith before he had scored. Alderman (eleven fours in 77) and Townsend (38) put on 105 for the third wicket in 90 minutes, only for the last six wickets to fall for 29 runs. Derbyshire were all out for 175, Gover taking five for 63.

Fifty years later 'an Old Supporter' recalled the match in an article in the year book. "On the Saturday of the Surrey match I arrived shortly after lunch to see the Derbyshire batting once more in a mess. The club had made a public commitment to play brighter cricket as they had done with much success in 1935 but now it was going wrong. As in the Kent match the batsmen had been hitting out too soon in their innings and not moving their feet to the ball. Denis Smith, having a thin start to the season, Stan Worthington and Les Townsend had all gone before I arrived but Albert Alderman was still there, battling it out against the bowling of Alf Gover and Freddie Brown. I saw both George and Alf Pope perish to adventurous strokes and Arthur Richardson dolly a catch to cover and return dejectedly to the pavilion... Alderman compiled an unattractive but invaluable 77 and Gover, without looking as hostile as at other times, took most of the wickets."

When Surrey began their innings Andy Sandham and Robert Gregory saw off Copson's early burst. He could find neither length nor direction and was soon replaced. The hundred was passed with only two men out, both victims of Mitchell to consecutive balls from the pavilion end. Tom Barling joined Sandham and Old Supporter said they seemed in little trouble when Copson was re-introduced at the Nottingham Road end. "He produced one of those spot-on balls that seemed to gain great pace off the pitch. Andy Sandham was clean bowled for 53." A five-over spell brought him three wickets for five runs. Seven wickets were down for 116 before Barling, driving and pulling well for 87 not out, which included four fours in an over from Mitchell, and Jack Parker took the score to 187 by the close. It had been Surrey's day – just – and honours between the fast bowlers were about even.

On Monday, Barling was bowled by Copson for 95 and Surrey's lead restricted to 43. Copson took five for 33 and Mitchell four for 89. Derbyshire gave another moderate display in their second innings, only Alderman (43) offering prolonged resistance. Surrey wanted 94 to win and reached 49 for two; 45 needed with eight wickets left.

With the outcome looking such a foregone conclusion, nobody on the ground, neither the teams nor the spectators, wanted to bother with the tea interval but the umpires Ernest Cooke and Charlie Parker invoked the rules and said there had to be one. When the teams returned to the field, half the spectators had gone home. It is stating the obvious to say they must have regretted it for what happened next stretched credibility. Copson, bowling irresistibly, demoralised Surrey. After tea his great pace and length earned him six wickets for eight runs in a spell of seven overs. He was almost unplayable, only Laurie Fishlock, unbeaten with 17 in 50 minutes, resisting for long and even he was beaten five times in one over. Surrey were all out for 77, Copson took seven for 19 in 14 overs – which gave him a match analysis of twelve for 52 – and Derbyshire had gained their opening victory of the 1936 County Championship season by 16 runs. The last wicket to fall was that of Gover. He believed he was wrongly given out, caught at the wicket off Copson, and stayed in the middle after the other players left the field, to make his point.

The *Derby Evening Telegraph* assessed the merits of the fast bowling rivals. "Gover was a hard worker, and looked capable of lasting longer than Copson, but at no time did he trouble the batsmen like the Derbyshire man. The Surrey pace bowler was not nearly so fast off the pitch as Copson, and his length was erratic. In contrast, Copson's length was so perfect and his deliveries so straight that the batsmen were compelled to play at every delivery."

Copson had pulled the fat out of the fire and the psychological aspects of this victory should not be underestimated. A second defeat by a Big Six county and the wrong end of a draw at Southampton would have been a start few envisaged. As it was the unexpected win over Surrey helped to change the course of the season.

Kent won at Edgbaston and led the Championship table with a hundred per cent record from four matches. Nottinghamshire, Leicestershire and Warwickshire followed, with Derbyshire in tenth place, a win, a draw and a defeat. They now had a short break before their next match, against Sussex at Queen's Park. Here Jack Nye bowled Alderman and Worthington with only 23 scored but Smith (53) and Townsend added 89 and Carrington helped in the recovery. This was completed by a fifth wicket partnership of 137 in 110 minutes between Townsend and Harry Elliott. Concerned by the middle order failings Richardson promoted Elliott in the order and he responded with 63. Townsend, missed at 33, was 165 not out by Saturday's close at 351 for seven and he went on to an unbeaten 182, which included a six and 22 fours. It was a more restrained innings than was usual from Townsend, given the recent batting collapses, but he drove superbly. Derbyshire made 387 and then Copson carried on where he left off against Surrey. Before lunch on the second day he took five for 27, Mitchell then claiming four victims as Sussex were routed for 129.

They followed on 258 behind, John Langridge and Harry Parks adding 109 for the second wicket but the innings fell away and Derbyshire won on the third morning by an innings and 25 runs, in good time for the journey down to Bristol for the next game. Copson's match analysis was eight for 78 and Derbyshire rose to sixth in the table.

At Bristol, George Pope, who had delivered 24 overs at Chesterfield without any ill effects, soon dismissed Reg Sinfield and Mitchell had Basil Allen stumped at 40. This brought Charlie Barnett and Wally Hammond together and the score had reached 50 when Pope left the field, a slip while bowling bringing about a reoccurrence of the knee trouble he had suffered at Oxford. There was to be no return this time. A damaged cartilage led to an operation in a Birmingham nursing home and Pope was out for the season. It was a grievous blow, *Wisden* commenting: "The extent of the loss of this fine cricketer, both in batting and bowling, could scarcely be estimated." George Pope played in four Championship matches in 1936, bowling 56.1 overs and taking five wickets at 25.60.

His brother soon bowled Hammond and Gloucestershire made only 164, Barnett top scoring with 59. Sinfield hit back and reduced Derbyshire to 85 for six before Harry Elliott (61) and Alf Pope (40) added 77 and there was a lead of 29. Gloucestershire's second innings lasted only two hours and they were all out for 123, Mitchell, Pope and Worthington getting the wickets. Alderman and Smith hit off the 95 needed in 90 minutes to record Derbyshire's third consecutive victory.

It left a vacant Friday to ease the travel and preparation for the Whitsuntide match against Essex at Derby. There was an enforced change, Storer replacing

George Pope. Essex, captained by Tom Pearce, had made a useful start to the season and had just beaten the Indians at Brentwood. Pearce and Richardson had at least one social engagement to fulfil, a flannel dance on the Saturday evening in aid of the pavilion extension fund. It proved to be the only bright spot that day. Drizzle set in before play could start and by mid afternoon the rain was falling steadily, ruling out the possibility of any cricket that day.

The weather was dry but cold on Whit Monday and, given this, a gate of 5,000 was satisfactory. The Derbyshire County Show was taking place that day, not far away at Swadlincote, and the 15,000 attendance there was the highest since 1919. Among the spectators at Derby was Old Supporter. He saw Derbyshire crash to 101 for eight against some hostile bowling by Nicholls and John Stephenson. "But Stan Worthington was now taking control. How often did we see Stanley mastering fast bowlers that others could not cope with. He beautifully middled the first ball he received, then, I believe, leg glanced the second for two and he was away, the pace men then holding no terrors for him. He was scoring quickly with lovely strokes while wickets were falling at the other end.

"When the eighth wicket fell, that man for a crisis, Tommy Mitchell, strode in. It is surprising how often at Derby he would come in and seem to make light of a situation which had inhibited the early batsmen." They were still together at lunch and afterwards "while Stan kept up his fine stroke play Tommy scored about as quickly with shots ranging from the classical to the comic." The pair added 77 in 45 minutes before Mitchell was out for 25. Worthington remained undefeated with 85 (13 fours) in a total of 179. Essex, helped by a fourth wicket partnership of 115 by Cutmore and Nicholls, were 193 for six by the close but nothing could be done on Tuesday and the match ended in a draw.

Derbyshire's run of good form placed them in the early pacemakers by Tuesday June 2. Kent still led. Surrey were second and Derbyshire held third place, ahead of Leicestershire.

Yorkshire, stuttering uncharacteristically, were fifth. They had outplayed Essex for two days at Hull but had been held to a draw, and a remarkable defeat by Worcestershire at Stourbridge had followed. Verity took 13 for 88 but a side which included Sutcliffe, Mitchell, Barber, Leyland and Hutton collapsed on a crumbling pitch against Howorth and Jackson in the quest for 118 and fell short by 11 runs. Somebody would pay and Glamorgan were beaten by ten wickets at Swansea and high-flying Kent put to the sword at Bramall Lane. In their second innings Kent were dismissed for 39, Verity taking nine for 12 to complete match figures of fifteen for 38. The champions remained favourites to retain the title in spite of their early-season setback.

The next round of fixtures found Derbyshire travelling to Northampton and making one change to their side, Wally Hunt coming in for his debut in place of Carrington. The move made sense. Hunt's spin would add variety to the attack. Carrington had struggled since his 72 in the opening match, his last eight

Championship innings producing only 85 runs. He promptly showed his character in a rain-ruined 2nd XI match against Nottinghamshire, top-scoring with 36 in Derbyshire's 94 for five.

Hunt's bowling was not needed. Percy Perrin, one of the Test selectors, was at the game and saw Townsend (four for three) and Mitchell wreck the home team's first innings for 59, Derbyshire struggling in turn on a difficult, rain-damaged pitch for 93, of which Townsend made 31. The weather caused the match to go into the final day, Copson taking six for 24 in Northamptonshire's second innings. Derbyshire needed 125 to win and although Alderman completed a pair, Smith's 59 helped them home by seven wickets. For Smith, it was a timely innings. He had made a poor start to the season and even after this match he was averaging only 23 in the Championship, a long way behind Townsend, Worthington and Alderman.

Gloucestershire were also challenging the front runners and this added spice to their visit to Derby on Wednesday June 10. There was one change in the Derbyshire team, Charlie Elliott coming in for Storer who was needed at Highfield Road. In this match Derbyshire gave a convincing demonstration of their power and an ability to win matches in limited time. Gloucestershire made a good start, 64 for the loss of one wicket and then 77 for two but they were all out for 95 in 105 minutes. Mitchell took seven for 26, the last six at a cost of nine runs. His tenth over included three of these and a six by Monks. Copson took three wickets and Harry Elliott held three catches. Worthington then drove powerfully, striking 13 fours in making 90, Harry Elliott, revelling in his promotion to number six to strengthen the middle order, helping in a fifth wicket partnership of 73. Leading by 105, Derbyshire dismissed the visitors for 194, Alf Pope taking four for 29. Alderman and Smith got the required 91 in 70 minutes, giving Derbyshire their fifth victory in eight Championship matches. In a repeat of Northampton, Smith batted beautifully, hitting eight fours in his unbeaten 63. Mitchell took his 1,000th wicket for the county in only his 207th appearance during this game. Only two points now separated Derbyshire from the leaders, Kent, with Middlesex third and Surrey in fourth place.

The leading pack continually looked over their shoulders in Yorkshire's direction. They were no higher than eighth but nobody felt that this state of affairs would last for much longer. Consequently, Saturday, Monday and Tuesday June 13, 15 and 16, when Yorkshire visited Queen's Park, were crucial days. The England selectors gave the home side a major advantage. Copson was absent, playing for the North against the South in a Test trial at Lord's but Yorkshire were missing Mitchell, Leyland and Verity, colleagues of Copson in the same match. For Derbyshire, Storer and Arnold Townsend replaced Charlie Elliott and Copson, the team being Alderman, Smith, Storer, Worthington, Leslie Townsend, Harry Elliott, Arnold Townsend, Hunt, Richardson, Alf Pope and Mitchell.

Will Taylor appreciated the importance of this game in the context of the County Championship but more than most he was aware of the financial implications. "We always hoped for fine weather and three exciting days for the Yorkshire and

Nottinghamshire matches at Chesterfield and Ilkeston," he said. Nobody was more disappointed when rain which set in on Friday evening ruled out play on Saturday. Taylor estimated the weather cost the club a £350 Saturday gate and increased the losses on such takings to more than £900 at that stage of the season.

It was 2.15pm on Monday before play could begin and Derbyshire made a deplorable start. Alderman, Smith and Storer had gone for only 18 and Worthington and Leslie Townsend faced the task of repairing the innings. Yorkshire then had a glorious opportunity to force home an advantage which could conceivably have brought victory. Townsend was dropped at slip by Turner before he had scored and the fielding error proved costly. Playing attractive cricket, the batsmen hit back in a brilliant partnership of 154 in 135 minutes, pulling the game around completely. Worthington, full of confidence, drove superbly and hit nine fours in making 80. Townsend went on to 101, his second century of the season occupying three hours and including two sixes and 12 fours. Derbyshire closed on 234 for nine, increasing this to 253 on the final morning.

When Yorkshire batted, Pope had Sutcliffe caught at the wicket and then Mitchell, cleverly varying his flight and pace, caused major problems. His first delivery removed Hutton and an opening burst of five for 20 reduced Yorkshire to 62 for seven. Arthur Wood and Frank Smailes added 37 but the champions were all out for 112, Mitchell six for 60, and were obliged, under two-day rules, to follow on 141 behind. Although Sutcliffe failed again, Hutton and Sellers batted cautiously and Yorkshire, 102 for one, easily saved the game. Realistically, it was the best Derbyshire could hope for, a result that pegged the champions further back. Kent's victory over Somerset extended their lead but Derbyshire were still not far behind.

Rain had also hit the Test trial, preventing play on Saturday. Around 6,000 spectators saw North make 321. Copson was a typical No 11 and any runs he scored were usually made very quickly, with healthily unorthodox strokes. On this occasion he lashed 24 out of a tenth wicket partnership of 39 with Hardstaff before being caught at the wicket off Robins. Gover took five for 93. In the last quarter-of-an-hour, South lost the wicket of Gimblett to Reg Perks. Copson bowled very fast, making the ball get up, and Barnett received a severe blow on the arm but on the final day he was punished as South totalled 363, Maurice Turnbull making 106 before Copson caught him off Verity. The Derbyshire bowler was hooked for six by Robins and conceded 103 runs in 33 overs, taking a solitary wicket, that of Errol Holmes. *The Cricketer* reported: "Copson has great pace off the ground, but he bowled short of a length and did not seem able to run the ball away. He has an economical action, and there is so much life in his deliveries that it is a pity he is so consistently short."

In the meantime, the county's amateurs kept themselves busy at club level, notably with the Friars. Seven who captained Derbyshire during their careers – Richardson, Hodgkinson, Alan Skinner, Walker, Blaxland, Guy Willatt and David Skinner – turned out for Friars in 1936. Guy Jackson skippered MCC in a match against Repton and Gilbert scored plenty of runs in local cricket.

The day following the Yorkshire match found Somerset facing Derbyshire at Ilkeston, Copson and Carrington returning to the exclusion of Arnold Townsend and Hunt. Although Somerset were capable of shocking anybody on their day, it should have been easy for Derbyshire. Five defeats and only one win in eight matches, the last three all lost, was not the form of a team with a tradition for upsetting its betters. Yet Derbyshire were rolled over by ten wickets on a pitch affected by rain. Hubert Hunt, a 24-year-old off-spinner, had the day of his cricketing life with seven for 49 and despite some good bowling from Mitchell and Worthington, the visitors led by 38. By the close Derbyshire had lost two wickets for 15 and the batting disintegrated to 62 all out on the second morning, Somerset recording a sensational victory.

That round of matches opened up the race for the Championship. Yorkshire defeated Essex and Nottinghamshire placed themselves among the contenders as Larwood and Voce routed Kent on the Angel Ground at Tonbridge. On the evening of Friday June 19, the pacemakers had settled themselves down into a pattern. Kent remained top with six wins from 10 matches, 65.33 per cent of the points possible. Derbyshire, 12 points behind after 10 games, were on 57.33, Nottinghamshire 55.23, Middlesex 51.33 and Yorkshire 48.88.

Licking their wounds, Derbyshire headed for Edgbaston with one change in their side, Charlie Elliott for Carrington, who had fallen to Wellard in each innings for a pair at Ilkeston. Richardson won the toss and decided to bat but must have had misgivings by noon as Danny Mayer got rid of Smith and Storer with a mere nine runs on the board. Worthington, missed at 17, started a recovery, driving and pulling vigorously for 81 (13 fours) and then Charlie Elliott, going in at the fall of the fourth wicket, fully justified his selection. He made 97, belying a reputation for stodginess with two sixes and nine fours. He should have been out before he scored and escaped again on 65 but added 92 for the fifth wicket with Alderman, combining sound defence with well-timed hitting on the leg side. Elliott fell to a catch off Eric Hollies but 280 for six was not a bad Saturday night score after the early shocks.

Play was delayed until 1.15pm on the second day and Warwickshire, caught on a drying pitch, were forced to follow on after some fine bowling by Townsend and Mitchell. Wyatt (72) made a fight of it on Tuesday but Townsend took seven for 46, bringing his match analysis to 50-15-90-12 and Derbyshire were home by an innings and 10 runs. George Paine was dismissed hit-wicket bowled Mitchell in both innings, the only instance in first-class cricket of that dismissal by the same bowler twice in one match.

It was a timely success, for Kent defeated Worcestershire and Nottinghamshire, again with Larwood and Voce in prime form, and won at Old Trafford. The leading three had opened a sizeable gap as Yorkshire had to be satisfied with a five-point draw. Kent played 11, won seven, points 113, 68.48 per cent; Derbyshire played 11, won six, points 101, 61.21 and Nottinghamshire played eight, won four, 60.83. Middlesex and Yorkshire followed, with Hampshire now the only undefeated county.

The following round of matches turned the race on its head. Derbyshire were back at Queen's Park on Wednesday with an unchanged team for the Worcestershire match. The start was sensational. Copson clean bowled Charles Bull with the first delivery of the match, a ball which came back from outside the off stump to hit leg. Harry Gibbons made 99 but Worcestershire were dismissed for 233, Copson taking five for 34, clean bowling all his victims. Townsend held the Derbyshire innings together with 76, which included four sixes and nine fours, typical of the aggressive approach taken by the batsmen at this stage of the season.

They led by 14, and some accurate and varied bowling found them requiring 149 for victory on the last day. Smith went early, bowled by Perks for the second time in the match. He made 2 and 0 and with a Championship average of 21 his form was giving increasing cause for concern. Fortunately Storer, who had also been having a lean time, rediscovered his touch. He made 62, sharing a partnership of 86 with Worthington (35). Perks then brought about a breakdown with five for 63 but Alderman was still there with 29 when Derbyshire claimed their seventh win of the season, edging home by three wickets.

Kent had also been involved in a close finish at Aigburth but they found themselves on the wrong end of it, Lancashire scraping home by two wickets. Yorkshire won at Bath but the key result was at Trent Bridge, where Nottinghamshire crushed Warwickshire by an innings. It was their third consecutive victory and it took them to the head of the Championship table. Nottinghamshire had won five and lost one of nine matches, obtaining 88 points, 65.18 per cent of the 135 possible. Derbyshire were second, seven wins and two defeats in 12, 116 points and a percentage of 64.44. Kent had slipped to third, three points behind Derbyshire with seven wins and three defeats in 12 and a percentage of 62.77. Yorkshire had climbed to fourth, four wins and a defeat in 11, 86 points, 52.12 per cent.

Meanwhile Lancashire, the champions of two years earlier, had fallen on relatively hard times. They won only two matches until after the August Bank Holiday and although proving difficult to beat, were never in contention but they gave an unchanged Derbyshire side a difficult time in a rain-affected match at The Park, Buxton, dismissing them for 61 in reply to a total of 194 on the first day. Copson (four for 35) and Pope (five for 53) bowled unchanged in a Lancastrian second innings of 94. Derbyshire required 228 to win in 180 minutes but opted for safety on the rain-affected pitch, ending at 92 for four. Denis Smith was demoted to number four in the order in this match, Storer opening first with Worthington and then with Alderman. At least Will Taylor had a smile on his face after a Saturday gate of 3,968 paying spectators produced record gate receipts for Buxton of £260. An estimated 5,000 people were on the ground. Among them was the club president, the Duke of Devonshire. When a ball crashed through the windscreen of his car the Duke promptly offered £5 to any batsman who could repeat the shot.

Kent regained the lead after beating Essex, Nottinghamshire taking three points for a loss on the first innings at Hove. This encounter gave the lie to any woolly thinking that now Carr had gone Nottinghamshire were a soft touch. Five minutes of the extra half hour remained when Sussex began their second innings needing nine to win. Voce bowled the first over, from which Jim Parks scored two runs and extras brought the total to seven. Two to win and slight rain began to fall. Nottinghamshire's captain George Heane spoke to the umpires, Claude Woolley and Jack Newman, and led his team from the field, the match ending in a draw. Sussex protested and threatened to discontinue fixtures with Nottinghamshire but the trouble soon subsided.

Derbyshire were unchanged for the third consecutive match when they visited New Road on Wednesday July 1: Storer, Alderman, Smith, Worthington, Townsend, the two Elliotts, Richardson, Pope, Mitchell and Copson. Yet again there was rain about, but Storer (52) and Alderman (61) gave their side an excellent start with an opening partnership of 108 in 160 minutes. By the close four wickets were down for 135, Perks bowling Worthington with a ball which sent a bail 35 yards. No play was possible until 3pm on Thursday, Charlie Elliott (49) and Alf Pope (28 not out) adding 54 for the eighth wicket before Richardson declared at 234 for eight.

Copson and Pope then proceeded to wreck the home side. By the close Worcestershire were 39 for six but even this represented something of a recovery, half the team being out with only six runs scored. Play did not begin on the third day until after lunch, when Worcestershire lost 14 wickets for 72. They were all out for 64, Copson five for 38, Pope four for 12, and fared even worse the second time around, lasting only 80 minutes for 47. Copson took a wicket with the first ball of the second innings and returned figures of 13-6-16-7 – a match analysis of twelve for 54. Harry Elliott claimed seven wicketkeeping victims, five of them in the first innings. Derbyshire's emphatic victory, by an innings and 123 runs, was quite awesome for Worcestershire were not at all a bad side in 1936, occupying 12th position in the final table for the second consecutive year.

Again the leadership changed hands, Nottinghamshire heading the table after ending Hampshire's unbeaten run of 15 matches with an innings victory at Basingstoke. Kent and Yorkshire each took five points from their matches and the situation at the halfway stage of the season remained tight: Nottinghamshire 106 points from 11 matches, 64.24 per cent; Derbyshire 134 from 14, 63.80; Kent 133 from 14, 63.33. Middlesex and Yorkshire, each just over 49 per cent, trailed.

This fascinating struggle now centred on Derbyshire's first-ever cricket week, with matches at Queen's Park against Warwickshire and Hampshire from Saturday July 4 to Friday July 11. Again the team was unchanged, the same eleven players having now taken the field for the past five games.

The week began well, Warwickshire being dismissed in two hours for 117, Mitchell five for 52, Copson four for 38 and Pope one for 18. Copson worked up a fine pace and made the ball swerve disconcertingly, taking three of the first five wickets at small cost. Derbyshire lost their openers for 26 but Worthington took charge with a fine display of driving and pulling. He was missed before he had scored, but raced to 114 not out by the close of play, 235 for four, with Charlie

Elliott on 48. Earlier Townsend hit a six and five fours in 36 and Smith made 24.

On Monday, Elliott added only a single, he and Worthington having shared a fifth wicket partnership of 127 in 90 minutes. Harry Elliott (40) helped Worthington put on 63 and Derbyshire's 381 gave them a first innings lead of 264. Worthington's 163 was his second hundred of the season and it included one five and 17 fours. He was at the crease for four hours.

Warwickshire had reduced the arrears by a single when rain ended play at 3pm. On the final day, Pope dismissed Arthur Croom and Aubrey Hill in his first over and despite Wyatt's 40 the last four wickets fell for one run. Warwickshire were all out for 105, Copson, Pope and Townsend taking three wickets apiece and Derbyshire had won by an innings and 159 runs – their second single innings victory in consecutive matches.

Yorkshire beat Surrey but, with Kent not playing, Nottinghamshire were unable to take full advantage. They had the better of their match against Middlesex at Trent Bridge, gaining a first innings lead of 87. Rain held them up and a third-day declaration at 4.15pm set Middlesex a target of 189 in 120 minutes. They settled for a draw and Nottinghamshire had to be content with first innings points.

It cost them the lead. Derbyshire moved into first place that evening, Tuesday July 7 1936, with nine victories in 15 matches and 149 points from a possible 225, 66.22 per cent. Kent were second, eight wins in 14, 133 points and 63.33 per cent and Nottinghamshire third, having won half of their 12 matches to give them 111 points at 61.66 per cent. Yorkshire, 52.85, and Middlesex, 47.22, followed.

Having watched the first and third places change between Kent and Nottinghamshire on three occasions without moving from second place, Derbyshire had taken the lead. Furthermore, they had a batsman, Stan Worthington, high in the national batting averages and Bill Copson among the first six bowlers. There might be rain about but it augured well for the second half of the Chesterfield Cricket Week.

Chapter 29
Border Battles

HAMPSHIRE arrived at Chesterfield in the early hours of Wednesday morning weary after a long journey from Portsmouth.

The players were tired but they were in good spirits. The side had bounced back from defeat at Trent Bridge with a victory over Sussex, winning by four wickets with five minutes to spare. There was general relief when Moore won the toss and elected to bat. It meant avoiding the chore of fielding after what was virtually a sleepless night but having to face Copson, Pope and Mitchell on a damp, soft Queen's Park pitch, with the destruction of Warwickshire fresh in the memory.

They were soon taking up their fielding positions, having been bowled out for 88 in 75 minutes. Copson made the early inroads, getting rid of Neil McCorkell and Phil Mead and half the side were out for 50. Pope, maintaining an immaculate length and making the ball break back sharply, took four for 15 after conceding 11 runs before meeting with success. In his last six overs he took three wickets for three runs. At first Derbyshire struggled, three wickets going for 74, including that of Alan Skinner. Free from law studies for a period, he replaced Storer, having got into practice by making 124 for the Friars against Notts Amateurs at the County Ground. After tea the pitch eased and Leslie Townsend drove powerfully. He was 153 not out by close of play, hitting four sixes off Creese and 19 fours during a stay of under four hours.

Only 30 minutes play was possible on the second day, which began at 5pm. Derbyshire declared at their overnight 336-8, a lead of 248, and Copson and Pope took a wicket apiece, leaving Hampshire facing almost certain defeat at 10 for two. Then the rain set in and not a ball could be bowled on the last day.

It was a disappointing end but the game provided another example of Derbyshire's power during the wet months of June and July. They owed almost everything to the bowlers and to two batsmen, Worthington and Townsend. The county's batting averages at this stage, including the Oxford match, showed Worthington leading with 938 runs with an average of 42.63. Townsend had 836, 39.80, Alderman 598, 26.00 and Smith, with 77 at The Parks still his best effort, 545 at 23.69. Harry Elliott had respectable figures and his nephew was currently in good form but too much depended on Worthington and Townsend. Contrast this with the bowling, where Copson had 88 wickets at 10.07, hotly pursued by Mitchell, Pope and Townsend. The rain affected all the matches involving the leading teams and there was no change in the table.

The poor weather followed Derbyshire to Old Trafford, the rain ruining the fixture. No play was possible on the first two days and the contest became subject to one-day rules, with ten points for first innings lead. Time ran out. Sibbles took full advantage of a drying pitch after Richardson had won the toss and Derbyshire had reached 84 with only one wicket down. Townsend hit seven fours in his 46, Alderman spent 130 minutes over 32 and Sibbles enjoyed a spell which brought him six for nine in seven overs; seven for 36 in the innings. The declaration at 116 for eight left Lancashire only 75 minutes batting and after 37 runs had come in three-quarters of an hour without loss, the match was abandoned. Each side received four points.

Posterity usually relegates such a match to a mere footnote but this one became historic, although nobody could possibly be aware of it at the time. Derbyshire had made one change, Hunt replacing Skinner in what was an all-county born team: Arthur Richardson, born at Quarndon, Harry Elliott (Scarcliffe), Albert Alderman (Allenton), Stan Worthington (Bolsover), Leslie Townsend (Long Eaton), Denis Smith (Somercotes), Charlie Elliott (Bolsover), Alf Pope (Tibshelf), Wally Hunt (Doe Lea), Tommy Mitchell (Creswell) and Bill Copson (Stonebroom).

That third and final day, Tuesday July 14, was the last occasion Derbyshire has fielded an all-county born side. There is a touch of pedantry about this. Robin Buckston, who was born in Kensington of a Derbyshire family, succeeded Richardson as captain and led out an otherwise all-county born team in 1937. Bert Rhodes, born at Tintwhistle in Cheshire but who moved to Hadfield in Derbyshire, also came into the team that year and it was only his presence which prevented an all-county born side occurring after the war. Theoretically it could have happened in the 1970s, although the batting would have been a bit thin and it would have meant leaving out Bob Taylor. A far cry from modern times, when teams have taken the field without a single county born player: although the creation of a Derbyshire Cricket Academy, 21st century heir to the nursery, and a £4.5 million indoor school at the County Ground, acts as a statement for the future.

In 1936, 21 players appeared in Derbyshire's 30 first-class matches. Fifteen were professionals; 14 county-born plus Storer, who was raised in Derbyshire. Of the six amateurs, Richardson, Gilbert and Jackson were born in the county and Hill-Wood came from a Derbyshire family. An all-Derbyshire born team was fielded on six occasions, increasing to 15 if Storer is included. In 27 matches at least ten Derbyshire-raised players took the field, with nine in the remaining three.

More pertinent at the time was the Championship table. Four points was not an unsatisfactory return from Old Trafford: it could have been better but then again it could have been a great deal worse. Nonetheless there were some anxious looks in the direction of Bradford, where Yorkshire entertained Nottinghamshire and Blackheath, where there was another local derby involving Kent and Surrey. Rain failed to prevent Kent and Surrey producing a sparkling match, dominated by the faster bowlers, Watt and Todd on the one hand and Gover and Watts on the other. Arthur Fagg's 121 was instrumental in Kent's first innings lead of 115; Gover's seven for 36 caused a second innings collapse which meant that Surrey had to make 191 in 150 minutes. They got them with six minutes and four wickets to spare, the 46-year-old Sandham showing the value of an old hand in such a situation by making 78.

At Bradford, Yorkshire were robbed. They needed only 44 for victory with Sutcliffe and Hutton getting nine of these when the weather closed in at 3.30pm, play having continued for some time in heavy rain. The match was abandoned but not without comment, *Wisden* saying: "The behaviour of some of the spectators when, after a two-hours' wait, the wicket remained unfit for further play, was most unseemly."

As a result, Derbyshire increased their lead, 158 points from 17 matches registering 61.96 per cent. Kent, with a match in hand, were 21 points behind, 57.08 per cent, Nottinghamshire, 55.71, remaining in third place. It heightened interest in what amounted to shoot-outs, Derbyshire and Kent at Burton-on-Trent, followed in the next round of fixtures by the return between Nottinghamshire and Yorkshire at Trent Bridge and a visit to Maidstone by Middlesex.

The Kent match was played in Staffordshire on Burton-on-Trent Cricket Club's Town Ground. The prevailing smell of beer from the breweries appropriately greeted the cricketers from the hop county as they arrived at Burton. Bill Bestwick, on the umpire's list, would probably have given his eye teeth to stand in such a game.

Both teams were weakened by the Gentlemen v Players game at Lord's. Copson got another taste of representative cricket, while Hopper Levett kept wicket for the Gentlemen. With Les Ames a long-term absentee because of ill health, Kent gave the wicketkeeping gloves to Fagg. Skinner took Copson's place in the Derbyshire team.

Sadly, Wednesday's was a familiar tale, rain restricting play to 50 minutes in which Derbyshire made 62 for the loss of Worthington. On the second day Townsend set about making up for lost time. Powerful drives earned him two sixes and 15 fours and except for a chance offered on 74 he made no mistake in 115 at a run a minute, his fourth hundred of the summer. He scored 77 out of 106 added for the third wicket with Skinner (49) and Derbyshire reached 268. Freeman and Wright found plenty in the pitch, dismissing the last seven batsmen for 78. In reply, Kent started badly, three men being out for 32 but Frank Woolley got 61, Brian Valentine, the captain, 43 and Ted Watt 30 – three sixes and three fours and a sequence of 6-4-4-6 off consecutive deliveries from Mitchell, who conceded 84 runs in 14 overs, with only one wicket to show for it. Kent's 184 left them 84 behind, Alf Pope doing most of the damage with five for 48, Townsend taking three for 32 and Worthington, sharing the new ball with Pope, one for 19. Alderman and Worthington had increased the lead by 50 at the close, Derbyshire having established a commanding position.

On Friday, Worthington (53) and Townsend (78 not out) scored quickly enough for Richardson to declare at lunch, setting Kent a target of 289. They were never close, admirable bowling and fielding restricting them to an all-out total of 147. By 4.35pm the match was won, just ten minutes before a storm swept the ground. This defeat effectively ended Kent's challenge for the title. After beating Essex at Tunbridge Wells on June 29 they did not win again until August 21 and by then it was too late. At least the *Derby Evening Telegraph* offered the visitors some consolation. "Derbyshire beat Kent on a pitch that seemed to change its mind with feminine frequency," it reported.

It was a signal victory in Derbyshire's campaign, tasting all the better for the losses on the first innings suffered by Yorkshire and Nottinghamshire in their matches. A large gap had suddenly opened: Derbyshire 10 wins and two defeats in 18 games, 173 points, 64.07; Kent eight wins and now five losses in 17, 137 points, 53.72; Nottinghamshire 120 points from 15, 53.33; Yorkshire 122 from 17, 47.84 and Middlesex 90 from 13, 46.15.

There was good news, too, from Lord's. After a blank first day the Gentlemen v Players game became a pace-fest, Gover (six for 41, from the Nursery end) and Copson (four for 29) excelling for the professionals and JWA Stephenson (Army and Essex) taking nine for 46 for the Gentlemen. Gubby Allen declared (Copson nought for 25 in the second innings) leaving the Players to make 132 in 75 minutes but some extreme speed by Kenneth Farnes put paid to that and the game was drawn. Pelham Warner's view was consistent with that of most cricket writers of the day: "Copson was apt to bowl short of a length, but he made great pace off the pitch."

By now the Test selectors – the chairman Pelham Warner, Percy Perrin and Tommy Higson snr – had taken a good look at the fast bowling choices. Gover, Allen, Perks and Copson had featured in the South v North Test trial. Gover had been omitted from the original 12 for the first Test, leaving Allen as the solitary fast bowler and the emphasis on spin. Since then Gover, Copson, Allen, Farnes, unavailable for the Tests, and Stephenson had been on view in Gentlemen v Players, all of these matches having taken place at Lord's. Soon Bill Voce, unlike Larwood, would make his peace with the authorities after the bodyline crisis and return to the fold. Although two Test matches against India remained, the party for Australia was the main talking point. This was chosen by the three selectors and Allen, the captain, with Sir Stanley Jackson (chairman), Lord Cobham and HDG Leveson-Gower representing MCC. Copson and Gover were still striving for a place in the side. Bowes, of slower pace than his colleagues, played four times against South Africa in 1935 but was not selected again for three years. Now Copson returned home for another opportunity, the match against the Indians at Derby.

Far more importance was attached to matches against the tourists than is the case today. They were crowd pullers and gave players a chance to impress – "what has he done against Yorkshire?" was a yardstick for the selectors in the 1930s but they also took note of the performances against teams from overseas.

Guy Jackson came in as captain because Richardson was attending his brother's wedding, leading Derbyshire out for what was to be his final time. Copson and Carrington replaced Hunt and Smith. India quickly got a dose of the unpleasant conditions at the bleak County Ground when the weather was unkind. High winds on the first day caused the bails to be removed at the pavilion end and play could not begin until after lunch on the Monday. In spite of this, the tourists had the best of it, leading by 68 but declaring too late to allow the county a chance of scoring 301 for victory. Copson, five for 44 and two for 42, took his 100th wicket of the season when he had Merchant caught at the wicket in the second innings and did his Test hopes no harm at all. The Elliotts – Charlie made 77 and received his county cap – added 88 after six wickets had fallen for 51 and Alderman and Townsend made useful runs when the pressure was off in the second innings.

There was plenty of satisfaction from the match but more from results elsewhere. At Mote Park, Middlesex were deprived of almost certain victory by rain, having to be content with five points to Kent's three. At Trent Bridge, 12,000 people watched a rain-interrupted first day in Harold Larwood's benefit match against Yorkshire. Larwood and Voce were upstaged by Butler but Yorkshire took the first innings points and Nottinghamshire settled for a draw.

As a result, Derbyshire's lead over Kent was now 33 points, each having played 18 matches. Nottinghamshire, Yorkshire and Middlesex followed – and Derbyshire's next two fixtures were against Yorkshire at Sheffield and Nottinghamshire at the Rutland Recreation Ground in Ilkeston.

Norman Yardley and Sandy Jacques replaced Maurice Leyland and Cyril Turner, who were suffering from groin injuries, in the Yorkshire side. Derbyshire made two changes, Richardson for Jackson and Smith taking Carrington's place, the team being in batting order: Alderman, Worthington, Townsend, Skinner, Smith, Elliott (CS), Elliott (H), Richardson, Pope, Mitchell and Copson. There was a sense of history in the making. Yorkshire, champion county, lording it over everybody between the wars, for years treating the likes of Derbyshire with contempt, now had to make all the running. Nothing less than victory would serve: a draw, even a first innings loss, would do very nicely for Richardson and his men. Accordingly, when Brian Sellers won the toss he took the only realistic option open to him. He sent Derbyshire in to bat.

At once the stage was set for the return confrontation between Worthington and Jacques. The latter had bowled well at Swansea in May and had been in the team at Aylestone Road for the Leicestershire game but he made only three Championship appearances in 1936, with one other first-class outing at Fenner's. Opportunities for fringe players were rare in the Yorkshire team: they had to make their mark quickly or spend their days in the 2nd XI. Worthington, remembering the fractured jaw, prepared to face one of the most hostile new ball attacks in the country, for Bowes, with his great height, remained a difficult customer. Worthington, too, might have reflected that he had been out of touch as an opening batsman since his big innings against Warwickshire nearly three weeks earlier, his last six innings producing 109 runs.

The morning was sunny, but it became overcast with a threat of rain when play started in indifferent light. Worthington hooked Jacques for three but at 23, with extras already contributing nine of the runs, the bowler saw Alderman survive a chance to wicketkeeper Wood. Sellers rang the changes but when Jacques returned for a second spell, Worthington pulled him square for four, turned him to the leg boundary and then off-drove him for his fifth four. Smailes had Alderman caught at 59 and Verity sent back Townsend with the score on 85 but Worthington continued to dominate. Three more leg-side boundaries off Jacques put an edge to his appetite for lunch, when Derbyshire, 123 for two, could reflect on a highly satisfactory morning. Worthington was still there, with 13 boundaries in 82, Skinner keeping him company.

Yorkshire now showed their fighting qualities. Skinner was bowled by Verity at 154 and the middle order crumbled, the innings closing for 216. Worthington stayed 216 minutes for his third hundred of the season. *Wisden* said: "How much Derbyshire owed to Worthington can be realised from the fact that he scored 135 out of 211, and his innings was all the more creditable in view of the almost complete failure of his colleagues, seven of whom scored only 25 runs between them. First in and eighth out, Worthington timed his strokes admirably and using the on-drive and pull with special skill he hit 21 fours. But for this individual effort, the tactics of Sellers must have been successful." The next highest score was 17 by Skinner. Bowes and Verity each took three for 47, Jacques ending with Richardson's wicket at a cost of 64 in 18 overs. Skinner ranked this as one of the best innings Worthington played. "He made the game seem very easy and I was finding it very difficult at the other end."

Copson removed Sutcliffe before he had scored – another example of his ability to get top batsmen out before they had settled – and Yorkshire had Arthur Mitchell's undefeated 54 to thank for a closing score of 102 for four. The second day was blank and the match developed into an absorbing struggle for the first innings lead. Mitchell went on to register his first hundred of the season but when the last man, Bowes, came in six runs were still needed. He lifted his first ball but Smith, running from first slip, got both hands to it but could not hold on. Yorkshire just scraped ahead, by two runs before the innings ended. Copson, six for 60 in 30 overs, and Pope, four for 58 from 31.5, took the wickets. The remainder was academic, Townsend making 50 out of 148 for five and Smith getting some vital practice with 37 not out.

Yorkshire had been held and with none of their rivals winning, Derbyshire maintained a comfortable lead.

Now the circus moved to Ilkeston and a fixture in which the third placed team challenged the leaders on their own patch. It was Saturday July 25 and that state of affairs would be perfectly proper had it been a Roses encounter, or a meeting between Middlesex and Surrey, or, indeed, between any of the Big Six. Four of the top five positions were occupied by Big Six counties, Surrey were not far away and the odd one out was Derbyshire. They had avenged their defeat by Kent, beaten Surrey and twice held Yorkshire to a draw. Now came the gathering of old friends and enemies, Derbyshire and Nottinghamshire at the Rutland Rec and a real tussle in prospect.

It should be emphasised that, some members apart, the average follower had little opportunity to watch cricket in the 1930s. The economy was improving but a crust still had to be earned and the shilling admission for a day's cricket had to be weighed against the demands of the family budget. The year book's Old Supporter, for example, was present for part of only four days' play at the County Ground in that momentous year. Personal memories cite my father, who recalled watching Saturday's play at Ilkeston but could not spare the time or the money for much more in 1936. Given the circumstances, he regarded the Nottinghamshire match as sacrosanct, aware that my mother's reciprocal treat was Fred Astaire and Ginger Rogers at the local cinema. Derbyshire's membership in 1936 rose slightly to 2,220. By contrast, Yorkshire had 6,592 members, Surrey 5,465 and Lancashire 4,649. Derbyshire's gate receipts were £3,090. The number of paying spectators at Derbyshire's home matches in 1936 was 76,077, compared with Yorkshire's 153,383.

Given the situation that July, the parochial aspects of the Derbyshire v Nottinghamshire game gained an extra competitive edge. It was unfortunate that the match coincided with the second Test at Old Trafford, for Hardstaff was missing from the Nottinghamshire team and Worthington was summoned when the injured Leyland withdrew. Both did well in England's 571 for eight declared, Hardstaff making 94 and Worthington 87. In the latter's place, Derbyshire brought in Arnold Townsend, who had scored heavily for Warsop Main in the Bassetlaw League that season. Carrington now felt completely out of favour but he reminded Cadman and the cricket committee that he could not be disregarded with a century for Blackwell against Derby LMS.

There was also a tactical change, Richardson restoring Denis Smith to his opening role in Worthington's absence. Again, this was a match in which Nottinghamshire's need for victory was greater than Derbyshire's. For a time, the skipper must have felt all was well with the world. He won the toss and looked on as Smith and Alderman began well against Larwood, now operating off a shortened run, and Voce. The partnership produced 55 runs before Alderman was out for 23, caught off Gunn. The innings now crawled to a virtual standstill as the batting demonstrated a distinct lack of confidence and enterprise on a pitch which offered the bowlers little assistance. Gunn, finding a bit of turn with his leg breaks, took three for 12 in one spell but Nottinghamshire did not help their cause by missing at least four slip catches. Smith battled away for nearly three hours, scoring 59 before he fell to a catch at the wicket by Ben Lilley off Voce. By the close, Derbyshire were 154-6, with Arnold Townsend on 16 and Richardson one. My father remembered it as one of the most intense day's play he ever saw. "It was slow going but nobody seemed to give an inch and both sets of supporters were thoroughly absorbed by it all," he said.

The game resumed in brilliant sunshine on Monday morning, with about 1,500 people on the ground. They saw Larwood and Voce polish off the tale, Derbyshire being dismissed for 187 in 91 overs. Larwood returned figures of 29-10-54-3, Gunn taking three for 22 in 18 overs and Voce two for 45 in 27. Nottinghamshire had the

(Clockwise from top left) Guy Jackson, Arthur Richardson, Harry Elliott and Harry Storer.

(Clockwise from top left) Leslie Townsend, Alf Pope, Stan Worthington and Albert Alderman.

(Top) The 1924 team: (back row) Storer, Bestwick, Carter, Horsley, H Elliott, Hutchinson. (front row) Morton, A Jackson, G Jackson (capt), Cadman, Bowden. (Below) The 1930 team. Only Hutchinson, Storer, Guy Jackson and Harry Elliott were left. (back row) Alderman, Hutchinson, Townsend, Smith, Worthington, Mitchell, Storer. (front row) Slater, Clarke, Jackson (capt) Lee, H Elliott. (courtesy Derby Evening Telegraph)

(Top) A Players cigarette card of Bill Copson (left) and Denis Smith.
(Bottom) Sam Cadman, the Lancashire-born all-rounder who helped lay the foundations
for Derbyshire's remarkable decade in the 1930s.

1930 and it rained then as well. Denis Smith, Alf Pope (with umbrella) and coach Sam Cadman examine the matting pitch laid over the sodden ground. (courtesy Derby Evening Telegraph)

Denis Smith.

Tommy Mitchell.

Harry Elliott (with wicketkeeper's gloves) leads out Derbyshire as captain.

advantage, although it had taken them long enough to achieve the upper hand. Even without Hardstaff they had plenty of batting and as Keeton and Harris went out to begin the innings there was talk around the ground of a healthy lead.

Both were back in the pavilion with only seven runs scored, Keeton leg-before to Pope, Harris caught by Skinner off Copson. Walker and Gunn raised the score to 71 but Nottinghamshire struggled against this superb attack, Mitchell, in particular causing major problems. Cleverly varying pace and flight he took six wickets in one spell for just over five runs each. Walker stayed two hours for 58 but having taken nine wickets for 126, Derbyshire looked forward to a valuable lead. They achieved it, but only by a margin of five runs. Larwood and Woodhead hit out in a last-wicket partnership which produced 56. Leslie Townsend put a stop to the nonsense and then Smith and Alderman set about restoring the initiative. The score reached 83 without loss but by the close Smith (36) and Leslie Townsend had gone, Alderman having 49 out of 94 for two.

One way or another a result was likely on Tuesday as Derbyshire sought to build on a lead of 99, with about one thousand people present. Alderman reached his half-century with a four to fine leg in Voce's first over, but was then caught by Lilley off the same bowler at 98. Although Skinner sent the hundred up with a square cut to the boundary, a cautious approach by Derbyshire proved to be their undoing. Larwood and Voce knocked the stuffing out of the batting. Larwood bowled six consecutive maidens in a spell of three for eight; Voce took five for 22 in 12 overs during the morning. The innings caved in as eight wickets went down for 31 in 75 minutes. Mitchell defiantly straight drove Voce for four, but only slightly dented figures of six for 43. Larwood took three for 29, and although Charlie Elliott seemed to be on the wrong end of a decision by Bill Reeves, given out caught at the wicket when he appeared not to touch the ball, there were no excuses. The batsmen had been outclassed by what was still the best fast bowling combination in county cricket and Nottinghamshire faced a comparatively easy task of getting 131 runs for victory.

Comparatively easy against anything but this Derbyshire attack; but for once things did not go well. At lunch, Nottinghamshire were 26 without loss. Keeton was missed twice in getting eight runs and Harris was dropped on 17. Pope raised hopes when he dismissed Keeton at 27 but Harris (43) and Walker (28) brought Nottinghamshire within touching distance. The game ended at 4pm, Nottinghamshire winning by six wickets. Nottinghamshire had now moved into second place with 143 points, 52.34 per cent of those possible. Derbyshire stayed top, with 58.66 per cent.

A day later – Wednesday July 29 – there was some consolation for Derbyshire when Stan Worthington and Bill Copson were selected for the MCC team which was to tour Australia. Seven names had been announced a week earlier but no fast bowlers, other than Allen, had been picked. There was plenty of speculation over whether Copson or Gover would be chosen and, among the all-rounders, Townsend was also mentioned. Worthington and Copson were among the four names announced in addition to the original seven. Gover was not chosen for the trip, although he took 200 wickets at 17.73 in 1936. Rumours that Will Taylor would go as manager were dashed when Rupert Howard was appointed.

The return match between Derbyshire and Nottinghamshire, scheduled for Worksop in mid-August, was already being written-up as the Championship decider. Nobody had yet ruled out Yorkshire and an innings victory over fellow-challengers Middlesex at Scarborough came as a reminder of their power. Derbyshire had no match in this round of fixtures and Kent, still hopeful of restoring their fortunes, came close to victory at Trent Bridge. Larwood took ten wickets in the game, but a bid to get 276 in 210 minutes foundered against Wright and the last pair, Heane and Woodhead survived the last five minutes to save the game.

On the eve of the August Bank Holiday games, Derbyshire were in first place, having won half and lost three of their 20 games, 176 points representing 58.66 per cent of those possible. Nottinghamshire had seven wins in 19, with only a single defeat and 146 points: 51.22 per cent. Kent were still in contention at this stage, eight wins and five losses in 21, 153 points and a percentage of 48.51. Yorkshire's win at Scarborough was their sixth in 21 matches, 152 points giving them 46.76 per cent. Their victims Middlesex had slipped further behind, 103 points. 40.39 per cent.

The holiday fixture at Chelmsford had an added ingredient, Essex including three pace bowlers, Nicholls, Farnes and Stephenson, who were of international quality and enjoyed notable success in 1936. They lost no time in making an impact. The pitch was damp on Saturday and five Derbyshire wickets fell for 29. The recovery was minimal as only Skinner, Worthington, back in the side to the exclusion of Arnold Townsend, and Harry Elliott reached double figures. Derbyshire were all out for 80 in 130 minutes, Farnes taking five for 20, which included ten runs from his final over.

Ninety minutes play was lost to rain during the Essex innings, but by the close they were 102 for four, with O'Connor going well. He went on to 87 on Monday, striking three sixes and seven fours before succumbing to a catch by Alderman off Leslie Townsend. Farnes took five consecutive twos off Pope as Essex established a first innings advantage of 139. Skinner recalled: "Ken Farnes, using the only stroke he had, was hitting Alf Pope on the up so high that the ball had snow on it when it came down. Five times in succession he played the shot, two runs a time, and five times an unfortunate Derbyshire fielder was running round in circles trying to size up the immense hit that was swaying in the wind as it was coming down, and five times the ball went to earth but Alderman finally held him." Copson finished with four for 64 and Pope three for 40.

Derbyshire fought back, passing the hundred with only one wicket down but the middle order fell away against Peter Smith's leg spin. Alderman, first in and seventh out, gave a splendid defensive display in making 79, but Monday's play ended with Derbyshire 195 for seven, only 56 ahead. Pope made an invaluable 33 and they were all out for 240 by 12.18pm on the final day, leaving Essex 102 to win.

Fifty-seven of these were obtained with only three wickets down but Mitchell, coming on at 2.30pm with the score 51, completely changed the course of the match. Using the googly to full advantage, he took six for 25 in five overs. Essex lost their last seven wickets for 24 and Derbyshire won by 20 runs. Once again, they had given a demonstration of a never-say-die spirit, a bloody-minded refusal to accept defeat while the slightest chance of avoiding it remained.

Yorkshire got their noses in front in a rain-affected Roses fixture but ran out of time in their quest for victory. Again, they could blame the weather, Old Trafford looking anything but a venue for a holiday game with its drizzle, showers and piles of sawdust. An attack including Bowes, Smailes and Verity occupied more than 184 overs in taking 20 Lancashire wickets – and Lancashire started the match third from the bottom – whereas Derbyshire required 133 to dismiss Essex twice. There was always the feeling that Bowes and Verity could surpass anything achieved by Copson and Mitchell, but Derbyshire were winning matches when only limited time was available. In other words, their bowlers were beating the weather.

So were Larwood and Voce, the former having a match analysis of twelve for 80 as Nottinghamshire won a thrilling contest at The Oval by 45 runs. Middlesex, the young Denis Compton and the veteran Patsy Hendren sharing a century partnership, gained a crushing victory at Hove but Kent could only take three points from Hampshire at the start of the Canterbury Festival. Hampshire's first innings lead was enough to raise them into third place, ahead of Yorkshire, Kent, Surrey and Middlesex. The East Midlands' counties had pulled further away: Derbyshire 191 points from 21 games, 60.63 per cent, Nottinghamshire 161 from 20, 53.66 per cent.

Unchanged, Derbyshire remained in the south for their next match, against Surrey at The Oval. This was the occasion of Alderman's wonder catch which sent back Barling for 57 on the Wednesday when Surrey were dismissed for 204, Mitchell and Copson again doing most of the damage. Smith, at long last, found his touch, putting on 152 for the third wicket with Skinner (58) and driving and cutting splendidly in making his first century of the season. His 106 included eleven fours and then Harry Elliott (79 not out) and Alf Pope (39) added 88 for the eighth wicket. *Wisden* commented: "Elliott gave one of the best batting displays of his career and showed sound discrimination in cutting and driving."

Derbyshire's total of 321 gave them a lead of 117, but Barling and Fishlock, profiting from fielding errors, got going for Surrey on Friday with a big partnership which left the game evenly poised. Rain and bad light ended proceedings with Surrey, 315-7, leading by 198. Nottinghamshire drew and there were victories for Yorkshire and Middlesex in the other games.

The team now returned home for a match against Leicestershire at Derby, beginning on Saturday August 8 – the first Championship fixture at the County Ground since June 11. Only the visit by the Indians had broken the drought. No wonder members from the county town complained: Chesterfield had had four matches, Ilkeston two and Buxton and Burton-on-Trent one each since

Gloucestershire had visited Derby. This was the last game scheduled for Derby; the club's headquarters relegated in the latter half of the season almost to a virtual out-ground. Attendances were generally better elsewhere and the executive can be applauded for taking cricket around the county but a mere four Championship fixtures in such a year was difficult for the county town to swallow.

That said, the Leicestershire fixture attracted satisfactory crowds, around 7,000 on Saturday and 3,500 on Monday. The match was dominated by the bowlers. Copson took five for 40, including three in four balls, *Wisden* saying he kept a capital length and made the ball leave the turf at bewildering pace. Mitchell had five for 57 as lowly Leicestershire were dismissed in 155 minutes for 117. When Harry Elliott caught Berry off Mitchell, he completed his 1,000th dismissal, 729 caught and 271 stumped. Derbyshire struggled in turn with George Geary proving difficult, but Alderman made a solid 35 in three hours and Richardson 31, crucially when six wickets were down for 100. The lead was 42. Richardson, who had been in poor form, attacked the bowling, driving straight or through the covers. Geary's first 15 overs yielded only six runs and he took five for 39 in 33.4 overs. On Monday it was Copson and Mitchell again as Leicestershire's second innings of 94 occupied only 115 minutes. Derbyshire cruised home by nine wickets, Alderman finding enough time to complete 1,000 runs for the season. The game lasted only nine hours.

Alderman was the third Derbyshire batsman to reach a four-figure aggregate. Townsend headed the averages at this point of the season with 1,260 runs at an average of 38.18, marginally ahead of Worthington, 1,257, 38.09, followed by Alderman 1,023, 33 and Smith 865, 26.21. The bowling averages were led by Copson, 123 wickets at 11.60, Townsend 54 at 16.40, Alf Pope 74 at 17.32, Mitchell 114 at 20.82 and Worthington 20 at 26.50, although he was used on far fewer occasions than in past seasons, . It illustrated the dependence on key batsmen, for while Skinner and the two Elliotts produced respectable but far from outstanding figures, Storer (his season now ended with an average of 15.76) and Carrington (11.60) were well below par.

There was competition from players in the 2nd XI. Carrington made 62 against Warwickshire 2nd at Belper Meadows and two youngsters who were to enjoy notable post-war careers with the county, Bert Rhodes and the 20-year-old trialist Cliff Gladwin enjoyed spectacular success against Nottinghamshire 2nd at Darley Dale. Rhodes scored 63 and took six for 37 and two for 28; Gladwin 108 not out and two for 45 in the first innings, Wally Hunt polishing off the Nottinghamshire second innings.

Another feature of the Darley Dale match was an innings of 83 and some fine bowling by George Langdale. Harry Storer had already told the club that Coventry City would release Charlie Elliott from soccer duties until the County Championship had been decided and when Worthington was selected for the third and final Test at The Oval, Langdale came into the side for the return match with Nottinghamshire at Worksop.

Chapter 30
The Push for the Title

GIVEN its Bassetlaw League background, Worksop was a fitting choice of venue for a match which might decide the destiny of the 1936 County Championship.

There was a precedent. Nottinghamshire and Derbyshire met there in 1921 in the first home game Nottinghamshire played away from Trent Bridge for 17 years, when the teams had played on the Duke of Portland's beautiful ground at Welbeck Abbey. Worksop were the Bassetlaw League's first champions in 1904 and won the title five times before the 1914-18 war.

Interest reached fever pitch and the league gave its full backing by recommending that "clubs should forego fixtures on August 15 in order to support the players in both county sides we had special reason to be proud of." George Langdale, who was making his first-class debut in the match, said it might never have been played at Worksop. "When it became obvious that it would be a vital clash, the Nottinghamshire committee wanted to switch the game to Trent Bridge and asked Worksop to accept the game against Leicestershire on August 19 instead. The Worksop club rose up in arms and sent a sub-committee to Trent Bridge to point out that £70 had been spent on a new scoreboard and that it was Derbyshire or no game at all."

After the Leicestershire match, Derbyshire sat out a round of county games in which Nottinghamshire and Yorkshire each obtained five points from Warwickshire and Leicestershire respectively. Neither were satisfied. At Scarborough, there were crowds of 10,000 on the first and second days, Bowes took 13 for 96 in the match, there was the inevitable rain and Yorkshire once again ran out of time. A fourth-wicket partnership of 142 by Francis Prentice and George Watson when Leicestershire's second innings was at a vulnerable stage blunted the push for victory and the visitors earned their draw.

At Edgbaston, Nottinghamshire were frustrated by Wyatt's undefeated 109. He was struck on the head by a ball from Voce on 45 and had defied the attack for 260 minutes when his declaration left Nottinghamshire only 90 minutes to chase 200. Kent suffered an innings defeat at the hands of Essex and Middlesex beat Hampshire.

On the evening of Friday August 14 the leading positions were: Derbyshire played 23, won 12, lost three, 211 points, 61.15 per cent; Yorkshire played 25, won eight, lost one, 192 points, 51.20 per cent; Nottinghamshire played 23, won eight, lost one, 176 points, 51.01 per cent; Middlesex played 21, won seven, lost three, 153 points, points 48.57. "Despite Derbyshire's clear lead in the Championship, Nottinghamshire and Yorkshire are so close that a falling-off in form, even for one match, might prove disastrous," said the *Derby Evening Telegraph*.

Derbyshire found fortune on their side. They lost Worthington to England but Nottinghamshire were without Voce who was also at The Oval, Hardstaff and Larwood. Derbyshire's side was: Alderman, Smith, Skinner, Townsend, Elliott (CS), Elliott (H), Langdale, Richardson, Pope, Mitchell and Copson. Nottinghamshire fielded Keeton, Harris, Walker, Knowles, Heane, Gunn, Staples, Woodhead, Wheat, Butler and Robinson. The hours of play were 11.30am to 7pm on the first two days and 11am to 4pm or 4.30pm on the final day.

Sixteen players with Bassetlaw League associations took part in the game and on the first day the teams were entertained to lunch by WE Longbottom, of Worksop, the president of the league. Richardson won the toss and Alderman, wearing his cap, and Smith, bare-headed, began the innings before a crowd of around 2,500. After half-an-hour Derbyshire were 26 without loss, Smith having made 20 of these. Smith (22) left at 31; when Alderman was 13 he was missed by Frank Woodhead at second slip and Skinner was out with the score on 50. At lunch Derbyshire had made 82 for two, Alderman having 28 and Townsend 15.

The crowd grew to 4,000 after lunch and saw the hundred go up after 135 minutes but Derbyshire then collapsed from 100 for two to 112 for five. Alderman spent 136 minutes over 31 and had Gunn held on to a skier from Harry Elliott at 110 Nottinghamshire might have broken through completely. As it was Langdale got off the mark from his first ball with a stroke through the covers, only to be missed in the slips on eight. At tea the score was 143 for six, Langdale having left for 14, and at 151 Elliott finally perished, lashing out at George Robinson to be caught by Keeton at mid-on. He had batted two hours for 17.

Eight wickets were down for 160 but Tommy Mitchell produced a typically mixed bag of strokes to make 45, his highest score of the season. It was both entertaining and frustrating at the same time and, in company with Copson, he added 44 for the last wicket in 30 minutes. It raised the total to 218 in 116 overs. As at Ilkeston, Derbyshire's batting had been tediously slow but 218 represented currency in the bank. When Alf Pope bowled Keeton with a ball which swung across him and got Harris with a fast, rising delivery that was edged to Skinner in the slips, the total began to look formidable. Nottinghamshire were three for two, with their famed opening pair back in the pavilion, a triumph, indeed, for Pope. Worse was to follow for the home team. At 11, Walker was run out and they closed at 16-3, with Joseph Knowles and Heane each on four. It had been Derbyshire's day.

Play got under way ten minutes late on Monday because of George Heane's late arrival. The Nottinghamshire skipper was involved in a motoring mishap on the way. Again there was a good crowd, some 2,000 at the start, and Nottinghamshire suffered a further blow when Knowles was bowled by Copson at 23. A fifth wicket fell at 49 but Heane (57) and Staples (47) repaired the damage with a sixth wicket partnership of 62 and at lunch the score was 126-7. The innings closed for 152, Copson taking four for 47 and Mitchell three for 51.

Leading by 66, Derbyshire sought first to consolidate their advantage and then seek the victory that could seal the Championship. Smith hit freely, reaching 40 out of 50 in 40 minutes. The openers put on 78 before Alderman was caught at the wicket for 29 in 68 minutes. Smith reached his half-century after 75 minutes and went on to make 85 before being caught off Gunn. Skinner scored 60 and at the close Derbyshire, 254 for seven, led by 320. They were in charge of the game.

Richardson continued the innings on the final morning. Twenty minutes batting produced 16 runs before the declaration at 270 for eight left Nottinghamshire to make 337 at 80 an hour. It was a pragmatic approach. Victory was highly desirable; so too was ensuring that Nottinghamshire did not win. Nottinghamshire, in turn, began steadily, Keeton and Harris scoring 22 in the first half hour. Mitchell was on for Pope at 11 and Richardson rang the changes but the openers were still there at lunch: 103 without loss, Keeton 57 and Harris 45. They remained in control, Keeton refusing to be intimidated by Copson's persistent short bowling in a hostile second spell.

The match fizzled out into a draw with Nottinghamshire 215 without loss in 79 overs. Not a chance was given, Keeton hitting eight fours in his 100, Harris 12 in 107. But Derbyshire emerged from the match with more satisfaction than their neighbours.

The fixture provided interesting statistics on how people travelled to games in the 1930s. Bus and train remained the most popular but the number of cars parked at Worksop was estimated at 500, 750 and 100 respectively during the three days. Gate receipts – admission was a shilling – were £360 on Saturday, £399 on Monday and £73 on the third day.

At The Oval, Worthington made 128 for England but the focus was on the Championship. While the Worksop match had been in progress, Yorkshire, without Leyland and Verity, on Test duty, butchered Somerset at Bramall Lane in two days. It sounded alarm bells. Derbyshire, 216 points, 60 per cent; Yorkshire 207 points, 53.07 per cent; Nottinghamshire 179 points, 49.72 per cent, Middlesex 158 points, 47.87 per cent. Mathematicians were suddenly in demand and the *Derby Evening Telegraph* came to the rescue. It said that backs of bus tickets, newspapers and old letters were being pressed into service for hastily pencilled calculations to fathom the odds of Yorkshire catching up. Derbyshire and Yorkshire each had four matches remaining.

If Yorkshire won all four of these they would finish the season with a percentage of 59.33. In that case Derbyshire would need at least 34 points to return 59.52 per cent. Three victories and a defeat for Yorkshire would register 56 per cent. But three victories and first innings points from the other game would give them 57.11 per cent. One Derbyshire win and first innings lead in the other three would produce

58.57 per cent. Other calculations related to Yorkshire winning two and losing two, 52.63 per cent, and winning one and losing three, 49.33 per cent. Nottinghamshire also had four matches left and if they won all of them, then they would finish on 56.90 per cent. "Yorkshire have come up with such a rush that Nottinghamshire, challengers for the greater part of the season, have been overlooked," the *Telegraph* said, adding that they still had an outside chance.

Such was the position on Tuesday August 18 as Derbyshire set off from Worksop for a lengthy trip to Eastbourne, Worthington joining the team from The Oval to the exclusion of Langdale. Yorkshire were next door, facing Kent at Dover while Nottinghamshire entertained Leicestershire at Trent Bridge.

Richardson did his weary team a big favour by winning the toss and Smith and Alderman began at The Saffrons against the bowling of Maurice Tate and Jack Nye. Sussex had fallen from the heights of two years earlier and came to Eastbourne on the back of defeats at Weston-super-Mare and Cheltenham. But they had cause to feel satisfied with most of Wednesday's play as they dismissed the Championship leaders for 228. Derbyshire had started well, recovering from the early loss of Alderman to reach 89 before Smith fell for 34. Worthington (56) and Skinner (62) lifted them into a position of some prosperity at 153 for three. Worthington drove powerfully for 70 minutes and Skinner attacked attractively all round the wicket but the last six wickets fell in 45 minutes for 30 runs.

Pope and Copson accounted for Jim Parks and John Langridge before the close and a third wicket fell at 33 but that was the extent of Derbyshire's success. Tom Cook made 53 before he was caught by Mitchell at forward short leg off Copson, the fieldsman being knocked out in the process of taking the catch. Then James Langridge (126) and Harry Parks (75) put on 185, carrying the score to 291 for four. Copson cleaned up the tail to end with six for 87 in 35 overs, the last six wickets going down for 25. A total of 316 gave Sussex a first innings lead of 88 and Derbyshire lost both of their openers to Nye by the close of the second day when they were still 47 in arrears.

Worthington and Townsend batted soundly on the final morning but half the side had gone for 125, only 37 ahead. At lunch the score was 135 for five, but the two Elliotts spent two hours on the defensive, raising the score to 163 before Harry fell for 11. Charlie remained undefeated with 39 as Derbyshire, 191-6, batted for more than a day – 129 overs, although Tate had been unable to bowl because of a strain – to save the game. Derbyshire were unperturbed by some barracking at the slow batting. One of the umpires, Harry Baldwin or Denis Hendren, most likely Baldwin, rebuked the crowd, saying "the shouting when a batsman was about to make his stroke was reducing cricket to the level of American baseball".

It was far from pretty, but it saved three points and these became even more priceless when the news came through that Kent had beaten Yorkshire at Dover. It had gone wrong from the start at the Crabble Athletic Ground for the champions, Sutcliffe, Hutton, Mitchell, Leyland and Barber being back in the pavilion with a mere 37 scored. Ames made 120 as Kent piled up 406 to lead by 198, and although Hutton got 71 in the second innings, the home side won easily by nine wickets. At Trent Bridge, Nottinghamshire were left to rue the cost of missed catches as Leicestershire escaped with a draw but they still remained in the hunt.

Each of the top three counties had three matches remaining. Derbyshire had 219 points, 58.40 per cent, Yorkshire 207, 51.11 and Nottinghamshire 184, 49.06. Yorkshire's maximum percentage was 56, Nottinghamshire's 54.52, so Derbyshire needed 18 more points to reach 237 and register 56.42 per cent to ensure they won the Championship. Fifteen points would give them 234, 55.71, which would be too many for Nottinghamshire.

Those fifteen points appeared to be there for the taking as Derbyshire arrived at Queen's Park, Chesterfield, for the last home match of the season, beginning on Saturday August 22. Their opponents were Northamptonshire, anchored at the bottom of the table after failing to win any of their 23 Championship matches. Heavy defeats at Worcester and Old Trafford preceded the Chesterfield game and although Northamptonshire were not quite the chopping blocks of some seasons – 14 of the 23 matches ended in a draw, which owed something to the wet summer and no little determination – they were generally in disarray. Five different captains point to the lack of continuity and at Queen's Park it was Beau Brown, a useful and enthusiastic batsman, who tossed up with Richardson. It was Northamptonshire's final match of the summer and it was probably greeted with something approaching relief.

Derbyshire made one change, Langdale coming in for Charlie Elliott. In the other important matches, Yorkshire continued their southern tour with a game at The Oval and Nottinghamshire were at Clacton.

The weather did not relent and the light was poor when play began at Queen's Park before about 1,000. Northamptonshire were in trouble immediately, Pope bowling the openers Bakewell and Northway with only eight scored. They never really recovered and were all out for 144 in 165 minutes. Copson and Pope each took four wickets and Mitchell two. Derbyshire struggled and by the close had lost seven wickets for 167, Townsend top-scoring with 67, including eight fours. The first aim – securing a first innings lead – had been achieved.

At The Oval, Yorkshire were all out just before the close for 315. Honours were even at Clacton; Nottinghamshire 40 without loss in reply to 300 by Essex.

By Monday, the weather had improved and a heat wave developed over the next few days. After lunch on the second day, the attendance at Chesterfield grew to 4,000. Derbyshire's first innings ended at 209, a lead of 65, but they paid a high price. Tommy Mitchell was struck twice on the right thumb by deliveries from Reg Partridge. He was taken to Chesterfield Royal Hospital, where the thumb was found to be broken at the joint.

Throughout the season, Copson and Mitchell had formed the cutting edge of the Derbyshire attack. Now the team had been deprived of half of the combination. They had no bowler capable of turning the ball away from the bat

– a key ingredient of Championship-winning sides in those days – and it was to prove costly on that hard pitch.

At first there was no apparent problem. Carrington fielded as twelfth man, Pope struck twice and two batsmen were out for 53, still 12 runs behind. Fred Bakewell and Jack Timms added 93 for the third wicket before Timms fell leg before to Pope for 41. Three wickets down for 146, the lead 80. Satisfactory enough for Derbyshire, with the likelihood that they would not require much above 200 to all but make certain of the title.

But Bakewell was still there. He was 27 years of age, at the height of his powers and in that bleak Northamptonshire season he played some brilliant innings. A two-eyed stance, with a slight crouch at the crease, belied a wide range of strokes which carried him into the England side on six occasions. Harry Elliott and Leslie Townsend knew him well; they had been colleagues on Jardine's 1933-34 tour of India. Now he began to attack the bowling and there was no Mitchell to deceive him in flight, beat him with spin or tempt him into indiscretion.

Bakewell was joined by Dennis Brookes, not yet 21 but a batsman rich in promise who was to score more runs for Northamptonshire than anyone else. Brookes settled in and watched as Bakewell completed his fifth century of the season in 150 minutes. The hundred partnership was logged, then 150, then 200 as the pair took the game away from Derbyshire in one of the most astonishing turnarounds of the 1936 season. They wrested full advantage from a fast outfield and the relatively short boundaries at Queen's Park. For once, indeed for what was really the first time that season, the Derbyshire attack seemed toothless. Copson came in for heavy punishment. Nought for 80 in 26 overs were not the sort of figures which won Championships.

The score was 357 when at long last a wicket fell, that of Brookes, bowled, inevitably, by Pope. He made 81, then his highest innings for the county, and struck nine fours. Brookes and Bakewell had added 211 for the fourth wicket in 190 minutes and by the close of play Northamptonshire were 374-4, with Bakewell 221 not out. He had been at the crease for 295 minutes when he completed his double century. Northamptonshire's lead was 309 and it was a weary team of champions-elect which wended its way into the pavilion at the close. At least they heard some cheering news: Surrey 416 for seven against Yorkshire, a lead of 101. And Nottinghamshire's match at Clacton was in the balance. Fourteen in arrears on the first innings, they had got four Essex wickets down for 161 and still had much to do.

The third day's attendance at Queen's Park was just over one thousand, bringing the match receipts up to £526. Brown declared the Northamptonshire innings closed just before noon: 411 for six, Bakewell 241 not out, Alf Pope six for 129 in 42 overs. He had toiled away manfully to carry an attack in which Copson and Townsend had combined figures of nought for 170. Bakewell's chanceless innings contained 19 fours and occupied six hours and 10 minutes.

Derbyshire were set 347 to win and it was soon obvious that they were intent on saving the game and five first innings points. There seemed little danger as the home side crawled to 25 in the first hour, Smith getting 19 of these, with four byes and Alderman having made two. At lunch the score was 35 without loss after 80 minutes batting.

Nobby Clark, the mercurial Northamptonshire left-arm fast bowler, had soon had enough of this. He began after lunch to a passive Alderman with two slips, a gully, silly point and two short legs. But it was Partridge who removed Alderman for 14, Clark accounting for the England batsmen Smith and Worthington. Soon Derbyshire were in all sorts of trouble at 64 for five. Skinner and Langdale increased this to 94 when change-bowler Bakewell, who took only 22 wickets in his entire career at 57 each, had Langdale caught by his captain.

Arthur Richardson joined Skinner at 4pm and the fielders crowded around the bat, with neither side now concerned about runs. A few boundaries were conceded which might have been saved by more orthodox field placing but these were the least of Northamptonshire's worries. Skinner (41) had been at the crease for two hours when he fell to Partridge under the new lbw rule. It was five minutes to five and seven wickets were down for 121. The unthinkable, the Championship leaders defeated by the bottom county, was still a possibility. Spectators with a sense of history recalled Nottinghamshire's defeat at Swansea in similar circumstances nine years earlier.

With Alf Pope as his partner, Richardson continued his dogged, back-to-the-wall innings. "Whatever the bowling, he refused to let it beat his bat or tempt him to give the slightest encouragement to the ring of keyed-up fieldsmen gathered all about him. Twice in one over, as though to relieve his feelings, he hit Grimshaw violently for four, and then he resumed the old relentless game of resolute defence," reported the *Derby Evening Telegraph*. Will Taylor recalled the tension. "I attempted to give the impression that I was perfectly cool and during the struggle a member who was probably more het up even than I was, said, 'I cannot understand how you can be so calm under these circumstances,' my reply was 'If you could only look inside, you would see my stomach turning over and over.'"

Mitchell was prepared to bat if necessary but Richardson and Pope gave not the semblance of a chance, in spite of the anxiety. At 5.42pm, Northamptonshire accepted the inevitable and called off the hunt. Derbyshire had made 173-7 in 107 overs, a tardy rate of scoring to say the least but they had saved the game. Richardson's undefeated 27 in 100 minutes represented one of the finest innings of his career.

In his 90th year, Dennis Brookes retained vivid memories. "Derbyshire were definitely the best side in the Championship that season and if they had beaten us they would have been champions. Instead, we held them up and nearly beat them ourselves. We might have won but Albert Alderman was given not out after he had trod on his wicket in the second innings and he stayed a long time.

"I remember them as a magnificent bowling side. Bill Copson was fast, about as quick as anybody in the country at that time and Tommy Mitchell took a lot of wickets with his leg breaks and googlies. They were not an outstanding batting side, although Stan Worthington did well and Denis Smith and Leslie Townsend were good players, but they generally made enough runs. In the field they were a hard team. They were a good fielding side which caught well although they were not particularly fleet of foot."

Yet again Derbyshire had provided a demonstration of the stubborn bloody-mindedness and recuperative powers which made them such a difficult side to beat. Those five points were priceless and the team gave their skipper a few pats on the back that evening.

Next day came news of the most shocking kind which put the cricket into perspective. Fred Bakewell normally travelled by car with Jack Timms but this time left Chesterfield with the 30-year-old amateur Reggie Northway driving. Years later he gave a poignant account of the journey to David Frith of *Wisden Cricket Monthly*.

"Of course, everybody thought: last match of the season and we'd been on the booze. But they were wrong. Reggie Northway was driving. He was practically a teetotaller. The Sunday before we'd driven all round the Derbyshire hills. Absolutely marvellous driver."

They stopped for a drink at the Trip to Jerusalem in Nottingham. Northway had a half-pint and drank only half of this. Then, around midnight, the car was involved in an accident on the A50 near Kibworth in Leicestershire. Bakewell told Frith that he did not think anybody knew what really happened. He thought the car – a little sports car with no roof – might have struck one of many round stones on the road at a slight bend. "It was kind of a windy night, and you could hardly hear one another to talk to, you know. That's how I kind of got down, and probably dozed off. Whether Reggie dozed off or not nobody will ever know."

The car came over a humpback bridge, missed a telegraph pole, struck a kerb and finished up on its side in a hedge. Two other Northamptonshire players, Jack Timms and Arthur Cox, were travelling in a car in front. When they realised their colleagues were not following they turned back and found Bakewell lying semi-conscious in the road and Northway's body in a ditch. Bakewell spent weeks in hospital. He appeared to have made a full recovery but his right arm was so badly broken that he never played county cricket again. His final innings was 16 short of his best score but it was one of his greatest.

"It was a wonderful innings and it was a privilege to be at the crease with him during our partnership," said Brookes. "My recollection of it was that the Test selectors had been waiting for him to make a big score and it was so sad that it was to his final innings."

Walter Goodyear, the groundsman at Queen's Park, also has clear memories. "I can remember lifting the bags into Northway's car that afternoon when they were getting ready to leave Chesterfield. It had been a fine match and Bakewell had played a magnificent innings."

Meanwhile Derbyshire made the lengthy trip to Wells, where they were to meet Somerset the following day, Wednesday August 26. During the journey emotions were mixed; relief at escaping with a draw, irritation that they had allowed such lowly opposition to dictate, dismay that Mitchell was absent and a measure of delight when they discovered that far from winning at The Oval, Yorkshire only just managed to avoid an innings defeat. Nottinghamshire were beaten by 34 runs at Clacton and this put them out of the running.

It meant that Derbyshire were now certain of a share of the Championship and needed mathematically a point, in practical terms three points for losing on the first innings in a drawn game, to prevent Yorkshire drawing level. Derbyshire's percentage of points was 57.43, Yorkshire's 50. The position was that if Derbyshire lost their two remaining matches and Yorkshire won both theirs, the two counties would be level with a percentage of 53.33. Or, to put it another way, Derbyshire had to avoid defeat in one of these games to become outright champions. Rain would do it and for once Will Taylor would not have minded for both fixtures were away, to Somerset and Leicestershire. Yorkshire would complete their traditional tour of the southern counties at Hove and Bournemouth, finishing the season by entertaining the MCC at Scarborough.

Derby's Grand Theatre staged *No! No! Nanette*; the cinemas were showing Henry Hall and the BBC Dance orchestra in *Music Hath Charms*. For those with a more adventurous taste, James Cagney starred in *Cisco Kid* and Walter Huston in *Rhodes of Africa*. Soccer fans looked forward to Saturday and Derby County's match against West Bromwich Albion and Chesterfield's visit to Southampton.

But for many people, even those with only a passing interest in sport, it was the news from the West Country that demanded attention.

Chapter 31
Champions

WELLS was an unlikely arena for such a crucial match. The old cathedral city at the foot of the Mendips was famed for its bishop's palace, with an associated theological college. Paper, brushes and textiles provided jobs for its 5,000 inhabitants and although it could trace its connections with cricket back to the mid-19th century, it had staged only one County Championship match. That had taken place the previous year, in July 1935, when Worcestershire had won by an innings.

The Wells Athletics Ground at Rowden Road was an unprepossessing little ground, originally without sightscreens and lacking a scoreboard. The match details to a crowd containing a healthy sprinkling of clergymen and theology students were broadcast from the scorers' box by loudspeakers. Nevertheless it became part of Somerset's policy to take the game around the county, with festivals at Bath and Weston-super-Mare and matches at Frome and Glastonbury. Not all the cricketers were impressed with the the ground, Bill Andrews describing the pavilion as "only the size of a small cowshed". Somerset's slow left-arm bowler Horace Hazell did not take kindly to having to find a penny in order to visit a toilet there. Such was the life of a pro in the 1930s. Few concessions were made on out-grounds. The *Bristol Evening Post* also had misgivings after that first match. "It still lacks some of the things which are generally deemed essential," it said. At least the sight screens were in place for the Derbyshire match.

Derbyshire made two changes, one enforced. Charlie Elliott came in for Langdale and the slow left-arm bowler Tommy Armstrong – who took 60 wickets at seven apiece for Ollerton in the Bassetlaw League that year – was called up in Mitchell's absence. The team was: Arthur Richardson (captain), Harry Elliott (wicketkeeper), Albert Alderman, Denis Smith, Stan Worthington, Leslie Townsend, Alan Skinner, Charlie Elliott, Alf Pope, Tommy Armstrong and Bill Copson.

Somerset had had an enjoyable season. They moved up seven places to finish seventh. Their opening batsmen Harold Gimblett and Frank Lee each topped one thousand runs while Arthur Wellard, Bill Andrews and Horace Hazell were the leading bowlers; Wally Luckes a dependable wicketkeeper. No fewer than 34 players turned out for the county in 1936, 24 of whom were amateurs. It was hardly a settled side but it played attractive cricket and was very popular. At Wells, Reggie Ingle, a Bath solicitor, skippered a team which included five amateurs, sparse by early-1920s yardsticks but a relatively high proportion in 1936. The umpires were Charlie Parker and Tom Oates.

The news from Kibworth cast a cloud over the day. It was all the more poignant because Reggie Northway, a steady batsman who was born in Ceylon, had played for Somerset before moving to Northamptonshire.

In contrast to the recent heat wave, there was a cold wind and an overcast sky when play started, the hours on the first two days being 12.15 to 7.15pm. Such was the sporting nature of the pitch that no arrangements had yet been made for Friday's hours.

Richardson won the toss but Somerset struck an early blow when Alderman was bowled at 27. Smith and Worthington then got going and by lunch the score was 106 for one, Smith 65, Worthington 31. Wellard soon removed Worthington and after Smith was fourth out at 153 the batting subsided. The left-hander batted for 140 minutes and hit a six and 12 fours in his 93. Charlie Elliott battled away for an unbeaten 29 but the innings closed at 216; Andrews five for 42 and Wellard four for 52. Somerset were soon in trouble, four wickets going down for 53. The left-handed amateur Bunty Longrigg (40 not out) pulled them round and by close of play the score was 116 for five. Fortunes had changed throughout but in the end it had been Derbyshire's day. It was a similar story at Hove, where Yorkshire dismissed Sussex for 225 and ended on 56 without loss.

Glorious sunshine greeted the teams on Thursday. Longrigg added only four more to his overnight score and Pope (five for 35) and Copson (three for 55) removed the tail. Somerset lost five wickets for 30 runs in half-an-hour's play during the morning and were dismissed for 146. Derbyshire had started the game requiring three points: now, if they avoided defeat, they would have an extra two for first innings lead.

That lead was a healthy 70 runs and it was quickly placed in perspective by Wellard, who shot out Smith, Worthington and Townsend with a mere 26 scored. Skinner made 39 but seven wickets were down for 98, only 168 in front, before Richardson and Pope rescued matters, just as they had in the Northamptonshire match. They added 66, Richardson driving and pulling admirably in making 50 and Pope getting a spirited 30. The total reached 200, disappointing for the home side but a source of satisfaction for Derbyshire. Wellard remained a handful, five for 47 and match figures of nine for 99 going a long way towards keeping Somerset in the match. Their target, 271, was a stiff one but Lee and Gimblett soon made inroads with an opening stand of 67. Copson accounted for both of them and by the close, 98 for two, Somerset needed another 173, with Longrigg and Jack Meyer at the wicket. At Hove, Yorkshire established a first innings' lead of 103, Sussex being ten without loss at the close.

The Championship was in Derbyshire's sights, but they needed early wickets on Friday morning. They got them; a Copson in-swinger bowling Meyer and Cameron being run out by Richardson from short leg. Four down for 115, 156 required. Tommy Armstrong was brought into the attack at 120, Longrigg driving him for six, but the bowler gained his revenge when he had the batsman caught by Smith in front of the sight screen. Longrigg had made 38 and five wickets had gone for 140.

Ingle, surviving a chance to Harry Elliott – who did not concede a bye in the match – off Pope before he scored, was now joined in the middle by Wellard, an opening bowler good enough to play Test cricket, who was also capable of delivering off-breaks from around the wicket. He was 33 years old and had played for Somerset since 1927. In 1936 he took 146 wickets and was among the leading fast-medium bowlers in the country. Standing 6ft 2ns, strong and with a broad physique, Wellard adopted a healthily uncomplicated approach to batting. He had a sound enough defence, but, with minimal backlift, earned renown as one of the most successful hitters in county cricket. David Foot, a writer specialising in West Country cricket, wrote that he aimed for the clouds. "The clouds could usually be relied on to convey the ball to chimney stacks, open bedroom windows, passing streams, or, in one case, a passing goods wagon." But Wellard was no mere slogger, as a career batting average of 19.73 from 12,575 runs gathered with a 2lb 11oz bat indicates. He made just two hundreds, 112 at Old Trafford in 1935 his highest, but in the relatively short time he was at the crease he could cause mayhem.

He had already made his mark at Wells the year before. Somerset, following on against Worcestershire, were in deep trouble in their second innings when Wellard and Andrews added 69 for the eighth wicket in less than 20 minutes. Andrews struck one ball into a garden and Wellard hit four sixes and four fours in 50. It was a losing cause but it was a forerunner of another feat of big hitting at Wells when Wellard hit five consecutive sixes in making 31 off one over from Frank Woolley in 1938. He was dropped on the boundary off the sixth ball. In that match he scored 57 and 37 and took thirteen wickets for 115 runs against Kent, his native county.

So Wellard was a hitter capable of changing the course of a game but one who could also be dismissed quickly. And, although the pitch played better as the game went along, 131 was a lot of runs to make against such an attack as Derbyshire's, particularly with half the team back in the pavilion. It nearly became insurmountable when Wellard, having made a single, put one foot down the wicket and lashed a ball from Armstrong to Smith, fielding in the deep. The fieldsman could not hang on to the catch and in the same over Wellard launched two massive drives over the sight screen. The over cost 17 runs.

Richardson removed his slow left-arm bowler from the slaughter but brought him back again with the score at 180. Wellard pushed the first ball of the over to short leg and drove the next five for six. Two were powerful drives over mid-wicket into the car park. The next three, hit straight, cleared long-off, two over the sight screen into an adjoining field. Raymond Robertson-Glasgow, his playing career over, was watching the match from outside the boundary and caught the third hit. He said the two balls which soared out of the small ground rained down on some pigsties. Wellard, he added, appeared as unruffled as the west front of Wells Cathedral. Thirty from the over. It placed the name of TR Armstrong in the record books for all the wrong reasons.

Wellard made 66 (seven sixes and four fours) out of the 77 added in 45 minutes with Ingle for the sixth wicket. But Ingle was caught in the slips off Copson and four wickets remained with 54 runs needed. Wellard was now joined by Andrews. The equation was simple. If these two remained for very long they would make mincemeat of the target. Richardson's options were limited. He had no Mitchell and had been forced to take Armstrong out of the fray. Worthington had pulled a muscle and was unable to bowl. It was almost inevitable that he should turn to Copson.

Fast bowlers tend to wane in August, as the pitches harden and the season's graft takes its toll. Not so Copson in 1936. Opposing batsmen remained in peril. In seven crucial games that month, beginning with Essex and ending with Somerset, he took 45 wickets at 14.77 each. Mitchell's haul before his injury was 29 at 19 and Alf Pope, who sent down more overs (295) than anybody in those games, had 25 at 25. Only Townsend, a mere seven at 58, deteriorated.

Wellard had made 20 of the 25-run partnership he shared with Andrews when he skied a ball from Copson and was caught at mid-off by Leslie Townsend. He hit 86 out of 102 scored while he was at the wicket in only 62 minutes. His innings included seven sixes, all off Armstrong, and eight fours, 74 in 15 scoring strokes. A spectator remembered him, sweat pouring from his face, making his way round the ground to the beer tent straight after his dismissal. Others recalled jumping over fences into gardens to retrieve cricket balls. The score was now 242-7. Twenty nine runs were needed with three wickets left. Andrews and McRae added nine in 20 minutes before lunch to take the score at the interval to 251.

Peter McRae was then a 20-year-old medical student at St Mary's Hospital, where he made a name for himself as a dashing three-quarter who appeared in a rugby international trial. He was born in Buenos Aires and went to St Mary's from school at Christ's Hospital. He captained Scotland at squash and was a graceful, correct batsman and excellent fieldsman.

After lunch Richardson, amidst tremendous tension, opened the attack with Copson and Pope. Six overs, five of them maidens, produced only four runs. Doggedly determined, Andrews and McRae stole singles and on two occasions McRae was perilously close to being run out. Pope bowled five maidens and Copson conceded four runs in five overs before Richardson made a double change, bringing on Townsend and Armstrong as the suspense mounted. McRae hit Armstrong to the leg boundary but at 263, Andrews, who had batted for 70 minutes, was caught by Alderman in front of the pavilion off Townsend. Two runs later Luckes was yorked by the returning Copson: 265-9, six runs needed, one wicket remaining. McRae was still there, partnered by the last man, Hazell.

Earlier in the season, at Bath, Hazell had scored 28 runs from an over by Verity, hitting the England slow left-arm bowler for four sixes but a seasonal batting average of nine did not auger well. Indeed, Alf Pope recalled asking Richardson to move Charlie Elliott to silly mid-on when he came in. Elliott just managed to get a hand to a ball driven by Hazell and it was deflected onto the wicket at the bowler's end. An appeal was rejected because the umpire was unsighted. In any event, one ball from

Copson would surely be enough. Instead Hazell off-drove the fast bowler, scourge of so many batsmen in 1936, to the boundary.

Somerset were 269-9 and now it was Townsend to bowl. McRae turned him for a single, leaving Hazell to face. Short and on the tubby side, the 27-year-old was an unlikely hero but a hero he became that day. He lifted Townsend's fifth ball over cover's head, sending it racing away to the boundary. Somerset, 274-9, had won by one wicket, completing the double over Derbyshire. McRae, who had played a fine defensive innings, 14 not out in 70 minutes in the crisis, and Hazell were carried shoulder-high from the field. Bill Andrews said Hazell's two cover drives matched Woolley at his best. That evening Wells rang to the celebrations of players and supporters alike.

Surgeon Lieutenant FM McRae was a victim of the war, when the destroyer HMS Mahratta was torpedoed in the Barents Sea while escorting a Russian convoy in February 1944.

Copson's effort had been magnificent, six for 81 in 30 overs. Alf Pope failed to take a wicket but conceded only 64 runs in 34 overs. Poor Tommy Armstrong had gone for 64 in eight overs, with a solitary maiden and a single wicket amidst the carnage. And all this with his wedding only eight days away. Gallows humour helped lift the gloom. Armstrong said that next time he came to Wells he would place his fielders in the Mendip Hills. But although the ground was used for fixtures for a time after the 1939-45 war, this was Derbyshire's solitary visit.

Skinner said that the wider Armstrong bowled the further Wellard hit him. "We then went on to lose the match by one wicket after what was certainly one of the most exciting games of cricket I have ever played in. I should perhaps add that I didn't help matters very much by dropping McRae in the gully at a crucial moment."

Exciting or not, Derbyshire were displeased. They had not wanted to lose this one, had expected to win it, and they had contested the game with the utmost intensity. The team left Wells convinced they ought to have won, indeed should have won. During the match four catches were missed: "Perhaps we tried too hard," said Denis Smith, laconically, years later. There may have been another contributing factor. William Richardson said his father told him about the team over-indulging and celebrating the Championship success prematurely. "My father was very angry when he learned about this. Travel arrangements had to be made for the next match at Oakham which involved getting to Bristol and changing trains at, I believe, Leicester. Charlie Elliott, the junior professional, was sent to ask father about the arrangements for leaving Wells. Still furious, father replied: 'Tell them to bloody well walk.'"

"Derbyshire beaten by Wellard's mighty hitting" read the headline in the *Derby Evening Telegraph*. "There is still an 'if' about the County Championship," it reported.

Thus Derbyshire were reliant on Sussex at Hove, where they started the day 93 runs behind Yorkshire with all of their second innings wickets in hand. The champions set about chiselling them out, the first wicket falling at 43. Then Melville produced some attractive strokes, the score rising to 135 before the second wicket fell. The scores filtered through to Wells, 162 for two, Melville 78 not out, and then Melville was gone, caught off Hutton for 90. But others made runs until AJ Holmes declared at 297 for seven, setting Yorkshire a target of 195 in 90 minutes. It was just about possible, but 130 an hour from, as it transpired, 25 overs – 7.8 runs per over – was too much to realistically expect. Modern cricketers, their fast-scoring skills honed on a diet of limited over matches, might attempt it, might even achieve it. But Sussex had Tate to apply the brakes if matters got out of hand. They did not and Mitchell and Hutton gathered 71 runs without due hurry or concern and without being separated.

Old Supporter (Derbyshire County Cricket Year Book 1986) wrote that news of the defeat at Wells arrived in Derby before tea time. "In the early evening the news arrived – Yorkshire had been held – Derbyshire were champions."

Yorkshire had to be satisfied with five points for the first innings lead. It cost them second place in the table, their 49.42 per cent being overtaken by Middlesex, who had beaten Worcestershire at New Road and now registered 50.13 per cent. Derbyshire led with 224 points from 27 matches, 55.30 per cent. More importantly, Yorkshire's maximum possible had decreased to 51.11, short of Derbyshire's minimum of 53.33 per cent.

On Friday August 28 1936, Derbyshire suffered defeat by Somerset at Wells but within a few hours knew they had won the County Championship.

Chapter 32
Celebrations

IMMEDIATE celebrations had to be put on hold for there was a match next day and the journey – by train and not on foot – to the Oakham School ground in Rutland. Nevertheless the mood was celebratory. Dudley Carew wrote of fun-filled hours shared with some members of the team after the match which definitely won them the Championship, whatever their nearest rivals did. "There was a glorious enjoyment in the railway carriage that night," Carew said. Bill Bestwick, umpiring at Worcester on the day the title was won, doubtless raised a glass to his old club.

Far from competing in key matches at the major Test grounds, Derbyshire were enjoying the climax of their triumphant season at outgrounds; Worksop, Wells and now Oakham. The town itself had strong links with cricket history. The mansion of Burley-on-the-Hill was the home of George Finch, the 9th Earl of Winchilsea, the man regarded as the chief founder of MCC, and the town club ground is just off Brooke Road. But it has been the school ground which has staged first-class cricket. Two MCC games were played in 1907 but the first Championship match did not take place until 1935, when Leicestershire defeated Kent by an innings. There was a charming, thatched pavilion on the west side of the ground at the time of Derbyshire's visit.

They were greeted by ideal weather and a warm welcome from the large crowd, which applauded the champions as they took the field, Leicestershire having won the toss. Storer recalled Charlie Elliott to Coventry City, Langdale coming in. With the pressure off, Derbyshire enjoyed themselves. They dismissed the home side for 151, Copson taking four for 34, and by the close were 103 for one. On Monday, Smith (169, one six and 13 fours) and Worthington (102, one six and seven fours) took their second wicket partnership to 209 in 190 minutes. Derbyshire made 338, removed half the Leicestershire side before close of play and finished the job before lunch on Tuesday morning, the margin being an innings and 66 runs. Pope took four for 44 in the second innings and Armstrong returned match figures of 25-8-31-3, some consolation for the shredding he received at Wells. For the first time that summer, results elsewhere could be ignored but Middlesex and Yorkshire both won and Gloucestershire defeated Nottinghamshire to ease past them into fourth place.

In the meantime, Will Taylor had been busy. "It was suggested to me that when the Championship was won there should be a public reception for the team on their return to Derby following the match against Leicestershire at Oakham and I immediately set to work. The Drill Hall was booked and I made contact with our president, the Duke of Devonshire, who was grouse shooting at Bolton Abbey and who came post haste to Derby. The mayors of the five towns in the county where we played were invited and were present. All arrangements were made for refreshments, and always having the financial position in view, the band of the Sherwood Foresters was booked for a dance after the reception of the team and a charge (of a shilling) made to non-members of the club. Everything went according to plan and we had a wonderful evening."

The reception was held on the evening of Tuesday, September 1. The principal guests were the Duke of Devonshire, Lord Lieutenant of the county and the club's president, Alderman John Clark, the mayor of Derby, and the mayors of Glossop, Ilkeston, Chesterfield, Buxton and Burton-on-Trent. Arthur Richardson led his team out to a roar of cheers. Former players included Joe Humphries, LG Wright, now aged 74 and GB Barrington (79), who first played in 1880, but Tommy Mitchell, of the current side, was unable to attend. None looked more delighted than the former captain Guy Jackson and the secretary Will Taylor. Jackson had cause for a double celebration. That month, at the age of 40, he announced his engagement to Shelagh Tollhurst, from Gravesend. They were married the following April and had two sons and a daughter.

The Duke congratulated the team, singling out Richardson, Guy Jackson, George Buckston, Will Taylor and Sam Cadman for individual praise. He said that while the match against Somerset was in progress he had stood on top of a hill in Yorkshire in one of the most severe thunderstorms he had ever known. "I could not help wishing that they were having some of it in Wells," he said. He also congratulated Stan Worthington and Bill Copson on their selection for the 1936-37 tour of Australia.

Richardson expressed his delight about the Championship, which he suggested should have been won a long time ago. He said he had received 300 letters of congratulation in the past three days. "In front of you now I thank my side for the wonderful way in which they backed me up this season." Whenever he asked his team for extra effort in a crisis he had always received it. This was a team which never gave up. Derbyshire were never beaten until the last run had been scored. The congratulations poured in. Lord Hawke said: "Know you will be pleased. Accept Yorkshire's and my own personal congratulations." Richardson said there were tributes from Brian Sellers and George Heane, "our fiercest foes and at the same time our best friends". And from Maurice Turnbull, captain of Glamorgan: "Congratulations on winning the Championship. Especially creditable performance as you did not use Glamorgan for fodder".

Alderman Clark said one of the most delightful features of the success was that all the players were from Derbyshire. He appealed for sportsmen to increase the finances of the club so that it would not have a heavy loss in a momentous season marred only by the weather. A testimonial fund for the players raised £600 and each received a watch.

Thus the natural progression to the Championship, third in 1934 and runners-up in 1935, was accomplished in 1936. It was especially satisfying given the loss of George Pope early in the season. Derbyshire moved to the top on July 7 during Chesterfield Cricket Week and remained there, despite the lapses in August involving four consecutive matches without a victory.

Derbyshire's 13 victories consisted of doubles over Gloucestershire, Leicestershire, Warwickshire and Worcestershire and wins over Essex, Kent, Northamptonshire, Surrey and Sussex. Defeats were inflicted by Somerset (twice), Kent and Nottinghamshire. First innings points were won against Yorkshire, Hampshire, Surrey, Nottinghamshire and Northamptonshire, and lost against Hampshire, Essex, Lancashire, Yorkshire and Sussex. There was no result in the Lancashire match at Old Trafford. Four games – Gloucestershire (twice), Surrey and Leicestershire – were won in two days, although two of the losses, against Kent and Somerset, came within a similar period. Seven of the wins were in home matches – three each at Derby and Chesterfield and one at Burton-on-Trent. Six away fixtures were won and there were two defeats at home, both at Ilkeston. Derbyshire won the toss 15 times and lost it on 13 occasions, being put in twice by Somerset and Yorkshire. Richardson himself called correctly on 14 occasions and lost 12.

Another point relates to team selection. Nine players played in 26 or more matches out of the 28 in the Championship. Alderman, Harry Elliott, Alf Pope, Leslie Townsend and Smith were ever-presents, Copson, Mitchell, Richardson and Worthington each missed only two games. It was a team effort in every sense of the word. Above everything, they never gave up and mastered the art of keeping going and making something happen when things were going astray. The side had grown up together, Will Taylor writing: "By their skill and acumen, Jackson and Richardson gradually moulded Derbyshire into a match-winning combination, and, with the flair for discerning the potentialities of young players, Cadman produced from the cricket nursery no fewer than eight of the Championship team".

Wisden – which included Copson and Worthington in its Five Cricketers of the Year – said: "Magnificent bowling – they possessed probably the deadliest and best varied attack of any side in the country – teamwork rather than individual brilliance, and a will-to-win spirit no matter the position of the game, were the salient factors which made Derbyshire stand out head and shoulders above most of their rivals.

"It must be confessed that the batting frequently revealed striking limitations; but paradoxically though it may appear, this very weakness influenced Derbyshire's triumph. Had the side put together big totals, their bowlers would never have found the time or opportunity to get rid of opponents for reasonably small scores. Derbyshire's policy of scoring quickly was proved the right one. It is sufficient to state that the county won 13 of their 28 matches and suffered only four defeats. No other team gained so many victories. There were, of course, times when Derbyshire found themselves compelled by circumstances to cast aside their customary bright, attractive methods, and on at least two occasions they baulked their rivals by dogged defence."

Celebrations

Wisden commented on the injury to George Pope, Smith's indifferent form for much of the season and Mitchell's broken thumb. "While Worthington, Copson, Townsend and H Elliott revealed wonderful form, full praise must be given to AW Richardson. First leading Derbyshire in 1931, Richardson again captained the eleven with shrewdness and a geniality which brought the best out of the cricketers under him. He proved his foresight in promoting Worthington to opening batsman when Smith was clearly suffering from temporary lack of confidence, and results justified his decision to place Elliott (H) higher in the batting order on occasions when the side fared badly. "For his handling of the bowling, Richardson deserved the highest commendation and undoubtedly his astuteness in 'nursing' Copson had a great deal to do with the young fast bowler's striking advance."

Wisden added that Worthington combined sound defence with hitting as powerful and at times devastating as it was entertaining; Townsend found fewer wickets to suit his bowling but was in capital form with the bat and Smith and Alderman also registered a thousand runs. Alan Skinner often batted attractively and fielded well in the slips, Charlie Elliott improved and stiffened the middle order and Harry Elliott played a number of sound defensive innings.

Alf Pope sent down more overs than anybody else and bowled with unflagging zeal to take 99 wickets but it was Copson and Mitchell who carried off chief honours in a deadly bowling combination. "Physically much stronger than in 1935 when he broke down in health, Copson bowled consistently and with great effect and, for the first time in his career, claimed 100 wickets. Altogether, in Championship matches he dismissed no fewer than 140 batsmen for an average of 12.80 as compared with 71 at just over 16 runs apiece the previous season, and in 13 games he obtained five or more wickets. Like most other bowlers of pace able to swing the ball, he gained increased effectiveness by reason of the new lbw rule and accomplished two great performances in dismissing 12 Surrey batsmen for 52 runs at Derby and securing 12 Worcestershire wickets at a cost of 54 at Worcester. Carefully handled, Copson left no doubt of his ability to stand up to the strain of an arduous summer. His fiery bowling at the beginning of an innings frequently gave Derbyshire the whip hand, and his exceptional 'nip' off the pitch, swing and swerve, allied to a good length, demoralised many batsmen before they gained a proper sight of the ball."

Wisden said Mitchell, with his cleverly-varied slows, proved an admirable foil to the pace of Copson and Pope. "True, Mitchell's leg-breaks were at times terribly expensive but on his day he could run through the best batting side in the land." He might have fared even better with more support in the field. Derbyshire dropped too many catches and though the fielding on the whole reached a fair standard it left much room for improvement, the almanack continued. But it pointed out that Elliott's wicketkeeping remained as reliable as ever. In 25 completed innings he did not concede a bye. "Many good judges hold Elliott to be as fine a wicketkeeper as any in the country; his claims to recognition in representative matches appear to have been overlooked."

"A review of the Derbyshire season would not be complete without reference to Sam Cadman, the former Derbyshire player, in charge of the nursery. The fact that most of the players who helped to win the Championship graduated from the nursery forms in itself a tribute to the judgment and perseverance of Cadman and those collaborating with him. The Derbyshire committee, too, are to be congratulated upon the success of this scheme to develop likely talent."

Similar points were made in *The Cricketer*, which said Derbyshire's success was immensely popular. "Well as Worthington, Townsend, Smith (in August), Alderman, AF Skinner and the two Elliotts batted on many occasions, Derbyshire's real strength lay in bowling and fielding. Thoroughly fit after some winter training with the Chesterfield football team, Copson had a great season, and was most definitely a match-winner. Very quick off the wicket and possessing the ability to make the ball come in from the off, the only criticism one can make of Copson's bowling is that he is inclined to bowl short of a length. However, his record is eloquent of ability, and he is the type of bowler who always appears to be attacking the batsman."

He received admirable support from Alf Pope, who bowled very accurately, and although there were occasions when Mitchell's indifferent length resulted in heavy punishment he had days when he was as deadly as ever. Townsend was the most successful all-rounder in the side.

Worthington, too, received praise, particularly for his 135 against Yorkshire – "undoubtedly his greatest achievement" – the magazine adding that he was a good field and there could be few safer catchers in first-class cricket. "Smith could do nothing right for the first three months of the season. He appeared to lose confidence, and the experiment of putting him in at either four or five met with little success. However, at the beginning of August, when he was once again used as an opening batsman, he scored 106 against Surrey at The Oval, and from thence onwards he was the Smith who had played so well in 1935." *The Cricketer* also had a word for Storer – "still a very good batsman; and if meeting with less success than usual, his top score of 62 played a prominent part in the first victory over Worcestershire" – and for Carrington – "plenty of time to re-establish himself, for he is only 22. He is a very promising off-side player, and has worked hard to consolidate his defence. He is the type of player who requires a hard wicket." It added: "AW Richardson has maintained the traditions of GR Jackson, who exercised so good an influence over the eleven both on and off the field."

Rev Henry Ellison mentioned committee colleagues "who had helped to bring about this state of affairs during the past 15 years: RB Chambers, Mr Aitken of Borrowash, Canon Browne, Colonel W Jelf, Mr Moult, Mr Eastwood, of Chesterfield, Mr Bottomley, Rev Clifton Smith and Mr Charles Wright, of Heanor".

Ellison felt Smith did not appreciate the soft wickets in the earlier part of the season – a good point this, which seems to have been missed by some others. "Constant 'feeling for her' took away his usual confidence; however, he finished well. Tom Mitchell has every reason to be satisfied with his season; the new lbw rule has undoubtedly helped him; that quick-moving googly has collected many wickets. Leslie Townsend slightly declined on his 1935 figures, but was most consistent, putting up one more century but dropping eight wickets – he has well earned a benefit in 1937. AV Pope has actually done slightly less bowling, but he has secured five more wickets; this is due to experience and sheer grit. He shouldered much of the responsibility of the attack after his brother's injury and his consistently accurate bowling won him praise and admiration from many critics. Charlie Elliott will never look back. We look to him to occupy Storer's place in the side. Harry cannot give up enough time from his football duties to do himself justice. To play first class cricket one must be a regular performer."

Worthington had fairly forced his way into the England side. "Copson has doubled his crop of wickets, due no doubt to better physique and greater experience. I still think he bowls too short to be a 'classic'. No batsman should be allowed to play back five balls out of six. He has the merit, however, of making his opponents play the ball." Ellison still felt Carrington was capable of making the grade and had real ability and there was more praise for Richardson. But he rued the absence of a really good slow left-arm bowler.

Above all, Ellison emphasised the value of the nursery. He said that it was one thing to organise it; quite another to decide how much promise a player had and if it was possible to bring that promise out. Ellison's maxim was temperament and confidence without over-confidence. "Once he has got a big score in public, or once he has taken five wickets, the player feels he can do it again, and there lies the secret of success."

The *Derby Evening Telegraph* said Derbyshire had a claim to be the greatest bowling side in the country. The title had been well-deserved and a key factor was an ability to complete matches. It said batsmen had been demoralised by Copson's remarkable pace off the pitch and Mitchell had also played a crucial part. Praise, too, for the captain's decisions to promote Harry Elliott in the order, Worthington to opener and his nursing of Copson. As for the nursery: "Without it Derbyshire may still be near the bottom of the table; with it we can look to the present standard being maintained," said the paper.

Dudley Carew said winning the title was a splendid thing for Derbyshire and for the county competition as a whole. "Only Warwickshire before them, in 1911, had broken into the charmed circle of the counties which had made the Championship their own since its inception. Derbyshire were a tough, well-balanced side with the bulk of their strength just where it is most needed – in their bowling. They had, too, a more than generous proportion of all-rounders." These represented a solid nucleus of all-round cricketing strength. "If Copson and Mitchell were the bowlers pure and simple, and Smith and Alderman corresponded to them in batting, then there were the two Popes, George and AV, Townsend and Worthington to bat and bowl, to say nothing of a batsman-wicketkeeper in Elliott. Here, then, was a side which could bat down to No 9, not sketchily but in strength, and with enough variety in bowling to ensure that no one need ever be overworked."

Terence Prittie found them a keen, consistent, well-balanced team. "Worthington and Townsend batted as well as at any time in their lives. Almost every man on the side could make runs. The attack was hostile and varied, the fielding sound rather than spectacular. Elliott was as good as any other wicketkeeper in England." But in comparing them to other champion counties between the wars, Prittie found them in no way outstanding. "In 1936 the Derby team lacked players of the very highest class. Perseverance, determination and dependability were all theirs. But personality and genius were missing. Their success was due to guts, keenness and opportunism, and to the fact that this particular year produced no really outstanding team. They are the most deserving but the least convincing or spectacular champion side of the whole period." One can take issue with this; surely Derbyshire would have been a match for the Middlesex team of the early 1920s and Nottinghamshire in 1929. Prittie's point about the fielding, however, was enlarged by Sir Home Gordon, who found it "first rate, apart from a tendency to stop the ball with the feet before the hands get down to it."

John Arlott, well aware of their ability as a contemporary follower of the game but looking back in a retrospective piece in *Wisden Cricket Monthly* to mark the 50th anniversary of the Championship success, said Derbyshire were undoubtedly the strongest – and their opponents would say the hardest – side in the 1936 competition.

"Their success was founded on the ability to score runs quickly, but, above all, to get other sides out cheaply with a quite excitedly varied and balanced attack."

Of Richardson, he wrote: "Tactful and encouraging, he had no need to be a driver – that team drove itself. Indeed it is difficult to recall a side more purposeful or more ruthlessly abrasive than that Derbyshire winning side. Their success was more the remarkable for the fact that a major all-rounder, George Pope, did not play after injury late in May; that Denis Smith lost form quite alarmingly until August; and at the end Tommy Mitchell effectively missed three matches. Their extremely hostile bowling was matched by absolutely aggressive, if not always faultless, fielding."

After discussing the individual merits, Arlott added: "Essentially, though, this was a single unit, and it may seem hard to convey to the ordinary follower of today what an atmosphere they could create: especially on south country grounds they made the cricket bristle with competition. Shall we ever see a side of quite such gladiatorial quality in the English county game again? There is no sign of it."

And what of the players? Alan Skinner's affection for that season was obvious more than 30 years later. "The side had a magnificent attack, both in depth and variety, for all sorts of wickets, and we fielded well with plenty of good close-to-the-wicket experts. It was, of course, not a great batting side, but we were in the first three of the Championship for four years so it could not have been all that bad! We had a number of batsmen who could score quickly and this meant that in uncertain weather our bowlers had time to get the opposition out twice and we could usually finish a match without a contrived ending.

"Actually, I always felt the 1935 side played better cricket. So far as I can recall we had a better record and were a bit unlucky not to win the Championship that year. Yorkshire were always our toughest opponents during those seasons, although, oddly enough, I usually managed to make a few runs against them. It is interesting to compare the Championship attack with bowlers like Jackson and Gladwin in later years. I should say there was little to choose between these two and Copson and Pope, but the latter had the advantage of being supported by Townsend, Mitchell and George Pope, when he was fit, and this helped to maintain the pressure."

Leslie Townsend said that while they never got big scores they made enough runs to give the bowlers a chance. "We bowled for every wicket," he said – another to emphasise the aggressive nature of this fine team. Tommy Mitchell paid warm tribute to Harry Elliott. "In my opinion, he was the best everyday keeper in the world because of the variety of bowling he took."

Charlie Elliott said the key factor was the balanced attack on the uncovered pitches of the day. "Bill Copson had the knack of getting any batsman out early on and Tommy Mitchell, when it was his day, was a great bowler who could bowl sides out twice in a match. They were supported by Alf Pope and Leslie Townsend, who was a very good all-rounder, and it really was an attack of Test match quality."

The old Warwickshire player Tom Collin recalled Mitchell as "a very big spinner of the ball." He said Larwood was the fastest bowler but bracketed Copson with Jim Smith and Alf Gover in the next category.

Reflecting on 1936, Arthur Richardson told Gerald Mortimer of the *Derby Evening Telegraph*: "Copson and Mitchell were at the heart of the Championship victory. Two killers, both positive bowlers and both likely to run through a side. Their personalities were as different as their bowling styles. Bill gave nothing away. Tommy was always tempting them with his leg spinners and was liable to be hit. But he was equally liable to get wickets and get them quickly.

"Unfortunately, we lost George Pope in May of 1936 with cartilage trouble after he had really developed during the previous two seasons. But his brother Alf did wonderfully well. He was a most willing player. I would sometimes tell him that he might have to bowl until close of play and he would just say; 'I like bowling, skipper,' and come bounding in for hours.

"I wanted Leslie Townsend to make runs, so I did not use his off-spinners nearly as much as Guy Jackson had done. He became a perfect complement to Stan Worthington. Stan enjoyed fast bowling: Leslie was infinitely happier against spin. I pushed Stan up the order and, therefore, he did not bowl much. I was more interested in specialists than all-rounders. Stan Worthington was a wonderful cricketer. There were times, watching him from the edge, when it was hard to tell if it was Stan or Wally Hammond at the crease. I cannot pay him a bigger compliment than to compare him with Hammond.

"Denis Smith was a most beautiful hitter. He was inclined, like all hitters, to be erratic, but his record over the years provides an answer to that. So, with Albert Alderman an unassuming opener and a fine fielder, the top batting was good enough. With Copson and Mitchell in the side, we did not need too many runs and as a result, the games were always open.

"Alan Skinner has never been given the credit due to him. He did not win a Blue at Cambridge, but he was one of the best amateur cricketers in the country. He scored a lot of his runs down to third man, and those who did not know him thought he was snicking the ball. In addition, he was a superb catcher. I owe him a great deal of debt for the way he filled in when Harry Storer went off to manage Coventry City. Harry, I'm sure, would have played for England if he had not always had football at the back of his mind.

"Harry Elliott, of course, was a great wicketkeeper and a wonderful influence on the side. Think of the best regimental sergeant-major you have ever known – that was Harry Elliott. It was a privilege for me to play in company with such fine cricketers and such wonderful people."

It was reciprocal. Among Arthur Richardson's most treasured possessions was a silver cigarette case, inscribed with the signatures of the Championship side.

It carried a simple dedication: "To the Skipper, from the lads."

Chapter 33
1874 and All That

ON the day Derbyshire were crowned champions, Madrid suffered its first air raid of the Spanish Civil War. The conflict marred the closing years of an old man, who, if life taken a different course, might have been an honoured guest at the Drill Hall celebrations as captain of what some claimed was the first Derbyshire Championship-winning side.

Sam Richardson (no relation to the 1936 captain) was skipper of the 1874 team which became a subject of debate as the 1936 season approached its close. He had fled to Madrid in 1890 after robbing the county and soccer club during his period as assistant secretary. He had issued tickets for football and cricket matches, helping himself to "considerable portions of the receipts". Richardson, who changed his name to John Roberts, used the cash to establish a tailoring and outfitting business in the city. As it flourished, members of his family joined him.

They were turbulent times. Maria Cristina, widow of Alfonso XI1, was Regent until her 16-year-old son became Alfonso XI11 in 1902. During the 1914-18 war, neutral Spain entered a period of prosperity. Whole districts were industrialised to meet the needs of the belligerents and stock of all kinds rose. Roberts did remarkably well. He was patronised by the court, becoming tailor to Alfonso. Under the military directory which replaced Parliament in the 1920s his success continued as he entered mellow old age. But in 1931 the monarchy collapsed and the Republicans sent Alfonso into exile. The best part of Roberts' custom vanished and, nearing 90 years of age, he was too old to begin a recovery.

He was the oldest British resident in Madrid and when the city came under siege he moved into the Anglo-American Nursing Home. Here he spent his last few months and, on January 18 1938, he died at the age of 93. The British cemetery in Madrid was in the war zone so the old cricketer was buried in a Spanish civil cemetery.

Towards the end of his life he received financial help and good wishes from friends in Derby. A small fund was raised by AG Elliott, who was apprenticed to him 50 years earlier and had corresponded with him regularly. In a touching letter of thanks, Richardson said he felt himself very alone in the world – most of his relatives were dead – but he sent his best wishes to many Derby people whom he knew in brighter days. Given his circumstances, the speculation over whether Derbyshire had been champions under his captaincy must have been of little concern to him.

From 1911-1962 *Wisden* listed Derbyshire as champions in 1874, replacing them with Gloucestershire in 1963. This followed research, commissioned by *Wisden*, into the early county champions by Rowland Bowen, a cricket historian. No official Championship existed before 1890 but champion counties can be traced back to 1826. The sporting press acted as unofficial arbiters, compiling orders of merit by the 'least lost' method. In such cases, the county with the smallest number of defeats, notwithstanding how many matches it had played, was accepted as champions.

In 1874 Derbyshire played four county matches, defeating Kent (twice) and Lancashire and having the worst of a rain-affected draw with Lancashire. Gloucestershire defeated Yorkshire (twice), Surrey and Sussex in their six matches, with a draw against Sussex and one defeat, by Surrey. Outside of the county programme, Derbyshire drew two matches with Yorkshire United, a breakaway organisation from the main club. Sixteen of Derbyshire defeated Nottinghamshire at Trent Bridge and a Derbyshire XV1 defeated the United South of England (including WG) at Derby. That meant five victories and three draws in eight fixtures and no defeats.

The journals of the day acknowledged that Derbyshire were the only unbeaten county but, in the main, said Gloucestershire were champions. Even the *Derby Mercury* carried a piece which acknowledged Gloucestershire as champion county. There was no contemporary claim to the title, either from the club or the local press. The closest was that of John Cartwright, a founding father and great supporter of Derbyshire, who covered cricket for local newspapers. He wrote to *Sporting Life* in August 1887 in an attempt to retain the club's first-class status, referring to a sketch he had written in 1875 about the county's performance in 'the season when Derbyshire stood number one among the counties on account of not losing a match.'

Bowen was to write: "At the time, Gloucestershire were accepted as champions, and claimed to be champions; Derbyshire were not and did not." So how did Derbyshire ever come to be regarded as champions? In January 1893 Rev RS Holmes wrote an article on the Championship for the magazine *Cricket*. In October 1894 it was expanded into a series. A year later Alfred Gibson's *County Cricket Championship* appeared. Holmes updated his articles into a similar book in 1896. Both writers worked back to 1873 – the year that rules governing qualification were introduced – using least-lost as a yardstick from 1873-86.

Thus undefeated Derbyshire were named as the 1874 champions, *Wisden* gradually adopting what became the official list. In the county itself, WJ Piper's 1897 history made no such claim, although it said they stood alone as the only unbeaten county. The *Derbyshire Cricket Guide* in 1896 did make the claim – but by then the Holmes-Gibson findings were becoming accepted. Fifty years after the event FS Ashley-Cooper's *Derbyshire Cricket* named the county as 1874 champions.

Piper ended a period of 35 years as Derbyshire's scorer in 1927. He was succeeded by Harry Parker, who began scoring in away matches two years earlier. Parker was born in Codnor but lived most of his life in Ripley, where he managed the lamp wick factory of James Crossley and Co Ltd for 32 years. Parker's scorebooks recorded the

1936 season. He received a life membership of the county in 1935 for his services on the committee and as honorary scorer and was to be succeeded by Sam Peters, from North Wingfield.

As for Piper, he dealt with mounting correspondence relating to the 1874 controversy, notably from Pelham Warner and *The Cricketer* and from *Wisden's* editor, who disputed its validity.

The Cricketer Annual examined Derbyshire's claim, using the theme of "can this claim to a previous triumph 62 years ago be established or not?" It found that if it was accepted that the smallest number of defeats decided the order of merit then no county could be placed above Derbyshire. "Their record, as far as it went, was creditable enough, but there was no suggestion from themselves or from anybody else, that they were the strongest county, or even among the stronger counties. Problems like this one, of ancient County Championships, are interesting, but the interest is, after all, only academic. In their own era, they never arose, and we settle them half a century after the event, on modern lines, and by the application of modern tests." In that light, the magazine published an 1874 table as it would have been according to the 1936 method of reckoning. It placed Derbyshire first with 80 per cent, Gloucestershire second with 72.22, Yorkshire third with 69.44 and Nottinghamshire fourth, 62.50.

The 1937 *Wisden* commented that Derbyshire had "some claim" to be considered champions in 1874. While acknowledging the doubt, it added: "The fact remains that no claim has been made to the Championship title of 1874 by any other county".

It would have been interesting to know what the members of the 1874 team thought about the controversy. Many of them, including RP Smith, John Smith, John Platts and William Hickton, were alive when Holmes and Gibson published their findings, although the key bowler, William Mycroft had died. Seven members remained in 1911, the year *Wisden* acknowledged Derbyshire as champions. Tom Foster lived until 1929.

The last survivor was Sam Richardson. Captain of a champion county or not, he would have been welcomed alongside his successor and namesake at the celebrations as the grand old man of Derbyshire cricket. But his actions of nearly half-a-century earlier ruled out even the remotest possibility of that.

Chapter 34
From the Nottingham Road End

WINNING the Championship was no flash in the pan. There were few changes in personnel as this team, raised in the coalfields and packed with experience, attitude and talent, remained a side to be feared for the remainder of the decade.

One change was at the top: Arthur Richardson could not see a way to continue as captain owing to the claims of business. He was urged to reconsider but the announcement came in October. Alan Skinner was the logical choice as successor, but as a law student he was preparing for his final exams and could not spare the time. There was a suggestion that Skinner and Richardson should share the captaincy, Richardson leading the side until the middle of July and Skinner then taking over the reins. But this was a non-starter. Instead, after some persuasion, Robin Buckston, an old Etonian and a schoolmaster in Bournemouth, was appointed. Buckston, son of George Buckston, who led the side in 1921, became a popular captain at the age of 28 and the intention was that he should remain in the post for ten or 15 years. He had a place in the public school's history books. In Eton's match against Winchester in 1927, nine wickets were down for 108 when Buckston, the wicketkeeper, came out to join ER Sheepshanks. They added 144 for the last wicket, Sheepshanks scoring 116 and Buckston 39 not out. Sheepshanks died in 1937 while acting as special correspondent to Reuter's in the Spanish Civil War. Buckston made his county debut in 1927, keeping wicket when Harry Elliott was injured but apart from a couple of games for MCC against Wales he played no other first-class cricket until 1937.

The staff for the 1937 season consisted of Buckston, Harry Elliott, Alderman, Smith, Worthington, Leslie Townsend, Charlie Elliott, George Pope, Alf Pope, Copson and Mitchell. Carrington, Rhodes, Arnold Townsend and Gladwin were on the nursery staff.

On the opening two days of the new season this team reached possibly its highest peak. Not only were Derbyshire the champions, but at Old Trafford on Saturday and Monday May 1 and 3 1937 they played like champions. It was a full-strength side: Alderman, Smith, Townsend, Worthington, George Pope, Carrington, Harry Elliott, Alf Pope, Buckston, Mitchell and Copson. Derbyshire recovered from the loss of Alderman and Townsend for 26 to end the first day on 341 for seven – Worthington 103, George Pope 64, Smith 58, Carrington 42 not out – going on to 427 on Monday, Carrington 49, Alf Pope 46 and Mitchell a career-best 57. Lancashire were bowled out for 258, Mitchell taking six for 73, and forced to follow-on, had made four without loss on Monday night. When Copson bowled Hopwood without addition on Tuesday victory appeared likely but the pitch lost its fire and Eddie Paynter saved the match with 150.

It became typical of the season. Derbyshire played some splendid cricket, winning 14 Championship matches and defeating the New Zealanders. Smith made 1,914 first-class runs and Worthington 1,774, both averaging more than 40. Worthington's 238 against Sussex at Derby was the highest of his career, spoiled by his retirement with cramp caused by a pad strap being too tight when he was within 36 of Davidson's record. George Pope, Alderman and Leslie Townsend, who suffered from ulcers, also exceeded a thousand runs and Skinner did well when he was available. Smith and Alderman were fully established as the regular openers, notably against Leicestershire at Queen's Park when they began with a stand of 233. Mitchell and George Pope were the leading wicket takers and although Alf Pope scored more than 700 Championship runs he took 27 fewer wickets at higher cost than 1936. Carrington and Charlie Elliott were not re-engaged for the 1938 season, financial reasons being a factor.

On paper, Derbyshire looked a better side than in their Championship year but batting collapses caused problems early on and two defeats by Yorkshire proved costly. It was close enough at Chesterfield, the visitors winning by six wickets, but the return at Bramall Lane was a rout. Derbyshire made 145 and then suffered as Yorkshire piled up 525 for four declared, Hutton batting for seven hours in making an undefeated 271. Smith made a great effort when Derbyshire went in again, 380 behind, and hit a six and 15 fours in 158. Townsend (51) helped him add 123 for the third wicket but the rest failed and Yorkshire won by an innings and 99 runs. It left Derbyshire as onlookers as Yorkshire and Middlesex battled it out at the top, the issue being settled in the last week of August in Yorkshire's favour. Derbyshire were usually among the top four and some late victories earned them third place.

If Copson was the key to success in 1936 his absence from a dozen Championship games with a knee injury proved crucial in 1937. He failed to win a place in the England team for the 1936-37 Test series in Australia but headed the tour bowling averages with 27 wickets at 19.81. In 1937 he performed the first hat-trick of his career against Lancashire at Burton-on-Trent. Then a knee injury put him out for a month and when he returned for the Warwickshire match at Derby on Saturday July 17 he had taken only 38 wickets for the county at a cost of 21 runs each.

A fortnight earlier Warwickshire made 523 for seven against Derbyshire with Bob Wyatt (232) and Tom Dollery (128) sharing a fourth wicket partnership of 253. They were in confident mood when they arrived at Derby, with several other good batting displays behind them. In Copson's absence, Alf Pope had opened the attack with Bert Rhodes, who had bowled well in the previous match at Taunton. So when Aubrey Hill and Norman Kilner began the Warwickshire innings Skinner – captaining the side in Buckston's absence – gave the new ball to Copson and Rhodes.

Alf Pope recalled the occasion. "It was about the only time in my career with

Derbyshire that I was not given the new ball. It was a lovely day and a good hard track and I remember we thought in the pavilion before the match started that whoever lost the toss would be in for plenty of leather hunting."

Copson began the attack from the Nottingham Road end with Rhodes operating from the old pavilion end. "This was always the case," said Pope. "Bill would have the benefit of bowling down the hill and I would usually bowl into the wind. When Bert came off after four overs I took over at the pavilion end."

Copson quickly made inroads. With the fifth ball of his first over he had Hill caught in the slips by Smith and in his second over he bowled Fred Santall: two wickets without conceding a run in his first two overs. Three runs, a two and a single, came from his third over and he conceded a single in his fourth over. At this point, Rhodes, who had bowled four overs for 11 runs, was replaced by Pope and the rot quickly set in. Copson had Kilner caught for seven by Skinner. Pope then took two vital wickets when he dismissed John Buckingham and Wyatt. Warwickshire had lost five wickets for 18 and Copson's analysis read 5-2-5-3.

A single came from the last ball of his sixth over and another from the first ball of the seventh but with his fourth ball Copson bowled Ord, his fourth victim at a cost of only seven runs in seven overs. Dollery and Peter Cranmer were now at the crease and Dollery struck a boundary from the third ball of Copson's eighth over. But he was bowled by the fifth, and the sixth delivery clean bowled Mayer. If Copson could take a wicket with the first ball of his ninth over he would perform the second hat-trick of his career.

There was a hush around the ground as Copson ran in to begin his next over, broken by a tremendous shout of glee as the ball shattered William Fantham's stumps. Warwickshire were 28 for nine and still the slaughter continued. With his next ball Copson bowled Eric Hollies, his fourth wicket in four balls. Warwickshire were all out for 28. Copson had taken eight wickets for 11 runs in eight overs and two balls, two of which were maidens. Pope had two for five in four overs and there was much speculation about what might have happened if he had opened the bowling.

Copson had bowled at great speed and obtained devastating lift from what was described as a good wicket although it had some early life. He made the ball swing appreciably either way and batsmen forced to play late defensive strokes seemed utterly powerless to cope with him. Six of his eight victims were clean bowled, testimony to his splendid line and length.

Memories of the day remained awe-inspiring. Cranmer, who ended with two not out, felt it was a particularly shrewd move to view the mayhem from the non-striker's end, while Smith, who stood at slip, said it was "a bit like being under fire. Bill always seemed to be faster off the pitch than through the air but that day the ball seemed to fizz through. At times it kept low, at others he got a lot of lift but there wasn't all that much in the pitch to help him. Warwickshire had a strong batting side but they seemed at a loss and it was just a procession to and from the pavilion."

Pope also found it difficult to explain why the visitors collapsed so dramatically.

"It was just one of those things that happen in cricket. Bill bowled well but they seemed to have a blackout or something. They used to talk about green pitches at Derby but we could bowl sides out just as quickly away from home. Warwickshire got plenty of runs in their second innings so you could not blame the pitch. It was just inspired bowling."

Leslie Townsend and Alan Skinner regarded it as the best bowling performance they ever saw by a Derbyshire player. Skinner recalled that Copson's wickets were taken mostly by fast shooters. "I am sure that at his quickest Bill Copson didn't know whether he was bowling a leg-cutter or an off-cutter so it wasn't surprising that the batsman didn't know either."

Derbyshire passed Warwickshire's score before lunch and went on to make 227, a lead of 199. Copson struck seven boundaries in 30 not out and dealt out more shocks when Warwickshire went in again on Saturday evening. He bowled Kilner with his second ball to take his sequence of wickets to five in six balls, and then dismissed Santall. It was his sixth wicket, all bowled, in 13 deliveries, giving a sequence of four in four, five in six, six in 13, seven in 23 and nine in 50. Hill and Dollery held on to the end, 81 for two, still 118 behind. On Monday, Hill (105) and Dollery, caught off Copson for 98, carried their third wicket stand to 213 but the remaining batsmen could do little against Mitchell (five for 80) and Warwickshire were all out for 291. Copson took three for 82 in 32 overs to return match figures of 40.2-6-93-11. Derbyshire made 93 for five to win during extra time on the second day, Mayer taking all five to bring his match analysis to ten for 122.

Copson had another inspired day when he took eight for 64 against high-flying Sussex at Derby but during 1937 he bowled only 470 Championship overs, taking 72 wickets at 18.65, fair enough but far below 1936. He was back to something like his peak in 1938, 101 wickets for the county at 19.75 and he began the following season with 58 wickets at 11 each, including ten for 92 in the match against the West Indians. He produced more devastation against Oxford University at The Parks: ten for 21 in the match including a hat-trick and four wickets in five balls.

At last, Copson made his Test debut, against the West Indies at Lord's in 1939, taking five for 85 and four for 67 in a comfortable England victory. In Bowes and Copson and with Farnes free from his Worksop College duties later, England appeared to have found a formidable new-ball trio. All three impressed in the Gentlemen v Players match and Bowes and Copson did well in the rain-affected second Test at Old Trafford. Copson now had twelve wickets at 15.41 each in the series – only to find himself left out of the team for the final game at The Oval. His place went to Reg Perks, who produced some outstanding figures in the Championship while Copson's form declined slightly. It seemed a harsh decision. Copson finished 1939 with 146 wickets at 15.36, including George Headley's on three occasions, twice in Tests and once at Derby.

His fitness problems were behind him and it was likely that he would have appeared in the Test matches against South Africa in 1940 and in Australia the following winter. Instead, with the outbreak of war, he found himself back in the coal industry and playing local league cricket and in charity matches.

In 1940, Joe Roper, a Ripley haulier and coal merchant, was determined to bring league and cup success to his local club, Butterley. Roper (his son Cyril married Larwood's daughter June) offered jobs with JH Roper Ltd, transport, to Copson and Leslie Townsend, who became captain. Copson, who had taken the new ball for England at Lord's a year earlier, now found himself operating on club grounds similar to those on which he had started his career. One such match at the Rutland Recreation Ground saw him taking five for 41 for Ripley Co-operative Society against Ilkeston Tradesmen.

Butterley won the Championship, Copson having 78 wickets in 187 overs at 5.19 each, including all ten against Stainsby for 20 in eight overs, eight of them clean bowled. At Codnor Park, with a refreshing breeze at his back and five slips and a backward point, he took seven for 15, all clean bowled. There was one setback, Heanor defeating Butterley by six wickets in a Bayley Cup semi-final on a very slow pitch at the Heanor Town Ground. Butterley were all out for 121 and Heanor's curate, Rev WEG Payton, who played for Derbyshire nine years later, then made 56 not out. He shared a crucial partnership with Jim Sharman, who became deputy head of a Ripley secondary school. Sharman, who scored 33, said: "The pitch did not help Copson and the ball came through too slowly to be really dangerous but he was always a handful." Copson took only one wicket in the game. He also played in a couple of matches for Clay Cross in the Derbyshire League, suffering in both competitions as edges flew to the boundary through a slip cordon unaccustomed to such pace.

Copson played nearly all of his wartime cricket with Saltaire and then Windhill in the Bradford League. A number of Derbyshire professionals – Leslie Townsend, the Popes, Smith and Mitchell – appeared in the competition and from 1940-45 Copson took 313 wickets at 8.70, George Pope 358 at 9.96 and Alf Pope 330 at 10.82.

Copson rejoined the county in 1946. At the age of 39 he shared the new ball for England with his county colleague Cliff Gladwin against South Africa at The Oval in 1947. He was still as fast as anyone in the country for a few overs and took three for 46 in the first innings. In three Test matches during his career his return was 15 wickets at 19.80 each. In 1948, when England's batsmen needed practice against pace to prepare for the Lindwall-Miller onslaught, Copson opened The Rest's attack in a Test trial at Edgbaston. He dismissed Washbrook, Yardley and Compton at a personal cost of 39 in 13 overs. His last county match was in 1950.

Statistics meant little to him. Will Taylor recalled how, near the end of a season, Copson was on the verge of his hundred wickets. "I asked him how many more he needed. He did not know. 'I'm not bothered how many wickets I take as long as the side is doing well' he said. That was Bill Copson. An absolute team man, who always put the interests of the club first." His son Michael confirmed this. "He was never an effusive man and he hated people promoting themselves," he said.

Denis Smith said he would always keep going. "I think this was partly because he had worked down the pits and knew what hard work was. I've seen him bowl with 12 yards of bandage holding him together and, even then, he made the batsman play at every ball. He always seemed to be quicker off the pitch than through the air, bowled a good line, and like Les Jackson, always delivered the ball from the same place. In one match at Buxton, I stood further back to him in the slips than I have ever stood in this country. I never saw Bill collared by a hitter. In his third game, he dropped one short at Frank Woolley, who hit him past point for six. He was always ready to learn from things like that."

There was humour, too. Basil Easterbrook wrote that Copson did not walk, he trudged; possibly a legacy of his back trouble. "On one occasion, watching him come up from third man to bowl, Denis Smith said, 'Bill, tha bloody walks like Groucho Marx'. 'Ay, and sometimes tha bats like him', replied Bill, his features as immobile as Buster Keaton's."

Arthur Richardson said: "He was the perfect example of the cricket professional, in the way he played, the way he dressed and the way he behaved. He was a great team man, always helpful to everyone and a wonderful example to us all."

Frank Peach wrote: "As the players used to come out of the professionals room on the old pavilion at Derby one could often hear him saying 'Come on lads, let's get at 'em.'"

Peter Brookes, a batsman who played for the seconds when Denis Smith was coach, and had a long career in county league cricket, recalls playing against Copson. "He was employed at the Clay Cross Works and I batted against him there," he said. "Of course, he was a long way past his best then but he was very accurate and you could tell what a great bowler he must have been. Before I went in, Denis Smith said 'you won't score any runs off him but if you play straight you'll be all right' and this was what happened."

After he retired Bill Copson played league cricket in Yorkshire for Lidget Green and, with his wife, took over a sweet and general provisions shop in Clay Cross. He was an umpire from 1958-67, finishing because of ill health. But it was never quite the same as playing, and he once said there were too many laws to think about. It was rumoured that he gave his decisions with two fingers, as though still manipulating the seam. Nevertheless, he did not shirk his duties, no-balling the South African Geoff Griffin at the height of the throwing controversy in the tourists' match against Nottinghamshire at Trent Bridge in May 1960 – one of seven umpires to do so that year. An umpiring colleague paid tribute: "Bill was a fine and very understanding umpire. He knew all about the ups and downs of life in county cricket, and the pressures of playing in Test cricket. These attributes, plus his calm manner, sound powers of analysis and sense of fair play made him a very good, and popular umpire."

Fred Trueman tells a tale which reflects how the pragmatism of Copson and the 1930s team continued during his umpiring days. Brian Statham was once bowling with Copson standing at his end and things were not going well. Brian looked ruefully at the ball, which had seen quite a bit of service in that innings, and remarked conversationally to Bill, "This seam's as flat as a fart". The umpire responded, "Well, lift it then. That's what I used to do".

William Richardson said Copson once offered laconic advice after no-balling a seam bowler who ran a mile before delivering the ball at gentle pace. "I could bowl faster than that standing still," Copson said.

The point was that he probably could.

Chapter 35
Loose-all

GRADUALLY the sun began to set on the glory years. Derbyshire dropped to fifth in 1938 but played positive cricket, 19 of 28 Championship games ending with a decision, eleven in the county's favour.

There were many highlights. Lancashire were beaten in May. There was a double over Nottinghamshire, at Ilkeston where Worthington celebrated the birth of a son with a century in each innings, and at Trent Bridge where he made another hundred. Alf Pope scored the only century of his career and Copson took six for 36 in an innings win at Edgbaston, and there was a partnership of 215 for the third wicket between Alderman and Townsend at Eastbourne. Set against these were two defeats by Yorkshire and an innings loss against the Australians – Bradman did not play – at Chesterfield. Worthington made 67 out of 151, the tourists declared at 441 for four, Bill Brown 265 not out, and Derbyshire were humbled for 56 in their second innings. And Warwickshire avenged their 1937 defeat in magnificent fashion at Derby. Needing 311 to win they lost half their side for 39 before Buckingham and Dollery added 220, the visitors winning by four wickets.

Placing cricket in perspective was the Markham colliery disaster near Chesterfield. Nine men had died there in January 1937; a month later seven were killed at South Normanton's Winterbank Colliery. At the Staveley Company's Markham pit on May 10 1938 the toll was 79, with 38 injured. An explosion occurred at 5.45am as the miners prepared to leave the pit after the night shift ended. It left a hundred men trapped underground; had it occurred 30 minutes later it would have involved 250 miners coming on for the day shift. Eric Marsh, a nephew of Stan Worthington and a post-war player who found greater fame as coach at Repton, was then aged 17. He was knocked unconscious but survived to help with the rescue work. A few days afterwards Derbyshire beat Surrey at Queen's Park in a match said to be watched by widows who went because their husbands would have been there. Marsh said a fixture was arranged between Derbyshire and a Derbyshire League XI in aid of the Markham Colliery Disaster Fund, in which he made 52 out of 104. "It prompted Tommy Mitchell to ask how an inexperienced boy had managed to 'read' him. He was not overjoyed to learn that Harry Elliott had told me of every ball that Tommy was going to deliver."

The Championship-winning team was still virtually intact in 1939 but this year, overshadowed by the threat of war, marked the end of the era in which they were among the top six for six consecutive seasons. Ten matches ended in victory but they fell to ninth place, their ranking during the inter-war period, the top six being Yorkshire, Lancashire, Nottinghamshire, Kent, Surrey and Middlesex. The attack remained a force; Copson in superb form, the Popes and Mitchell forming a set of bowlers which six times dismissed Championship opponents for less than a hundred. Harry Elliott kept wicket smartly and George Pope headed the batting averages and was not far away from repeating his double of 1938. But the batting fell away, Smith, Worthington and Alderman, while passing their thousand runs, averaging between 25 and 31 in a wet summer. Leslie Townsend had a poor time, losing his place to his brother Arnold in August, and the slump was typified by the team's dismissal for 20 (Alf Pope top scored with six) at Sheffield in June, when Cliff Gladwin made his debut.

There were times when Derbyshire touched their best. At Derby they beat Kent by five wickets, Smith batting throughout the first innings with 57 out of 112 and Copson and the Popes taking the wickets. After trailing by four runs against Worcestershire at Chesterfield, Derbyshire declared at 421 for nine, Smith 123, Alderman 91, and won by 315 runs, Alf Pope taking six for 47. Surrey were routed by an innings at Guildford; Copson took ten in the match against Essex at Chesterfield which Derbyshire won by ten wickets and there was a six-wicket win over Middlesex at Derby, again thanks mainly to Copson.

In an exciting match at Cheltenham, Gloucestershire were beaten by one run. The home side needed 261 for victory and made a good start. Although they claimed the extra half-hour, 14 were still required with three wickets in hand at the close of the second day's play. On the third morning, Edward Scott hit Mitchell for a boundary but was caught and bowled in his next over. Goddard took two twos off Copson and then fell to a catch by Arnold Townsend at mid-off and when George Lambert joined William Neale four were wanted. Each got a single before Neale skied Mitchell and was caught by Smith.

In the final home game of 1939, Nottinghamshire were beaten at Ilkeston, George Pope making 121. After this match, Harry Elliott – by now the oldest professional on the circuit – stood down to allow Gladwin to play in the final three games, Alderman keeping wicket. There was a fine performance at Taunton, where Arnold Townsend scored his maiden century. Derbyshire needed 260 to win and Smith was out for 27 but a partnership of 188 between Townsend and Alderman changed the whole course of the game. Alderman made 55 and Townsend an unbeaten 142 in a seven-wicket victory.

Then, on Wednesday August 30 1939, Derbyshire began their final match of the season at Leicester: Smith, Arnold Townsend, Alderman (wicketkeeper), Worthington, George Pope, Rhodes, Alf Pope, Gladwin, Buckston (captain), Mitchell and Copson. They made 226, Alderman 91, and dismissed Leicestershire for 174, Copson six for 39. Smith and Alderman shared a second-wicket partnership of 102 in the second innings and at the close of the second day Leicestershire needed

236 to win with nine wickets in hand. But rain prevented play on Friday – the day Hitler invaded Poland – and two days later Britain was at war with Germany.

Major Arthur Richardson served in Gibraltar with the Light AA Regiment. Lieutenant Robin Buckston, invalided out of the same regiment, was listed in 1944 as Captain and Adjutant Home Guard. Captain Gilbert Hodgkinson (Sherwood Foresters) was severely wounded in France, taken prisoner and subsequently repatriated. Others serving in the forces included Captain Stanley Worthington (commissioned in the Royal Electrical and Mechanical Engineers after service with the AA in Gibraltar), Lance Bombardier Bert Rhodes (Light AA Regiment), George Pope (Royal Corps of Signals, discharged through injured knee), Flight Sergeant Harold Pope, Leading Aircraftman Arnold Townsend (Royal Observer Corps), Charlie Elliott and Sam Cadman (National Fire Service), Cliff Gladwin (Home Guard) and Albert Alderman (warden and stretcher bearer as well as Home Guard). Those engaged on munitions, war work or in the collieries were Bill Copson, Tommy Armstrong, Harry Elliott, Tommy Mitchell, Alf Pope, Denis Smith, at a wireworks in Yorkshire, and Leslie Townsend.

Guy Jackson was appointed chairman of the general committee when Rev Henry Ellison left the county. During the war Derbyshire played a few friendly games and the remnants of the 1936 team gathered again a decade later when the County Championship resumed. Hodgkinson was invited to captain the side, with Worthington, a professional, as vice-captain. Alderman, Armstrong, Copson, Charlie Elliott, Harry Elliott, George Pope, Smith and Arnold Townsend, of the Championship-winning team, also appeared in the post-war seasons, some more frequently than others. Langdale played for Somerset, Alan Skinner once for Northamptonshire.

Their best days were behind them but they were still capable of turning a game. Smith headed the batting averages in 1946, Copson took 93 wickets and Worthington captained the team on nine occasions when Hodgkinson was unavailable, Smith also skippering the side once, at The Oval. It was a poor season, 15th place in the table, and some of the battle-hardened pros from the 1930s were not easy to handle. Eddie Gothard succeeded Hodgkinson as captain. Worthington, grammar school education and a wartime commission, felt with some justification that he should have been considered but, although attitudes were softening, amateurs were to remain at the helm until 1963.

In that year, 1947, George Pope and Copson were still deemed good enough to play Test cricket, Pope enjoying a remarkable match at Chesterfield when Somerset were defeated in a single day. Charlie Elliott and Arnold Townsend each made a thousand runs and Pope took 114 wickets. He surpassed this with a double of 1,152 runs and 100 wickets in 1948, which included the highest score of his career, 207 not out at Portsmouth when he shared an unbroken partnership of 241 for the seventh wicket with Rhodes. On August 18 Derbyshire were joint leaders of the Championship with Glamorgan, the eventual winners, but they faded to sixth place.

Now new products from the coalfields were making their mark. Les Jackson and Cliff Gladwin emerged; the finest opening attack in the county's history. Copson, used in short bursts, Gladwin and Jackson formed the pace battery on the hard, dry pitches of 1949 but the batting failed and sometimes the bowlers wilted in the heat.

By 1950 the team had been reshaped but one swansong remained. On June 3, Derbyshire travelled to Bradford for a match against Yorkshire, who were to finish third in the Championship behind the joint holders Lancashire and Surrey. It was a powerful side, studded with players of Test status, with an attack consisting of the youthful Trueman, Coxon, Wardle and Leadbeater. Derbyshire made an indifferent start but Denis Smith, now aged 43, batted splendidly for 122 not out in a total of 289, hitting two sixes and 12 fours. It was to be the last of his 30 centuries for the county and his third against Yorkshire. Jackson dismissed Hutton in the first over and although Lowson batted well they were 60 behind on the first innings. Derbyshire lost four wickets for 40 but Smith (36) and Rhodes added 61 and Yorkshire were set 299 to win in 160 minutes. Despite a century from Hutton they were beaten by 79 runs, Bert Rhodes taking six for 74 with cleverly flighted leg breaks which bit and turned. It was Derbyshire's first victory over Yorkshire since 1905 and it brought immense satisfaction, particularly to Smith, Rhodes and Charlie Elliott who remained from the pre-war team. A month later the trio were in the side at Old Trafford which defeated the joint champions.

One by one, the veterans were awarded a testimonial, Smith receiving £1,919 in 1947, Alderman £1,659 in 1948, Copson £2,500 in 1949, Charlie Elliott £1,667 in 1950 and Bert Rhodes £2,060 in 1952.

By 1953 the only member of the Championship-winning side still playing regularly was Charlie Elliott, who had forged a successful opening partnership with Arnold Hamer. But at the age of 41 time caught up. He was unable to find his touch and at one point of the season averaged only 14 from 20 innings. There were consolations, notably the famous innings victory over Surrey at Derby in two days during the period of the Londoners' run of seven consecutive Championships.

Elliott then batted all day for an unbeaten 132 against Northamptonshire at Chesterfield. A week later his delayed arrival at Queen's Park caused Derbyshire to start with Hamer and John Kelly and they registered a century stand against Kent. Elliott spent the rest of the summer in the middle order, not entirely without success, 48 not out against Middlesex at Derby and 82 at Dudley when he was run out.

On Tuesday August 18 1953, Derbyshire completed a 10 wicket victory over Leicestershire at the County Ground. It was overshadowed by England's deeds at The Oval, when the Ashes were won on the following day for the first time since 1932-33. On Saturday Hamer and Kelly had opened with 183 but rain ended play early. The innings closed at 290 for nine on Monday, wickets falling rapidly in the quest for quick runs. Elliott was run out for six in what proved to be his final innings. On the last day the visitors followed on. They looked like saving the game but in the end Derbyshire needed only four in 14 minutes, Hamer duly making these off a single over.

Elliott missed the last four games and finished the season with 692 runs, average 21.62 and 21 catches. It was time to go. His captain Guy Willatt paid tribute: "We were all sad to see the inability of Elliott to find his true form. No player has given himself more wholeheartedly to the cause of Derbyshire cricket, and although at times exasperatingly slow from a spectator's point of view, it was his determination and concentration which carried the side on so many occasions. From a personal point of view I cannot overestimate his value as a senior pro."

Charlie Elliott was the last member of the 1936 team to take the field in a first-class match. His retirement marked a 34-year span, since Guy Jackson had started his career in 1919.

Chapter 36
Farewells

FOR years, many of them were familiar figures at the County Ground and Queen's Park, unassuming and yet always interesting in modest recollections about their golden days. Reunions were held, some marking special anniversaries of the Championship, reflecting the unity of a team which included seven men who played for England but with a collective total of only 28 caps. Their pleasure was evident when Derbyshire won trophies at Lord's and came close to the title in 1954, 1991 and 1996.

Sam Cadman, coach until the outbreak of the 1939-45 war, died at his Glossop home on May 6 1952 at the age of 75. He had continued playing for Glossop after his county career ended and at the age of 70 scored 17 not out in a 2nd XI match. His son Archie enjoyed a career in league cricket which approached 50 years. A right-arm medium paced bowler, he led Glossop to the Lancashire & Cheshire League Championship in 1956, when they also won the Walkden Cup.

The first of the players to die was Niel Alexander McDonald Walker, who was born at Poona on August 22 1895, and did not play again after his solitary appearance in 1936. His death occurred at Park Hall, Spinkhill, near Sheffield on August 10 1960, aged 64. A middle-order right hand batsman and right-arm medium paced bowler, he had two games for the county, in 1931 against New Zealand and, as captain, against Kent at Gravesend in 1936. His four first-class matches (two for Europeans in India) produced 48 runs, average eight, and two wickets for 77.

Samuel Walter Hunt concentrated on his football career after 1936. He died suddenly at Rochdale on August 2 1963, aged 54. A middle-order right-hand batsman and right-arm leg break bowler, Wally Hunt appeared in five games in 1936. He also played for Northumberland and in Central Lancashire League cricket. After finishing with Derbyshire, he scored 32 goals in 31 matches for Carlisle in 1938-39. His first-class cricket career consisted of those 1936 games, which produced 48 runs, average 9.60 and no wicket for three runs.

Guy Rolfe Jackson, who lived at Higham Cliffe, was the only player to appear in all of the 18 seasons spanning the end of the First World War to the Championship year. Jackson died in Chesterfield Royal Hospital on February 21 1966 at the age of 69. Educated at Harrow, he was a middle-order right hand batsman and captained Derbyshire from 1922-30 and occasionally afterwards, leading the side on 226 occasions. Jackson served on the MCC committee from 1934-38 and was chairman of Derbyshire's committee from 1942-60. With his elder brother Col Humphrey Jackson, he was joint managing director of the Clay Cross Company and its associate firms. A JP, for a year he was High Sheriff of Derbyshire and during the 1939-45 war he held the rank of Lieutenant-Colonel in the Home Guard. His nephew TGH Jackson (son of Humphrey) was captain of Harrow in 1944, winning the cups for batting and fielding. His career lay in the army, where he became a Lieutenant-Colonel in the Royal Green jackets before his death in 1979.

When Jackson died, Will Taylor paid tribute in the 1967 year book: "Just before I commenced this article I was approached by Walter Goodyear, our head groundsman at Derby, who had heard I was writing it. He asked if I would mention how much he and his staff respected Captain Jackson, looked forward to his visits to Derby, and how greatly they appreciated the opportunity of co-operating with him when desired to do so."

After Guy died, 40 per cent of the Clay Cross Company's shares were issued to the public. It was bought by Ready Mixed Concrete in 1974, when the vice-chairman John Jackson retired from the board, ending 120 years of family involvement.

Guy Jackson's first-class career, 1919-36, saw him play in 280 matches, scoring 10,291 runs with 140 the highest of his nine centuries and an average of 23.07.

Harry Storer did not play first-class cricket again after 1936. Storer died in Derby on September 1 1967, aged 69. A sound opening right-hand batsman and right-arm leg-break bowler, he played club cricket in the Birmingham area for Coventry & North Warwicks and the Forty Club after his county career ended. He was a member of a County Championship winning side while managing a senior league football team, Coventry City, which won promotion in the same year. All of his 302 matches, 1920-36, were played for Derbyshire. He scored 13,513 runs, average 27.63, with 18 hundreds and a top score of 232. He took 232 wickets at 32.43 each.

William Henry Copson died suddenly at his home at Clay Cross on September 13 1971, aged 63. A right-arm fast-medium bowler with a short run, Copson was a tail end batsman who hit hard if he could connect. He enjoyed his best season in 1936, 160 wickets at 13.34, and took 1,094 wickets at 18.96 each during his first-class career of 279 matches from 1932-50; in three Tests 15 wickets at 19.80 each. Copson was one of the Five Cricketers of the Year in the 1937 edition of *Wisden*. He appeared for the Players against the Gentlemen at Lord's in 1936 and 1939.

Thomas Stanley Worthington received £720 from his testimonial in 1939 and, although still capable of making runs, he became injury-prone and was not re-engaged for the 1948 season. Worthington played for Todmorden in the Lancashire League in 1948 and was professional for Northumberland in 1949. In the same year he was appointed assistant coach at Old Trafford and when Harry Makepeace died in December 1952, Worthington, with his trademark trilby, cravat, blazer and cigarette, succeeded him as a chief coach who ruled with a rod of iron. He demanded a high degree of physical fitness and a strict regard for the ethics of the game at all levels. He remained in the post until 1963. During that time he worked closely with Harry

Crabtree, who promoted the cricket coaching courses at Lilleshall in Shropshire. He played a leading part in establishing the MCC Coaching Certificates in the north, training the first 12 people to win certificates away from Lord's.

Stan Worthington died in hospital at King's Lynn on August 31 1973, aged 68, after being taken ill while on holiday at Brancaster Staithe. In his first-class career, 1924-47, he appeared in 453 matches, scoring 19,221 runs and 31 centuries, with a highest innings of 238 not out and an average of 29.07. He took 682 wickets at 29.23 each and held 340 catches. He played in nine Test matches, scoring 321 runs, average 29.18, with one century, 128 against India at The Oval. His eight Test wickets cost 39.50 apiece. Worthington was one of the Five Cricketers of the Year in the 1937 edition of *Wisden*.

Harry Elliott became an umpire in 1946 but resigned at the end of the year to be county coach. Elliott kept wicket in four matches in 1947 when Denis Smith was injured, and, aged 55 years 276 days on the final day of the August Bank Holiday game against Warwickshire at Derby, became the oldest player ever to appear for the county. He donned a white coat again in 1952, continuing to stand until the close of the 1960 season and was aged 71 when he officiated in Derbyshire's match against the Pakistan Eaglets in 1963. He was joint owner of a sports business in The Spot in Derby with Sammy Crooks, the former Derby County and England winger, for many years. Harry Elliott died in Derby on February 2 1976, aged 84. His first-class career, 1920-47, consisted of 532 matches in which he made 7,580 runs, average 13.93 with a highest score of 94. His total of 1,206 dismissals consisted of 904 catches and 302 stumpings. He established a county record of 1,183 dismissals (caught 889, stumped 294) which was subsequently passed by Bob Taylor. Elliott played in four Test matches, with eleven dismissals.

William Thomas Taylor died suddenly at his home at Breadsall on August 17 1976, aged 91. He was secretary of the club from 1908 to 1959, honorary life member of MCC and one of Derbyshire's hon. secretaries from 1962-72. His presidency of the Derbyshire County Supporters' Club until 1976 and committee membership resulted in a 67-year period at management level. Of the other club officials in 1936, the president, the Duke of Devonshire died in 1938, the chairman George Buckston in 1942, the hon secretary Rev Henry Ellison in 1948 and the hon treasurer Major Llewellyn Eardley-Simpson in 1958.

Like Will Taylor, Denis Smith enjoyed a near-lifetime's association with the club. He retired after the 1951 season, succeeding Harry Elliott as club coach and making a single appearance during an emergency in 1952. Smith was coach for 20 years, finally ending his 44-year connection with the club in 1971, although he continued scouting until the end of the 1979 season, 52 years after his first-class debut. For many years he lived in a house at Sleetmoor Lane, Somercotes, which he called Orion after the boat on which he had sailed for Australia in 1935-36. His first wife was a granddaughter of William Mycroft, the great 19th century bowler. After being widowed, he married Mrs Marjorie Cresswell, a former member of Derby

Ladies Cricket Club, and moved to live in Derby. It was there that his sudden death occurred on September 12 1979. A few days earlier he had been meeting old friends and enjoying cricket at the Scarborough Festival. Although his health had not been of the best, his death was a shock. In his first-class career, 1927-52, Smith played in 443 matches, scoring 21,843 runs with an average of 31.65. He made 32 centuries, with a top score of 225 and held 379 catches, with five stumpings. He appeared in two Test matches against South Africa in 1935, making 128 runs, highest score 57, average 32. Smith was one of the Five Cricketers of the Year in the 1936 edition of *Wisden*. He appeared for the Players against the Gentlemen at Lord's in 1935.

It was fitting that Sir Wilfred Hill-Wood should have captained the team at Southampton in 1936 because, like Guy Jackson, he made his debut for the county in 1919, the first post-First World War season. Unlike Jackson, he appeared in only eight of the 18 seasons, 35 matches in all for the county, seven as captain. Wilfred William Hill-Wood was born at Chelsea on September 8 1901 and died at his Kensington home after a short illness on October 10 1980. He was aged 79. A memorial service was held in St Margaret's, Westminster in November. In later life WW Hill-Wood became a merchant banker and for many years was financial advisor to the Royal Family. His financial involvements included investment trusts, insurance, sugar manufacturing, British Celanese Ltd, textiles and plastics. In 1976 the Queen created him a Knight Commander of the Royal Victorian Order, a title which can be awarded only by the Monarch. He was also a Commander of the British Empire and during the 1939-45 war was in the intelligence service. Throughout his life he supported Derbyshire cricket – he attended the centenary dinner in 1970 – and was a vice-president of the club for many years. He was also a member of the MCC, serving on a number of committees, and a Free Forester. His final first-class match was for MCC in 1939 and during his career, 1919-39, he scored 2,848 runs, average 27.65, making three hundreds, the highest 122 not out. Hill-Wood took 65 wickets at 34.41.

The increasing calls of business restricted Alan Skinner's appearances, but during his career he captained Derbyshire in 28 matches. Skinner's post as assistant solicitor with Nottinghamshire County Council marked the start of a career in the law and local government which took him to Northamptonshire County Council as deputy clerk and then clerk to West Suffolk County Council. When local government was reorganised in 1974 he became the first chairman of the Anglian Water Authority, a post he held until he retired in 1978. Skinner, who made his home at Woolpit, near Bury St Edmunds, captained Northamptonshire against the New Zealanders in 1949, eleven years after his final appearance for Derbyshire, although he played for the county in 1945 when friendlies were staged. His brother David captained Derbyshire in 1949 so both brothers led a first-class county against the tourists in the same year. He was awarded the OBE during the war and became a deputy lieutenant of Suffolk in 1974. Alan Frank Skinner died at the West Suffolk Hospital, Bury St Edmunds on February 28 1982, aged 68. His first-class career, 1931-49, encompassed

86 matches and he scored 3,537 runs, average 26.20, with one century, 102.

When the news of Arthur Richardson's death was announced in 1983 the flag at Chesterfield was lowered to half mast during the match with Kent. Although the family leather business W and J Richardson – it continued until 1984 – demanded much of his time, he maintained his connection with Derbyshire after he skippered the Championship-winning team. He played for, and sometimes captained the 2nd XI up to the outbreak of war and served on the committee until 1974. With Edgar Wassell, he had a great deal to do with the reconstruction of the ground at Derby in 1955 when the old pavilion was demolished and the grandstand brought into use. The groundsman Walter Goodyear laid a new match square. After the war he acted as secretary to the Friars.

A week or two after Richardson's death, Frank Peach spoke to three members of his Championship side. "Whenever speaking of this shrewd, unobtrusive, genial gentleman he was always referred to as Mr Richardson," he said. Arthur Richardson's son William, a middle order right-hand batsman and left-arm fast-medium bowler, appeared for the county from 1959-65, captaining the team on seven occasions. William's son Alastair carried the family sequence to a third generation when he played his solitary match for the county at Cardiff in September 1992.

Arthur Walker Richardson died at St Mary's Nursing Home, Ednaston, on July 29 1983. He was aged 76. His 159 first-class matches from 1928-36 were all played for Derbyshire, 127 as captain. He scored 3,982 runs, highest score 90, with an average of 19.05.

Albert Alderman was a regular in 1936, despite a top score of only 79. But he exceeded a thousand runs for the third consecutive season and in 1937 posted his highest aggregate, 1,509, and career-best score, 175. He maintained his form during the next two years and continued in 1946 after the war. His final season, 1948, produced two centuries in seven matches. Coaching at Repton followed before George Langdale helped bring about a career change. Langdale was a civilian lecturer at the Royal Military Academy, Sandhurst, when it was decided to combine the role of cricket and football professionals in a single full-time post. Langdale recommended his old Derbyshire colleague and Alderman was interviewed and appointed in 1949. In addition to coaching and umpiring, Alderman managed the academy sports and fancy goods shop, helped by his wife Isobel. He played one match for Berkshire in 1950 and in 1966 became a first-class umpire, serving for three years before joining the Minor Counties list in 1969 as a reserve. Alderman spent his later years at Camberley in Surrey.

Albert Edward Alderman died at Frimley Park Hospital, Surrey, after being taken ill at his home, on June 6 1990 at the age of 82, leaving his wife, two sons and a daughter. His first-class cricket, 318 matches, was spent with Derbyshire. He scored 12,376 runs, average 25.14, with 12 centuries. Of his 202 catches, 16 were taken at the wicket and he made two stumpings.

Another of the amateurs who captained Derbyshire in 1936, John Gilbert, died in

1992. Of his eleven first-class matches for the county, 1930-36, three were as captain. In later years he became landlord at the Baginton Oak public house in Coventry and lived in Nottingham for many years until his death. John Dudley Harwood Gilbert died at Wollaton on June 24 1992 at the age of 81. He scored 106 runs in first-class cricket, with a top score of 25 and an average of 9.63.

Two of Derbyshire's greatest-ever all-rounders, Leslie Townsend and George Pope, died in 1993.

Leslie Townsend and his wife fell in love with New Zealand as a result of his two winters with the Auckland Club and he vowed that when his career ended he would emigrate. After his season with Butterley – his son Paul Richard was born at Ripley in 1944 – he played in the Bradford League and following the war spent three seasons with Northumberland in the Minor Counties, making 192 against Durham in 1946. He moved to New Zealand in 1949, a decision which was never regretted. He was engaged by the Canterbury Cricket Association, playing in Saturday club games but declined an invitation to appear in the Plunket Shield matches. In 1954-55 he became professional with the Nelson Cricket Association and also coached at Nelson College. Townsend and his wife made one visit home, in 1969 when the New Zealand team toured this country.

Leslie Fletcher Townsend died suddenly, although after a long illness, at a rest home in Stoke, near Nelson in New Zealand, on February 17. He was aged 89. In his first-class career he appeared in 493 matches from 1922-39, scoring 19,555 runs, highest score 233, with 22 hundreds and an average of 27.50. He took 1,088 wickets at 21.12 each and held 237 catches. Townsend played in four Tests, scoring 97 runs, average 16.16 and taking six wickets at 34.16. He was one of the Five Cricketers of the Year in the 1934 edition of *Wisden*. Townsend appeared for the Players against the Gentlemen at Lord's in 1929 and 1933.

George Pope returned fully fit for the 1937 season, scoring 1,318 runs, including his maiden century, and taking 92 wickets for the county. In 1938 he completed the double in all first-class matches and with 1,464 runs and 83 wickets was not far away in 1939. Pope did not play for Derbyshire in 1946 because he had league commitments with Colne. Fine all-round summers in 1947 and 1948 earned him his solitary Test cap. There was a remarkable performance at Chesterfield in 1947 when Somerset were beaten in a day, Pope taking six for 34 and seven for 16, thirteen for 50 in the match. No Derbyshire all-rounder was more combative, aggressive and intolerant in the field; he sometimes also took issue with the committee and his later captains off it. During the winter of 1948-49 his wife contracted rheumatic fever and was advised to live in Jersey. He sought his release from Derbyshire but the Popes stayed in the Channel Islands for only a short time before returning to Chesterfield. League cricket meant he would be absent from home for only short periods, hence a spell in Ireland and seasons with Heywood in the Central Lancashire League and player-coach with Sheffield United CC at Bramall Lane. He was a first-class umpire from 1966-74 and again in 1976 and an entertaining after-dinner speaker.

George Henry Pope died at his Chesterfield home on October 29 after being ill for some time. He was 82. In his first-class career, 1933-50, he appeared in 205 matches, scoring 7,518 runs, average 28.05. He made eight centuries, with 207 not out his top score. Pope took 677 wickets at 19.92 each and held 157 catches. He appeared in one Test match, scoring eight not out and taking one wicket for 85. He appeared for the Players against the Gentlemen at Lord's in 1939.

Arnold Townsend died a year after the death of his elder brother, Leslie. He was the last county cricketer to be capped before the war, in 1939, and served for six years in the RAF, spending some time in South Africa. Here he made his only first-class appearance outside of Derbyshire games, for South African Air Force XI against the Rest of South Africa at Johannesburg in 1942-43. Townsend was a key member of the team in 1946, when he made 1,188 runs, average 27.62, but was struck on the head when fielding close to the wicket in the final match of the season at Frome. The injury was serious and he spent a number of days in hospital. It was felt this affected his confidence, although there was little evidence of this in 1947, 1,348 runs, average 30.63. In 1948 he carried his bat for 102 out of 228 at Old Trafford but his form fell away the following year. After retiring, he coached young cricketers and was a regular at Derbyshire matches up to the time of his death. Arnold Frederick Townsend died in hospital in Derby on February 25 1994. He was aged 81. In 117 matches during his first-class career, 1934-50, he scored 4,327 runs, average 23.13, with five hundreds, the highest 142 not out.

Time was taking its toll and 1996 marked the deaths of Tommy Mitchell and Alf Pope.

Mitchell was the oldest surviving English Test cricketer and the last of the 1932-33 bodyline tourists. As such he was in demand for interviews from leading cricket writers. Mitchell was due to have a benefit in 1940. He played in the Bradford League during the war and for Derbyshire in the 1945 friendlies. When county cricket resumed in 1946 he was 44 and felt he was still good enough. He claimed that Derbyshire did not agree, saying they considered that he was too old, drank too much, and, at best, had only a season or so left in him. Mitchell declined the terms offered by the club, returning to the mines and spending several seasons playing in the Yorkshire Council with Hickleton Main, a South Yorkshire mining village. His son Thomas Lord Mitchell, thus named in homage to his father playing at the home of cricket, appeared in the leagues and for Derbyshire 2nd as a leg break bowler.

Thomas Bignall Mitchell died at the Sue Ryder Home for the elderly, Hickleton Hall, Doncaster on January 27 1996 after a long illness. He was aged 93.

Mitchell's first-class career from 1928 to 1939 saw him take 1,483 wickets in 328 matches at a cost of 20.59 each. He took a hundred in a season 10 times and appeared in five Tests, eight wickets at 62.25. He made one first-class fifty, averaging 7.97 with the bat and holding 132 catches. Mitchell appeared for the Players against the Gentlemen at Lord's in 1931 and 1934.

When the war started Alf Pope was directed by the Minister of Labour to return to the mines, his cricket being played in the Bradford League. After the conflict was over he had four seasons in the Birmingham League with Mitchells and Butlers as their professional before taking an engagement at Trinity College in Ontario, Canada. He returned in 1952 as professional to Forfarshire and in 1957 spent the winter coaching at Falcon College in Bulawayo. Pope then settled as coach and head groundsman at Berkhamstead School for 20 years. He worked part-time at Trent College for six years, playing until he was 69. For 30 years he also repaired bats and pads and re-faced wicketkeeping gloves. Scoring, umpiring or simply just watching, his love of cricket remained undiminished and he was a sparkling conversationalist, with an accurate memory of times past. His son Tony and grandson Tim played regularly in the Nottinghamshire and Derbyshire Border League/Derbyshire County League.

Alfred Vardy Pope died in the Derbyshire Royal Infirmary on May 11 1996, aged 86. His first-class career covered only ten seasons, 1930-39, in which he took 555 wickets at 22.54 – 99 in 1936 at 18.13 – and scored 4,963 runs, average 18.52, his top score, 103, being his only hundred.

Elijah Carrington went back to the mines. He did not maintain the promise he showed in 1935 and after averaging only 12 in six matches in 1937 was not retained. Carrington continued playing locally, with spells as a pro in Ayr and Bath, and he appeared again for the county in wartime friendlies against Nottinghamshire. Latterly, with his wife, he ran a fish and chip shop in Hilcote. Elijah Carrington died at his home at Hilcote on November 19 1998. He was aged 84. Carrington played 50 first-class matches from 1934-37, scoring 1,470 runs, average 20.13. The highest of his eight half-centuries was an innings of 80.

Tommy Armstrong recovered from his mauling at Wells to take seven for 36 against Gloucestershire at Buxton in 1937 and he headed the bowling averages in 1946 with 28 wickets at 17.60 from five games. He made solitary appearances in 1949 and 1950. In a two-day match at Coventry in 1945 he took seven for 52 against the Royal Australian Air Force when his colleagues in the Coventry and District XI included Charlie Elliott and Harry Storer. Thomas Riley Armstrong died in a nursing home at Markfield, Leicestershire on February 6 2000, aged 90. His 58 matches spanned 1929-50 and he took 133 wickets at 24.35, including five in an innings on seven occasions.

George Langdale had one more game for the county after the Championship year, in 1937, although he appeared in a 1945 friendly. He played for Norfolk in 1939 and following service in the army, when he was commissioned, he joined Somerset in 1946, scoring 146 against Yorkshire at Taunton. His career in education restricted him to 20 appearances for Somerset until 1949, although he produced some fine all-round performances during 12 seasons with Berkshire. In 1953 he took all ten Dorset wickets for 25 at Reading. Langdale spent ten years at the Royal Military Academy, Sandhurst. From 1956 until he retired in 1981 he was at Welbeck College and he played for Worksop in the Bassetlaw League. He was president of the league in 1985 and wrote *A History of the Bassetlaw and District Cricket League 1904-1978.*

George Richmond Langdale OBE died in the Bassetlaw General Hospital, Worksop, on April 24 2002, aged 86. He played four matches for Derbyshire, three in 1936 and one in 1937. His first-class career, 1936-53, consisted of 25 matches, 709 runs, average 18.17, with one century and 23 wickets at 40.82.

The last survivor, Charlie Elliott, was a youngster fighting to establish a place in the middle order in the Championship team but a man who achieved more in the wider context of the game than any of his colleagues. He played for Stourbridge in the Birmingham League during the war and returned to the county in 1946, although Warwickshire had shown an interest. He exceeded one thousand runs in six consecutive seasons from 1947-52 as a reliable, if somewhat dour opener who also became senior pro. In 1947 at Trent Bridge he made his highest score, 215, sharing a second wicket partnership of 349 with John Eggar, who was master-in-charge of cricket at Repton .

Elliott's greatest achievements came after his retirement. He joined the umpires' list in 1956 when Frank Chester retired, officiating in 42 Test matches between 1957-74, the first the famous game against the West Indies at Edgbaston when Peter May and Colin Cowdrey added 411 for the fourth wicket in England's second innings. The batsmen countered Sonny Ramadhin's bowling by using their pads and Ramadhin felt he should have had both of them lbw on numerous occasions. One Test was in New Zealand and he also stood in two England – Rest of the World XI games in 1970.

Another notable game was against Australia at The Oval in 1968 when Derek Underwood's bowling squared the rubber for England after volunteers from the crowd, armed with brooms and blankets helped the groundsman mop up after a thunderstorm flooded the ground. With only a few minutes left, one wicket remaining and ten men around the bat, John Inverarity, who had defied England for four hours, offered no stroke to a straight ball and was out leg before. It fell to Elliott to give the decision. "Charlie Elliott was a brave umpire," said Underwood. "If it was out, he would give it." This was the match in which Basil D'Oliveira, a late choice, made 158, only to be omitted from the team for South Africa. His subsequent selection, when Tom Cartwright withdrew with a shoulder injury, led to the cancellation of the tour. When D'Oliveira came out to bat at The Oval, everybody was aware of the significance. He was unbeaten on 23 overnight but on Friday morning played a couple of poor strokes. Quietly, from the non-striker's end, Elliott advised him to "get your head down". When he reached fifty, Elliott said: "Well played – my God you're going to cause some problems." And then, when D'Oliveira completed his century: "Oh Christ, you've set the cat among the pigeons now."

At the time of Elliott's retirement, when he was 62, only Frank Chester (48) had umpired more Tests. His last Test was at Lord's when Pakistan objected to play taking place in conditions they regarded as too wet. Water had leaked under the covers and

Underwood took 13 wickets. As senior umpire Elliott over-ruled complaints. He also told Brian Close, then the England captain, to "get on with it" in the controversial Yorkshire v Warwickshire match at Edgbaston, when Close adopted alleged delaying tactics. Close subsequently lost the England captaincy.

During the throwing controversy of the 1960s, he scrutinised the action of Harold Rhodes, the son of his former colleague Bert Rhodes, who had been called by Paul Gibb in 1960. In the early part of the 1961 season a throwing truce was in force for matches against the Australians and Rhodes played against the tourists for MCC at Lord's. He was reported by Elliott for having a doubtful action. Four years later, in June 1965, Rhodes was no-balled twice by Syd Buller. Then at Portsmouth, Elliott studied his action from square-leg and point before telling Derek Morgan, Derbyshire's captain, that he was not satisfied and would have to no-ball Rhodes if he continued. Rhodes, who had a hyper-extension of the arm, was eventually cleared and his basic action declared fair. But it took eight years and the blighting of a Test career. In 1966, Elliott warned the West Indian fast bowler Charlie Griffith after a venomous bouncer was just avoided by Tom Graveney. Elliott said: "You can bowl Charlie, but any more like that and I will have to call you."

Elliott, who always kept a big cigar in his top pocket, earned a reputation for making difficult decisions in a calm and efficient manner. "It's all to do with your temperament and the ability to make those decisions quickly," he said. He umpired in six Gillette Cup finals at Lord's, the last being in 1974, his final season on the list. In his later years as an official, Elliott, who stood in 458 first-class matches, was awarded a Churchill Travelling Fellowship that enabled him to study conditions and meet umpires around the world. It was this which took him to New Zealand in 1970-71. Bob Taylor said: "He was one of the old school of umpires and all the players had a lot of respect for him."

He was a Test selector from 1975-81, bringing years of experience as a player and an umpire to the panel. The period ended with a thrilling series against the Australians in which England, with Ian Botham outstanding, regained the Ashes.

Charlie Elliott received the MBE for services to cricket and was made an Honorary Member of MCC – a remarkable journey from the pit top at Glapwell Colliery. Elliott also gave something back to Derbyshire cricket. For many years he was a member of the committee and was chairman of the cricket committee at the time of Kim Barnett's appointment as captain in 1983. He was president of the club in 1993-94. In his 90th year he was still running a guest house in Nottingham which was festooned with cricketing memorabilia.

Charles Standish Elliott died at Nottingham on New Year's Day 2004. He was aged 91. In his first-class career, 1932-53, he appeared in 275 matches and scored 11,965 runs, average 27.25 with nine hundreds. He took eleven wickets at 47.81 and held 210 catches, stumping one batsman when keeping wicket in 1947.

As for the mines, the slump of the 1930s was consigned to history and the pits and their employees entered a time of prosperity, with high wages for coal face workers. When the industry was nationalised in 1947, there were still more than half-a-million miners in the country. High employment gave labour increased power in extracting concessions from employers. The Conservative government tried to rein in the power of the unions in 1970 only to meet massive TUC opposition. Widespread power cuts and a three-day working week led to Ted Heath's 'Who Governs Britain?' election on union power. He was defeated. But in 1979 a Conservative government which was committed to reforming trade union law was elected. Oil and North Sea gas reduced the demand for coal. Another strike brought a confrontation between Arthur Scargill, president of the National Union of Mineworkers, and Margaret Thatcher's Conservative government. The catalyst was the closure of Cortonwood colliery in South Yorkshire on March 1 1984. Now there were laws against secondary picketing and police to enforce them. Crucially, compared to the 1970s, coal stocks were high and also Nottinghamshire miners continued to work. A High Court ruled the strike was illegal and it fizzled out in March 1985. It marked the start of a seemingly terminal decline.

By the 21st century only nine deep pits remained in operation, three of them in Nottinghamshire. They had gone from Derbyshire, the last at Markham closing in 1994. One or two rows of former miners' cottages and a few conserved headstocks, winding wheels and miners' lamps remain. From time to time, UK Coal arouses the ire of local protest groups with applications to opencast areas which still have coal to be mined. Some of the colliery sites became industrial estates. Homes such as the Stonebroom Blocks were demolished.

The clearing up continues. East Midlands Development Agency has launched a £140.5 million reclamation project at the former Avenue Coking Works at Wingerworth, near Chesterfield, which has stood idle since it closed in 1992 with the loss of 500 jobs.

The 242-acre site is one of the most contaminated in Western Europe; the legacy of decades of mining activity and lime, iron and coke production. The operation includes proposals for woodland and footpaths and potential residential and commercial development. The work, due to be completed in 2012, is funded through the English Partnerships National Coalfield Programme.

The coalfields left their scars but the industrial belt, some 30 miles long and 10 miles wide in the east of the county, with its mining, ironworks and engineering, was the forcing ground which produced Derbyshire's greatest-ever side. The skipper's family tanning business had grown out of farming in Horsley Woodhouse, within the coal belt. Tommy Armstrong, Elijah Carrington, Bill Copson, Harry Elliott, Charlie Elliott, Tommy Mitchell, Alf Pope, and Stan Worthington worked either in the mines or in mining related jobs. Guy Jackson's family were colliery owners and Harry Storer and Denis Smith worked for ironworking companies. Albert Alderman was employed in the Rolls-Royce offices. The Townsends' family associations were with the lace industry. Success on the cricket field brought them into contact with dukes and knights of the realm; they played in the Test match arenas, visited towns and cities and seaside grounds and travelled to parts of the British Empire which a few years earlier they had known only as red adornments to their village school atlases. Cricket enabled them to cross social divides and, to a man, brought them a better way of life away from the coal face, although some returned to the mines afterwards.

Derbyshire's success in 1936 has to be measured against the dominance of the Big Six, which endured for more than 70 years, although in the closing stages it was sustained only by Surrey and Yorkshire. For most of this period, Yorkshire, Kent and Nottinghamshire subscribed to a home-grown policy; Lancashire, Middlesex and Surrey happily using players born outside the county boundaries. The grip of the Big Six was loosened by Warwickshire in 1911 and 1951, when players came from within the county and others from further afield. Welsh fervour justifiably greeted Glamorgan's success in 1948 but recruits from Middlesex stiffened the side. When Hampshire won the title in 1961, Barbados and Antigua featured among the birthplaces alongside a sprinkling of Southamptons. Yorkshire won five of the next seven Championships, Worcestershire's 1964-65 teams again breaching the county border, before other clubs began to enjoy shares of the spoils. No county outside the Big Six which won the title – and only three within it – was as fully representative as Derbyshire; decidedly so when the greater resources available to some of the others are considered. Football has few similar parallels; perhaps Celtic, European Cup winners in 1967 with a team born within 30 miles of Glasgow, the nearest.

The key members of the Derbyshire and Nottinghamshire Championship-winning teams between the wars were coalfield products. Appropriately – and perhaps inevitably – the last words should be left to Tommy Mitchell. "Whenever the team was in trouble and one or two of us didn't do very well there was always somebody who either made runs or took wickets."

Mitchell, who once said: "I was as good a workman down the pit as I was on the cricket field," adding: "It was just a case of pulling together – and everybody did."

It is a fitting epitaph for that remarkable team.

Final table – 1936

1st Inns Points

	P	W	L	W	L	No Rslt	Poss		Obt	%
Derbyshire	28	13	4	5	5	1	420		239	56.90
Middlesex	26	10	4	8	3	1	390		203	52.05
Yorkshire	30	10	2	12	4	2	450		230	51.11
Gloucestershire	30	10	7	4*	8	1	450		203	45.11
Nottinghamshire	28	8	3	9	8	0	420		189	45.00
Surrey	30	9	7	6	6	2	450		191	42.44
Somerset	26	9	10	2	3	2	390		162	41.53
Kent	28	9	9	4	5	1	420		174	41.42
Essex	26	8	8	5	5	0	390		160	41.02
Hampshire	30	7	5	9	9	0	450		177	39.33
Lancashire	30	7	6	7	5	5	450		175	38.88
Worcestershire	28	7	9	4	7	1	420		150	35.71
Warwickshire	24	4	8	2	7	3	360		103	28.61
Sussex	30	4	10	7	6	3	450		125	27.77
Leicestershire	24	2	5	8	8	1	360		98	27.22
Glamorgan	26	1	12	6	5	2	390		68	17.43
Northamptonshire	24	0	9	5*	9	1	360		61	16.94

Includes ten points for a win on the first innings in a match played under the Laws for one-day games.

County Championship averages

Batting

	Matches	Ins	Not Out	Runs	Highest Ins	100s	Average
Worthington	26	40	3	1322	163	3	35.72
Townsend LF	28	43	4	1322	182*	4	33.89
Smith	28	46	5	1256	169	2	30.63
Alderman	28	46	4	1074	79	0	25.57
Skinner	12	20	0	441	62	0	22.05
Elliott H	28	41	9	639	79*	0	19.96
Elliott CS	18	26	3	426	97	0	18.52
Storer	9	13	0	205	62	0	15.76
Carrington	7	11	0	157	72	0	14.27
Pope AV	28	38	6	441	40	0	13.78
GR Langdale	3	5	0	64	29	0	12.80
AW Richardson	26	34	4	378	50	0	12.60
Mitchell	26	32	7	267	45	0	10.68
Hunt	5	5	0	48	17	0	9.60
Pope GH	4	6	0	50	14	0	8.33
Armstrong	2	3	1	16	8*	0	8.00
Townsend AF	2	3	0	23	21	0	7.66
Copson	26	29	13	89	17	0	5.56

Also batted: W W Hill-Wood, 10 and 38; Captain N A MacD Walker, 13 and 7.

Bowling

	O	M	R	W	Average
Copson	788.3	203	1792	140	12.80
Pope AV	815.1	256	1666	94	17.72
Townsend LF	518.3	158	1062	54	19.66
Mitchell	639.2	68	2373	116	20.45
Armstrong	33	9	95	4	23.75
Pope GH	56.1	11	128	5	25.60
Worthington	222.5	45	584	19	30.73

Also bowled: Langdale 26-3-95-0; Elliott CS 2-0-9-0; Hunt 1-0-3-0; Skinner 3-0-15-0; Smith 3-1-13-1; Townsend AF 6-1-23-0; MacD Walker 2-0-10-0.

Catches: Elliott (H), 50, Smith 21, Worthington 18, Mitchell 14, Townsend (LF) 14, Skinner 12, Copson 11, Alderman 10, Elliott (CS) 8, Pope (AV) 7, Richardson 7, Storer 7, Hill-Wood 2, Pope (GH) 2, Carrington 1.

Stumpings – Elliott 12.

1936 Match-by-Match

Hampshire v Derbyshire

Played at County Ground, Southampton, on May 6, 7, 8
Toss won by Hampshire
Match drawn

Hampshire

*Mr R H Moore	c Smith b Townsend	11	lbw b A V Pope	100
†N T McCorkell	c Hill-Wood b Townsend	41	b A V Pope	1
Mr C G A Paris	st H Elliott b Mitchell	1	b Worthington	101
C P Mead	c G H Pope b Mitchell	62		
J Arnold	c Worthington b Townsend	8	(4) b Copson	65
W L C Creese	b G H Pope	36	(5) c Hill-Wood b Copson	25
G S Boyes	b Mitchell	25	(8) b A V Pope	13
A E Pothecary	c Townsend b Mitchell	7	(6) not out	20
G Hill	run out	10		
H M Lawson	not out	36	(7) c G H Pope b A V Pope	0
O W Herman	b G H Pope	5		
Extras	(B 6, LB 6, W 1, NB 1)	14	(B 1, LB 8)	9
Total		256	(7 wickets, dec)	334

Fall: 1st inns 1/21, 2/30, 3/82, 4/92, 5/167, 6/167, 7/179, 8/206, 9/241,10/256

2nd inns 1/8, 2/191, 3/221, 4/293, 5/304, 6/307, 7/334

Derbyshire

A E Alderman	b Lawson	25	c Herman b Hill	23
D Smith	c Pothecary b Lawson	8	c McCorkell b Creese	34
L F Townsend	b Herman	5	(4) b Herman	67
T S Worthington	b Herman	9	(3) b Herman	44
E Carrington	c Pothecary b Herman	72	b Creese	1
G H Pope	b Creese	12	c Paris b Creese	4
A V Pope	c Paris b Boyes	10	c McCorkell b Boyes	1
*Mr W W H Hill-Wood	c Moore b Boyes	10	c McCorkell b Herman	38
†H Elliott	not out	35	not out	1
T B Mitchell	c Lawson b Herman	8	not out	27
W H Copson	b Lawson	3		
Extras	(LB 5, NB 2)	7	(B 4, LB 8, W 1, NB 2)	15
Total		204	(8 wickets)	255

Fall: 1st inns 1/20, 2/33, 3/49, 4/49, 5/82, 6/113, 7/136, 8/179, 9/195,10/204

2nd inns 1/64, 2/64, 3/148, 4/155, 5/173, 6/174, 7/220, 8/235

Derbyshire

	o	m	r	w	o	m	r	w
Copson	17	6	26	0	22	6	74	2
A V Pope	16	3	45	0	29.5	3	122	4
Mitchell	28	5	93	4	9	0	52	0
Townsend	33	15	43	3	2	0	14	0
G H Pope	18.1	4	35	2	8	1	26	0
Worthington					11	1	37	1

Hampshire

	o	m	r	w	o	m	r	w
Lawson	19.4	4	41	3	19	8	31	0
Herman	16	1	57	4	29	7	88	3
Creese	12	3	24	1	28	10	40	3
Boyes	15	2	65	2	18	8	27	1
Hill	4	1	10	0	13	5	28	1
Arnold					4	0	26	0

Umpires: L C Braund and F Chester

Close of play scores: First day: Derbyshire (1) 40/2 (A E Alderman 21, T S Worthington 4)
Second day: Hampshire (2)235/3 (J Arnold 26, W L C Creese 2)

Oxford University v Derbyshire

Played at The Parks, Oxford, on May 9, 10, 11
Toss won by Derbyshire
Derbyshire won by an innings and 130 runs

Derbyshire

D Smith	c Kimpton b Darwall-Smith	77
A E Alderman	b Darwall-Smith	9
T S Worthington	c Scott b Ballance	174
L F Townsend	c Grieve b Murray-Wood	48
E Carrington	b Ballance	34
G H Pope	not out	62
*Mr J D H Gilbert	b Dyson	16
A V Pope	c Mitchell-Innes b Darwall-Smith	14
†H Elliott	b Mitchell-Innes	5
T B Mitchell	c sub b Darwall-Smith	4
W H Copson	b Darwall-Smith	0
Extras	(B 10. LB 3)	13
Total		456

Fall: 1st inns 1/31, 2/170, 3/306, 4/329, 5/370, 6/404, 7/429, 8/447, 9/456,10/456

Oxford University

Mr M R Barton	b Copson	0	(5) b Copson	70
Mr M M Walford	b G H Pope	8	(4) c Elliott b Copson	4
Mr C F Grieve	c Smith b G H Pope	6	(6) c and b Mitchell	2
*Mr N S Mitchell-Innes	not out	67	(1) lbw b G H Pope	9
†Mr R C M Kimpton	lbw b Mitchell	12	(3) run out	15
Mr B H Belle	lbw b Mitchell	0	(7) b G H Pope	2
Mr W Murray-Wood	b Copson	0	(8) st Elliott b Townsend	42
Mr R F H Darwall-Smith	b Copson	0	(9) b Mitchell	23
Mr J B Scott	b Copson	3	(11) c Elliott b A V Pope	0
Mr T G L Ballance	b A V Pope	16	not out	1
Mr J H Dyson c Alderman	b Townsend	35	(2) c Elliott b A V Pope	1
Extras	(B 2, LB 4)	6	(LB 2, NB 2)	4
Total		153		173

Fall: 1st inns 1/4, 2/15, 3/20, 4/37, 5/39, 6/42, 7/42, 8/54, 9/82, 10/153
2nd inns 1/6, 2/16, 3/25, 4/31, 5/43, 6/47, 7/142, 8/168, 9/172,10/173

Oxford University

	o	m	r	w
Darwall-Smith	24.5	0	134	5
Scott	16	1	57	0
Mitchell-Innes	14	1	81	1
Murray-Wood	12	1	90	1
Ballance	12	2	37	2
Dyson	7	3	20	1
Grieve	5	0	24	0

Derbyshire

	o	m	r	w	o	m	r	w
Copson	12	5	14	4	14	3	27	2
A V Pope	12	6	13	1	12.5	2	29	2
G H Pope	12	4	17	2	8	1	16	2
Mitchell	23	1	91	2	13	0	57	2
Townsend	2.3	0	9	1	5	0	28	1
Worthington	2	0	3	0	5	1	12	0

Umpires: J H King and D Hendren

Close of play scores: First day: Derbyshire (1) 456 all out

Kent v Derbyshire

Played at Bat and Ball Ground, Gravesend, on May 13 and 14
Toss won by Derbyshire
Kent won by ten wickets

Derbyshire

A E-Alderman	b Freeman	47	lbw b Wright	20
D Smith	st Levett b Freeman	17	c Ashdown b Watt	12
T S Worthington	c Levett b Wright	7	c Todd b Watt	0
L F Townsend	st Levett b Freeman	9	b Watt	4
E Carrington	b Freeman	1	c Valentine b Wright	25
C S Elliott	st Levett b Wright	3	b Freeman	0
A V Pope	c Wright b Freeman	10	b Freeman	18
*Capt N A MacD Walker	c Lewis b Freeman	13	c and b Wright	7
†H Elliott	not out	4	not out	5
T B Mitchell	c Lewis b Freeman	2	b Wright	1
W H Copson	c Fagg b Wright	1	b Wright	0
Extras	(B 5)	5	(B 7)	7
Total		119		99

Fall: 1st inns 1/42, 2/53, 3/68, 4/72, 5/89, 6/99, 7/103, 8/112, 9/115, 10/119
2nd inns 1/19, 2/19, 3/27, 4/62, 5/63, 6/81, 7/87, 8/93, 9/99, 10/99

Kent

W H Ashdown	c H Elliott b Pope	2	not out	17
A E Fagg	b Copson	14	not out	25
F E Woolley	c Copson b Mitchell	34		
*Mr B H Valentine	lbw b Mitchell	28		
L J Todd	c H Elliott b Copson	55		
Mr I S Akers-Douglas	c Smith b Mitchell	12		
D V P Wright	b Copson	21		
†Mr W H V Levett	c Worthington b Copson	2		
A E Watt	c Alderman b Worthington	8		
A P Freeman	b Copson	0		
C Lewis	not out	1		
Extras	(LB 2)	2		
Total		179	(no wickets)	42

Fall: 1st inns 1/9, 2/33, 3/73, 4/86, 5/122, 6/157, 7/170, 8/171, 9/171, 10/179

Kent

	o	m	r	w	o	m	r	w
Todd	6	1	16	0	9	1	16	0
Watt	7	0	20	0	9	3	22	3
Freeman	16	7	29	7	11	2	23	2
Wright	14.1	1	49	3	7	1	31	5

Derbyshire

	o	m	r	w	o	m	r	w
Copson	16	2	57	5	5	1	26	0
Pope	9	1	36	1	4	0	11	0
Mitchell	11	1	52	3	1	0	5	0
Townsend	7	0	14	0				
Walker	2	0	10	0				
Worthington	2	1	8	1				

Umpires: J A Newman and D Hendren
Close of play scores: First day: Derbyshire (2) 10/0 (A E Alderman 0, D Smith 6)

Derbyshire v Surrey

Played at Derby, on May 16, 17, 18
Toss won by Derbyshire
Derbyshire won by 16 runs

Derbyshire

D Smith	c Brown b Gover	0	c Watts b Parker	15
A E Alderman	b Gover	77	c Brooks b Brown	43
T S Worthington	lbw b Watts	1	c Cover b Parker	11
L F Townsend	c Parker b Brown	38	c Brooks b Parker	3
E Carrington	c Parker b Gover	12	b Brown	10
G H Pope	c Fishlock b Brown	14	c and b Brown	9
*Mr A W Richardson	c Barling b Brown	0	c Barling b Brown	4
A V Pope	c Fishlock b Brown	9	lbw b Gover	1
†H Elliott	b Gover	6	b Watts	24
T B Mitchell	b Gover	3	st Brooks b Brown	3
W H Copson	not out	5	not out	0
Extras	(B 3, LB 5, NB 2)	10	(B 9, LB 2, NB 2)	13
Total		175		136

Fall: 1st inns 1/1, 2/4, 3/109, 4/126, 5/146, 6/146, 7/150, 8/166, 9/166, 10/175
2nd inns 1/37, 2/59, 3/67, 4/87, 5/97, 6/102, 7/103, 8/122, 9/136, 10/136

Surrey

A Sandham	b Copson	53	b Copson	5
R J Gregory	lbw b Mitchell	22	lbw b A V Pope	0
H S Squires	lbw b Mitchell	0	st Elliott b Mitchell	20
H T Barling	b Copson	95	b Copson	23
L B Fishlock	c and b Mitchell	0	not out	17
E W Whitfield	b Copson	1	lbw b Copson	0
E A Watts	b Mitchell	3	b Copson	8
*Mr F R Brown	b Copson	0	b Copson	2
J F Parker	not out	18	b Copson	0
†E W J Brooks	lbw b Copson	0	c Smith b A V Pope	0
A R Gover	c Worthington b A V Pope	9	c Elliott b Copson	0
Extras	(B 9, LB 7, NB 1)	17	(LB 1, W 1)	2
Total		218		77

Fall: 1st inns 1/46, 2/46, 3/102, 4/103, 5/104, 6/115, 7/116, 8/207, 9/209, 10/218
2nd inns 1/2, 2/10, 3/49, 4/53, 5/53, 6/63, 7/73, 8/75, 9/76, 10/77

Surrey

	o	m	r	w		o	m	r	w
Gover	18.5	4	63	5		16	6	25	1
Watts	8	3	22	1		8.1	4	19	1
Parker	8	1	21	0		15	4	26	3
Brown	15	2	52	4		20	7	53	5
Gregory	1	0	7	0					

Derbyshire

	o	m	r	w		o	m	r	w
Copson	16	6	33	5		14	5	19	7
A V Pope	20.5	5	50	1		9	3	8	2
Worthington	9	2	19	0		4	1	20	0
Mitchell	23	5	89	4		8	0	28	1
Townsend	6	1	10	0					

Umpires: E Cooke and C W L Parker

Close of play scores: First day: Surrey (1) 187/7 (H T Barling 87, J F Parker 8)

Derbyshire v Sussex

Played at Queen's Park, Chesterfield, on May 23, 25, 26
Toss won by Derbyshire
Derbyshire won by an innings and 25 runs

Derbyshire

A E Alderman	b Nye	0
D Smith	c John G Langridge b Tate	53
T S Worthington	b Nye	9
L F Townsend	not out	182
E Carrington	b J H Parks	35
†H Elliott	b Wensley	63
G H Pope	c J H Parks b Tate	4
*Mr A W Richardson	c Holmes b J H Parks	5
A V Pope	c Cornford b Nye	2
T B Mitchell	c Jas. Langridge b J H Parks	0
W H Copson	c Holmes b J H Parks	17
Extras	(B 9, LB 5, NB 3)	17
Total		387

Fall: 1st inns 1/0, 2/23, 3/112, 4/177, 5/314, 6/321, 7/351, 8/366, 9/367, 10/387

Sussex

J H Parks	c Elliott b Copson	3	c Smith b A V Pope	3
John G Langridge	b Copson	3	c Worthington b G H Pope	58
H W Parks	lbw b Mitchell	15	c Worthington b G H Pope	52
G Cox	not out	42	c Worthington b Copson	39
Jas. Langridge	lbw b Mitchell	0	b Copson	27
*Fl-Lt A J Holmes	run out	1	lbw b Townsend	5
M W Tate	b Copson	34	c A V Pope b Townsend	6
C Oakes	b Copson	0	b Copson	31
A F Wensley	b Copson	1	not out	5
†W H Cornford	c Copson b Mitchell	7	b A V Pope	0
J K Nye	c Copson b Mitchell	14	c Elliott b A V Pope	0
Extras	(B 2, LB 7)	9	(LB 7)	7
Total		129		233

Fall: 1st inns 1/6, 2/7, 3/35, 4/35, 5/37, 6/86, 7/86, 8/88, 9/105,10/129
2nd inns 1/4, 2/113, 3/126, 4/163, 5/172, 6/184, 7/227, 8/228, 9/229, 10/233

Sussex

	o	m	r	w
Nye	24	2	100	3
Tate	27	7	42	2
Wensley	31	8	78	1
J H Parks	25.1	7	56	4
Oakes	11	3	36	0
Jas Langridge	19	2	58	0

Derbyshire

	o	m	r	w	o	m	r	w
Copson	17	5	42	5	18	7	36	3
A V Pope	8	4	7	0	16.2	7	14	3
G H Pope	6	3	7	0	18	3	42	2
Mitchell	14.4	2	64	4	19	0	97	0
Worthington					5	2	11	0
Townsend					21	12	26	2

Umpires: W A Buswell and J A Newman

Close of play scores: First day: Derbyshire (1) 351/7 (L F Townsend 165) Second day: Sussex (2) 223/6 (Jas Langridge 26, C Oakes 27)

Gloucestershire v Derbyshire

Played at Bristol, on May 27, 28
Toss won by Gloucestershire
Derbyshire won by ten wickets

Gloucestershire

R A Sinfield	b G H Pope	9	lbw b A V Pope	9
C J Barnett	b Copson	59	b A V Pope	11
Mr B O Allen	st Elliott b Mitchell	1	c Copson b Worthington	18
W R Hammond	b A V Pope	20	c Elliott b Worthington	8
W L Neale	run out	16	st Elliott b Mitchell	28
E J Stephens	b Copson	5	b Mitchell	22
*Mr D A C Page	c Elliott b A V Pope	7	b Mitchell	0
C J Monks	b Copson	12	b Mitchell	17
†V Hopkins	c Elliott b Mitchell	2	c and b Mitchell	0
T W J Goddard	b Copson	23	c sub b A V Pope	4
Mr G P Surman	not out	2	not out	0
Extras	(LB 8)	8	(B 3, LB 2, W 1)	6
Total		164		123

Fall: 1st inns 1/37, 2/40, 3/94, 4/94, 5/99, 6/110, 7/132, 8/135, 9/139, 10/164
2nd inns 1/11, 2/40, 3/40, 4/53, 5/84, 6/84, 7/110, 8/110, 9/119, 10/123

Derbyshire

A E Alderman	lbw b Sinfield	42	not out	40
D Smith	b Surman	1	not out	51
T S Worthington	b Surman	8		
L F Townsend	c Hammond b Sinfield	6		
E Carrington	c Hammond b Sinfield	0		
†H Elliott	c Hopkins b Sinfield	61		
*Mr A W Richardson	b Sinfield	7		
A V Pope	c Monks b Goddard	40		
G H Pope	b Sinfield	7		
T B Mitchell	not out	5		
W H Copson	b Sinfield	2		
Extras	(B 5, LB 8, NB 1)	14	(LB 2, W 1, NB 1)	4
Total		193 (no wicket)		95

Fall: 1st inns 1/7, 2/19, 3/33, 4/33, 5/71, 6/85, 7/162, 8/172, 9/183, 10/193

Derbyshire

	o	m	r	w	o	m	r	w
Copson	20.3	2	72	4	6	1	26	0
A V Pope	18	6	26	2	13	3	30	3
G H Pope	6	0	18	1				
Mitchell	12	1	33	2	10.1	2	40	5
Worthington	4	0	7	0	8	0	21	2

Gloucestershire

	o	m	r	w	o	m	r	w
Surman	15	1	60	2	8	2	23	0
Monks	5	2	3	0	5	2	4	0
Goddard	33	12	62	1	10	3	29	0
Sinfield	23.3	8	54	7	10	1	23	0
Neale					4.3	0	12	0

Umpires: L C Braund and J A Newman

Close of play scores: First day: Derbyshire (1) 109/6 (H Elliott 33, A V Pope 5)

Derbyshire v Essex

Played at Derby, on May 30, June 1, 2
Toss won by Derbyshire
Match drawn

Derbyshire

A E Alderman	b Nichols	26
D Smith	b Nichols	5
H Storer jun	b Nichols	0
L F Townsend	b Stephenson	5
T S Worthington	not out	85
E Carrington	c Ashton b Stephenson	1
†H Elliott	lbw b Smith	9
*Mr A W Richardson	lbw b Smith	10
A V Pope	b Smith	0
T B Mitchell	b Evans	25
W H Copson	b Smith	1
Extras	(B 9, LB 2, NB 1)	12
Total		179

Fall: 1st inns 1/19, 2/21, 3/43, 4/43, 5/53, 6/79, 7/99, 8/101, 9/178, 10/179

Essex

J R Sheffield	c Pope b Copson	24
R M Taylor	lbw b Worthington	14
M S Nichols	c Smith b Mitchell	76
J O'Connor	b Worthington	1
J A Cutmore	c and b Mitchell	45
Mr C T Ashton	not out	13
*Mr T N Pearce	st Elliott b Mitchell	6
Extras	(B 4, LB 9, W 1)	14
Total	(6 wickets)	193

Mr J W A Stephenson, V J Evans, †T H Wade and T P B Smith did not bat

Fall: 1st inns 1/41, 2/41, 3/47, 4/162, 5/175, 6/193

Essex

	o	m	r	w
Nichols	17	2	66	3
Stephenson	15	' 6	41	2
Smith	10.2	1	32	4
Evans	9	1	28	1

Derbyshire

	O	M	R	W
Copson	16	5	32	1
Pope	15	2	40	0
Worthington	12	1	31	2
Mitchell	9.5	0	52	3
Townsend	13	5	24	0

Umpires: J A Newman and H W Lee

Close of play scores: First day: No play second day: Essex (1) 193/6 (C T Ashton 13)

Northamptonshire v Derbyshire

Played at Northampton, on June 3, 4, 5,1936
Toss won by Northamptonshire
Derbyshire won by seven wickets

Northamptonshire

A H Bakewell	b Copson	6	(4) b Copson	0
N Grimshaw	st Elliott b Mitchell	11	(1) b Copson	0
D Brookes	c Richardson b Pope	5	(2) b Copson	26
J E Timms	lbw b Mitchell	0	(3) lbw b Townsend	69
A L Cox	c Copson b Townsend	12	st Elliott b Mitchell	2
†K C James	lbw b Mitchell	0	c Mitchell b Pope	29
*Mr H J H Lamb	c Townsend b Mitchell	17	b Copson	8
A D G Matthews	c Smith b Townsend	0	b Townsend	4
R J Partridge	c Elliott b Townsend	2	not out	3
G C Perkins	not out	4	c Elliott b Copson	14
E W Clark	c and b Townsend	0	b Copson	0
Extras	(LB 2)	2	(LB 3)	3
Total		**59**		**158**

Fall: 1st inns 1/6, 2/23, 3/23, 4/23, 5/23, 6/47, 7/51, 8/53, 9/59, 10/59
2nd inns 1/0, 2/63, 3/71, 4/78, 5/120, 6/132, 7/147, 8/154, 9/158,10/158

Derbyshire

A E Alderman	c Matthews b Clark	0	(2) lbw b Matthews	0
D Smith	c and b Matthews	4	(3) c Bakewell b Clark	59
H Storer jun	c Bakewell b Clark	12	(1) c Partridge b Clark	18
L F Townsend	c and b Matthews	31	not out	17
T S Worthington	c Bakewell b Clark	9	not out	30
†H Elliott	b Matthews	4		
S W Hunt	c Cox b Perkins	17		
*Mr A W Richardson	b Matthews	2		
A V Pope	c Clark b Matthews	8		
T B Mitchell	b Perkins	0		
W H Copson	not out	0		
Extras	(B 1, LB 2, W 2, NB 1)	6	(B 1)	1
Total		**93**	(3 wickets)	**125**

Fall: 1st inns 1/0, 2/4, 3/25, 4/36, 5/47, 6/75, 7/77, 8/93, 9/93, 10/93
2nd inns 1/0, 2/78, 3/79

Derbyshire

	o	m	r	w	o	m	r	w
Copson	11	3	15	1	22	13	24	6
Pope	8	3	7	1	14	3	33	1
Townsend	10.3	7	3	4	16	5	30	2
Mitchell	16	4	32	4	22	1	68	1

Northamptonshire

	o	m	r	w	o	m	r	w
Clark	24	12	24	3	12	1	39	2
Matthews	31.1	9	42	5	13	5	23	1
Perkins	8	2	16	2	12	2	25	0
Bakewell	1	0	2	0				
Partridge	1	0	3	0	13.4	2	37	0

Umpires: J Hardstaff snr and A Skelding

Close of play scores: First day: Derbyshire (1) 25/2 (H Storer jun 12, L F Townsend 7)
Second day: Northamptonshire (2) 55/1 (D Brookes 23, J E Timms 30)

1936 match by match

Derbyshire v Gloucestershire

Played at Derby, on June 10,11,1936
Toss won by Gloucestershire
Derbyshire won by ten wickets

Gloucestershire

C J Barnett	c H Elliott b Mitchell	39	(3) lbw b Pope		27
R W Haynes	c Copson	8	(1) b Copson		16
W L Neale	b Mitchell	21	(4) c Smith b Pope		6
E J Stephens	c H Elliott b Copson	8	(6) b Mitchell		16
R A Sinfield	c Worthington b Mitchell	1	not out		41
C C R Dacre	c H Elliott b Mitchell	4	(7) c H Elliott b Copson		0
*Mr D A C Page	b Mitchell	2	(8) b Mitchell		10
J F Crapp	not out	4	(9) c Smith b Pope		22
C L Monks	b Mitchell	6	(10) b Mitchell		2
†V Hopkins	c and b Mitchell	0	(2) b Mitchell		16
T W J Goddard	b Copson	0	c H Elliott b Pope		29
Extras	(W 2)	2	(B 6, LB 2, W 1)		9
Total		95			194

Fall: 1st inns 1/18, 2/64, 3/77, 4/79, 5/80, 6/83, 7/88, 8/94, 9/94,10/95
2nd inns 1/26, 2/52, 3/64, 4/69, 5/90, 6/96, 7/115, 8/154, 9/157,10/194

Derbyshire

*Mr A W Richardson	c Crapp b Monks	3			
A E Alderman	c Dacre b Stephens	0	not out		23
D Smith	run out	14	(1) not out		63
L F Townsend	c Page b Sinfield	20			
T S Worthington	c and b Haynes	90			
†H Elliott	c Crapp b Goddard	22			
S W Hunt	b Goddard	16			
C S Elliott	b Neale	18			
A V Pope	c Page b Neale	11			
T B Mitchell	b Haynes	3			
W H Copson	not out	2			
Extras	(LB 1)	1	(LB 4 W 1)		5
Total		200	(no wicket)		91

Fall: 1st inns 1/0, 2/6, 3/31, 4/70, 5/143, 6/153, 7/172 8/195, 9/198,10/200

Derbyshire

	o	m	r	w		o	m	r	w
Copson	12.5	2	34	3		19	2	48	2
Pope	7	3	19	0		16.3	6	29	4
Worthington	5	1	14	0		4	0	10	0
Mitchell	10	2	26	7		30	4	98	4

Gloucestershire

	o	m	r	w		o	m	r	w
Stephens	8	1	24	1		6	0	30	0
Monks	8	1	35	1		6	0	12	0
Goddard	27	5	65	2					
Sinfield	25	10	39	1					
Neale	5.1	0	18	2		4	2	6	0
Haynes	7	1	18	2		9.5	1	22	0
Page						5	3	16	0

Umpires: F L Walden and J A Newman

Close of play scores: First day: Gloucestershire (2) 1/0 (R W Haynes 0, V Hopkins 1)

215

Derbyshire v Yorkshire

Played at Queen's Park, Chesterfield, on June 13, 15, 16
Toss won by Derbyshire
Match drawn

Derbyshire

A E Alderman	c Smailes b Bowes	4
D Smith	lbw b Bowes	9
H Storer jun	lbw b Smailes	1
T S Worthington	c Sellers b Turner	80
L F Townsend	c Sellers b Smailes	101
†H Elliott	b Bowes	17
A F Townsend	c Sellers b Bowes	1
S W Hunt	lbw b Fisher	10
*Mr A W Richardson	lbw b Bowes	5
A V Pope	not out	7
T B Mitchell	run out	12
Extras	(B 3, LB 3)	6
Total		253

Fall: 1st inns 1/11, 2/14, 3/18, 4/172, 5/201, 6/208, 7/227, 8/229, 9/234, 10/253

Yorkshire

H Sutcliffe	c H Elliott b Pope	6	c H Elliott b L F Townsend	11
L Hutton	lbw b Mitchell	8	not out	56
*Mr A B Sellers	c and b Mitchell	2	not out	25
Q Turner	b Mitchell	8		
Mr J R S Raper	lbw b Mitchell	15		
J H Pearson	b L F Townsend	10		
Mr G A Wilson	b Mitchell	4		
†A Wood	b Pope	26		
T F Smailes	b Pope	13		
H Fisher	c Worthington b Mitchell	1		
W E Bowes	not out	10		
Extras	(B 3 LB 6)	9	(B 4, LB 6)	10
Total		112	1 wicket)	102

Fall: 1st inns 1/13, 2/14, 3/21, 4/24, 5/44, 6/48, 7/62, 8/99, 9/100, 10/112
2nd inns 1/36

Yorkshire

	o	m	r	w
Bowes	33	12	66	5
Smailes	24	5	60	2
Fisher	24	10	60	1
Turner	13	3	40	1
Hutton	2	0	9	0
Wilson	7	2	12	0

Derbyshire

	o	m	r	w	o	m	r	w
Worthington	12	1	19	0	6	0	13	0
Pope	14.2	6	14	3	18	9	15	0
Mitchell	18	0	60	6	10	1	26	0
L F Townsend	5	1	7	1	7	4	15	1
Hunt	1	0	3	0				
A F Townsend	6	1	23	0				

Umpires: T W Oates and H G Baldwin

Close of play scores: First day: No play Second day: Derbyshire (1) 234/9 (A V Pope 1)

Derbyshire v Somerset

Played at Rutland Recreation Ground, Ilkeston, on June 17, 18
Toss won by Somerset
Somerset won by 10 wickets

Derbyshire

H Storer jun	lbw b Hunt	18	lbw b Wellard	2
D Smith	c Hazell b Hunt	22	c Luckes b Andrews	11
T S Worthington	c Andrews b Hunt	21	c Bennett b Andrews	2
L F Townsend	c Hazell b Hunt	0	c Wellard b Andrews	0
A E Alderman	lbw b Wellard	18	c Bamwell b Buse	3
E Carrington	c Lee b Wellard	0	c Gimblett b Wellard	0
†H Elliott	lbw b Hunt	14	c Gimblett b Wellard	4
*Mr A W Richardson	c Andrews b Hunt	19	run out	7
A V Pope	c Lee b Wellard	23	b Andrews	18
T B Mitchell	c Andrews b Hunt	6	c Gimblett b Wellard	4
W H Copson	not out	0	not out	3
Extras	(B 6, LB 5)	11	(B 2, LB 5, NB 1)	8
Total		152		62

Fall: 1st inns 1/44, 2/49, 3/49, 4/76, 5/77, 6/87, 7/114, 8/124, 9/146,10/152

2nd inns 1/12, 2/15, 3/17, 4/17, 5/20, 6/21, 7/22, 8/38, 9/53, 10/62

Somerset

H Gimblett	c Mitchell b Townsend	43	not out	15
F S Lee	c Carrington b Worthington	32	not out	10
*Mr R A Ingle	c Alderman b Mitchell	10		
Mr G M Bennett	b Mitchell	18		
H F T Buse	st H Elliott b Worthington	37		
A W Wellard	c Worthington b Mitchell	3		
W H R Andrews	lbw b Mitchell	14		
†W T Luckes	b Worthington	8		
Mr C J P Bamwell	c Alderman b Mitchell	3		
H Hunt	not out	11		
H L Hazell	b Worthington	7		
Extras	(B 2, LB 2)	4		
Total		190	(no wicket)	25

Fall: 1st inns 1/48, 2/60, 3/89, 4/127, 5/138, 6/160, 7/160, 8/167, 9/176, 10/190

Somerset

	o	m	r	w	o	m	r	w
Wellard	14	3	43	3	11.2	1	29	4
Andrews	3	0	12	0	10	0	21	4
Hazell	12	2	37	0				
Hunt	19.2	7	49	7				
Buse	2	1	4	1				

Derbyshire

	o	m	r	w	o	m	r	w
Copson	20	3	0	2	2	0	18	0
Pope	4	0	12	0				
Mitchell	22	2	90	5				
Townsend	15	6	50	1				
Worthington	17.2	4	31	4	3	0	7	0

Umpires: W Reeves and F L Walden

Close of play scores: First day: Derbyshire (2) 15/2 (D Smith 10)

217

Warwickshire v Derbyshire

Played at Edgbaston, Birmingham, on June 20, 22, 23
Toss won by Derbyshire
Derbyshire won by an innings and 10 runs

Derbyshire

H Storer	lbw b Mayer	3
D Smith	c Smart b Mayer	0
T S Worthington	c Kilner b Mayer	81
L F Townsend	b Hollies	23
A E Alderman	lbw b Wyatt	34
C S Elliott	c Mayor b Hollies	97
†H Elliott	c Paine b Hollies	33
*Mr A W Richardson	c Croom b Paine	32
A V Pope	not out	6
T B Mitchell	b Hollies	3
W H Copson	run out	3
Extras	(LB 3)	3
Total		318

Fall: 1st inns 1/0, 2/9, 3/79, 4/116, 5/208, 6/246, 7/298, 8/308, 9/315, 10/318

Warwickshire

N Kilner	c Townsend b Mitchell	13	b Townsend	48
A J W Croom	c C Elliott b Townsend	11	c Smith b Copson	0
W A Hill	c Storer b Townsend	0	b Copson	4
*Mr R E S Wyatt	c Storer b Townsend	14	b Townsend	72
F R Santall	b Mitchell	18	c H Elliott b Townsend	0
H E Dollery	c Alderman b Mitchell	22	lbw b Townsend	4
E G Barber	c Worthington b Townsend	13	b Townsend	9
G A E Paine	hit wicket b Mitchell	0	hit wicket b Mitchell	41
†J A Smart	c Smith b Mitchell	7	c and b Townsend	2
J H Mayer	not out	7	b Townsend	3
W E Hollies	b Townsend	1	not out	8
Extras	(LB 3)	3	(LB 8)	8
Total		109		199

Fall: 1st inns 1/25, 2/25, 3/25, 4/59, 5/61, 6/92, 7/94, 8/96, 9/105, 10/109
2nd inns 1/0, 2/8, 3/88 4/88, 5/94, 6/108, 7/149, 8/169, 9/179, 10/199

Warwickshire

	o	m	r	w
Mayer	26	9	48	3
Wyatt	21	8	44	1
Santall	8	3	17	0
Hollies	35	10	114	4
Paine	30	8	83	1
Croom	2	0	9	0

Derbyshire

	o	m	r	w	o	m	r	w
Pope	7	3	10	0	7	3	8	0
Worthington	4	1	10	0	8	5	8	0
Townsend	18	4	44	5	32	11	46	7
Mitchell	15	2	42	5	23.4	2	99	1
Copson					22	7	30	2

Umpires: A Dolphin and H G Baldwin

Close of play scores: First day: Derbyshire (1) 280/6 (H Elliott 22, A W Richardson 18)
Second day: Warwickshire (2) 45/2 (N Kilner 16, R E S Wyatt 21)

Derbyshire v Worcestershire

Played at Queen's Park, Chesterfield, on June 24, 25, 26,1936
Toss won by Worcestershire
Derbyshire won by three wickets

Worcestershire

C H Bull	b Copson	0	lbw b Copson	0
Mr E G Righton	lbw b Mitchell	19	run out	1
S H Martin	b Copson	41	c Storer b Townsend	48
H H I H Gibbons	b Copson	99	lbw b Mitchell	12
†Mr B W Quaife	lbw b Mitchell	15	b Townsend	16
J Horton	b Copson	34	c Storer b Townsend	16
*Hon C J Lyttelton	b Pope	4	not out	44
R Howorth	b Pope	3	c Pope b Mitchell	5
V Grimshaw	b Copson	0	b Townsend	1
R T D Perks	not out	4	c Copson b Pope	9
P F Jackson	c Storer b Pope	0	run out	1
Extras	(LB 14)	14	(B 5, LB 3, W 1)	9
Total		233		162

Fall: 1st inns 1/0, 2/30, 3/83, 4/106, 5/216, 6/225, 7/227, 8/229, 9/231,10/233
2nd inns 1/1, 2/1, 3/28, 4/67, 5/91, 6/96, 7/121, 8/134, 9/160, 10/161

Derbyshire

H Storer jun	c Quaife b Jackson	26	lbw b Perks	62
D Smith	b Perks	2	b Perks	0
T S Worthington	b Jackson	33	b Perks	35
L F Townsend	st Quaife b Howorth	76	b Howorth	7
A E Alderman	lbw b Howorth	25	not out	29
C S Elliott	b Jackson	0	c Quaife b Perks	0
†H Elliott	b Perks	30	c Grimshaw b Howorth	4
*Mr A W Richardson	not out	23	b Perks	2
A V Pope	c Jackson b Perks	0	not out	1
T B Mitchell	c Perks b Howorth	10		
W H Copson	b Perks	0		
Extras	(B 11, LB 10, NB 1)	22	(B 2, LB 3, W 1, NB 3)	9
Total		247	(7 wickets)	149

Fall: 1st inns 1/7 2/51, 3/92, 4/175, 5/176, 6/176, 7/224, 8/224, 9/247,10/247
2nd inns 1/0, 2/86, 3/99, 4/120, 5/122, 6/143, 7/145

Derbyshire

	o	m	r	w		o	m	r	w
Copson	27	8	34	5		18	4	38	1
Pope	25	9	41	3		14	6	22	1
Mitchell	23	0	83	2		13	1	59	2
Worthington	7	1	32	0					
Townsend	12	3	29	0		13	3	34	4

Worcestershire

	o	m	r	w		o	m	r	w
Perks	20.2	2	56	4		20	4	63	5
Jackson	34	10	64	3		4	1	8	0
Howorth	25	8	79	3		19.1	4	56	2
Martin	15	6	26	0		5	0	13	0

Umpires: T W Oates and L C Braund

Close of play scores: First day: Derbyshire (1) 100/3 (L F Townsend 20, A E Alderman 8)
Second day: Worcestershire (2) 143/8 (Hon C J Lyttelton 35, R T D Perks 1)

Derbyshire v Lancashire

Played at Park Road Ground, Buxton, on June 27, 29, 30
Toss won by Lancashire
Match drawn

Lancashire

F B Watson	lbw b Mitchell	29	lbw b Copson	11
J L Hopwood	lbw b Mitchell	13	c H Elliott b Copson	17
J Iddon	lbw b Copson	51	c H Elliott b Pope	15
E Paynter	b Worthington	15	lbw b Copson	7
C Washbrook	lbw b Worthington	0	c Townsend b Pope	8
N Oldfield	c and b Copson	44	c Worthington b Copson	6
†W Farrimond	lbw b Copson	0	(10) b Pope	0
*Mr W H L Lister	c Worthington b Townsend	0	b Pope	0
R Pollard	c H Elliott b Copson	5	(7) not out	16
F S Booth	b Worthington	20	(9) run out	5
F M Sibbles	not out	5	b Pope	3
Extras	(LB 12)	12	(B 4 LB 2)	6
Total		**194**		**94**

Fall: 1st inns 1/30, 2/65, 3/89, 4/89, 5/154, 6/154, 7/155, 8/161, 9/166, 10/194
2nd inns 1/16, 2/45, 3/53, 4/61, 5/70, 6/70, 7/71, 8/78, 9/78» 10/94

Derbyshire

H Storer jun	b Sibbles	1	lbw b Iddon	10
T S Worthington	c Farrimond b Booth	3	(3) lbw b Sibbles	25
L F Townsend	c and b Sibbles	1	(4) b Oldfield	23
D Smith	c Pollard b Booth	0	(5) not out	11
A E Alderman	lbw b Booth	18	(2) lbw b Hopwood	15
†H Elliott	c Watson b Booth	11	not out	1
C S Elliott	lbw b Booth	5		
*Mr A W Richardson	b Booth	7		
A V Pope	c Farrimond b Pollard	0		
T B Mitchell	not out	4		
W H Copson	b Pollard	0		
Extras	(B 2, LB 5, NB 4)	11	(B 2, LB 3, W 1, NB 1)	7
Total		**61**	**(4 wickets)**	**92**

Fall: 1st inns 1/3, 2/5, 3/5, 4/7, 5/24, 6/29, 7/54, 8/55, 9/61, 10/61
2nd inns 1/30, 2/30, 3/76, 4/89

Derbyshire

	o	m	r	w	o	m	r	w
Copson	17	6	35	4	16	3	35	4
Pope	8	3	10	0	15.4	0	53	5
Worthington	18.3	8	28	3				
Mitchell	19	2	68	2				
Townsend	16	3	41	1				

Lancashire

	o	m	r	w	o	m	r	w
Booth	18	6	18	6	10	2	18	0
Sibbles	16	5	17	2	14	5	19	1
Pollard	10.5	2	15	2	4	2	5	0
Hopwood	18	3	27	1				
Iddon	9	4	9	1				
Watson	3	0	7	0				
Oldfield	1	1	0	1				

Umpires: E J Snaith and A E Dipper

Close of play scores: First day: Derbyshire (1) 61 all out Second day: Lancashire (2) 25/1
(J L Hopwood 6, J Iddon 4)

Worcestershire v Derbyshire

Played at Worcester, on July 1, 2, 3
Toss won by Derbyshire
Derbyshire won by an innings and 123 runs

Derbyshire

H Storer	c King b Grimshaw	52
A E Alderman	b Perks	61
D Smith	c Lyttelton b Jackson	25
T S Worthington	b Penes	1
L F Townsend	c Martin b Howorth	1
C S Elliott	b Jackson	49
†H Elliott	c Horton b Martin	1
*Mr A W Richardson	c Howorth b Martin	10
A V Pope	not out	28
Extras	(B 3, LB 3)	6
Total	(8 wickets, dec)	234

T B Mitchell and W H Copson did not bat

Fall: 1st inns 1/108, 2/119, 3/121, 4/122, 5/156, 6/162, 7/180, 8/234

Worcestershire

C H Bull	c H Elliott b Copson	2	(5) b Copson		1
V Grimshaw	b Pope	0	(9) c H Elliott b Copson		6
S H Martin	c Worthington b Pope	1	c Townsend b Mitchell		3
H H I H Gibbons	lbw b Copson	1	c C S Elliott b Copson		3
†Mr B W Quaife	b Copson	0	(6) lbw b Copson		4
*Hon C J Lyttelton	st H Elliott b Mitchell	11	(1) b Copson		0
J Horton	c H Elliott b Copson	22	not out		15
R Howorth	c H Elliott b Copson	7	b Copson		1
B P King	c H Elliott b Pope	10	(2) c Smith b Copson		0
R T D Perks	b Pope	4	c H Elliott b Mitchell		10
P F Jackson	not out	6	c and b Mitchell		0
Extras	(LB 4)	4			
Total		64			47

Fall: 1st inns 1/2, 2/2, 3/4, 4/4, 5/6, 6/27, 7/43, 8/48, 9/57, 10/64
2nd inns 1/0, 2/1, 3/5, 4/7, 5/7, 6/12, 7/16, 8/28, 9/47,10/47

Worcestershire

	o	m	r	w
Perks	21	4	50	2
Jackson	17.4	2	64	2
Howorth	37	17	61	1
Martin	16	4	44	2
Grimshaw	4	2	9	1

Derbyshire

	o	m	r	w	o	m	r	w
Copson	18	2	38	5	13	6	16	7
Pope	16.3	10	12	4	5	4	1	0
Mitchell	2	0	14	1	9.4	1	26	3

Umpires: T W Oates and W A Buswell

Close of play scores: First day: Derbyshire (1) 135/4 (D Smith 10, C S Elliott 5) Second day: Worcestershire (1) 39/6 (J Horton 20, R Howorth 4)

Derbyshire v Warwickshire

Played at Queen's Park, Chesterfield, on July 4, 6, 7
Toss won by Warwickshire
Derbyshire won by an innings and 159 runs

Warwickshire

N Kilner	c Pope b Copson	12	c H Elliott b Pope	14
A J W Croom	b Mitchell	7	c Storer b Pope	1
W A Hill	b Mitchell	5	c H Elliott b Pope	0
*Mr R E S Wyatt	c H Elliott b Copson	1	lbw b Townsend	40
F R Santall	b Copson	2	b Mitchell	3
H E Dollery	st H Elliott b Mitchell	22	b Copson	29
T Collin	b Pope	23	c Richardson b Townsend	14
J H Mayer	c Richardson b Copson	24	c Pope b Townsend	2
†J A Smart	b Mitchell	7	c Mitchell b Copson	0
K Wilmot	st H Elliott b Mitchell	1	c Storer b Copson	0
W E Hollies	not out	13	not out	1
Extras	(NB 1)	1		
Total		117		105

Fall: 1st inns 1/15, 2/24, 3/25, 4/27, 5/27, 6/67, 7/81, 8/101, 9/102, 10/117
2nd inns 1/1, 2/1, 3/35, 4/47, 5/70, 6/94, 7/104, 8/104, 9/104, 10/105

Derbyshire

H Storer jun	c Wyatt b Mayer	0
A E Alderman	c Hollies b Wilmot	7
T S Worthington	c Collin b Hollies	163
L-P Townsend	b Collin	36
D Smith	lbw b Mayer	24
C S Elliott	lbw b Mayor	49
†H Elliott	c Collin b Hollies	40
*Mr A W Richardson	b Collin	1
A V Pope	b Wilmot	28
T B Mitchell	not out	16
W H Copson	c Smart b Wilmot	11
Extras	(B 4, LB 2)	6
Total		381

Fall: 1st inns 1/0, 2/26, 3/82, 4/131, 5/258, 6/321, 7/326, 8/332, 9/365, 10/381

Derbyshire

	o	m	r	w	o	m	r	w
Copson	15	3	38	4	10 4	2	31	3
Pope	12	5	18	1	10	5	12	3
Mitchell	12.5	0	52	5	10	0	26	1
Townsend	4	19	0	11	6	1	9	3
Worthington	3	0	16	0				

Warwickshire

	o	m	r	w
Mayer	21	4	61	3
Wyatt	11	4	37	0
Wilmot	18	2	75	3
Hollies	30	3	100	2
Collin	20	2	80	2
Santall	5	2	11	0
Croom	4	1	11	0

Umpires: C W L Parker and A E Dipper

Close of play scores: First day: Derbyshire (1) 235/4 (T S Worthington 114, C S Elliott 48)
Second day: Warwickshire (2) 1/0 (N Kilner O, A J W Croom 1)

Derbyshire v Hampshire

Played at Queen's Park, Chesterfield, on July 8, 9,10
Toss won by Hampshire
Match drawn

Hampshire

J Arnold	c Skinner b Pope	24	not out	6
†N T McCorkell	lbw b Copson	3	lbw b Copson	2
A E Pothecary	c H Elliott b Pope	2	c Worthington b Pope	1
C P Mead	lbw b Copson	1	not out	1
*Mr R H Moore	lbw b Mitchell	7		
W L C Creese	b Pope	14		
Mr W Lancashire	b Mitchell	13		
G S Boyes	c H Elliott b Pope	1		
W L Budd	lbw b Mitchell	4		
H M Lawson	not out	11		
O W Herman	b Mitchell	5		
Extras	(LB 2, W 1)	3		
Total		88	(2 wickets)	10

Fall: 1st inns 1/20, 2/23, 3/24, 4/38, 5/50, 6/54, 7/66, 8/68, 9/80,10/88
2nd inns 1/7, 2/8

Derbyshire

A E Alderman	b Boyes	9
T S Worthington	c McCorkell b Creese	17
L F Townsend	not out	153
Mr A F Skinner	st McCorkell b Boyes	19
D Smith	c Pothecary b Lancashire	28
C S Elliott	run out	17
†H Elliott	b Herman	6
*Mr A W Richardson	b Herman	4
A V Pope	c Arnold b Moore	37
T B Mitchell	not out	27
Extras	(B 6, LB 9, NB 4)	19
Total	(8 wickets, dec)	336

W H Copson did not bat
Fall: 1st inns 1/35, 2/51, 3/74, 4/125, 5/175, 6/212 7/218, 8/284

Derbyshire

	o	m	r	w	o	m	r	w
Copson	6	1	24	2	5	3	3	1
Pope	11	5	15	4	5	1	7	1
Mitchell	6	1	46	4				

Hampshire

	o	m	r	w
Herman	26	5	92	2
Lawson	8	1	27	0
Creese	21	7	72	1
Boyes	19	3	56	2
Budd	7	1	19	0
Lancashire	6	0	23	1
Moore	5	0	28	1

Umpires: T W Oates and L C Braund

Close of play scores: First day: Derbyshire (1) 336/8 (L F Townsend 153, T B Mitchell 27)
Second day: Hampshire (2) 10/2 (J Arnold 6, C P Mead 1)

Lancashire v Derbyshire

Played at Old Trafford, Manchester, on July 11, 13,14
Toss won by Derbyshire
Match drawn

Derbyshire

A E Alderman	b Sibbles	32
T S Worthington	c Nutter b Sibbles	1
L F Townsend	b Sibbles	46
D Smith	b Sibbles	5
A V Pope	c Washbrook b Sibbles	3
C S Elliott	not out	10
S W Hunt	c Duckworth b Sibbles	0
†H Elliott	c Hudson b Sibbles	3
T B Mitchell	c Iddon b Booth	6
Extras	(B 6, LB 2, NB 2)	10
Total	(8 wickets, dec)	116

*Mr A W Richardson and W H Copson did not bat

Fall: 1st inns 1/3, 2/84, 3/89, 4/93, 5/94, 6/94, 7/107, 8/116

Lancashire

J L Hopwood	not out	21
C Washbrook	not out	15
Extras	(LB 1)	1
Total	(no wicket)	37

J Iddon, E Paynter, N Oldfield, A E Nutter, *Mr W H L Lister, †G Duckworth, F M Sibbles, F S
Booth and Mr G N Hudson did not bat

Lancashire

	o	m	r	w
Booth	18.1	4	24	1
Sibbles	19	4	36	7
Hudson	10	3	25	0
Nutter	7	4	7	0
Hopwood	4	0	14	0

Derbyshire

	o	m	r	w
Worthington	5	0	19	0
Pope	8	4	10	0
Townsend	4	2	7	0

Umpires: E Cooke and A Dolphin

Close of play scores: First day: No play Second day: No play

Derbyshire v Kent

Played at Burton-on-Trent CC (Town) Ground, Burton-on-Trent, on July 15, 16, 17
Toss won by Derbyshire
Derbyshire won by 141 runs

Derbyshire

A E Alderman	run out	25	c Ashdown b Lewis	39
T S Worthington	c Valentine b Watt	15	c Watt b Lewis	53
L F Townsend	c and b Lewis	115	not out	78
Mr A F Skinner	c Ashdown b Wright	49	c Watt b Lewis	12
D Smith	b Wright	4	not out	20
C S Elliott	b Freeman	12		
S W Hunt	b Wright	5		
A V Pope	c Watt b Freeman	9		
*Mr A W Richardson	b Freeman	19		
T B Mitchell	c Todd b Freeman	5		
†H Elliott	not out	0		
Extras	(B 4 LB 6)	10	(B 2)	2
Total		268	(3 wickets, dec)	204

Fall: 1st inns 1/26, 2/84, 3/190, 4/195, 5/216, 6/225, 7/242, 8/243, 9/264, 10/268
2nd inns 1/80, 2/133, 3/178

Kent

W H Ashdown	lbw b Worthington	4	c Alderman b Pope	5
†A E Fagg	b Pope	1	c Alderman b Pope	46
F E Woolley	c C S Elliott b Townsend	61	b Worthington	21
P R Sunnucks	lbw b Townsend	5	c Richardson b Worthington	0
L J Todd	b Mitchell	23	b Worthington	0
*Mr B H Valentine	b Pope	43	c H Elliott b Pope	26
T W Spencer	c Worthington b Pope	4	not out	23
D V P Wright	c Townsend b Pope	12	lbw b Townsend	0
A E Watt	c Skinner b Townsend	30	c Smith b Townsend	4
C Lewis	b Pope	0	c Richardson b Mitchell	9
A P Freeman	not out	0	c Smith b Townsend	12
Extras	(LB 1)	1	(LB 1)	1
Total		184		147

Fall: 1st inns 1/4, 2/6, 3/32, 4/83, 5/100, 6/130, 7/151, 8/174, 9/184, 10/184
2nd inns 1/15, 2/45, 3/45, 4/51, 5/96, 6/106, 7/111, 8/115, 9/133, 10/147

Kent

	o	m	r	w		o	m	r	w
Watt	16	3	47	1		15	3	42	0
Todd	9	0	24	0		6	1	16	0
Freeman	22.2	1	89	4		11	2	27	0
Wright	18	3	53	3		7	1	34	0
Lewis	9	1	45	1		17	1	83	3

Derbyshire

	o	m	r	w		o	m	r	w
Pope	25.2	9	48	5		16	7	30	3
Worthington	7	2	19	1		11	3	29	3
Townsend	12	3	32	3		17	1	59	3
Mitchell	14	0	84	1		6	1	28	1

Umpires: A Dolphin and F I Walden

Close of play scores: First day: Derbyshire (1) 62/1 (A E Alderman 17, L F Townsend 25)
Second day: Derbyshire (2) 50/0 (A E Alderman 15, T S Worthington 35)

Derbyshire v Indians

Played at Derby, on July 18, 20, 21
Toss won by Indians
Match drawn

Indians

V M Merchant	lbw b Worthington	23	c H Elliott b Copson		75
S Wazir Ali	b Pope	2	(3) c Townsend b Worthington		10
S Mushtaq Ali	lbw b Worthington	9	(2) c sub b Townsend		27
*Maj C K Nayudu	lbw b Pope	60	c Alderman b Townsend		30
L P Jai	b Copson	43	c Skinner b Copson		11
C Ramaswami	c Skinner b Copson	0	not out		40
M Jahangir Khan	b Copson	9	c Worthington b C Elliott		21
M Baqa Jilani	not out	33	c Skinner b Townsend		9
C S Nayudu	c Pope b Mitchell	3			
S N Banerjee	b Copson	28			
†K R Meherhomji	b Copson	0			
Extras	(B 6, LB 11, NB 1)	18	(B 5, LB 4)		9
Total		228	(7 wickets, dec)		232

Fall: 1st inns 1/3, 2/22, 3/55, 4/134, 5/134, 6/140, 7/158, 8/169, 9/226, 10/228
2nd inns 1/76, 2/109, 3/114, 4/135, 5/163, 6/195, 7/232

Derbyshire

A E Alderman	lbw b C K Nayudu	1	not out		61
T S Worthington	b Banerjee	9	b C S Nayudu		14
L F Townsend	b Banerjee	7	b Banerjee		77
Mr A F Skinner	b Banerjee	2			
C S Elliott	lbw b Jahangir Khan	77			
*Mr G R Jackson	lbw b C S Nayudu	4			
E Carrington	b Banerjee	2	(4) not out		6
†H Elliott	lbw b Jahangir Khan	42			
A V Pope	st Meherhomji b C S Nayudu	5			
T B Mitchell	c Jai b Jahangir Khan	1			
W H Copson	not out	6			
Extras	(B 1, LB 2, NB 1)	4	(B 9, LB 1, W 1)		11
Total		160	(2 wickets)		169

Fall: 1st inns 1/8, 2/12, 3/14, 4/27, 5/48, 6/51, 7/139, 8/152, 9/154, 10/160
2nd inns 1/27, 2/162

Derbyshire

	o	m	r	w		o	m	r	w
Copson	25	9	44	5		24	6	42	2
Pope	21	8	26	2		27	7	61	0
Worthington	18	7	42	2		11	4	34	1
Mitchell	25	4	72	1					
Townsend	11	3	26	0		22	4	73	3
C Elliott						3.5	1	13	1

Indians

	o	m	r	w		o	m	r	w
Banerjee	13	0	51	4		7	1	22	1
C K Nayudu	5	2	14	1		5	0	30	0
Jahangir Khan	10	3	28	3		17	4	28	0
Jilani	7	4	5	0		1	0	5	0
C S Nayudu	8	0	45	2		7	1	37	1
Mushtaq Ali	5	2	13	0		8	1	16	0
Ramaswami						4	0	11	0
Wazir Ali						2	0	3	0
Jai						3	2	6	0

Umpires: J Hardstaff, snr and E J Smith

Close of play scores: First day: Indians (1) 219/8 (M Baqa Jilani 28, S N Banerjee 24) Second day: Indians (2)37/0 (V M Merchant 21, S Mushtaq Ali 15)

Yorkshire v Derbyshire

Played at Bramall Lane, Sheffield, on July 22, 23, 24
Toss won by Yorkshire
Match drawn

Derbyshire

A E Alderman	c Barber b Smailes	13	c Mitchell b Smailes		23
T S Worthington	c Wood b Bowes	135	c Mitchell b Bowes		13
L F Townsend	c Hutton b Verity	9	c Barber b Smailes		50
Mr A F Skinner	b Verity	17	c Barber b Jacques		16
D Smith	lbw b Bowes	1	not out		37
C S Elliott	run out	2	st Wood b Yardley		1
†H Elliott	lbw b Verity	4	not out		3
*Mr A W Richardson	b Jacques	4			
A V Pope	c Yardley b Bowes	13			
T B Mitchell	b Smailes	5			
W H Copson	not out	0			
Extras	(B 7, LB 6)	13	(LB 3, NB 2)		5
Total		216	(5 wickets)		148

Fall: 1st inns 1/59, 2/85, 3/154, 4/155, 5/164, 6/177, 7/182, 8/211, 9/216, 10/216
2nd inns 1/18, 2/89, 3/90, 4/128, 5/129

Yorkshire

H Sutcliffe	c Skinner b Copson	0
L Hutton	c H Elliott b Copson	31
A Mitchell	c C S Elliott b Pope	103
Mr N W D Yardley	lbw b Pope	12
H Verity	c Skinner b Copson	0
W Barber	b Copson	8
*Mr A B Sellers	c H Elliott b Copson	0
†A Wood	b Copson	24
T F Smailes	c Richardson b Pope	22
T A Jacques	c Worthington b Pope	8
W E Bowes	not out	3
Extras	(B 1, LB 6)	7
Total		218

Fall: 1st inns 1/0, 2/68, 3/101, 4/102, 5/114, 6/120, 7/182, 8/186, 9/211, 10/218

Yorkshire

	o	m	r	w	o	m	r	w
Bowes	21.4	3	47	3	8	2	10	1
Jacques	18	1	64	1	8	1	19	1
Smailes	13	4	45	2	11	1	44	2
Verity	18	4	47	3	14	2	50	0
Yardley					7	1	10	1
Hutton					5	2	10	0

Derbyshire

	o	m	r	w
Copson	30	7	60	6
Pope	31.5	10	58	4
Mitchell	10	0	41	0
Worthington	6	1	30	0
Townsend	9	3	22	0

Umpires: J Hardstaff snr and F I Walden

Close of play scores: First day: Yorkshire (1) 102/4 (A Mitchell 54) Second day: No play

Derbyshire v Nottinghamshire

Played at Rutland Recreation Ground, Ilkeston, on July 25, 27, 28
Toss won by Derbyshire
Nottinghamshire won by six wickets

Derbyshire

A E Alderman	c Voce b Gunn	23	c Lilley b Voce	53
D Smith	c Lilley b Voce	59	b Voce	36
L F Townsend	c Woodhead b Larwood	8	b Woodhead	2
Mr A F Skinner	b Gunn	2	lbw b Voce	5
C S Elliott	st Lilley b Gunn	16	c Lilley b Larwood	2
A F Townsend	b Larwood	21	b Voce	1
†H Elliott	lbw b Woodhead	14	not out	10
*Mr A W Richardson	run out	6	c Lilley b Larwood	1
A V Pope	c Knowles b Voce	2	b Voce	0
T B Mitchell	c Lilley b Larwood	14	b Voce	7
W H Copson	not out	1	c Voce b Larwood	0
Extras	(B 12, LB 9)	21	(B 4 LB 4)	8
Total		187		125

Fall: 1st inns 1/55, 2/62, 3/69, 4/107, 5/121, 6/150, 7/169, 8/171, 9/174,10/187
2nd inns 1/83, 2/94, 3/98, 4/105, 5/110, 6/110, 7/111, 8/112, 9/120,10/125

Nottinghamshire

W W Keeton	lbw b Pope	4	c C S Elliott b Pope	14
C B Harris	c Skinner b Copson	1	c and b L F Townsend	43
W Walker	b Mitchell	58	lbw b L F Townsend	28
G V Gunn	c and b Mitchell	34	c Smith b Pope	12
J Knowles	c Pope b Mitchell	0	not out	23
A Staples	c H Elliott b Mitchell	0	not out	11
W Voce	lbw b Mitchell	9		
†B Lilley	c and b Mitchell	7		
*Mr G F H Heane	c H Elliott b Pope	2		
H Larwood	not out	38		
F G Woodhead	c Mitchell b L F Townsend	24		
Extras	(B 2, LB 3)	5	(LB 2)	2
Total		182	(4 wickets)	133

Fall: 1st inns 1/3, 2/7, 3/71, 4/77, 5/97, 6/107, 7/117, 8/118, 9/126, 10/182
2nd inns 1/27, 2/83, 3/96, 4/106

Nottinghamshire

	o	m	r	w		o	m	r	w
Larwood	29	10	54	3		18.2	7	29	3
Voce	27	7	45	2		23	6	43	6
Woodhead	12	2	34	1		9	3	16	1
Staples	5	1	11	0		4	1	11	0
Gunn	18	11	22	3		7	1	18	0

Derbyshire

	o	m	r	w		o	m	r	w
Copson	19	4	41	1		14	4	29	0
Pope	21	4	41	2		17	9	25	2
Mitchell	25	6	87	6		12	3	49	0
L F Townsend	6.1	0	8	1		11	2	28	2

Umpires: W Reeves and W A Buswell

Close of play scores: First day: Derbyshire (1) 154/6 (A F Townsend 16, A W Richardson 1)
Second day: Derbyshire (2) 94/2 (A E Alderman 49)

Essex v Derbyshire

Played at Chelmsford, on August, 1, 3, 4
Toss won by Derbyshire
Derbyshire won by 20 runs

Derbyshire

A E Alderman	c sub b Farnes	0	c Wade b Farnes	79
D Smith	b Stephenson	8	b Stephenson	15
T S Worthington	c Wade b Stephenson	13	c Wilcox b Smith	42
L F Townsend	c Wilcox b Farnes	0	lbw b Smith	8
Mr A F Skinner	lbw b Nichols	19	lbw b Smith	7
C S Elliott	b Farnes	4	b Smith	4
†H Elliott	lbw b Stephenson	11	b Smith	14
*Mr A W Richardson	b Nichols	2	c Wade b Stephenson	14
A V Pope	lbw b Farnes	9	b Stephenson	33
T B Mitchell	b Farnes	0	lbw b Nichols	6
W H Copson	not out	9	not out	3
Extras	(B 1, LB 4)	5	(B 7, LB 4, NB 4)	15
Total		80		240

Fall: 1st inns 1/8 2/22, 3/23, 4/23, 5/29, 6/52 7/56, 8/68, 9/70,10/80
2nd inns 1/35, 2/103, 3/118, 4/148, 5/156 6/172, 7/186, 8/223, 9/236, 10/240

Essex

Mr L G Crawley	b Copson	6	b Copson	1
*Mr D R Wilcox	lbw b Pope	9	lbw b Townsend	15
M S Nichols	lbw b Copson	21	c Townsend b Pope	10
J O'Connor	c Alderman b Townsend	87	b Mitchell	21
Mr B H Belle	b Mitchell	0	lbw b Mitchell	10
Mr C T Ashton	lbw b Copson	10	lbw b Mitchell	0
T P B Smith	b Pope	6	b Townsend	8
Mr J W A Stephenson	b Townsend	20	lbw b Mitchell	0
L C Eastman	c Mitchell b Copson	31	lbw b Mitchell	6
†T H Wade	not out	6	c Skinner b Mitchell	8
Mr K Farnes	c Alderman b Pope	11	not out	1
Extras	(B 10, LB 1, NB 1)	12	(LB 1)	1
Total		219		81

Fall: 1st inns 1/16, 2/16, 3/77, 4/80, 5/103, 6/112, 7/165, 8/176, 9/202,10/219
2nd inns 1/12, 2/26, 3/28, 4/57, 5/57, 6/66, 7/66, 8/71, 9/77,10/81

Essex

	o	m	r	w		o	m	r	w
Nichols	9	2	27	2		18	3	51	1
Farnes	13	6	20	5		27	5	56	1
Stephenson	11.3	4	27	3		18.5	4	56	3
Eastman	3	2	1	0					
Smith						24	3	62	5

Derbyshire

	o	m	r	w		o	m	r	w
Copson	31	8	64	4		13	6	20	1
Pope	27.1	11	40	3		7	1	16	1
Townsend	19	7	38	2		15	8	19	2
Worthington	5	2	5	0					
Mitchell	11	1	60	1		5	0	25	6

Umpires: H G Baldwin and G Brown

Close of play scores: First day: Essex (1) 102/4 (J O'Connor 49, C T Ashton 10) Second day: Derbyshire (2) 195/7 (A W Richardson 10, A V Pope 3)

Surrey v Derbyshire

Played at Kennington Oval, on August 5, 6, 7
Toss won by Surrey
Match drawn

Surrey

R J Gregory	c Townsend b Copson	2	c C S Elliott b Copson	15
H S Squires	lbw b Mitchell	36	b Copson	16
H T Barling	c Alderman b Copson	57	c Smith b Townsend	102
L B Fishlock	lbw b Copson	10	c Skinner b Copson	71
*Mr E R T Holmes	lbw b Mitchell	11	(7) not out	38
T McMurray	c Townsend b Copson	0	(5) c Alderman b Smith	35
E A Watts	b Mitchell	51	(6) b Pope	18
†E W J Brooks	b Townsend	18	run out	1
A R Gover	lbw b Mitchell	0	not out	9
K W C King	c C S Elliott b Mitchell	11		
J V Daley	not out	4		
Extras	(LB 4)	4	(B 5, LB 5)	10
Total		204	(7 wickets)	315

Fall: 1st inns 1/2, 2/93, 3/103, 4/115, 5/117, 6/119, 7/173, 8/188, 9/189, 10/204
2nd inns 1/26, 2/45, 3/205, 4/208, 5/247, 6/289, 7/292

Derbyshire

A E Alderman	lbw b Daley	14
D Smith	b Gover	106
T S Worthington	c and b Gover	2
L F Townsend	b Watts	0
Mr A F Skinner	c Brooks b Daley	58
C S Elliott	lbw b Gover	3
†H Elliott	not out	79
*Mr A W Richardson	lbw b Holmes	8
A V Pope	c Fishlock b King	39
T B Mitchell	b Daley	0
W H Copson	c Squires b King	6
Extras	(NB 6)	6
Total		321

Fall: 1st inns 1/18, 2/19, 3/171, 4/176, 5/185, 6/187, 7/208, 8/296, 9/298, 10/321

Derbyshire

	o	m	r	w		o	m	r	w
Copson	17	5	41	4		23	8	60	3
Pope	16	4	47	0		36	8	86	1
Mitchell	24	1	88	5		16	1	73	0
Townsend	10	3	20	1		22	6	56	1
Worthington	4	2	4	0		3	0	8	0
Smith						3	1	13	1
C S Elliott						2	0	9	0

Surrey

	o	m	r	w
Gover	30	5	92	3
Watts	17	2	41	1
King	13.1	0	61	2
Holmes	6	2	21	1
Daley	24	2	88	3
Gregory	3	0	12	0

Umpires: G Brown and F Chester

Close of play scores: First day: Derbyshire (1) 51/2 (D Smith 93, A F Skinner 51) Second day: Surrey (2) 82/2 (H T Barling 29, L B Fishlock 19)

Derbyshire v Leicestershire
Played at Derby, on August 8,10
Toes won by Leicestershire
Derbyshire won by nine wickets

Leicestershire

G L Berry	c H Elliott b Mitchell	19	b Copson	4
F T Prentice	b Mitchell	5	lbw b Mitchell	6
N F Armstrong	st H Elliott b Mitchell	37	lbw b Copson	16
*Mr C S Dempster	c Smith b Copson	4	c Skinner b Copson	16
G S Watson	b Copson	21	b Pope	0
H C Graham	lbw b Copson	0	b Mitchell	1
G Geary	b Copson	2	b Mitchell	0
W E Astill	c Skinner b Mitchell	22	c Smith b Mitchell	14
H A Smith	c Mitchell b Copson	3	c Copson b Mitchell	17
†P Corrall	c H Elliott b Mitchell	0	c Smith b Copson	2
W H Marlow	not out	0	not out	17
Extras	(B 4)	4	(LB 1)	1
Total		117		94

Fall: 1st inns 1/18, 2/27, 3/34, 4/74, 5/74, 6/76, 7/94, 8/115, 9/117, 10/117
2nd inns 1/4, 2/24, 3/36, 4/39, 5/40, 6/40, 7/58, 8/60, 9/72,10/94

Derbyshire

A E Alderman	b Marlow	35	not out	27
D Smith	c Dempster b Smith	16	lbw b Geary	13
T S Worthington	lbw b Geary	9	not out	13
L F Townsend	c Prentice b Astill	4		
Mr A F Skinner	b Smith	8		
†H Elliott	b Smith	1		
C S Elliott	lbw b Geary	17		
*Mr A W Richardson	c Corrall b Geary	31		
A V Pope	c Astill b Geary	10		
T B Mitchell	not out	5		
W H Copson	b Geary	6		
Extras	(B 13, LB 3, W 1)	17		
Total		159	(1 wicket)	53

Fall: 1st inns 1/38, 2/49, 3/54, 4/73, 5/77, 6/100, 7/121, 8/146, 9/147,10/159
2nd inns 1/28

Derbyshire

	o	m	r	w		o	m	r	w
Copson	18	5	40	5		13	1	39	4
Pope	11	4	13	0		11	3	12	1
Mitchell	19.3	3	57	5		13.3	1	42	5
Townsend	7	4	3	0					

Leicestershire

	o	m	r	w		o	m	r	w
Geary	33.4	16	39	5		7	0	16	1
Smith	26	5	60	3		8	1	33	0
Astill	12	3	27	1					
Marlow	5	0	16	1		0 2	0	4	0

Umpires: A Dolphin and W A Buswell

Close of play scores: First day: Derbyshire (1) 159 all out

Nottinghamshire v Derbyshire

Played at Worksop, on August 15, 17,18
Toss won by Derbyshire
Match drawn

Derbyshire

A E Alderman	b Woodhead	31	c Wheat b Robinson	29
D Smith	c Wheat b Robinson	22	c Harris b Gunn	85
Mr A F Skinner	b Staples	8	(4) c Wheat b Butler	60
L F Townsend	lbw b Butler	28	(3) c Keeton b Woodhead	6
C S Elliott	lbw b Robinson	6	b Butler	26
†H Elliott	c Keeton b Robinson	17	b Robinson	6
Mr G R Langdale	c Butler b Woodhead	14	b Robinson	29
*Mr A W Richardson	c Knowles b Robinson	11	not out	12
A V Pope	b Butler	5	c Harris b Robinson	2
T B Mitchell	st Wheat b Harris	45	not out	1
W H Copson	not out	7		
Extras	(B 16, LB 6, W 1, NB 1)	24	(B 6, LB 8)	14
Total		218	(8 wickets, dec)	270

Fall: 1st inns 1/31, 2/50, 3/100, 4/102, 5/112, 6/139, 7/151, 8/160, 9/174, 10/218
2nd inns 1/78, 2/87, 3/155, 4/214, 5/215, 6/245, 7/254, 8/268

Nottinghamshire

W W Keeton	b Pope	0	not out	100
C B Harris	c Skinner b Pope	5	not out	107
W Walker	run out	2		
J Knowles	b Copson	4		
*Mr G F H Heane	c Smith b Mitchell	57		
G V Gunn	lbw b Copson	17		
A Staples	lbw b Copson	47		
F G Woodhead	c Copson b Mitchell	5		
†A B Wheat	c Alderman b Mitchell	11		
H J Butler	not out	0		
Mr G W Robinson	b Copson	0		
Extras	(LB 4)	4	(LB 7, NB 1)	8
Total		152	(no wicket)	215

Fall: 1st inns 1/1, 2/3, 3/11, 4/23, 5/49, 6/111, 7/127, 8/151, 9/152 10/152

Nottinghamshire

	o	m	r	w	o	m	r	w
Butler	33	6	57	2	22	2	64	2
Woodhead	31	11	47	2	16	1	48	1
Robinson	35	17	54	4	26	4	87	4
Staples	17	8	36	1	17	5	42	0
Harris	0.4	0	0	1				
Gunn					7	0	15	1

Derbyshire

	o	m	r	w	o	m	r	w
Copson	23.4	6	47	4	13	2	27	0
Pope	17	4	25	2	23	5	54	0
Mitchell	21	5	51	3	17	2	49	0
Townsend	7	2	14	0	19	3	49	0
Langdale	4	1	11	0	7	2	28	0

Umpires: J A Newman and C V Tarbox

Close of play scores: First day: Nottinghamshire (1) 16/3 (J Knowles 4, G F H Heane 4)
Second day: Derbyshire (2) 254/7 (A W Richardson 3)

Sussex v Derbyshire

Played at The Saffrons, Eastbourne, on August 19, 20, 21
Toss won by Derbyshire
Match drawn

Derbyshire

A E Alderman	b Tate	6	c Jas Langridge b Nye	7
D Smith	c W L Cornford b Jas Langridge	34	c Holmes b Nye	7
T S Worthington	c J H Cornford b J H Parks	56	c Holmes b Jas Langridge	45
L F Townsend	lbw b Jas Langridge	32	c John G Langridge b Jas Langridge	46
Mr A F Skinner	c W L Cornford b Nye	62	lbw b J H Cornford	8
C S Elliott	lbw b J H Cornford	11	not out	39
†H Elliott	b Nye	8	lbw b John G Langridge	11
*Mr A W Richardson	lbw b J H Cornford	11	not out	8
A V Pope	b J H Cornford	1		
T B Mitchell	b J H Cornford	0		
W H Copson	not out	5		
Extras	(LB 1 NB 1)	2	(B 10, LB 8, W 1, NB 1)	20
Total		228	(6 wickets)	191

Fall: 1st inns 1/8, 2/89, 3/99, 4/153, 5/198, 6/209, 7/216, 8/217, 9/217, 10/228
2nd inns 1/14, 2/33, 3/110, 4/117, 5/125, 6/163

Sussex

J H Parks	lbw b Pope	9
John G Langridge	lbw b Copson	0
Mr B L Cumming	c Skinner b Pope	14
T E R Cook	c Mitchell b Copson	53
Jas Langridge	c H Elliott b Mitchell	126
H W Parks	b Copson	75
*Fl-Lt A J Holmes	c Worthington b Copson	5
M W Tate	c Mitchell b Copson	0
†W L Cornford	c Copson b Mitchell	8
J K Nye	c and b Copson	5
J H Cornford	not out	6
Extras	(B 7, LB 6, W 1, NB 1)	15
Total		316

Fall: 1st inns 1/9, 2/9, 3/33, 4/106, 5/291, 6/295, 7/295, 8/302, 9/308,10/316

Sussex

	o	m	r	w		o	m	r	w
Tate	12	2	30	1					
Nye	13	1	40	2		31	7	67	2
J H Cornford	17.1	2	59	4		33	16	31	1
J H Parks	24	4	59	1		20	7	28	0
Jas. Langridge	21	3	38	2		27	17	16	2
Cook						8	1	17	0
John G Langridge						8	4	6	1
Cumming						1	0	5	0
Holmes						1	0	1	0

Derbyshire

	o	m	r	w
Copson	35	8	87	6
Pope	30	9	55	2
Townsend	25	8	52	0
Mitchell	21.3	4	81	2
Worthington	10	4	26	0

Umpires: H G Baldwin and D Hendren

Close of play scores: First day: Sussex (1) 30/2 (B L Cumming 11, T E R Cook 10) Second day: Derbyshire (2) 41/2 (T S Worthington 22, L F Townsend 3)

Derbyshire v Northamptonshire

Played at Queen's Park, Chesterfield, on August 22, 24, 25
Toss won by Northamptonshire
Match drawn

Northamptonshire

A H Bakewell	b Pope	3	not out	241
Mr R P Northway	b Pope	1	c Elliott b Pope	1
N Grimshaw	lbw b Mitchell	15	c Skinner b Pope	16
J E Timms	lbw b Pope	47	lbw b Pope	41
D Brookes	c Pope b Copson	14	b Pope	81
†K C James	lbw b Copson	8	(7) b Pope	12
A L Cox	b Pope	12	(6) c Elliott b Pope	2
*Mr W C Brown	not out	30	not out	13
R J Partridge	b Mitchell	2		
G C Perkins	lbw b Copson	3		
E W Clark	b Copson	2		
Extras	(B 4, LB 2, W 1)	7	(LB 4)	4
Total		144	(6 wickets, dec)	411

Fall: 1st inns 1/3, 2/8, 3/61, 4/86, 5/86 6/95, 7/113, 8/124, 9/132,10/144
2nd inns 1/2, 2/53, 3/146, 4/357, 5/376, 6/386

Derbyshire

A E Alderman	b Partridge	9	b Partridge	14
D Smith	b Partridge	31	b Clark	25
T S Worthington	c James b Partridge	15	b Clark	0
L F Townsend	lbw b Timms	67	lbw b Cox	1
Mr A F Skinner	lbw b Timms	1	lbw b Partridge	41
†H Elliott	b Clark	18	lbw b Clark	0
Mr G R Langdale	b Clark	8	c Brown b Bakewell	9
*Mr A W Richardson	c Bakewell b Clark	18	not out	27
A V Pope	c Perkins b Partridge	11	not out	13
T B Mitchell	c Brooks b Partridge	14		
W H Copson	not out	2		
Extras	(B 11, LB 3, W 1)	15	(B 21, LB 13, W 4, NB 5)	43
Total		209	(7 wickets)	173

Fall: 1st inns 1/45, 2/49, 3/73, 4/74, 5/111, 6/121, 7/167, 8/179, 9/201, 10/209
2nd inns 1/43, 2/43, 3/46, 4/56, 5/64, 6/94, 7/121

Derbyshire

	o	m	r	w		o	m	r	w
Copson	16.5	7	24	4		26	2	80	0
Pope	21	3	58	4		42	6	129	6
Mitchell	16	1	38	2					
Townsend	5	0	17	0		38	7	90	0
Langdale						11	0	45	0
Worthington						17	1	48	0
Skinner						3	0	15	0

Northamptonshire

	o	m	r	w		o	m	r	w
Clark	18	3	63	3		27	10	41	3
Partridge	26.3	5	69	5		29	16	22	2
Timms	15	4	40	2		12	6	13	0
Cox	7	1	17	0		17	13	12	1
Perkins	4	1	5	0		5	3	5	0
Bakewell						6	1	17	1
Grimshaw						11	6	20	0

Umpires: C V Tarbox and C W L Parker
Close of play scores: First day: Derbyshire (1) 167/7 (A W Richardson 9) Second day:
Northamptonshire (2) 374/4 (A H Bakewell 221, K C James 10)

Somerset v Derbyshire

Played at Rowden Road, Wells, on August, 26, 27, 28
Toss won by Derbyshire
Somerset won by one wicket

Derbyshire

A E Alderman	b Wellard	9	c and b Meyer	17
D Smith	b Andrews	93	b Wellard	2
T S Worthington	lbw b Wellard	35	lbw b Wellard	9
L F Townsend	b Andrews	7	b Wellard	5
Mr A F Skinner	c Meyer b Andrews	9	st Luckes b Meyer	39
C S Elliott	not out	29	b Andrews	6
†H Elliott	b Meyer	11	b Andrews	10
*Mr A W Richardson	b Wellard	8	c Meyer b Wellard	50
A V Pope	b Andrews	0	c Meyer b Gimblett	30
T R Armstrong	b Andrews	1	not out	8
W H Copson	b Wellard	1	c Luckes b Wellard	1
Extras	(B 4, LB 7, NB 2)	13	(B 6, LB 14, NB 3)	23
Total		216		200

Fall: 1st inns 1/27, 2/117, 3/147, 4/153, 5/162, 6/186, 7/212, 8/213, 9/215,10/216
2nd inns 1/6, 2/17, 3/26, 4/60, 5/85, 6/87, 7/98, 8/164, 9/196, 10/200

Somerset

F S Lee	b Pope	35	c H Elliott b Copson	27
H Gimblett	b Worthington	4	b Copson	41
Mr F M McRae	c H Elliott b Pope	2	(9) not out	14
Mr R J O Meyer	b Copson	2	(3) b Copson	14
Mr E F Longrigg	b Pope	44	(4) c Smith b Armstrong	38
Mr J H Cameron	lbw b Worthington	23	(5) run out	8
*Mr R A Ingle	lbw b Copson	8	(6) c Smith b Copson	16
A W Wellard	c C S Elliott b Pope	17	(7) c Townsend b Copson	86
W H R Andrews	c H Elliott b Pope	4	(8) c Alderman b Townsend	12
†W T Luckes	b Copson	1	b Copson	0
H L Hazell	not out	0	not out	8
Extras	(LB 6)	6	(LB 9, NB 1)	10
Total		146	(9 wickets)	274

Fall: 1st inns 1/23, 2/38, 3/41, 4/53, 5/99, 6/118, 7/122, 8/145, 9/146,10/146
2nd inns 1/67, 2/76, 3/98, 4/115, 5/140, 6/217, 7/242, 8/263, 9/265

Somerset

	o	m	r	w	o	m	r	w
Wellard	15.1	2	52	4	22.1	4	47	5
Meyer	24	6	53	1	17	3	46	2
Andrews	16	4	42	5	16	2	56	2
Gimblett	3	0	15	0	8	4	14	1
Hazell	9	1	41	0	7	4	14	0

Derbyshire

	o	m	r	w	o	m	r	w
Copson	21	3	55	3	30	6	81	6
Pope	20.1	3	35	5	34	13	64	0
Worthington	7	1	34	2	5	0	20	0
Townsend	4	0	16	0	17. 5	5	35	1
Armstrong					8	1	64	1

Umpires: C W L Parker and T W Oates

Close of play scores: First day: Somerset (1) 116/5 (E F Longrigg 40, R A Ingle 6) Second day: Somerset (2) 93/2 (R J O Meyer 13, E F Longrigg 8)

Leicestershire v Derbyshire

Played at School Ground, Oakham, on August 29, 31, September 1
Toss won by Leicestershire
Derbyshire won by an innings and 66 runs

Leicestershire

G L Berry	c Elliott b Copson	9	c Elliott b Copson	4
F T Prentice	c Richardson b Copson	7	c Worthington b Townsend	13
N F Armstrong	lbw b Copson	2	b Pope	42
H C Graham	c and b Townsend	8	c Elliott b Pope	1
G S Watson	b Pope	24	st Elliott b Armstrong	13
Mr M St J Packe	c Alderman b Townsend	3	b Armstrong	3
A W Shipman	not out	37	not out	21
G Geary	b Pope	9	b Copson	0
*W E Astill	c Elliott b Armstrong	29	b Copson	4
HA Smith	b Townsend	10	b Pope	8
†P Corrall	lbw b Copson	5	b Pope	12
Extras	(B 4, LB 4)	8		
Total		151		121

Fall: 1st inns 1/13, 2/18, 3/23, 4/43, 5/47, 6/57, 7/78, 8/120, 9/137, 10/151
2nd inns 1/6, 2/25, 3/28, 4/52, 5/56, 6/85, 7/86, 8/90, 9/101, 10/121

Derbyshire

D Smith	b Astill	169
A E Alderman	b Shipman	0
T S Worthington	b Smith	102
Mr A F Skinner	lbw b Shipman	1
L F Townsend	c Corrall b Smith	2
Mr G R Langdale	b Geary	4
†H Elliott	c Corrall b Smith	24
*Mr A W Richardson	b Geary	7
A V Pope	not out	3
T R Armstrong	st Corrall b Astill	7
W H Copson	c Graham b Astill	0
Extras	(B 7, LB 10, NB 2)	19
Total		338

Fall: 1st inns 1/0, 2/209, 3/212, 4/225, 5/240, 6/307, 7/328, 8/328, 9/338, 10/338

Derbyshire

	o	m	r	w	o	m	r	w
Copson	23.4	7	34	4	17	3	56	3
Pope	28	9	49	2	25.4	9	44	4
Armstrong	19	4	29	1	6	4	2	2
Townsend	18	2	31	3	11	5	8	1
Langdale					4	0	11	0

Leicestershire

	o	m	r	w
Shipman	16	2	49	2
Smith	34	3	119	3
Geary	31	3	85	2
Astill	21	1	52	3
Prentice	6	0	14	0

Umpires: E Cooke and F I Walden

Close of play scores: First day: Derbyshire (1) 103/1 (D Smith 49, T S Worthington 50)
Second day: Leicestershire (2) 59/5 (N F Armstrong 22, A W Shipman 3)

Bibliography

H S Altham and E W Swanton, *A History of Cricket*, George Allen & Unwin 1948.

Bill Andrews, *The Hand that Bowled Bradman*, Macdonald 1973.

John Arlott, Vintage Summer: 1947, Eyre & Spottiswood 1967.

F S Ashley-Cooper, *Derbyshire Cricket*, George W May 1924.

David Baggett, *Derbyshire County Cricket Club First-Class Records 1871-1994*, Limlow Books 1995.

Philip Bailey, Philip Thorn and Peter Wynne-Thomas, *Who's Who of Cricketers*, Newnes Books in association with The Association of Cricket Statisticians 1984.

Derek Birley, *A Social History of English Cricket*, Aurum Press 1999.

Rowland Bowen, Cricket: *A History of its Growth and Development throughout the World*, Eyre & Spottiswood 1970.

Bill Bowes, *Express Deliveries*, Stanley Paul 1949.

Walter Brierley, *Means-Test Man*, Methuen & Co Ltd 1935.

Robert Brooke, *A History of the County Cricket Championship*, Guinness Publishing 1991.

Julie Bunting, *The Earls and Dukes of Devonshire*, Derbyshire Heritage Series, Footprint Press 1996.

Neville Cardus, *Good Days*, Rupert Hart-Davis 1948; *Australian Summer*, Rupert Hart-Davis 1949; *The Roses Matches 1919-39*, Souvenir Press 1982.

Dudley Carew, *To the Wicket*, Chapman and Hall 1946.

Mike Carey, Les Jackson, *A Derbyshire Legend*, Tranters Derby 1997.

A W Carr, *Cricket with the Lid Off*, Hutchinson 1935.

Frank Chester, *How's That*, Hutchinson 1956.

Denis Compton, *End of an Innings*, Oldbourne Book Co 1958.

Michael Crick, *Scargill and the Miners*, Penguin Books Ltd 1985.

Christopher Douglas, *Douglas Jardine Spartan Cricketer*, George Allen & Unwin 1984.

L Eardley-Simpson, *The Rise of Derbyshire Cricket 1919-35*, GC Brittain & Sons Ltd 1935.

Alan Edwards, *Lionel Tennyson, Regency Buck*, Robson Books 2001.

Matthew Engel and Andrew Radd, *The History of Northamptonshire County Cricket Club*, Christopher Helm 1993.

David Frith, *Bodyline Autopsy*, Aurum Press 2002; *The Fast Men*, Van Nostrand Reinhold, Wokingham 1975.

Roy Genders, *League Cricket in England*, T Werner Laurie Ltd 1952.

Geoff Gration, *The Best Summers of Our Lives*, Breedon Books 2000.

John Heath, *The Illustrated History of Derbyshire*, Barracuda Books Ltd, Buckingham 1982.

Alan Hill, *Herbert Sutcliffe: Cricket Maestro*, Simon and Schuster Ltd 1991.

E R T Holmes, *Flannelled Foolishness*, Hollis and Carter 1957.

Gerald Howat, *Plum Warner*, Unwin Hyman 1987.

Len Hutton, *Fifty Years in Cricket*, Stanley Paul 1984.

Terry Judge, *The Clay Cross Calamities*, Scarthin Books 1994.

G R Langdale, *A History of the Bassetlaw & District Cricket League 1904-1978*, Bassetlaw League 1979.

Harold Larwood with Kevin Perkins, *The Larwood Story*, W H Allen 1965.

Jim Ledbetter, *First-Class Cricket A Complete Record, 1936*, Limlow Books 1994.

Derek Lodge, *Figures on the Green*, George Allen & Unwin, 1982.

Christopher Martin-Jenkins, *Wisden Book of County Cricket*, Queen Anne Press 1981; *The Spirit of Cricket*, Faber and Faber 1994.

Ronald Mason, *Plum Warner's Last Season*, Epworth Press 1970.

Gerald Mortimer, *Are the Fixtures Out?* Derby Evening Telegraph, Breedon Books Publishing 2003.

Peter Oborne, *Basil D'Oliveira*, Little, Brown 2004.

Gerald Pawle, *R E S Wyatt – Fighting Cricketer*, Allen & Unwin 1985.

Frank Peach, *Derbyshire Cricketers 1871-1981*, The Association of Cricket Statisticians 1982.

T C F Prittie, *Cricket North and South* (*Mainly Middlesex and Lancashire Hot-Pot*, Hutchinson & Co), The Sportsman's Book Club. 1955.

Harold Rhodes, *The Harold Rhodes Affair*, Breedon Books Sport 1987.

Anton Rippon and Andrew Ward, *The Derby County Story*, Breedon Books 1983.

RC Robertson-Glasgow, *46 Not Out*, Hollis & Carter 1948.

Peter Roebuck, *From Sammy to Jimmy, The Official History of Somerset County Cricket Club*, Partridge Press 1991.

Fred Root, *A Cricket Pro's Lot*, Edward Arnold & Co 1937.

Andrew Searle, *S F Barnes: His Life and Times*, Empire Publications 1997.

John Shawcroft, *A History of Derbyshire County Cricket Club 1870-1970*, Derbyshire CCC 1972; *Derbyshire Bowlers*, J H Hall and Sons Ltd 1986; *The History of Derbyshire County Cricket Club*, Christopher Helm 1989; *The Rise and Fall of Percy Perrin, Derbyshire v Essex 1904*, J W McKenzie 2000.

Ric Sissons, The Players: *A Social History of the Professional Cricketer*, Kingswood 1988.

E J Smith, *Tiger Smith of Warwickshire and England. The Autobiography of E J Smith as told to Patrick Murphy*, Lutterworth 1981.

Richard Streeton, *P G H Fender: A Biography*, Faber 1981.

Bibliography

Bob Taylor with Patrick Murphy, *Standing Up, Standing Back*, Willow Books, Collins 1985.

Peter Taylor, *With Clough by Taylor* (with Mike Langley), Sidgwick and Jackson 1980.

The Duchess of Devonshire, *Chatsworth*, Derbyshire Countryside Ltd.

The History Today Companion to British History, edited by Juliet Gardiner and Neil Wenborn, with 1914-79 by Dr John Stevenson, Worcester College, Oxford. Collins & Brown Ltd 1995.

A A Thomson, *Cricket: The Wars of the Roses*, Pelham Books 1967; *Vintage Elevens* (with Denzil Batchelor), Pelham Books 1969.

Fred Trueman and Don Mosey, *Talking Cricket*, Hodder and Stoughton 1997.

Pelham Warner, *Cricket Between Two Wars*, Chatto & Windus 1942; *Lord's 1787-1945*, George G Harrap & Co 1946; *Gentlemen v Players 1806-1949*, George G Harrap & Co 1950.

Roy Webber, *County Cricket Championship*, Phoenix Sportsbooks 1957.

Jack Williams, *Cricket in England, A Cultural and Social History of the Inter-War Years*, Frank Cass 1999.

J E Williams, *The Derbyshire Miners*, George Allen & Unwin 1962.

Anthony Woodhouse, *The History of Yorkshire County Cricket Club*, Christopher Helm 1989.

R E S Wyatt, *Three Straight Sticks*, Stanley Paul 1951.

Peter Wynne-Thomas, *The History of Nottinghamshire County Cricket Club*, Christopher Helm 1992; *Harold Larwood, Famous Cricketers Series No. 6*, The Association of Cricket Statisticians.

N W D Yardley and J M Kilburn, *Homes of Cricket*, Peter Garnett 1952.

Wisden Cricketers' Almanack, *The Cricketer International*, *Wisden Cricket Monthly*, *The Wisden Cricketer*, *Derbyshire County Cricket Yearbooks 1954-2005*, *The Cricket Statistician*, *Cricket Lore*, *The Times*, *The Daily Telegraph*, *Derbyshire Times*, *Derby Evening Telegraph*, *Derby Daily Telegraph*, *Derby Daily Express*, *Derby Mercury*, *Derbyshire Advertiser*, *Derbyshire Life and Countryside*, *Ilkeston Advertiser*, *Ripley and Heanor News*.

Index

Index

Index